Microprocessors and Microcomputers and Switching Mode Power Supplies

TEXAS INSTRUMENTS ELECTRONICS SERIES

Applications Laboratory Staff of Texas Instruments Incorporated ■ DIGITAL INTEGRATED CIRCUITS AND OPERATIONAL AMPLIFIER AND OPTO-ELECTRONIC CIRCUIT DESIGN

Applications Laboratory Staff of Texas Instruments Incorporated ■ ELECTRONIC POWER CONTROL AND DIGITAL TECHNIQUES

Applications Laboratory Staff of Texas Instruments Incorporated ■ MICROPROCESSORS AND MICROCOMPUTERS AND SWITCHING MODE POWER SUPPLIES

Applications Laboratory Staff of Texas Instruments Incorporated ■ MOS AND SPECIAL-PURPOSE BIFOLAR INTEGRATED CIRCUITS AND R-F POWER TRANSISTOR CIRCUIT DESIGN

Applications Laboratory Staff of Texas Instruments Incorporated ■ POWER-TRANSISTOR AND TTL INTEGRATED-CIRCUIT APPLICATIONS

Carr and Mize ■ MOS/LSI DESIGN AND APPLICATION

Crawford ■ MOSFET IN CIRCUIT DESIGN

Delhom ■ DESIGN AND APPLICATION OF TRANSISTOR SWITCHING CIRCUITS

The Engineering Staff of Texas Instruments Incorporated ■ CIRCUIT DESIGN FOR AUDIO, AM/FM, AND TV

The Engineering Staff of Texas Instruments Incorporated ■ SOLID-STATE COMMUNICATIONS

The Engineering Staff of Texas Instruments Incorporated ■ TRANSISTOR CIRCUIT DESIGN

Härtel ■ OPTOELECTRONICS: THEORY AND PRACTICE

Hibberd ■ INTEGRATED CIRCUITS

Hibberd ■ SOLID-STATE ELECTRONICS

The IC Applications Staff of Texas Instruments Incorporated ■ DESIGNING WITH TTL INTEGRATED CIRCUITS

Kane and Larrabee ■ CHARACTERIZATION OF SEMICONDUCTOR MATERIALS

Learning Center Staff of Texas Instruments Incorporated ■ CALCULATOR ANALYSIS FOR BUSINESS AND FINANCE

Luecke, Mize, and Carr ■ SEMICONDUCTOR MEASUREMENTS AND INSTRUMENTATION

Runyan ■ SEMICONDUCTOR MEASUREMENTS AND INSTRUMENTATION

Runyan ■ SILICON SEMICONDUCTOR TECHNOLOGY

Sevin ■ FIELD-EFFECT TRANSISTORS

Microprocessors and Microcomputers and Switching Mode Power Supplies

Edited by
BRYAN NORRIS

Manager, Applications Laboratory
Texas Instruments Limited

McGRAW-HILL BOOK COMPANY

New York St. Louis San Francisco Auckland Bogotá
Düsseldorf Johannesburg London Madrid Mexico
Montreal New Delhi Panama Paris São Paulo
Singapore Sydney Tokyo Toronto

Library of Congress Cataloging in Publication Data
Main entry under title:

Microprocessors and microcomputers and switching mode
power supplies.

(Texas Instruments electronics series)
Includes bibliographies and index.
1. Semiconductors. 2. Electronic apparatus and
appliances–Power supply. 3. Microprocessors.
4. Microcomputers. 5. Integrated circuits. I. Norris, Bryan.
TK7871.85.M52 621.3815'2 78-15110
ISBN 0-07-063756-3

1234567890 **HDHD** 7654321098

Contents

SECTION 1 SWITCHING MODE POWER SUPPLIES

SECTION 2 DEFLECTION CIRCUITS

SECTION 3 NEW CONSUMER SYSTEMS

SECTION 4 MICROPROCESSORS/MICROCOMPUTERS

Preface

The aim of this book is to provide up-to-date information on a broad range of semiconductor devices, and to give straightforward examples of how they may be applied in practice. Also, each chapter has been written by practicing professional engineers, to whom all thanks are given for their contributions and efforts involved.

The book is divided into four sections concerned with: power supplies; deflection systems; new consumer integrated circuits or systems to achieve sound, display, or touch switching; and the new pervasive semiconductor control device, namely the microprocessor/microcomputer.

As present designs of power supply are increasingly using switching mode techniques, section one has chapters describing the concepts, practical design, self oscillating forms, and i.c. types of switching mode power supplies respectively.

Section two begins with a combined power supply/deflection circuit, then discusses conventional horizontal deflectional stages, and finishes with i.c. vertical deflection stages.

A number of exciting consumer i.c.s and systems have been recently introduced and section three covers these, e.g. various applications of audio amplifier and touch control i.c.s. are explained. The advent of a module, having mini-computer complexity, which enables teletext signals to be decoded and the written information displayed on a domestic television screen, opens the door to a seemingly unlimited variety of new applications which will now be economically achievable. An insight into some of these is given, along with the description and method of use of the module, in Chapter 9.

The final section first introduces microprocessors, their technology and terminology, discusses how they can be used and programmed, and describes a particular 16 bit microprocessor. Specific examples of microprocessor/microcomputer use in A to D conversion, serial code generation, and consumer products are detailed.

Bryan Norris

Applications Manager
Texas Instruments Limited

I SWITCHING MODE POWER SUPPLY CONCEPTS

by
Mick Maytum and Peter Wilson

As discussed in the previous volume[1], the switching mode power supply is becoming a common form of generating the required voltages for a system. Now that reliable high voltage power transistors and control integrated circuits (i.c.s.) are available at economical prices, the complexity of the switching mode, with respect to the conventional series regulator power supply, can be allowed in order to obtain its major advantages; viz. high efficiency and small size and weight. Further features which add to its usefulness are the ability to regulate over a large range of input voltages, and ease of isolation and provision of a number of voltage supplies, as discussed in detail in subsequent chapters.

The supply's circuit examination can be broadly sectionalized into three as shown in Figure 1. The input rectification converts the a.c. supply to a smoothed d.c. voltage for the inverter. This voltage is then 'chopped' at high frequency (>20kHz) in the inverter. A small high frequency transformer fed from the 'chopped' voltage, is used to produce multiple outputs and isolation between a.c. supply and the output. Output rectification then gives the required d.c. voltages.

INPUT RECTIFICATION

Rectifier Specification

Figure 2 shows the commonly used rectification systems together with their relative costings. The European versions can operate from 185 to 270V a.c. 50Hz giving a 20% output voltage ripple at 200W and 'low' a.c. supply (185V). To maintain the same ripple on the USA version (100 to 130V a.c. 60Hz) the capacitors have to be at least three times larger in value although needing only half the voltage rating (smoothing and energy storage $\propto \frac{1}{2}CV^2$ but cost $\propto CV$). This accounts for most of the cost differential between the European and US circuits.

If required, dual supply voltage operation 117V/230V can be satisfied by the higher cost circuits (d) and (e). Australian legislation prohibits the use of rectifier circuits which cause unbalance (a d.c. component) in the a.c. voltage supply current. A similar piece of legislation is possible in Europe, as already the electricity generating companies are applying pressures for voluntary compliance. In this case circuits (b) and (e) would not be acceptable as they cause a d.c. component.

Thus the preferred circuits are:

(a) Full wave bridge for European/US single supply.

(d) Dual voltage for European/US compatible operation.

The overall efficiency of any of the rectification systems depend on the value of surge limiting resistor R1 (for a fixed value of smoothing capacitor). In the past the minimum value for this resistor was set by the rectifiers surge current rating. Today the limit is set by the contacting capability of the a.c. supply on/off switch. A survey of U.K. television switch suppliers showed typical switch 'on' surge contact ratings of 60 to 95A peak. B.S.415 illustrates a switch test circuit of 80A peak operating from 265V ±5V. Running from high mains and making contact at the voltage peak, the range of surge limiting resistor, R1, is 6.3 to 4Ω depending on the actual switch used. The resistors power loss is large (10-15W) and so there is a large incentive to use the lowest possible value. If higher rated current switches were available so that the rectifier defined the peak current, the surge limiting resistor could be considerably reduced; if fault conditions did not have to be comprehended. This is because the charging of the reservoir capacitor will normally take place in much less than a mains half cycle time and hence the peak rectifier current is set on an i^2t basis. For instance, the BY127 a mains rectifier, which is rated at 40A I_{FSM}, has an implied maximum peak rating of 500A for very short period. The data for this device indicates a minimum surge limiting resistor of 2.7Ω for a 400μF capacitor. This kind of information could be dangerous on two counts:

(i) It completely ignors the switch 'on' surge capabilities of the mains switches available leading to the unreliable operation of this component (welded contacts, etc).

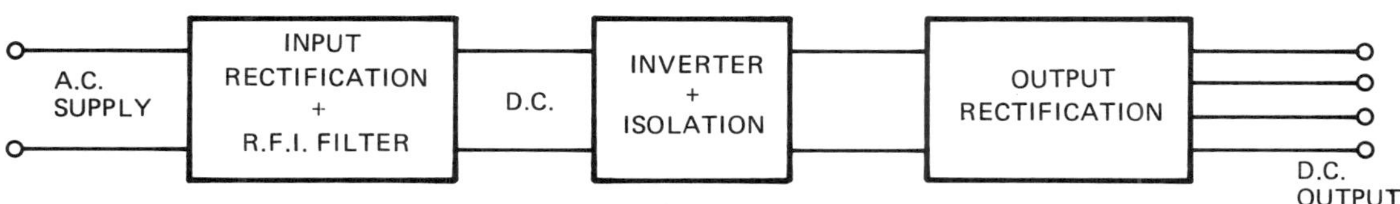

FIGURE 1. Basic Switching Mode Power Supply Sections

(a) Full Wave

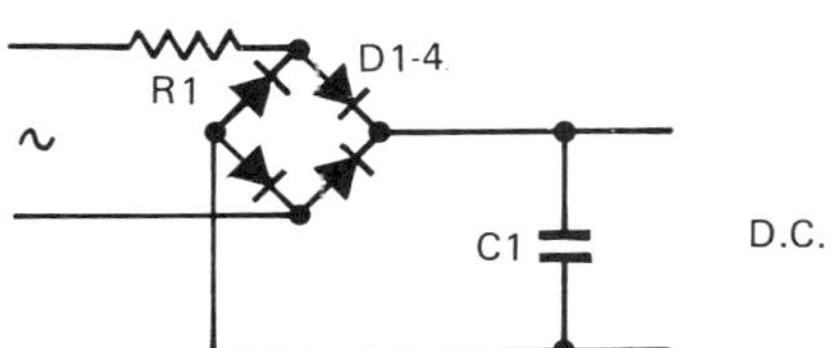

(b) Half Wave

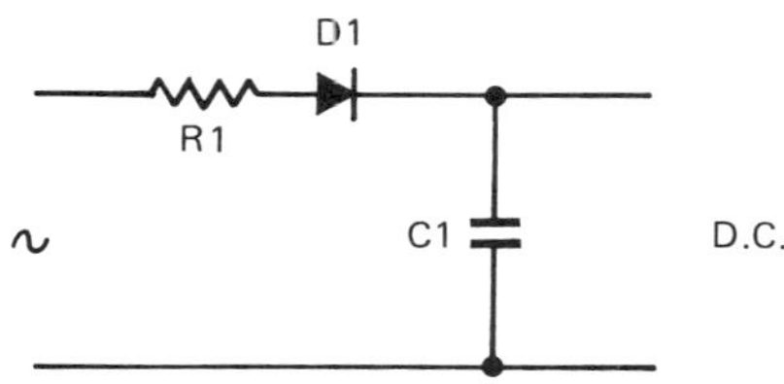

(c) Full Wave Voltage Doubler

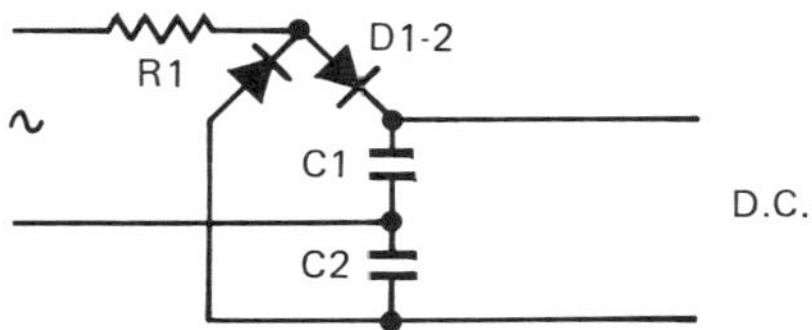

(d) Dual Voltage

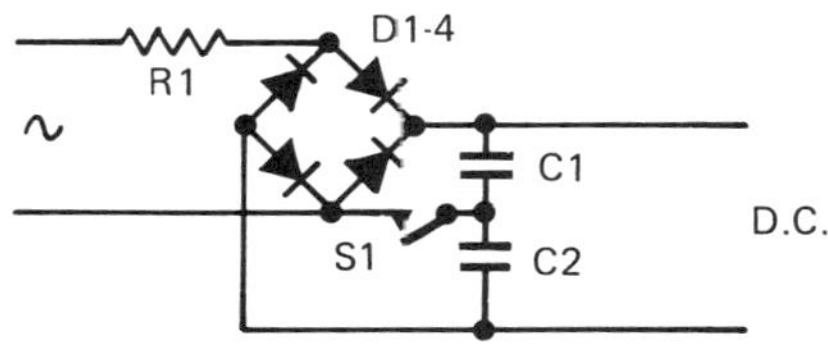

(e) Dual Voltage Doubler

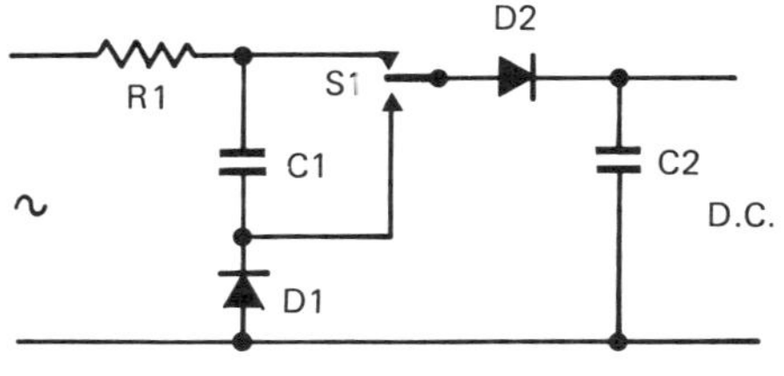

$ Costing for Same % Ripple

Europe		USA	
Absolute Value	Δ	Absolute Value	Δ
1.7	0	2.0	0
2.1	0.4	2.7	0.7
2.6	0.9	3.2	1.2
3.4	1.7	NA	NA
4.2	2.5	NA	NA

FIGURE 2. Input Rectifier Systems

(ii) It completely ignors fault conditions when the rectifiers must carry very heavy currents, outside even the single cycle rating, until the mains fuse opens.

Item (ii) raises the question of what is the current time characteristic of the mains fuse. The U.K. television manufacturer, for example, hopes the receiver will be fitted with a 3A fused plug on the mains lead at installation. Sometimes this could be a 13A fused plug through ignorance. So the fused plug should be regarded as the very last line of overload protection. The manufacturer does control the equipments internal mains fuse. The highest values used by the U.K. television manufacturer are typically 2AT (large – slow blow) in the 20 x 5 mm size. The fusing current/time characteristic of this is defined up to 20A by the BS4265 and IEC127 specifications. It is, however, difficult to obtain indications on the characteristics above 20A.

In summary – the rectifier maximum single cycle fault surge current is set by the mains on/off switch and the longer term (>20ms) surge capability by the internal mains fuse, Figures 3 and 4. The rating should apply at a reasonable initial junction temperature, say 70°C. The average d.c. output current of the bridge should be ≏1.2A at $T_{ambient}$ = 70°C.

The BY127 has a good reputation for reliability. Its V_{RRM} is 1250V which implies voltage excursions greater than 850V positive or negative from the a.c. supply rarely occur (some capacitance filtering of the a.c. supply is assumed). In normal operation the bridge diodes will only see the peak a.c. supply voltage (375V). Under voltage surge conditions the voltage developed across the bridge will depend on the filtering capacitor values and the leakage inductance of the main smoothing capacitor and its wiring is sufficient to apply most of the voltage surge to the bridge. The bridge Repetitive Reverse Maximum voltage, V_{RRM}, rating should therefore be set as 850V. A US specification is likely to have the same surge capability, but be lower in voltage and higher in average output current.

Recommended Bridge Rectifier Specification @ 70°C.

Maximum Reverse Repetitive Voltage,	V_{RRM}	850V
Maximum Reverse Working Voltage,	V_{RWM}	400V
Average Current	I_{AV}	1.2A
Maximum Forward Surge Current	I_{FSM} (single cycle)	95A. (see Figures 3 and 4).

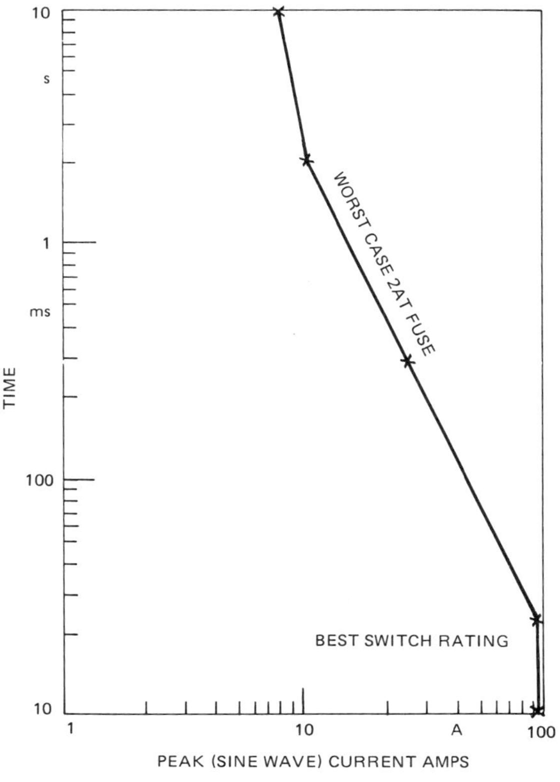

FIGURE 3. Bridge Peak Surge Current Capability

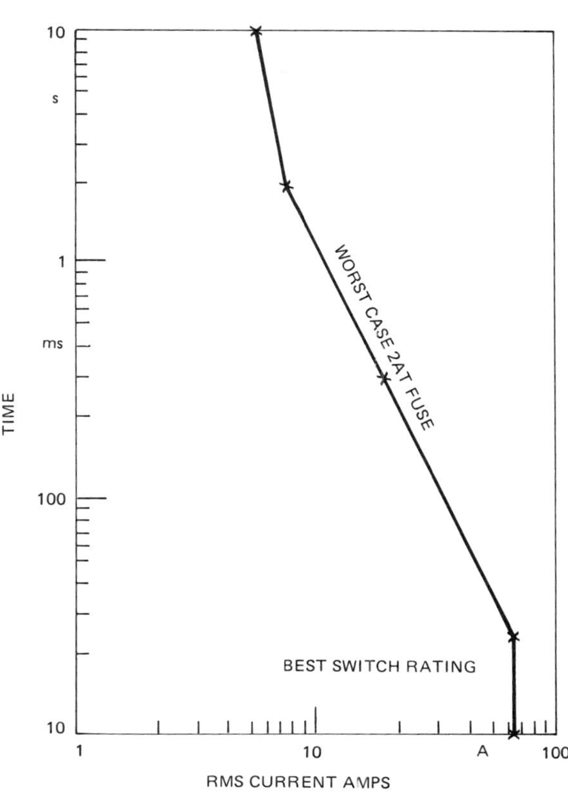

FIGURE 4. Bridge RMS Current Capability

Smoothing Capacitor Selection

The question of smoothing capacitor value has been fully detailed[2]. For easier reference larger versions of the published graphs appear in Figures 5 and 6. This section will deal with second order considerations in capacitor selection.

The function of the capacitor is two fold. First to provide smoothing of the rectified a.c. supply, reducing ripple current and so preventing switching 'hash' passing through the conducting rectifier diodes into the a.c. supply.

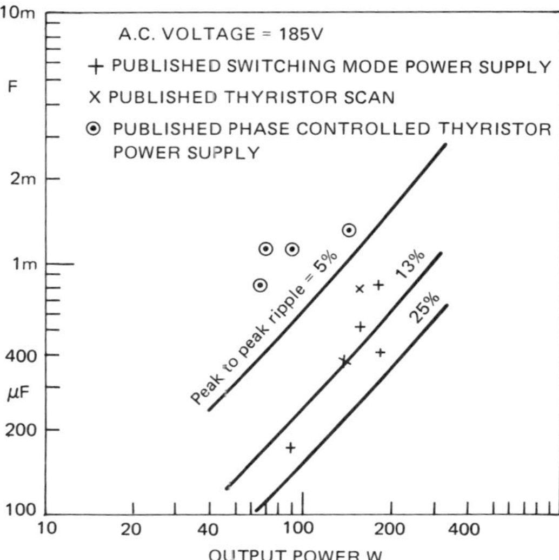

FIGURE 5. Smoothing Capacitor Value v Output Power (185V AC)

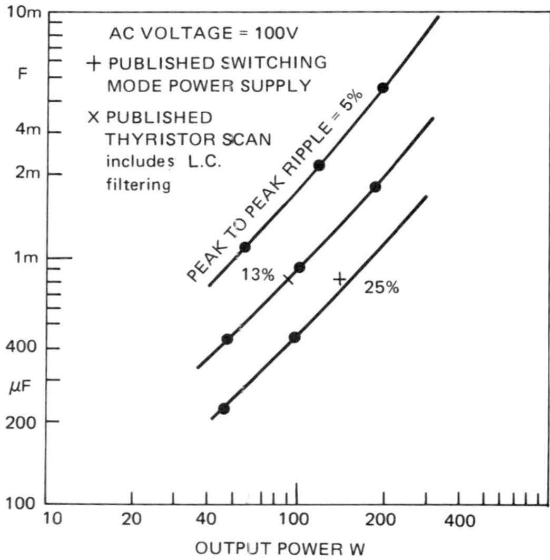

FIGURE 6. Smoothing Capacitor Value v Output Power (100V AC)

Figure 7 illustrates the problem. Besides possessing the property of capacitance there will also be small quantities of series resistance (e.s.r. – equivalent series resistance) and inductance. Both of these prevent the capacitance from being completely effective. The e.s.r. (the loss component) must be below a certain level to ensure the capacitor does not overheat.

FIGURE 7. Equivalent Capacitor Circuit

After discussions with various capacitor manufacturers, it was concluded that the e.s.r. was the most significant problem. As the effective rms ripple current through the capacitor exceeds the data sheet limit by about 40% in switching mode service, its maximum e.s.r. needs to be half of the normal maximum value (for the same power loss). As most capacitors are well below the maximum e.s.r. value this tightening of the e.s.r. limit is no problem. Further decoupling of the rectified rail close to the inverter by an extra 0.5-1μF non-electrolytic can be helpful in reducing high frequency ripple current.

Radio Frequency Interference (R.F.I. or E.M.I.) Filters

Filter formats are well established. However, most designs are of the universal type which can be added to any piece of mains operated equipment, Figure 8. Also some filters are unidirectional in that they will only suppress radiation coming from the equipment to the a.c. supply, or, if the input/output connections are reversed, only suppress radiation from an a.c. supply to the equipment. It would seem reasonable to suppress against both these radiations in the case of switching modes. The choice of L and C values can be made on the basis of BS800, but further optimisation of the values would be needed once the unit was mounted in the equipment.

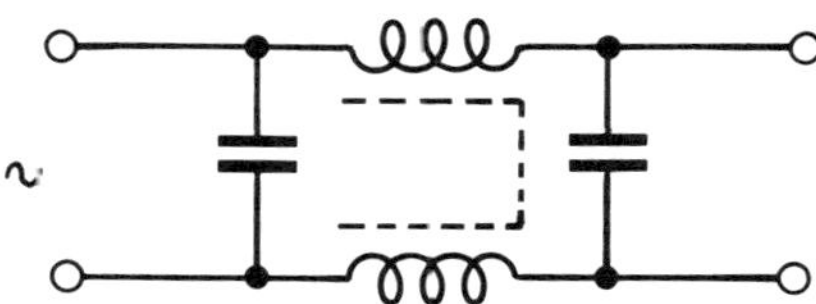

FIGURE 8. Typical R.F.I. Input Filter

Mains rectifiers can cause r.f.i. problems and are usually shunted by 1-4nF (some even have ferrite beads in series with them). A 'standard' r.f.i. suppression system is shown in Figure 9. From 50Hz current limitations (BS415) the primary to output capacitor is limited to 4n7F. The transformer primary to secondary winding capacitance (shown dotted) can be reduced by careful winding techniques or by the use of screens which will reduce the switching mode 'earth' loop current.

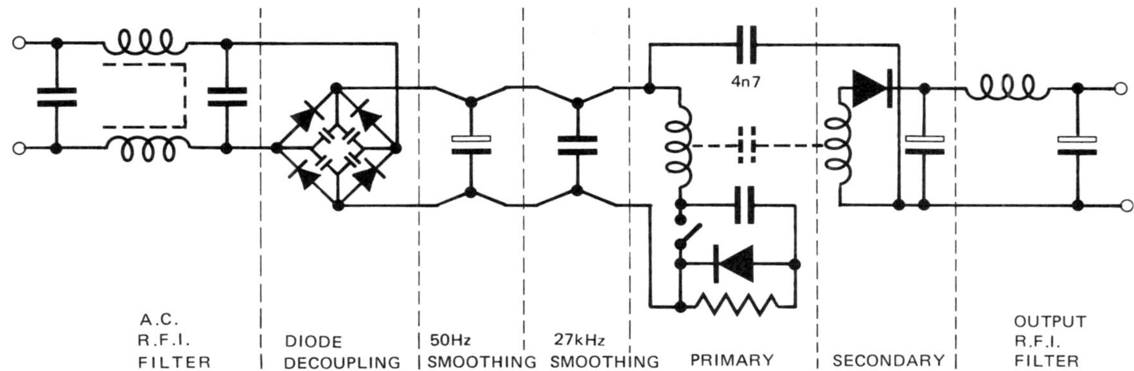

FIGURE 9. R.F.I. Suppression Features

INVERTER AND ISOLATION

General

Concept: The present cost of transformers, power semiconductors and control systems tend to dictate the choice of a single high voltage transistor shunt switching mode power supply as shown in Figure 10. Also this type of inverter easily produces a multi-rail output system. So, for example, output rails of 210V (video, tuner) 70-150V (horizontal deflection) and 30V (audio, signal processing, vertical deflection) can all be produced with reasonable stability and regulation.

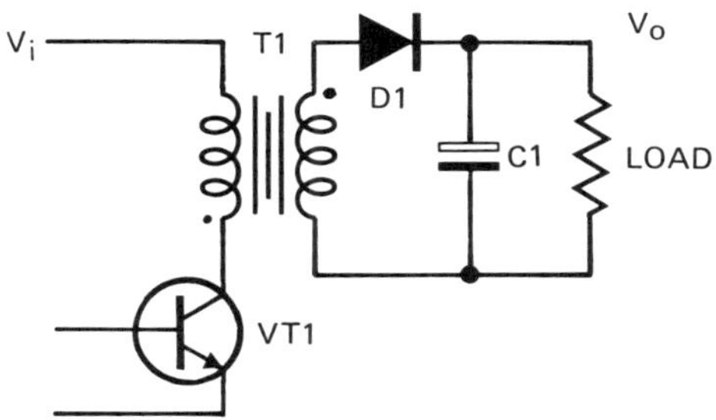

FIGURE 10. General Shunt Switching Mode Circuit

Principle: Voltage V_i is the rectified a.c. supply discussed in the input rectification section. When the transistor VT1 switches 'on', it applies V_i across the primary of transformer T1. The conduction time of the transistor controls the increase in magnetic energy of the transformer. When the transistor switches 'off' the stored energy reverses the transformer windings voltage polarities (back e.m.f.). When the secondary's winding voltage exceeds V_o (the load voltage), diode D1 conducts clamping the secondary winding voltage to V_o. If the primary/secondary turns ratio is N the primary voltage will be NV_o and the transistors voltage $V_i + NV_o$. In the transistors non-conduction time energy is passed out of the secondary winding via diode D1 being passed directly to the load and also stored on the output smoothing capacitor C1. If the transistor is switched 'on' again (to replenish the energy loss) before all the energy has been passed out to the secondary winding the system is called Incomplete Energy Transfer (i.e.t.). If all the energy had been transferred before the transistor is switched on the system is called Complete Energy Transfer (c.e.t.). The product of the output energy and the operating frequency gives the output power. Variation of the transistors conduction duty cycle changes the energy stored per cycle and so can be used to compensate for load and input supply changes.

Design Options

Stabilisation:

1. *Variation of transistor conduction period, δT, with a fixed operating frequency to maintain V_o constant.* This type of system is the easiest to design and troubleshoot. Also the losses in the collector voltage control circuits are much more defined. The biggest problem is the operation under 'standby' or light loading when the control circuit tries to make the transistor switch 'on' for less than 1μs. The system constraints are such that either such a small pulse width could never be achieved or very poor switching would result. When considering loads such as that of a colour television, this particular problem is not important as the load is relatively constant. As items such as remote control, games and Teletext become popular, this problem could however become more significant.
2. *Variation of transistor conduction period, δT, with a variable operating frequency to maintain the output voltage V_o constant.* This is the inherent operating mode (combined with c.e.t.) of the self oscillating switching mode supply. The positive points for this system are cost, simplicity and efficiency. The negative balance is design difficulty, variable performance/reliability. Performance/reliability problems can be overcome with the use of a Darlington transistor.
3. *Fixed transistor conduction period, δT, with variable operating frequency to maintain the output voltage constant.* This does not seem to have any particular system advantages, except for its wide stabilisation range.

Energy Transfer: This option determines the transformer T1 size, the peak transistor collector current, and the radiating properties of the system. Modern ferrite materials result in a transformer design which is core saturation limited rather than hysteresis loss limited, for the frequency (15-30kHz) and power (20-200W) range considered. With this saturation constraint only half the core volume is required for c.e.t. system, c.f. an i.e.t. one at the same minimum frequency.

C.e.t. also means the output rectifier D1 has stopped conducting when the transistor switches 'on' again, so there is minimal reverse recovery radiation from the diode and a minimal turn 'on' collector current spike due to the rectifier recovery. The i.e.t. system is the converse of this with the transistor switching 'on' when the output diode is still conducting resulting in collector current spikes caused by the output rectifier reverse recovery.

Under worst case conditions the peak collector current at turn 'off' in the c.e.t. system will be about 60% higher than in the i.e.t. system.

Summarizing:

1. *C.E.T.*
   Smaller transformer, lower inherent radiation from the output rectifiers and transistor turn on, higher peak transistor collector current.

2. *I.E.T.*
   Larger transformer, higher inherent radiation from the output rectifiers and the transistor turn on, lower peak transistor current.

Operating Frequency: Generally the higher the minimum operating frequency is, the smaller will be the transformer. If the transistor switching losses (including collector voltage control circuits) are constant per cycle then the higher the frequency the higher the switching losses resulting in a decreased power supply efficiency. Thus the choice of operating frequency range is basically a compromise between the above factors. Present constraints limit the range to 15-32kHz. To keep out of the audio range the limits become 19-32kHz.

1. *Variable Operating Frequency*
   The desirable operating range has been defined above. If the operating frequency goes above the 32kHz limit then it can be arranged that the self oscillating system goes into a burst (discontinuous) mode resulting in a lower overall loss, c.f. if the frequency had been allowed to rise. A potential problem of the variable operating frequency aspect is if this radiates into other parts of the receiver then varying interference problems can arise as the load power changes.

2. *Fixed Operating Frequency*
   This can either be related to the horizontal scan rate or independent. Figure 11 shows the frequency spectrum of concern. Prime frequency sources are shown above the line and their harmonics below it.

It can be seen that there is a relatively free frequency band between 25 and 29kHz which inherently will have the least interaction with other set functions in this frequency range. This result leads to the development of the 27kHz power supply concept described in the next chapter.

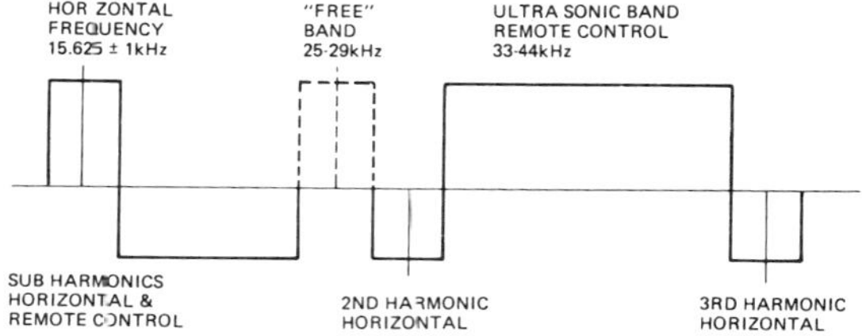

FIGURE 11. Frequency Spectrum

Table 1 gives a matrix which summarises the options and indicates the conditions under which some current systems operate. Figures 12 and 13 illustrate the effects of frequency and energy transfer on transformer size and transistor collector current.

Table 1

Energy Transfer \ Control	Fixed Operating Frequency: Locked to Horizontal	Fixed Operating Frequency: Free Run	Variable Operating Frequency
C.e.t.		27kHz	Y
I.e.t.	X	19kHz	

Primary Power Losses

The non-isolated section of the power supply will have *major* power losses in the following areas:

(a) Rectifier surge limiting resistor (5-15W)
(b) Control circuit supply (1-7W)
(c) Driver circuit supply (7-20W)
(d) Switching transistor base circuit power (1-10W)
(e) Switching transistor collector voltage control (7-18W)

(a) *Rectifier Surge Limiting Resistor:* This power loss will be decided by the mains on/off switch and the bridge rectifier ratings. As such it is a common loss to all forms of switching mode supply. Without any other power loss in the system this resistor reduces the 200W switching mode maximum efficiency into the 90-95% region.

(b), (c) *Supplies and* (d) *Base Power:* These three power losses are interactive and are thus considered as a group. There are three favoured systems of providing the initial supply start up power for (b), (c), (d). (Once the switching mode begins to operate additional power can be drawn from the output transformer.) These are:

(i) Small mains transformer.
   This implies a cost penalty, but the further isolated winding could be used for the remote control power in remote on/off applications and as a charger on the hand control unit.

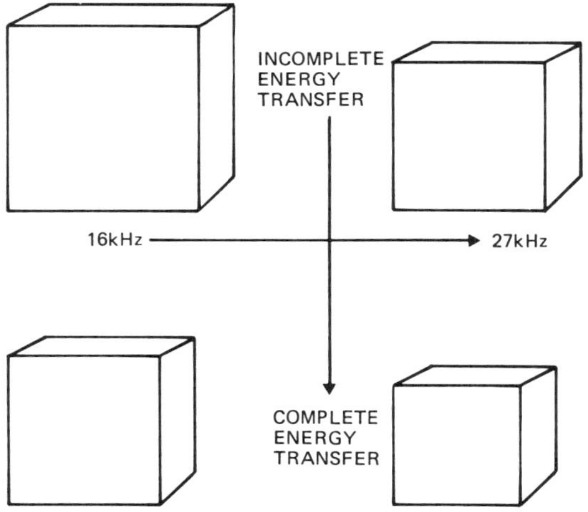

FIGURE 12. 200W Isolated Switching Mode Relative Transformer Size

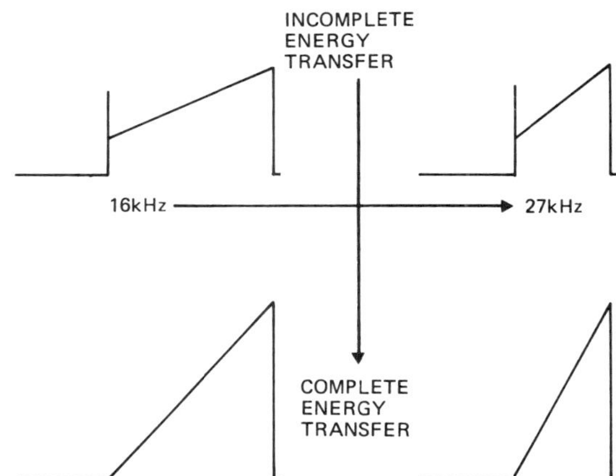

FIGURE 13. 200W Isolated Switching Mode Relative Collector Currents

(ii) High value resistors from the rectified mains. The problem here is the dissipation incurred, in producing currents of more than a few milliamps, reduces overall power supply efficiency and reliability. Table 2 shows the power rating required for different resistor values.

Table 2

Resistor Value kΩ ± 5%	Power Rating W	Current into low voltage rail Max mA	Min mA
680	0.25	0.52	0.29
330	0.5	1.07	0.58
150	1	2.4	1.3
82	2	4.3	2.3
56	3	6.3	3.4
33	5	11	5.8
18	8	20	11
15	10	24	13
12	12	30	16
9.1	16	39	21

In a fixed frequency system the amount of power lost in items (b), (c) and (d) should not exceed about 15W for reasonable switching mode efficiency (80-90%). In the 27kHz c.e.t. system described in the next chapter the driver (c) and control (b) circuits are series connected so that the same current is used twice functionally. The actual current available for the control circuit supply is shown in Table 2 for high and low input supplies. The maximum running loss for (b), (c) (d) in this system is about 15W. An equivalent 19kHz c.e.t. system loses about 13W. If transistor VT1 in Figure 10 is a Darlington device, as discussed later, obviously the power loss needs to be of the same order, and stacking of the control circuit and driver is not possible.

As the current for the driver (c) is not required when the Darlington is 'on', drawing its base power (d), and vice versa, it could be possible to use the same current for both functions and switch it between the two. Under worst case conditions something like 20mA would be available for the functions (b), (c) and (d). The control function would take about 6mA leaving 14mA for the driver and Darlington.

Self-oscillating variable frequency Darlington switching mode system require much less power for items (b), (c) and (d), i.e. about 5W. The real requirement for this system is a starting bias for the power transistor. A capacitive pump, or differentiating system, is favoured for providing a starting bias without the possibility of thermal runaway under quiescent conditions.

(iii) Capacitive pumps/differentiators.

A 'wattless' method of obtaining a 20mA low voltage supply is shown in Figure 14. This circuit is not particularly cheap but it is efficient. A

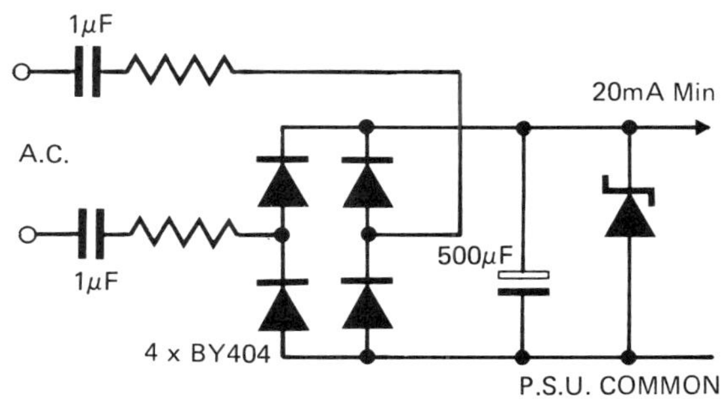

FIGURE 14. Capacitive Pump Circuit

variable frequency system uses a capacitive differentiator to apply a positive current pulse to the base of the self oscillating supply's power transistor, as shown in Figure 15. This produces a 3ms collector current pulse of $h_{FE}I_B$. If the circuit is functioning correctly oscillations will start. Under certain fault conditions the transistor will be turned 'on' with full supply voltage across it. This forward safe area stress may cause device failure as the h_{FE} and I_B values could vary over a large range.

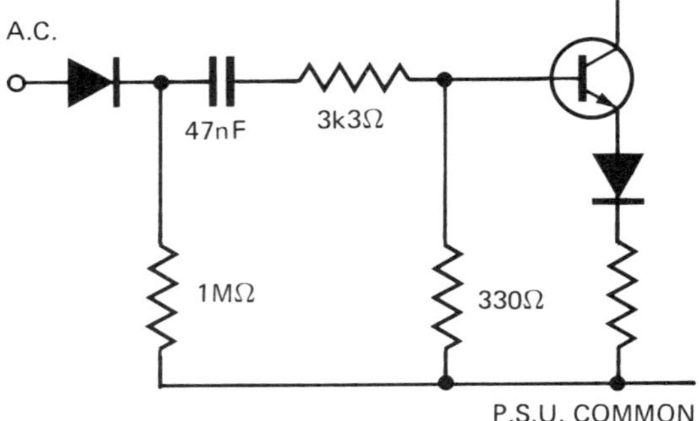

FIGURE 15. Starting Bias Circuit of a Variable Frequency

A better method would be to bias the transistor in common base and completely define the maximum collector current under 'stopped' fault conditions, as shown in Figure 16. Also the a.c. voltage at which the circuit starts is better defined in this system.

A self oscillating system draws minimal power for items (b) and (c). The only large power loss (d) is in the series base resistor which is in the range of 5-10W.

(e) *Switching Transistor Collector Voltage Control:* The two main power losses here are in the dV_{CE}/dt network and peak voltage clipper network discharge resistors. The 19kHz c.e.t. circuit loses 7W in each of these resistors giving a total loss of 14W. In the 27kHz c.e.t. system an extra voltage margin on the transistors BV_{CBO} rating and careful design allows the peak voltage clipper circuit to be removed.

Present transistor specifications for dV_{CE}/dt are 1000V/μs maximum. Any power reduction in the dV_{CE}/dt limiter can only come from increased dV_{CE}/dt ratings on the transistor. Another possibility would be to design a dV_{CE}/dt circuit where the power was fed back to the supply.

Figure 17 shows the dV/dt circuit power loss against BV_{CBO}. As can be seen there is an optimum where the power can be minimised. The values on the left hand vertical axis need to be multiplied by $f_0/5$(kHz) to give the power loss. The two right hand axes are for 20 and 27kHz 200W operation. This clearly shows the increased losses due to higher frequency and c.e.t. operation. The i.e.t. power loss is optimistic as a peak voltage clamp is likely to be needed because of the increased leakage inductance energy. As noted earlier in the 19kHz i.e.t. circuit the sum of the dV_{CE}/dt and $\hat{V}_{CE}$ powers is roughly equal to the 27kHz c.e.t. dV_{CE}/dt and $\hat{V}_{CE}$ power (the c.e.t. system has no $\hat{V}_{CE}$ limiter).

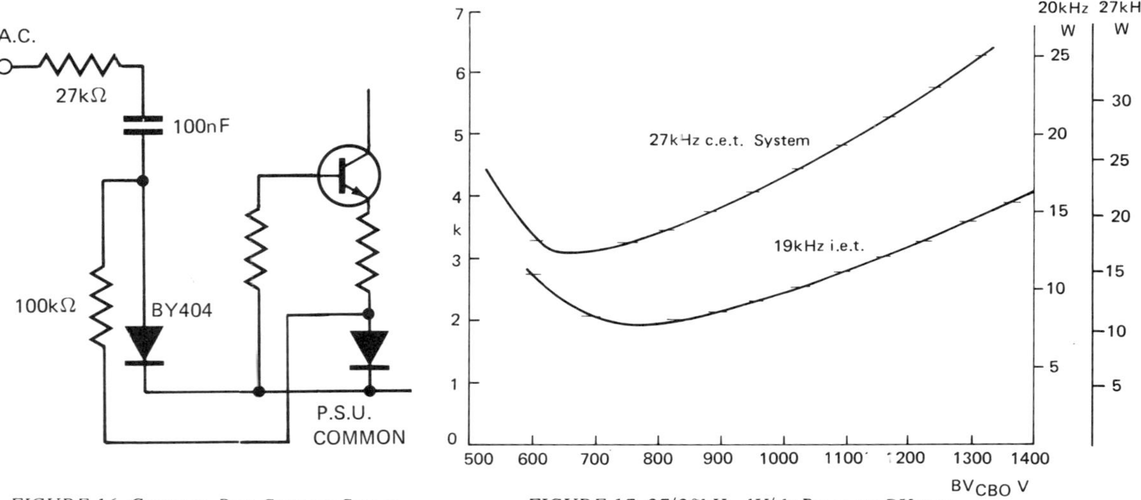

FIGURE 16. Common Base Start up System

FIGURE 17. 27/20kHz dV/dt Power vs BV_{CBO}

The Output Power Transistor

For a 200W switching mode power supply the output power transistor (VT1 in Figure 10) needs to be an 800V 4A device for Europe and 400V 8A device for the US. A number of advantages are obtained if it is possible to use a Darlington transistor in this position instead of a single transistor. These are:

- Moré consistant and faster switching over a large collector current range.
- It can be directly driven without the need of a driver transformer.
- A lower drive current leads to improved circuit efficiency and lower driver VA.
- In practical situations the device power loss is not substantially different to a single device.

Device V.A. Rating: Figure 18 shows the basic circuit analysed to produce the device VA ratings. The transformer's leakage inductance L_L was taken as 1/100th of the primary inductance Lp. This is realistic for c.e.t. types and optimistic for i.e.t. types. The calculations were done for c.e.t./i.e.t. operations and for 20 and 27kHz. The basic calculation procedure is:

Choose V_o and Lp for say V_i = 200V, and P_o = 200W.

For 1000V/μs collector voltage the control capacitor C2 = I_C nF; calculate L_L.

Calculate I_C for 370V inputs; calculate leakage energy in L_L and resultant peak voltage when in resonance with capacitor C2; calculate the transistors working V_{CE}.

Allow a 50% margin on the resonant voltage of capacitor C2 above the input voltage V_1 (370). This voltage relative to the common (emitter) is taken as the BV_{CBO}.

Allow a 20% margin on the maximum I_C at V_i = 200V for tolerancing.

The product of these two is the device VA rating.

This is shown in Figures 19 and 20 for 27kHz and 20kHz. It will be noted the device VA optimum is slightly lower for 27kHz operation. This is because the transformer leakage inductance energy decreases with increasing frequency resulting in a lower voltage at resonance with capacitor C2. As the c.e.t. system requires the highest VA it is wise to optimise for this system. This indicates BV_{CBO} = 800V is the best choice. The gain specification should be made at I_C = 4A, V_{CE} = 1.5V.

Darlington Gain Characteristics: The calculations in the primary power loss section established that for efficient operation the maximum available rectified mains drive current for the output Darlington is about 14mA. Assuming, as just indicated, an I_C of 4A, the required gain h_{FE} is 4/0.014 = 280 @ V_{CE} = 1.5V.

Alternatively the switching mode operation could be started with this 14mA and then additional current supplied from the switching mode transformer. The drive winding should produce about 12V (rectified) and the power loading (from an efficiency viewpoint) should be about 6W. This implies an additional base current of 270mA giving h_{FE} = 4/0.284 = 14. The drawbacks with this system are briefly:

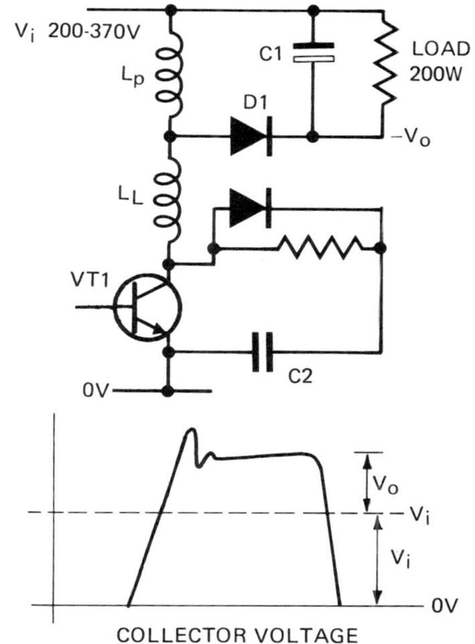

FIGURE 18. Circuit Analysed for VA Ratings

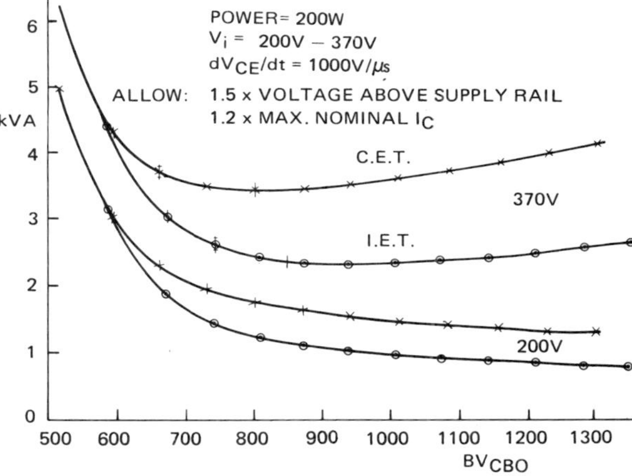

FIGURE 19. Device VA at 27kHz

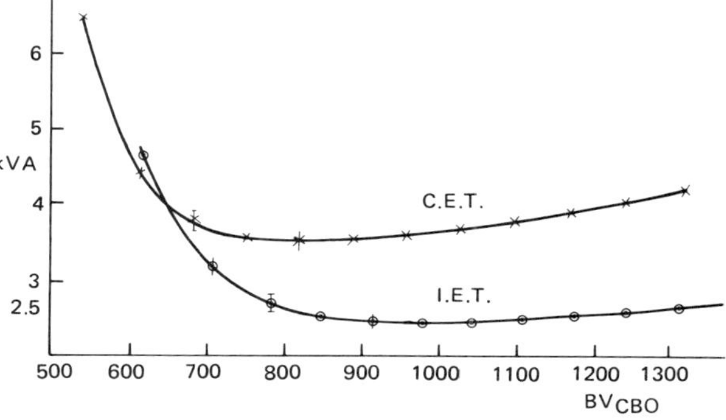

FIGURE 20. Device VA at 20kHz

1. added complexity/unreliability/power loss.
2. increase current for the Darlington turn 'off' driver.
3. some sensing would have to be added to the control function to restrict the pulse width during start up when only 14mA of drive was available. The extra circuitry required, shown in Figure 21, will, obviously, add a small amount to the overall cost.

A compromise to this system would be to draw, say, 30mA from the existing reference rail ($\simeq$25-35V). The required gain of the device would then be $4/.042 \simeq 100$ and the extra cost only about one third of the previous amount.

The Darlington Turn 'Off' Device: Experience with the BU180A Darlington transistor showed that turn 'off' base currents of 15 to 30% of the collector current gave acceptable switching times. So the turn 'off' driver device should have a gain specified at the 4A x 0.3 = 1.2A level. From earlier calculations the available base current for this device is about 14mA giving an h_{FE} of 85. For rapid switching the device could be overdriven by a factor of 2 to 3. Thus the minimum gain requirement becomes about 200 times. The device should not develop an excessive voltage across itself at 1.2A so the h_{FE} needs to be specified at V_{CE} = 1V. An approximate device specification would be as follows:

(a) npn Bipolar transistor.

Absolute maximum ratings:

Collector Emitter voltage $I_B = 0$	15V
Emitter base voltage	5V
Peak collector current (10% duty cycle)	1.5A
Continuous Dissipation @ 75°C ambient	200mW:

Electrical Characteristics:	min	max	
BV_{EBO} @ $I_E = 0.1$mA	5		V
I_{CEO} @ $V_{CE} = 12$V		1	μA
h_{FE} @ $V_{CE} = 1$V, $I_C = 1.2$A	200		

Such a device is the BSR59.

(b) F.E.T.

An alternative technique would be to use an n-channel junction f.e.t. to provide the turn 'off' drive, as illustrated in Figure 22. The peak current requirement for the f.e.t. would be about 1.2A. As the f.e.t. looks like a fixed resistance (below its pinch off) one would need a very large area to match the effective r_{sat} of the biopolar turn 'off' transistor ($\triangleq 1/1.2 = 0.8\Omega$).

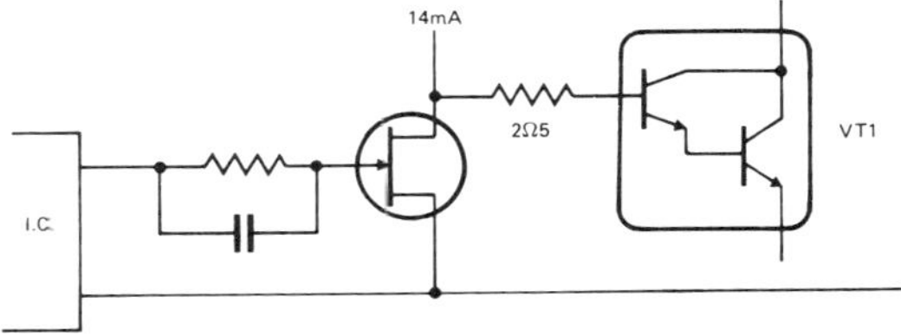

FIGURE 22. F.E.T. Turn 'Off' Circuit

One solution would be to use the r_{DS} of the f.e.t. to define the Darlington's $I_{B(off)}$ rather than by inductance. A series padding resistor equal to the r_{DS} maximum would reduce variations in $I_{B(off)}$ due to the f.e.t. r_{DS}. Assuming a voltage of 5V on the Darlington's base at turn 'off', the required $I_{B(off)}$ total resistance becomes $5/1.2 = 4\Omega$ giving $r_{DS} \triangleq 2\Omega$. This input capacity would be of the order of 100pF which does not represent any i.c. driving problem.

Thus an approximate F.E.T. Specification would be:

Absolute Maximum Ratings

V_{SG}	10V
V_{DS}	15V
V_{DG}	25V
Peak Drain Current (10% duty cycle)	2A
Continuous dissipation at 75°C ambient	400mW

Electrical Characteristics	max
$V_{DS(on)}$ @ $V_{GS} = 0$, $I_D = 1.2$A	2.5V*
$V_{GS(off)}$ @ $V_{DS} = 5$V, $I_D = 1\mu$A	–3V

*This value could need to be reduced to allow for temperature effects.

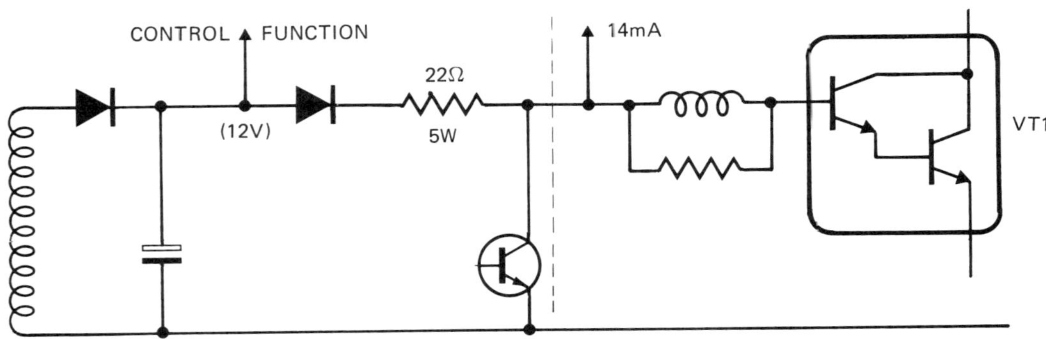

FIGURE 21. Extra Components for Low Gain Darlington

Both the above solutions (a) and (b) are inherently simple for, from a circuit point of view, interfacing between the control i.c.s. low drive capability and the Darlington's high turn 'off' current requirement. More complicated alternatives are (i) using a 'fast' Darlington (having V_{CEsat} and turn 'off' problems) or (ii) a parallel connected transistor/thyristor pair; (the thyristor would sink the Darlington 'off' current and the transistor would commutate the thyristor and sink the Darlington I_B (on)).

(c) Thyristor.
In a self oscillating power supply a thyristor turn 'off' system is adequate as the supply's operation automatically commutates the thyristor.
Salient features are:
(i) The device must not have a large 'on' voltage, V_T, or this will result in excessive power dissipation.
(ii) Its turn 'on' times must not be too slow or there will be power loss and poorly defined 'off' drive for the output Darlington.
(iii) The communication times must not be too long so as to result in premature 'burst mode' operation and reduction of power supply loading.

Thus an appropriate Thyristor Specification would be:

Absolute Maximum Ratings:	
Repetitive Peak off state voltage	20V
Repetitive Reverse voltage	10V
Average current @ 70°C ambient	300mA
Repetitive surge current	2A
Electrical Characteristics:	max
I_{GT} gate trigger current @ V_{AA} = 5V I_A = 1.5A	0.2mA
V_T on state voltage @ I_A = 1.5A	1.6V
Switching Characteristics:	
t_{gt}, gate controlled turn 'on' time @ I_G = 0.4mA I_A = 1.5A	1µs
t_q, circuit commutated turn 'off' time	5µs

Such a device would be the BRY59.

Control Circuit Features

Self Oscillating Systems: One form of control mechanism on a variable frequency system is as shown in Figure 23, i.e. that of peak current setting. Resistors R1 and R2 form a potential divider across the negative voltage source V1 (generated by a diode and capacitor from the base winding). When the transistor VT1 current through resistor R4 generates a voltage equal to that across resistor R1 plus the triggering voltage of the thyristor Th1, the thyristor fires commencing the turn 'off' process of the transistor. Extra current from the error amplifier reduces

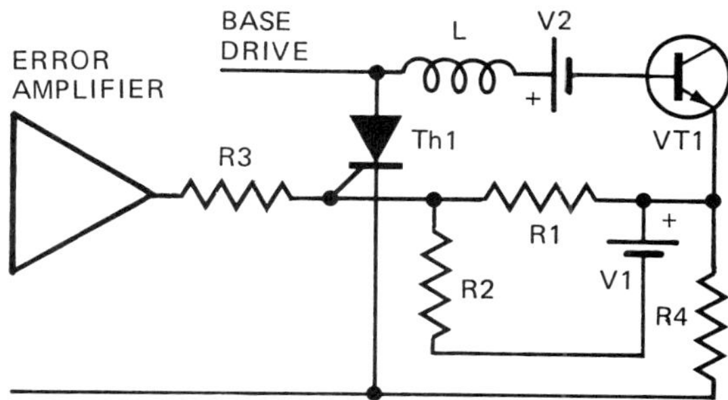

FIGURE 23. Variable Frequency Supply Control System

the voltage drop across resistor R1 and lowers the peak current to which the transistor ramps. When the thyristor fires it has to sink the transistor turn 'off' current (≏1.5A) plus the positive base drive (≏1.5A) giving a very high anode current for the thyristor. The turn 'off' base current slope for the transistor is controlled by the series base inductor L and the voltage source V2 (generated by a diode and capacitor from the base drive winding). Being a c.e.t. system the transistor remains 'off' until all the stored energy has been transferred; (the thyristor Th1 is commutated by the reversed base drive during this period ready for the next cycle). At the end of this period the circuit rings sufficiently to cause positive base current and initiates another cycle. As the load power decreases the operating frequency increases. A point is reached when the thyristor commutating time is longer than the energy transfer period and the thyristor latches 'on' stopping the oscillation. After period the circuit restarts and a further burst of operation occurs before the thyristor latches 'on' again. (As explained in the starting circuits in the primary power loss section). This system will typically go into the 'burst mode' below about 40% power loading. Its problems therefore, are:

(a) The turn-'off' thyristor suffers a high average dissipation due to the high peak currents.
(b) The point at which 'bursting' begins is very dependent on thyristor commutation time which itself is very temperature dependent.
(c) At supply start-up and close down the two voltage sources V1 and V2 are not well defined giving poor transistor switching.
(d) The transistor positive base drive current varies over a wide range giving poor switching.
(e) The whole performance of the power supply depends on the interaction of the transistor and thyristor which can give some very good, or bad, results.

These problems with the exception of (b) can be completely overcome by using a Darlington for the power switch and some circuitry changes as detailed in the voltage regulating transformer (v.r.t.) section of Chapter III. Producing a thyristor with a very short commutating time is not the complete answer, as this would allow the supply to oscillate to much higher frequencies (causing extra $dV_{CE}dt$ resistor loss) before 'bursting' set in.

Fixed Frequency Systems: The type of control circuits currently employed for this function are the SN76549, TDA 2640 and the SL442. They have the following features which are the basic minimum necessary for a control i.c.

(a) Current Consumption:
The start-up/run supply currents are relatively high considering the current has to come from the rectified a.c. supply so causing a large power loss i.e. 6/8mA TDA2640, 9/15mA SN76549, –/45mA SL442 (mains transformer recommended).

(b) Start Up/Close Down Voltage Features:
The principle here is that the i.c. should not produce any output until its supply rail is sufficiently high for all the necessary internal circuits to be functioning correctly. (In the SN76549 this is done by including a series zener in the output transistors feed from the i.c.s. supply rail).
A problem which arises when additional current is being supplied to the i.c. from the switching mode transformer once the system is running, is the resultant starting and stopping voltages of the complete power supply. A supply may start at 170V a.c. and run down to 110V a.c. Obviously such low voltage running is not good for the power switch. The problem can also occur at a.c. supply switch 'off' if the rectified supply rail falls more rapidly than that of the i.c. One answer is to have a current trip level close to the normal operating level so that the circuit shuts down quickly once the main supply rail starts to fall and the power switches peak current goes up. The disadvantage with this, is that operations which impose quite heavy short term loads on the power supply cause tripping and temporary shut down, if the current trip is set low. An alternative to this, used in the SL442, is to have a current trip which must be activated a certain number of times before the i.c. shuts down.
As on the SN76549 there should be a minimum output pulse limit ($\simeq 1\mu s$) in the interest of good switching from the power switch. To cope with loadings below 10% of the maximum output power the control system should go into a 'burst' mode as described for the variable frequency system.
Under certain conditions there may be ill-defined start-up and shut down of the power supply with a.c. mains. A good way to overcome this, is to have a control i.c. connection fed from an external resistive divider from the rectified mains, which, when its voltage is above a certain value, allows output pulses, and, when below another voltage, inhibits output pulses. Some hysteresis is required between the two voltage sense levels. This input is returned to the i.c. supply if such an operation is not required. By using this pin a remote controlled on/off could be achieved.

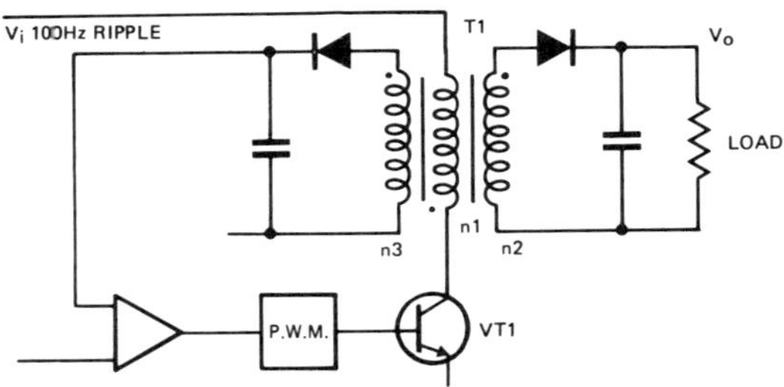

FIGURE 24. Feedback Loop.

(c) Feedback Loop:
Figure 24 shows the feedback loop which exists in all the current isolated switching mode supplies. Winding n3 is closely coupled to the output winding n2 so that its rectified voltage reflects the state of the load voltage. (The load voltage cannot be sensed directly as it is isolated from the rest of the circuit.) This voltage is compared with a reference voltage, the difference being amplied and applied to a pulse width modulator (p.w.m.) which then drives the power switch VT1. The p.w.m. is generally a circuit which gives out a pulse of predetermined time. If the d.c. input rail V_i were without any a.c. ripple this would be ideal. In practice V_i will have some ripple which will increase or decrease the voltage applied to the transformer T1 primary winding nl, for the conduction time of the power switch. Hence the energy stored at the end of the pulse will be greater or smaller than desired, with the result that ripple will be fed to the output, V_O. This is sensed by the feedback winding and so the modulators pulse width is varied to try and reduce the effect. In some cases ripple direct from V_i is fed to the error amplifier to anticipate the ripple which would be produced in V_O and remove it. Unfortunately, the compensation cannot be perfect because (i) the ripple spectrum shape in V_O is different to that in V_i, and (ii) the overall loop gain varies with V_i and loading. With a c.e.t. system at constant power loading P_O, zero ripple would occur on the output rail V_C, if each cycle passed a package of energy $1/2 L_p i_1{}^2$ equal to $P_O . \tau$. This system would completely reject the input supply V_i ripple voltage. As the primary inductance L_p is constant such an operation implies the power switch should be cut 'off' when its collector current reaches i_1. Thus in such a system, the power switch current would become part of the p.w.m. loop. A typical power switch current waveform is shown in

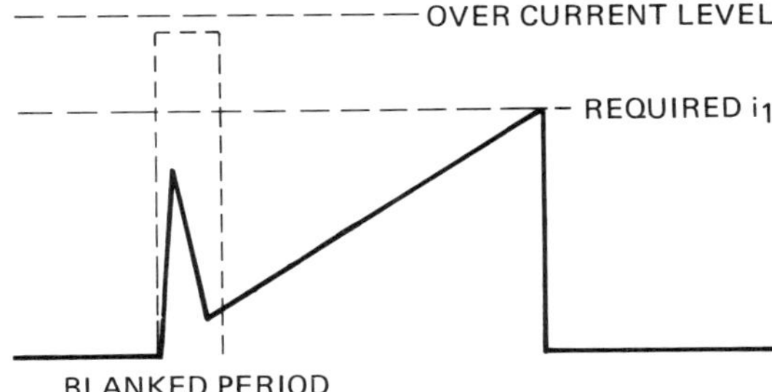

FIGURE 25. Current Waveform

Figure 25. The initial spike is the discharge of the dV_{CE}/dt capacitor and any other capacitances. It would seem reasonable to blank this period from the current amplitude sensing circuit for 1μs. Normally the control circuit would sense the current i_1 had been reached and turn 'off' the power switch. If the overcurrent limit was reached at any time the power switch would be cut off. The SL442 has a feature which allows a number of overcurrent detections before inhibiting any further output pulses. Thus, on long term overloads, the system shuts down but on load surges the circuit goes into a constant power mode. The vulnerability of such a system is that when the power switch current monitoring is lost, an open circuit could be detected as an overcurrent, but a short circuit would not be detected.

OUTPUT RECTIFICATION

Diode D1

Normally the diodes operating peak inverse voltage will be the primary power transistors working voltage, divided by the transformers turned ratio. If an optimum design is followed as for the primary section then the diodes voltage rating is $V_r \hat{=} 4V_O$ and its working value would be $\hat{=} 3V_O$. The maximum average diode current is $P_O/V_O = I_O$, while the actual forward current during the diodes conduction time will be $4 \times I_O \rightarrow$ zero for the c.e.t. mode and about $2.5 \times I_O \rightarrow 1 \times I_O$ for the i.e.t. mode. Only the forward losses need to be taken into account for c.e.t. systems. For i.e.t. systems the reverse recovery losses can represent a significant power loss and need to be examined. In an i.e.t. system running at 20kHz, the power output per mJ of transformer peak energy will be about 10W/mJ. Hence the transformers total peak stored energy is $P_O/10$mJ. The output winding inductance will be:

$$2P_O/\{10 \times (2.5 \times I_O)^2\} = 0.032P_O/I_O^2 \quad \text{mH.}$$

If the ratio of inductance to leakage inductance is about 80:1 then the output leakage inductance is

$$0.4P_O/I_O^2 \ \mu\text{H.}$$

Hence the turn 'off' current slope applied to the diode will be: $3 \times V_O \times I_O^2/0.4P_O = 7.4\ I_O$ A/μs.

Values of the output current I_O and turn 'off' current slope for various different diode ratings and three output power levels (50W, 100W and 200W) are given in Table 3.

A diode which is well suited for use in this position is the BY205.

So far only a single output system has been considered. Multi-output systems are much more complex. The above reasoning could be applied to any output of a multi system which provides, say, 60% of the total output power. Other lower power outputs need to be individually examined.

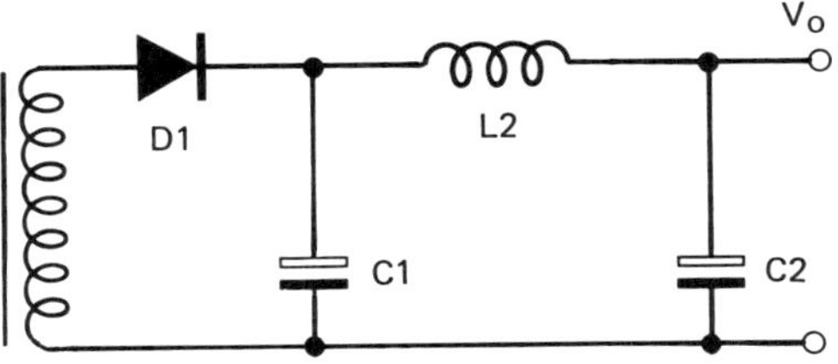

FIGURE 26. Output Rectification

Smoothing

The components following the diode smooth the rectified a.c. The additional sections, inductor L2 and capacitor C2 serve to reduce transient spikes across capacitor C1 caused by the inevitable r.f.i. and inductance. If the power is relatively lower, inductor L2 could be replaced by a resistor or the additional section entirely removed. A study on the total system stability and output ripple voltage showed 'optimum' performance resulted when capacitor C1 on the main output rail is as large as possible. Practically one aims for the resonant frequency of capacitor C1 and its transformer winding inductance to be about twenty times the operating frequency.

Spikes on the output rails can cause problems. Careful layout and the use of inductor L2 to 'feed off' the power supply board helps. In severe cases a coupled choke in the positive and the common rails might be needed.

Table 3

Diode Rating	V_O	V_R TEST	50W		100W		200W	
			I_O	dI/dt	I_O	dI/dt	I_O	dI/dt
V	V	V	A	A/μs	A	A/μs	A	A/μs
100	25	75	2	15	4	30	8	60
200	50	150	1	7.5	2	15	4	30
400	100	300	0.5	3.75	1	7.5	2	15
600	150	450	0.33	2.5	0.66	5	1.33	10
800	200	600	0.25	1.9	0.5	3.75	1	7.5
1000	250	750	0.2	1.5	0.4	3	0.8	6

REFERENCES

1. Applications Laboratory Staff of Texas Instruments Incorporated, *Electronic Power Control and Digital Techniques,* McGraw-Hill Book Company, New York, 1976, pp. 65-77.

2. Applications Laboratory Staff of Texas Instruments Incorporated, *Electronic Power Control and Digital Techniques,* McGraw-Hill Book Company, New York, 1976, pp. 4-10.

II DESIGN OF ISOLATED SWITCHING MODE POWER SUPPLIES

by
Peter Wilson

Switching mode power supplies, particularly in their isolated form, fill a niche which has arisen, for example, with the development of 'add on' units such as video cassette recorders and Hi-Fi sound, games, etc, in television receivers. In some parts of the world, e.g. Australia, isolation is mandatory for safety reasons. This is a trend which is likely to spread to European countries in future receiver designs. Cost, efficiency, performance and reliability are the design criteria. The cost of the isolated supply should not be prohibitively high, ideally being only marginally higher than current non-isolated units. Efficiency is becoming a selling point in the current environment of high cost energy. It is also important, from the reliability viewpoint, to design so that the system does not run normally at a high temperature, this being a common cause of component failure. The performance of the isolated supply should be at least as good as that of its non-isolated counterparts, particularly in respect of load regulation and line stabilisation, and overload and over voltage protection. Radiation, both into the input supply and into the rest of the t.v. receiver, also needs to be considered in order to meet the relevant regulations (e.g. VDE0872 in Western Germany). Similarly the isolation provided by the power supply must conform with the relevant standards, e.g. BS415 and the International Electrotechnical Commission (IEC) Recommendation 65.

The design procedures described in this chapter, therefore, lead to a supply which represents a good balance between cost, efficiency and performance, thus providing a realistic solution for an isolated power supply for a colour television receiver, but which is also applicable, in part or fully, to other supply applications.

PRINCIPLES

Basic System

For ease of isolation and multi-voltage output rails, a shunt switching regulator is the simplest approach to consider for a switching mode power supply. Figure 1 shows the basic circuit arrangement where transformer T1 provides the isolation. The drive pulse turns the output transistor VT1 'on' for a certain time to store up energy from the supply in the transformer. Then when the drive turns transistor VT1 'off' the energy is transferred via the diodes D1 and D2 to the outputs V_o. Capacitors C1 and C2 serve as energy storage devices reducing the ripple voltage at the outputs. Unlike the series type of power supply, chopper or conventional regulated, where if the transistor fails by going short circuit, the output voltage goes to the input value; the shunt chopper is fail safe as the fuse in the supply blows. Similarly if the transistor goes open circuit the output just goes to zero. With regulation tending to be

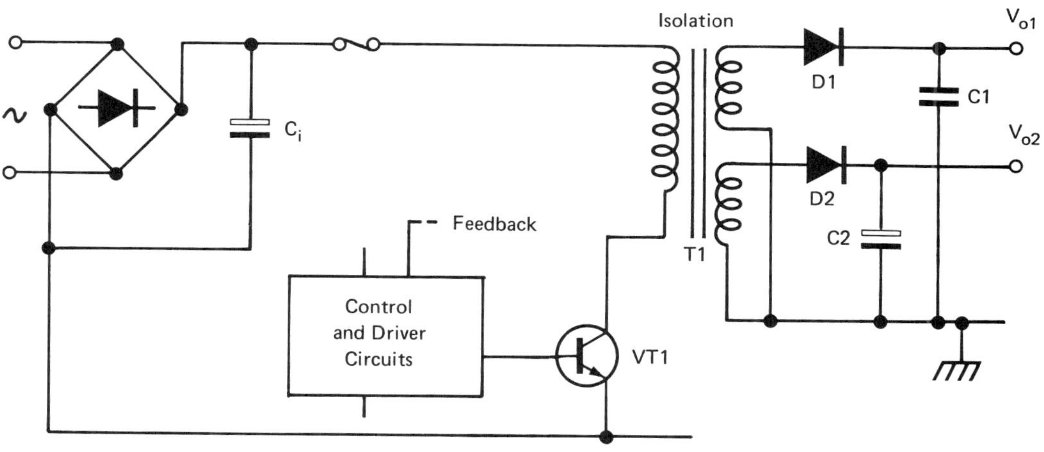

FIGURE 1. Basic Shunt Switching Regulator

poor at low power levels, it is usually necessary, to maintain a reasonably stable output voltage, to keep a minimum loading; but this is usually the case with a multiple output supply. The starting circuits for the shunt mode are, however, more complex than those required for the series mode.

A non-isolated version of the shunt switching regulator could use a choke in place of the transformer with taps to provide the required supply voltages. The reference voltage could then be derived directly from the output supply.

Energy Transfer

As explained in the Design Options section of the previous chapter, two distinct modes of operation are possible for the transformer/choke.

Complete Energy Transfer (c.e.t.) where all the energy stored in the transformer/choke is transferred to the secondary circuits before the switching transistor VT1 is turned 'on'.

Incomplete Energy Transfer (i.e.t.) where the energy stored in the choke/transformer is not completely transferred to the secondary circuits before the transistor VT1 is turned 'on'.

To achieve c.e.t. a relatively low transformer T1 primary inductance is required which results in higher peak collector currents in the switching transistor VT1. As a consequence, winding losses are increased, as is the ripple current in the input reservoir capacitor C_i. The higher peak current also indicates the need for a larger switching device. When all the energy stored in the transformer has been transferred to the secondary circuits, the reverse voltage across the switching device falls, eventually settling to the input supply voltage. Consequently, when the switching transistor is again turned 'on', the initial collector current is zero, and the collector emitter voltage substantially lower than that seen in an i.e.t. system. The net result is low dissipation in the transistor at turn 'on', and a reduction in fast transients which are known to give rise to interference. A c.e.t. design will result in the secondary rectifiers switching 'off' at low current levels, substantially reducing device dissipation and turn 'off' transients which would otherwise need to be filtered out of the supply lines.

The i.e.t. mode demands a high collector current flow at transistor turn 'on' and can lead to high device dissipation, even when the base waveforms are optimised. The higher transformer primary inductance, however, results in a lower peak collector current at the end of the

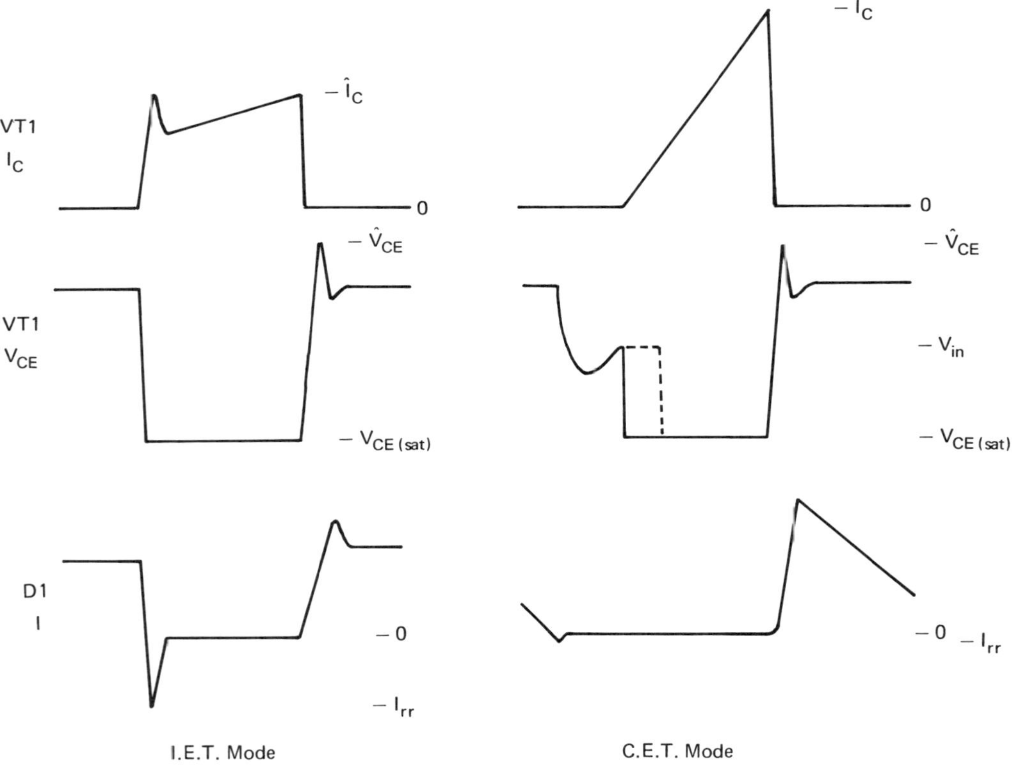

FIGURE 2. Comparison of Waveforms for I.E.T. and C.E.T. Modes

transistor conduction time than that experienced when using a c.e.t. system of equivalent output power. Since there is residual stored energy in the transformer core of an i.e.t. system, the core volume will be greater than for the c.e.t. system, other factors being equal. For typical systems, the effective core volume, V_e, in the c.e.t. mode approaches half that of the i.e.t. effective core volume.

Figure 2 shows a comparison of the waveforms for c.e.t. and i.e.t. systems.

Operating Frequency

With non-isolated regulators, some component saving could be made by operating at the horizontal scan frequency, the oscillator stage being common to both. However, the added complication of isolation detracts from this saving and a separate oscillator and control circuit are again a viable proposition. Provided that switching losses do not become disproportionate, operation at a higher frequency will result in a smaller transformer core being required, and in a reduction in the size of smoothing components. A frequency of 27kHz is chosen as it is not related to the horizontal scan frequency and so avoids spurious locking. It is also below the frequency band used by remote control units using ultrasonics and above its sub harmonics. The transformer core size is directly proportional to frequency. Thus, other factors being equal, operation at 27kHz results in a core size only 58% of the volume required at 15.6kHz, as illustrated in Figure 12 of the previous chapter.

DESIGN PROCEDURE

Circuit Arrangement

A basic block diagram of a switching mode power supply operating in the shunt mode is shown in Figure 3. The secondary windings on transformer T1 are chosen to give the required output supply voltages. In order to take advantage of the smaller transformer size the supply is operated in the c.e.t. mode and at 27kHz. The high voltage output device VT1 switches the current through the primary of transformer T1, its conduction time being controlled by the driver stage. To remove the need of an additional low voltage supply, a high voltage driver stage is used fed from the rectified a.c. line. The supply for the control circuit is therefore taken from the driver stage to reduce dissipation which is inherent with series dropping resistors. An additional transformer winding is used to provide a feedback signal for the control circuit, which modulates the width of the drive pulse.

A complete 200W isolated switching mode power supply circuit diagram is given in Figure 4. This, together with a suitable printed circuit board layout, is described fully later in the chapter. Such a supply features:

- Stable output(s) over a wide range of input voltage, 180-265V a.c.
- Good load regulation in the working range, 200-100W.
- High efficiency – better than 80%.
- Reliability using proven and currently available semiconductors.
- Cost effectiveness.
- Small size.
- Use of the SN76549 control i.c. giving:
  controlled operation at switch 'on', switch 'off' and in the event of loss of feedback signal; fast acting protection circuit with permanent shut down in the event of a persistant overload.

The Output Circuits

The output voltage supplies chosen for and generated by the circuit shown in Figure 4 are:

220V at 100mA i.e. 22W
160V at 900mA i.e. 144W
and 30V at 1A i.e. 30W, a total of 196W.

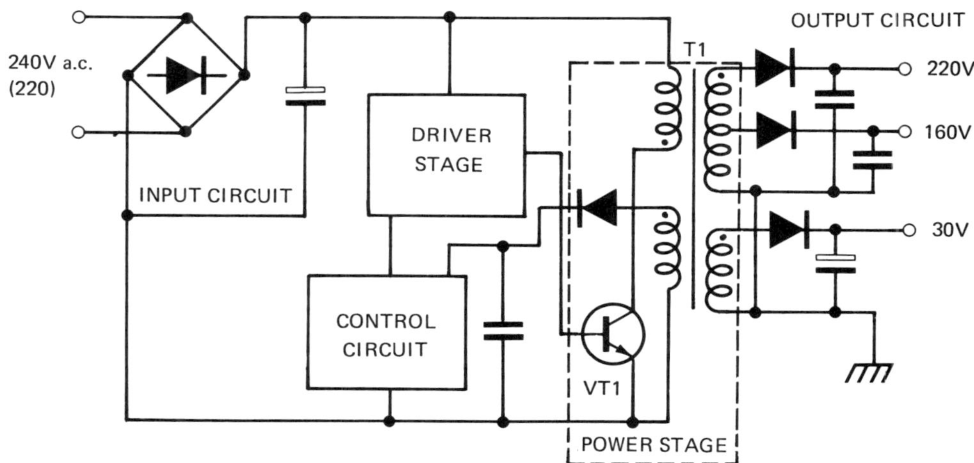

FIGURE 3. Basic Block Diagram of the Power Supply

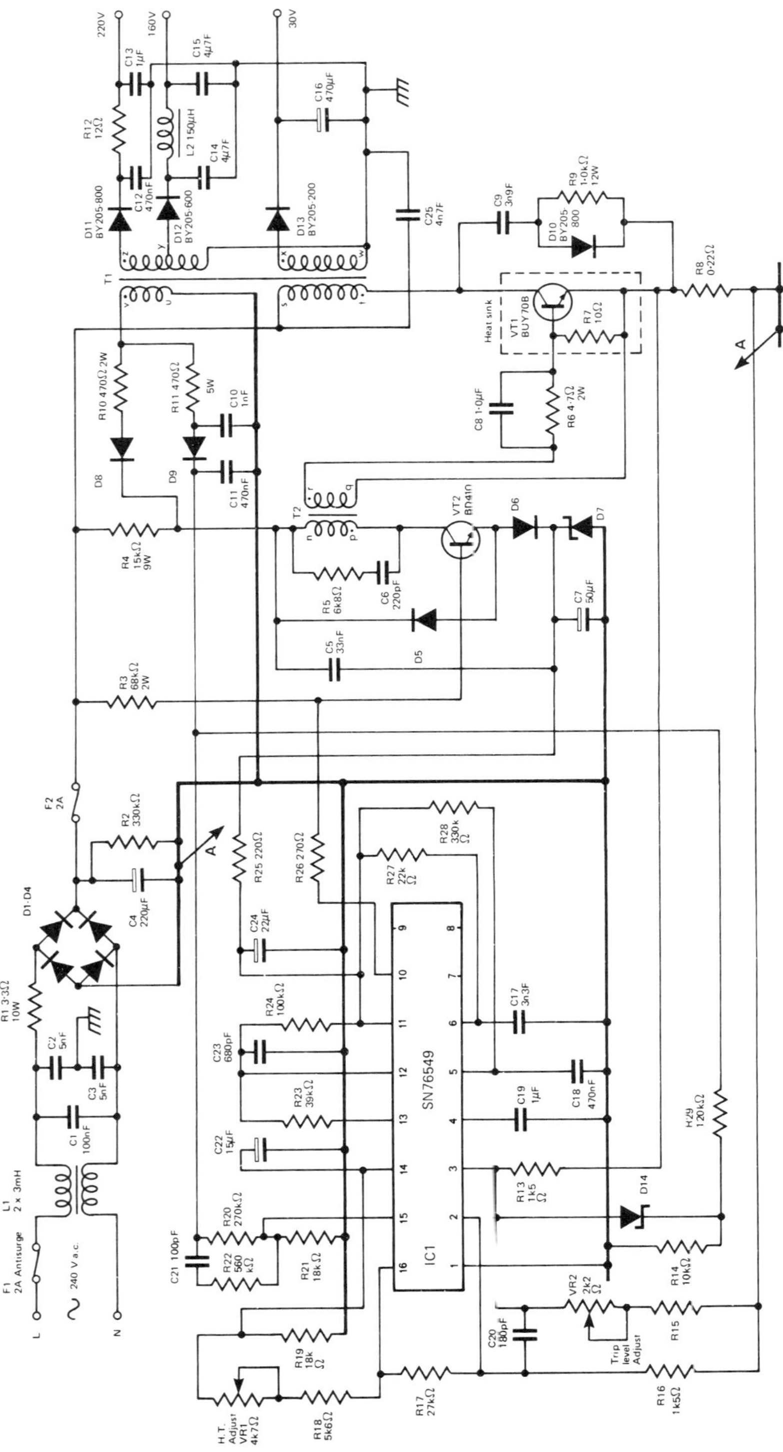

FIGURE 4. Complete 200W Isolated Switching Mode Power Supply

Such supplies would, for example, be adequate for:

a) the video output circuits

b) the deflection circuit

c) and the vertical deflection circuit, etc.

in a colour television receiver.

The C.E.T. Mode Transformer, T1

Considering the primary circuit, the basic inductance equation

$$E = L \times di/dt$$

is applicable for a switching mode circuit where

$E = V_{in}$, the rectified a.c. supply voltage

$L = L_p$, the inductance of transformer T1 primary winding

$di = \hat{I}_C$, the peak collector current of transistor VT1

and dt = the 'on' time of transistor VT1,δt

$= \delta/f$ where δ = transistor 'on' time/operating period

and f = the operating frequency

thus $V_{in} = L_p \times \hat{I}_C \times f/\delta$ ... 1

In the c.e.t. mode the output power, P_o, equals the energy stored per cycle times the operating frequency,

i.e. $P_o = \frac{1}{2} \times L_p \times \hat{I}_C^2 \times f$ ... 2

A limit condition occurs when the energy is completely transferred, just before the transistor switches 'on' again. This condition is approached at maximum output power and the lowest V_{in} value.

Thus choosing as the limit case $V_{in(min)} = 200V$

and $P_{o(max)} = 200W$

then for $\delta = 0.5$

from Equation 1 $\quad 200 = L_p \times \hat{I}_C \times 27 \times 10^3/0.5$

from Equation 2 $\quad 200 = \frac{1}{2} \times L_p \times \hat{I}_C^2 \times 27 \times 10^3$

Dividing $\quad 1 = \frac{1}{2} \times \hat{I}_C \times 0.5,$

i.e. $\hat{I}_C = 4A$

$L_p = 100/4 \times 27 \times 10^3$

$= 926\mu H$

To calculate the transformer turns ratio, the primary voltage, V_x, during the energy transfer must be known. In the above limit case, the relaxation time, i.e. shaded area in Figure 5, is at a minimum and the output rectifier(s) conduction time, t_1, approaches $(1 - \delta)t$. In steady state operation the transformer volt-second areas during the transistor conduction and during the energy transfer period will be equal, i.e.

$V_x \times t_1 = (V_{in} - V_{CE(sat)}) \times \delta t$ ... 3

As $t_1 = (1 - \delta)t = 0.5t,$

$V_x = (V_{in} - V_{CE(sat)}) \simeq 200V$

since $V_{in} \gg V_{CE(sat)}$

Thus the turns ratio to give output voltages of 220, 160 and 30 are:

220/200, 160/200 and 30/200

i.e. 1:1.1 $\quad$ 1:0.8 $\quad$ and $\quad$ 1:0.15

In practice these ratios could need slight modification to take account of rectifier volt drops and coupling factors in the transformer. The coupling factor should be as high as possible to keep the primary leakage inductance down, i.e. below 1% say.

Thus the effective electrical specification for transformer T1 is:

Primary inductance, L_p, 926μH at 4A peak.

Primary leakage inductance <9μH.

Secondaries:

220V; Turns ratio 1:1.1, average current 0.1A

160V; Turns ratio 1:0.8, average current 0.9A

30V; Turns ratio 1:0.15, average current 1.0A

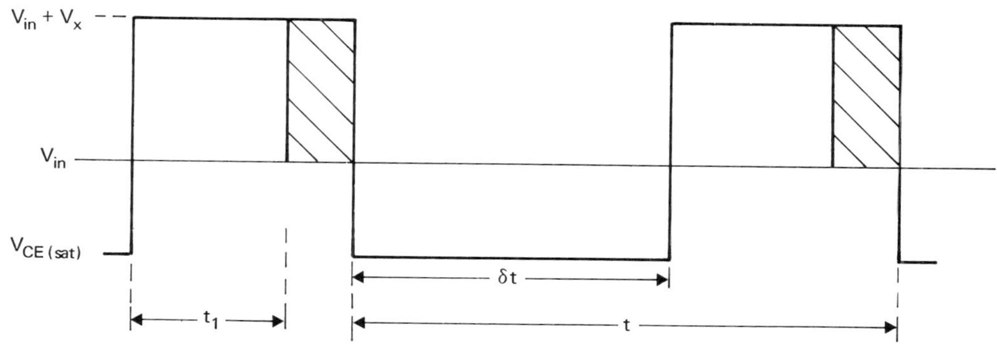

FIGURE 5. Output Transformer (T1) Primary Volt-second Area

To meet various safety and interference regulations additional parameters must be specified. A detailed magnetic design for this transformer is given in Appendix A. In order to determine the range of pulse widths required from the control section the minimum power, maximum input voltage case must be examined:

at $V_{in(max)}$ = 365V
and $P_{o(min)}$ = 100W, say

from Equation 2

$$\hat{I}_C^2 = 2 \times P_o/L_p \times f$$
$$= 200/926 \times 10^{-6} \times 27 \times 10^3$$
$$\hat{I}_C = 2.83A$$

from Equation 1

$$\delta = L_p \times \hat{I}_C \times f/V_{in}$$
$$= 926 \times 10^{-6} \times 2.83 \times 27 \times 10^3/365$$
$$= 0.19$$

and $\delta t = 0.19/27 \times 10^{-3} = 7.04\mu s$

Thus the pulse width range is $\delta = 0.5 \rightarrow 0.19$

Equating volt-second areas for this condition:

from Equation 3, the rectifier conduction time

$$t_1 = V_{in} \times \delta t/V_x$$
$$= 365 \times 7.04 \times 10^{-6}/200$$
$$= 12.8\mu s$$

The relaxation time is $t - t_1 - \delta t$ (shaded area in Figure 5)

i.e. $= 37 - 12.8 - 7.0$
$= 17.2\mu s$

The figure of 200W for the maximum power used in the design is considered the maximum likely to be taken by a t.v. receiver. The design procedure can, of course, be applied to the lower power units. Generally lower power results in lower values of peak collector current $\hat{I}_C$ required from switching transistor VT1 and higher transformer T1 primary inductance, e.g. a 150W power supply would work at 3.0A $\hat{I}_C$ with a transformer primary inductance of 1.2mH. Minimum power output at $\delta t = 7\mu s$ would be 75W.

The Output Device

The reverse voltage across the switching transistor, VT1, during the rectifier conduction time, t_1, is

$$(V_{in} + V_x).$$

To this must be added the voltage overshoot at transistor turn 'off'. In the high input voltage condition, $(V_{in} + V_x) = 565V$ and allowing a maximum of 200V overshoot, the switching transistor will require a working V_{CEX} of 765V. This factor, plus the 4A peak collector current requirement indicate the use of a transistor such as the BUY70B for the switching device VT1.

As described in the section on principles, use of the c.e.t. system involves switching 'on' the output device at near zero current and the collector current ramping up to a higher peak value than would be seen in an equivalent i.e.t. system. Power dissipation at turn 'on' is low and thus the reliability considerably improved. Turn 'off' dissipation is controlled by:

i) the base drive waveforms used, being defined by $I_{B(end)}$, $I_{B(off)}$ and dI_B/dt, and

ii) limiting the rate of rise of collector emitter voltage. A reasonable target here is to ensure that $V_{CE} < 500V$, $0.5\mu s$ after the collector current has fallen to 90% of its peak value.

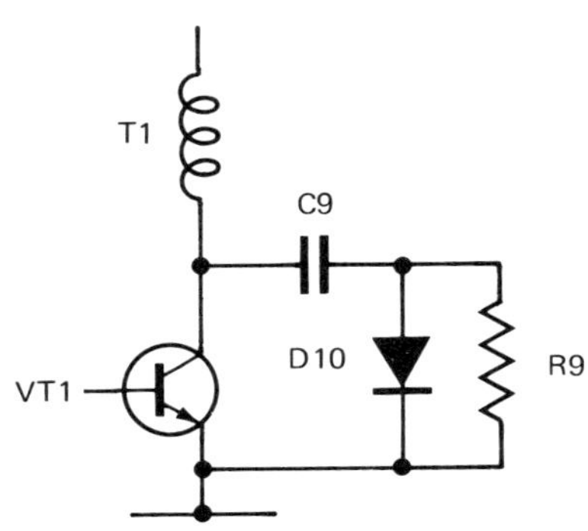

FIGURE 6. dV/dt Limiting Circuit

Figure 6 shows a dV/dt limiting circuit, comprising the components C9, R9 and D10 which protects transistor VT1 from a fast voltage rise at transistor turn 'off'. At transistor VT1 turn 'off', the collector current is diverted into capacitor C9 and to the common supply through diode D10. The rate of voltage rise is governed by the peak current flowing in transformer T1 at transistor turn 'off' and the value of capacitor C9. The value of resistor R9 is chosen to sufficiently discharge the capacitor during the shortest transistor conduction time, which occurs at the highest input supply voltage and minimum load. A lower resistor value results in higher discharge currents. A higher value will not sufficiently discharge capacitor C9 resulting in a fast initial rise in voltage across transistor VT1 at turn 'off', which will increase the transistor transient dissipation.

Calculation shows that a 1k ohm resistor is required for resistor R9 when the capacitor value is 3.9nF. Typical resistor dissipation is 7W, rising to 12W in the worst case. The diode D10 needs to be a fast, soft recovery type, minimising transistor turn 'on' dissipation and radiation. In the circuit in Figure 4, a BY205-800 diode is suggested.

The heatsink provided for transistor VT1 should be sufficient to maintain the case temperature within the thermal derating curve for the device, when operating at ambient temperatures up to 70°C. A heatsink of thermal resistance from transistor case to ambient of 4°C/W results in a case temperature of 102°C for a worst case device dissipating 8.0W. This operating point falls within the thermal derating curve for the device.

The Driver Stage

The design of the driver stage must start with the drive requirements of the power switching device VT1. A BUY70B requires a base current, $I_{B(end)}$, of 800mA at a collector current I_C of 4A. This is the minimum value which must be supplied under worst case conditions, i.e. at low supply voltage and maximum load.

Considering the volt second areas of the driver transformer T2 under steady state conditions and assuming a base resistor, R6, of value 4.7 ohm:

$$V_{on} \times t_2 = V_{off} \times (t - t_2)$$

i.e. $(V_{BE(sat)} + I_{B(end)} \times R6) \times t_2 = V_{off} \times (t - t_2)$

where

$V_{BE(sat)} = 1.5V$ max for VT1, the driver conduction time $t_2 = 17\mu s$ in condition described above, and the waveform period $t = 37\mu s$.

Hence $(1.5 + 0.8 \times 4.7) \times 17 = V_{off} \times 20$

$\therefore V_{off} = 4.5V$

The secondary leakage inductance of the transformer T2 defines the rate of fall of base current at turn 'off' and is important in controlling the operation of the output device.

Using the equation $E = L \times di/dt$

Secondary leakage inductance
$L_s = (V_{on} - V_{off})/dI_B/dt$

where,

$dI_B/dt = (I_{B(end)} - I_{B(off)})/t_s$

Substituting $t_s = 3\mu s$ and $I_{B(off)} = \hat{I}_C/3 = 1.3A$

$L_s = (1.5 + 0.8 \times 4.7) - (-4.5) \times 3/2.1 \ \mu H$

$L_s = 14\mu H$ (Ignoring voltage drop across resistor R6)

In this application the output device is overdriven in the majority of situations and optimum switching cannot always be expected. Figure 7 shows the base current waveform used in the 200W power supply.

The value of the primary inductance of transformer T2 controls the rate of fall of transistor VT1 base current during the normal conduction time. To minimise the base current droop, the criterion[1] is:

$$L_p/n^2 \geqslant V_{on} \times t_2/\Delta I_{B(end)}$$

Assuming a 20% droop in I_B
and a 25:1 turns ratio, n

$L_p = (25)^2 \times 5.26 \times 17/160$ mH

$L_p = 350$ mH

The 25:1 turns ratio assumed indicates a primary voltage swing in this instance of $(V_{on} - V_{off}) \times 25 = 244V$. The voltage overshoot at driver turn 'off' is damped by components R5, C6 across the primary winding.

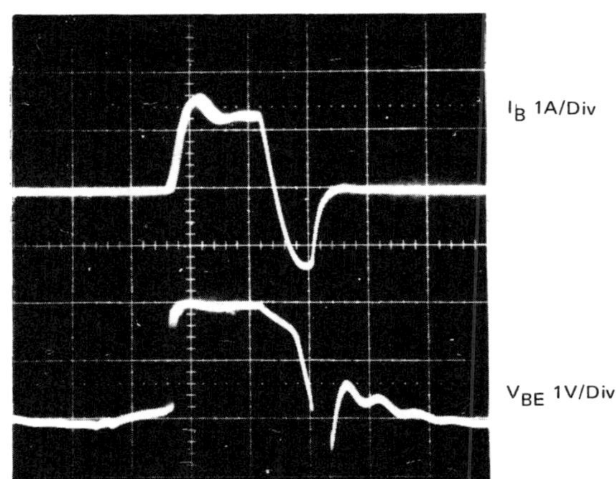

FIGURE 7. Output Transistor VT1 Base Waveforms

Having established the transformer detail, the power requirements of the driver stage can be examined. First, consider a supply derived from a single resistor from the input supply:

$R4 = (V_{in} - V_1) \times n \times t/I_{B(end)} \times t_2$

Assuming $V_{in} = 200V$ and the d.c. driver supply as 90V, (V_1)

R4 = 7k2 ohm, i.e. 6k8 ohm in practice.

Dissipation in this resistor would vary from approximately 3.0W at low input supply to 15W at high input supply, low load. Dissipation would also be high in the situation which occurs when the protection circuit latches 'on' permanently and the driver transistor VT2 is continuously 'on'. By taking power for the driver stage from the reference winding, the value of resistor R4 can be increased, improving overall efficiency. Dissipation at high input supply, low load is then reduced to approximately 7.5W. Resistor R3 provides base current for transistor VT2. Its value is governed by the base current requirement of transistor VT2 during the storage time of the output transistor VT1, i.e. 3mA to supply an 80mA peak collector current.

A suitable transistor for the driver device VT2 would be the BD410.

The Control I.C.

The integrated circuit to perform the control function, for a switching mode power supply, should ideally have the following features:

1. An internally regulated supply and a low start up current.

2. An error amplifier to compare the feedback voltage with an internal temperature-compensated reference voltage. This amplifier should be overriden in the start up

mode to avoid initial overstressing of the output stage.

3. An internal oscillator whose frequency is determined by an external resistor and capacitor (including the facility for locking to an external source).

4. A fast acting over voltage and over current protection circuit.

5. A permanent cut-out which will shut down the power supply after a preset number of trip circuit operations.

6. The output pulse should be delayed at switch 'on' until the internally regulated supply is established.

7. Its output transistor should be capable of providing fast switching of the driver stage.

Such a control i.c. is the SN76549. A description of the control circuit around a '549' i.c., as shown in Figure 4, is given later in the practical module section.

The Input Circuit

The operation of the input circuit, shown in Figure 4, is also given later.

PRACTICAL MODULE

The basic block diagram of the power supply was shown in Figure 3. The operation of the circuit can be conveniently discussed in these blocks:

a) The input circuit and filter components.
b) The control circuit.
c) The high voltage driver stage.
d) The power stage.
e) The output circuits.
f) The i.c. protection circuit.

Figure 4 gave the complete circuit of the 200W 27kHz supply.

a) Input Circuit and Filter Components

The main components are the rectifier bridge and the 100 Hz filter circuit. The rectifiers D1-D4 are chosen to have the capability of withstanding voltages greater than the peak input voltage. Some allowance must also be made for voltage transients on the supply, although the h.f. filter at the input will attenuate these. The 'single cycle' surge current rating of the rectifiers must be sufficient to take the surge current at switch on when the 100 Hz filter capacitor C4 is being charged. Series resistor R1 limits the surge current at switch on to below the lowest surge current rated component in the charging circuit (the 'on'/'off' switch, fuse F1, or the rectifiers). As resistor R1 is a source of power loss, the lowest practical value should be used. The value of the 100 Hz filter capacitor, C4, is chosen to reduce the supply ripple to 25V pk-pk,[2] the control circuit being capable of reducing to an acceptable level the residual ripple voltage transferred to the secondary supplies. In selecting a source of capacitor C4, one must bear in mind the 27kHz and 100 Hz ripple current capability, Resistor R2, shunting the capacitor, provides a discharge path when the supply is switched off. It is desirable, and mandatory in some countries, to restrict the level of interference fed back into the a.c. supply. At the time of designing this module, the IEC Recommendations covering the common market countries had not been published and so the German VDE0872 regulations were taken as a guideline. In the 27kHz supply, a coupled choke L1 is placed in the live and neutral lines which is wound to present a low impedance to the normal current flow, but high impedance to symmetrical components. Capacitors from both the live and neutral lines to earth, C2, C3, (max value 5nF as specified in BS415 'Electric Shock Hazard Under Normal Conditions') suppress asymmetric components, and reduce earth currents from the isolated supply. The capacitor C1 between live and neutral lines assists in reducing symmetric interference components.

b) The Control Circuit

The control function is built around the SN76549 switching mode supply control i.c. (operation of the circuit has been described elsewhere[3, 4]).

Supply current is fed through resistor R25 to pin 11 of the circuit. The supply rail (nominally 10.4V) is decoupled by capacitor C24. Ramp generator capacitor C23 is used to modulate the output pulse width. The capacitor is charged from pin 11 through resistor R24, which defines the minimum pulse width and through resistor R23 from the error amplifier output (pin 13). Discharge of capacitor C23 is through an internal 2k ohm resistor. Pins 14 and 15 on the i.c. are the error amplifier inputs. A reference voltage derived from the internal reference and defined by resistors R18, R19 and potentiometer VR1 is applied to pin 14. A feedback voltage from the power transformer is stepped down by the resistor chain R20, R21 and applied to pin 15. Pin 16 on the i.c. is an output from the internally generated reference voltage (nominally 8.4V).

The components attached to pin 6 on the i.c. are used to fix the frequency of operation of the power supply. Capacitor C17 is charged and discharged between voltage thresholds defined internally. Charging is through resistor R27 to a threshold of typically 4.8V, and the discharge is through an internal 680 ohm resistor to a lower threshold of typically 2.0V.

Pins 7, 8 and 9 on the i.c. are not used in this application. They relate to the phase locking circuit which is used when the internal oscillator is locked to an external source such as the horizontal oscillator in a television.

The components C18, R28 connected to pin 5 of the control circuit set the protection circuit delay time. When the protection circuit is fired, capacitor C18 is discharged through an internal resistor to approximately 2.8V. The output from the control circuit goes high as soon as the protection circuit is fired (i.e. after a propagation delay time of about 200ns). The output remains high until capacitor C18 has recharged to approximately 7.0V through resistor R28. The protection circuit delay time is the sum of the discharge and recharge times of C18 (130ms with the component values shown in Figure 2). Capacitor C19 on pin 4 of the i.c. provides the latch up facility. The capacitor is charged during the discharge time of C18. The protection circuit latches up when the capacitor is charged to 8.5V. The value of C19 defines the number of trip-restart cycles performed before the power supply shuts down. Once the power supply has shut down, it can only be restarted by switching the mains supply 'off' to allow capacitor C19 to discharge and then switching 'on' again.

The protection circuit has a differential input stage accessible on pins 2 and 3 of the control circuit. The input on pin 2 is biassed to a d.c. voltage of 400mV by resistors R17 and R16 from the reference voltage on pin 16. The input to pin 3 is taken both from the resistor R8 in series with the emitter connection of transistor VT1, and from the feedback winding by the resistor chain R14, R29 and zener diode D14.

Overload protection is provided by sensing the voltage drop across the emitter resistor R8 of output transitor VT1. A short circuit on the output of the power transformer (T1) will cause the emitter current to rise, increasing the voltage dropped across resistor R8 and firing the protection circuit.

The overvoltage protection circuit senses the voltage developed by the feedback winding. The feedback voltage is divided by R14, R29, zener diode D14 activating the protection circuit when the voltage at the junction of the resistors exceeds the sum of the zener voltage and the d.c. voltage applied to the other side of the differential input circuit. The offset voltage of the input circuit is of the order 30mV.

The open collector output from the control circuit, at pin 10, switches the driver transistor VT2. The resistor R26 limits the peak current at switch 'off' of transistor VT2 to 50mA.

The feedback voltage from the power transformer passes through the 'snubber' network C10, R11, which removes voltage overshoot eliminating the possibility of an erroneous feedback signal through peak rectification. The feedback voltage is rectified by diode D9 smoothed by capacitor C11 and then applied to the error amplifier by resistor chain R20, R21. The phase advance network C21, R22 across R20 improves high frequency response and prevents instability of the control loop.

c) The High Voltage Driver Stage

The use of a high voltage driver stage eliminates the need for an auxilliary low voltage supply. The low power consumption of the control circuit and the derivation of power for the driver stage from the reference winding on the power transformer make this a practical proposition. The components in the secondary circuit of transformer T2, together with the leakage inductance of the secondary winding of the transformer, define the base current waveform of the power transistor VT1. Resistor R6 limits its forward base current, $I_{B(end)}$, to 0.8A in the limit case when the input supply voltage is low and the load on the output a maximum. Capacitor C8 improves the turn 'off' of the power output transistor VT1 by assisting in the extraction of stored charge. The purpose of the resistor R7, which is mounted directly across the base emitter pins of transistor VT1, is to damp out ringing on the base-emitter voltage waveform which could otherwise result in the device being turned 'on' inadvertently as the voltage across it rises.

Power for the driver stage is taken from the input supply through resistor R4, and also from the reference winding on the power transformer through resistor R10 and diode D8. The resistor R3, which connects the base of the driver transistor VT2 to the input supply ensures that the driver is 'on' at power supply switch 'on' and switch 'off' when the control circuit is inoperative. The driver stage and the output device operate in anti-phase thus the output device is held 'off' in the situations mentioned above. The value of resistor R3 is set by the critical condition for transistor VT2 which arises when the output stage reaches the end of its storage time at turn 'off'. Transistor VT2 then passes a peak collector current equal to:

$$(I_{B(end)} + I_{B(off)})/n$$

where: $I_{B(end)}$ = forward base current end value
$I_{B(off)}$ = reverse base current peak value
and n = transformer T2 turns ratio

Resistor R3 provides sufficient base current to saturate transistor VT2 in this condition. Capacitor C5 decouples the top of transformer T2 primary at the operating frequency, and diode D5 provides a bypass for the transformer primary when the power supply is switched 'off'. In the absence of diode D5, transistor VT2 may conduct in the reverse direction driving transistor VT1 'on'. Diode D6 prevents the emitter base reverse voltage rating of VT2 being exceeded when the base terminal is pulled down by the control circuit. Components D7, C7 provide a shunt stabilised supply for the control circuit. Tuning components R5 and C6, across transformer T2 primary, damp the voltage overshoot seen across driver transistor VT2 to a safe value.

d) The Power Stage

Operating in the complete energy transfer (c.e.t.) mode, the normal current waveform through the power stage, transformer T1 and transistor VT1 is a ramp. This starts a near zero current, and reaches 4.0A peak in the 200W design. The BUY70 high voltage transistor, being characterised at 4A collector current, is particularly suitable for the switching device VT1.

As mentioned, the dV/dt limiting circuit comprises components C9, R9 and D10. The heat sink supplied for transistor VT1 maintains the device operating point within the thermal derating curve at ambient temperatures up to 70°C. A heatsink is also supplied for rectifier D10.

The power transformer T1 uses a pair of 42mm E cores. Stranded wire and sectionalised windings are used to reduce power loss due to high frequency effects. A core temperature rise – measured at the top of the centre limb – of only 40°C above ambient is thus achieved. Secondary windings on transformer T1 provide the required output voltages.

e) The Output Circuits

Three voltage supplies are generated:

220V at 100mA for video output circuits	22.0W
160V at 900mA for the deflection circuit	144.0W
30V at 1000mA for vertical deflection	30.0W
Total	196.0W

The 160V output is the main, regulated supply. A π filter is used to attenuate the 27kHz ripple. The capacitors C14, C15 need to have high ripple current capability (6A peak current) or the effect of series resistance becomes apparent. Switching transients are reduced by the use of a soft recovery diode and by careful attention to circuit layout. The rectifier D12 is a 600V type.

The 30V supply is decoupled by electrolytic capacitor C16. Ripple current rating is again important, both in h.f. ripple attenuation, and in component dissipation.

The 220V supply adopts a peak voltage clipping action, i.e. the diode D11 conducts during transistor VT1 voltage overshoot time. Conduction time is shorter than on the 30V and 160V supplies and the 27kHz ripple component is more significant.

Depending on the thermal environment, heat sinks may be required on rectifiers D12 and D13.

f) The I.C. Protection Circuit

The input to the i.c. protection circuit is a pnp differential pair. This means that the tripping threshold has common mode rejection and low temperature drift. Firing the trip circuit turns 'off' the input transistor on pin 3 of the control circuit so the input impedance is high. The time from firing of the trip circuit to the output on pin 10 going high is of the order 200ns. It is very important to have a short trip propogation time since the collector current of the power transistor VT1 rises sharply when driving into a short circuited load. It is also important that the trip circuit is properly set up.

Setting Up Procedure

A suitable printed circuit board (p.c.b.) layout for the complete 200W 27kHz switching mode power supply is shown in Figures 8 and 9. Figure 8 gives the p.c.b. copper side and Figure 9 the matching component position layout.

The correct setting up procedure for the module is given sequentially below and alternatively in flow chart form in Figure 10.

1. Check the circuit board for missing or damaged components, and ensure that flying leads are secured.

2. Attach supply leads to the tags marked 'L' and 'N'. As waveforms on the primary (non isolated) side of the supply are to be observed, an isolating transformer should be used when setting up the supply.

3. The regulated supplies generated are accessible from tags at the edge of the board. The required loads can now be applied.

4. Before switching 'on' disconnect the flying lead to the collector of the power transistor VT1 in order that the primary circuit may be set up prior to applying power to the regulated supplies. Check that fuses F1, F2 are the correct types.

5. Apply power, either by winding up a Variac, or simply by switching 'on'. The pulse width modulator circuit will output a minimum width pulse which can be traced through the circuit from the output of the control i.c. (pin 10) to the base-emitter of the power device VT1; as shown in waveform diagrams given in Figure 11 a, b and c. Should there be no pulse waveform, follow the check list:

   a) Observe the waveform on pin 6 of the i.c. There should be a sawtooth waveform at the operating frequency, 27kHz, as illustrated in the photograph, Figure 11d. If the sawtooth waveform is not there check the supply to the i.c. on pin 11 which should be approximately 10.4V d.c. If the supply voltage is correct, check the oscillator components, C17, R27. If the fault is not here switch 'off' and change the control circuit. In the absence of supply voltage on pin 11 check the high voltage driver stage.

   b) Fuse F2 blowing will indicate a fault in the driver stage.

   c) Fuse F1 blowing will indicate a fault in the input filter, and bridge rectifier circuit.

6. Having checked that the primary circuit is operating correctly, switch 'off' and reconnect the flying lead to the collector of VT1. Disable the feedback loop by removing resistor R20. Set the preset potentiometers VR1 and VR2 to mid range and switch 'on'. The power supply will operate at minimum pulse width. (The output waveforms are shown in Figure 11e.) If the protection circuit fires continually, a fault in the output circuit is indicated. The regulated supplies can be disconnected one by one to isolate a fault in the secondary side. It is not advisable to disconnect more than one of the secondaries at one time as this could cause overvoltage failure in the remaining circuits. Should a fault not be found, then the output device VT1 and the dV/dt limiting circuit C9, D10, R9 should be checked. Finally check the transformer T1 for shorted or faulty windings.

7. When operation at minimum pulse width has been checked, switch 'off' and close the control loop by replacing R20. Switch 'on' and monitor the main supply rail, adjusting VR1 to obtain the correct voltage. Potentiometer VR2 will need a final adjustment to ensure correct operation of the protection circuit.

FIGURE 8. Copper Side of Printed Circuit Board

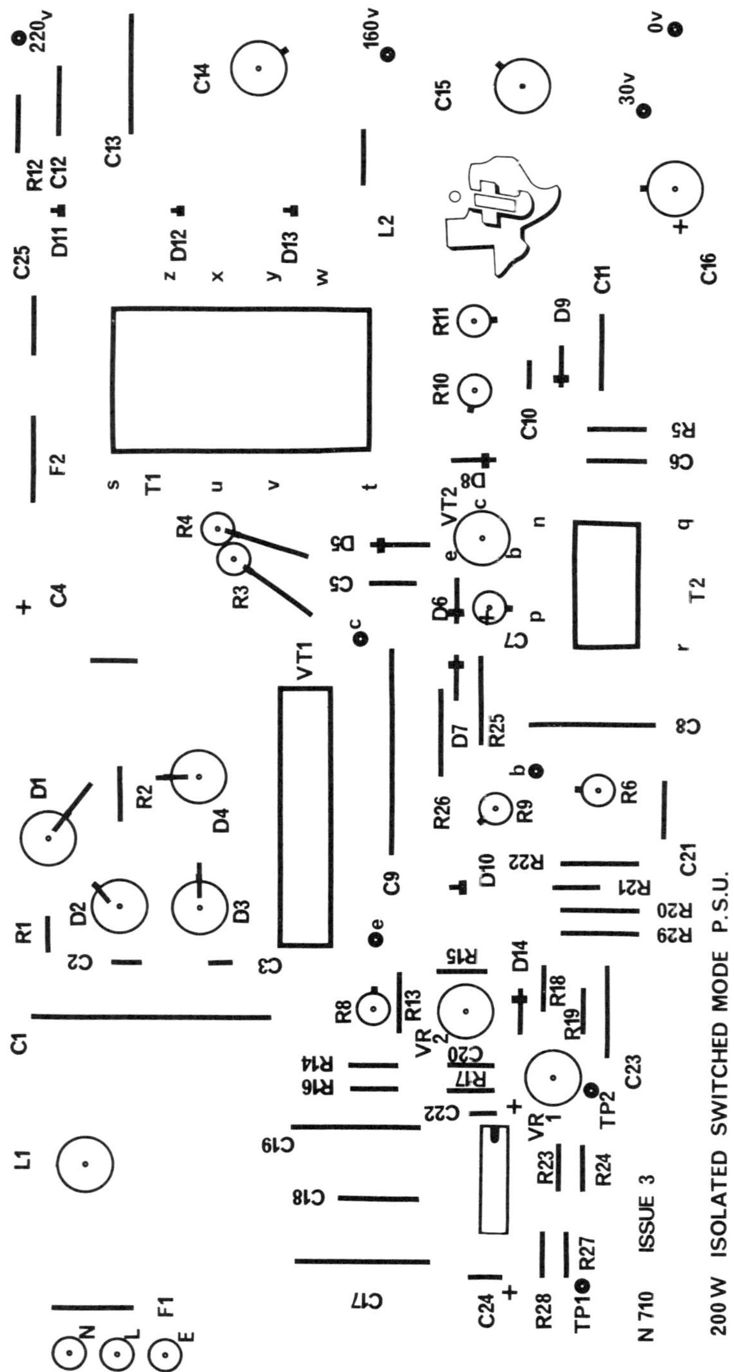

FIGURE 9. Component Side of Printed Circuit Board

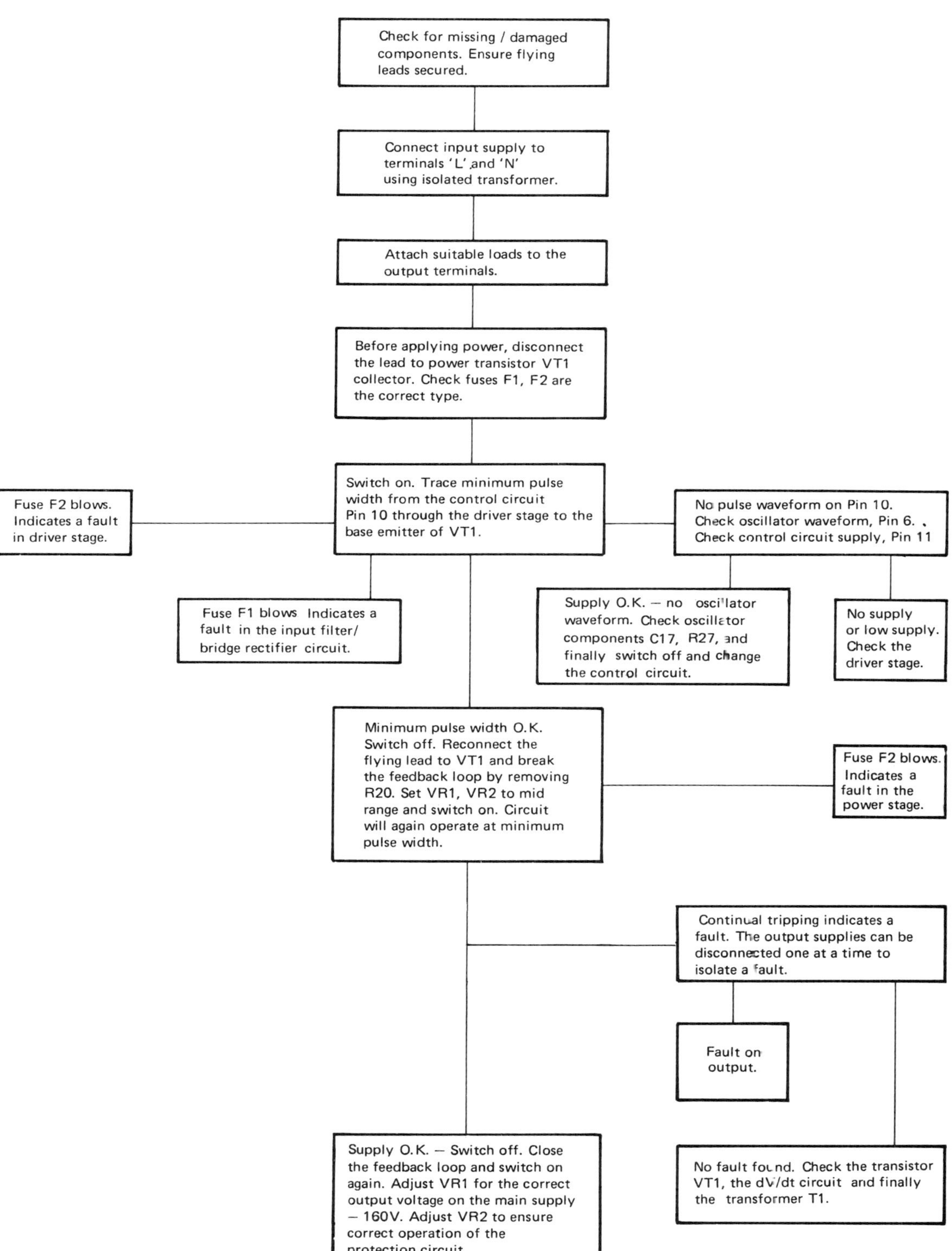

Figure 10. Module Setting Up Flow Chart

Waveforms

Figure 11 gave the circuit waveforms useful to set up the module for correct operation. Figures 12, 13 and 14 show the module waveforms under normal operating conditions. Figure 12 shows the driver, power and output stage waveforms under normal operating conditions. Figure 13 shows the operation of the power supply at switch 'on' and switch 'off', and Figure 14 illustrates the action of the protection circuit when the main output supply goes short circuit.

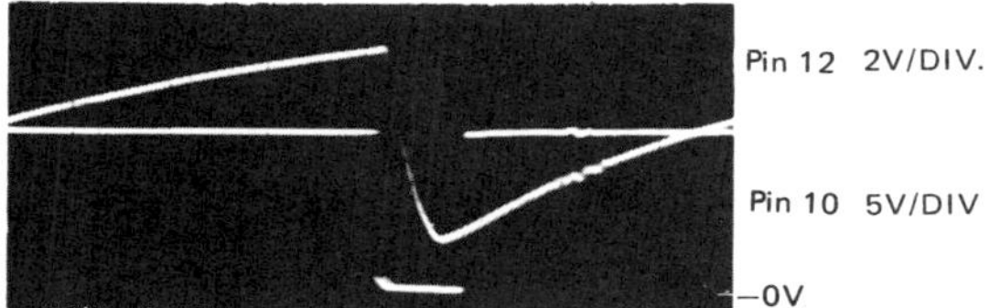

a) ICI Pin 10 output waveform (minimum pulse width) Pin 12 pulse width modulator ramp waveform

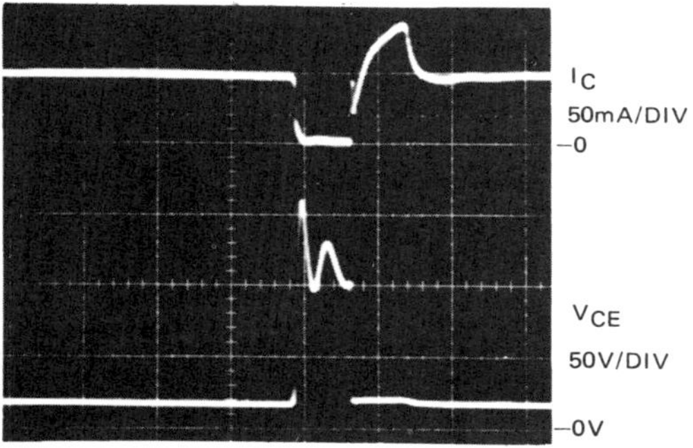

b) Driver stage (VT2)

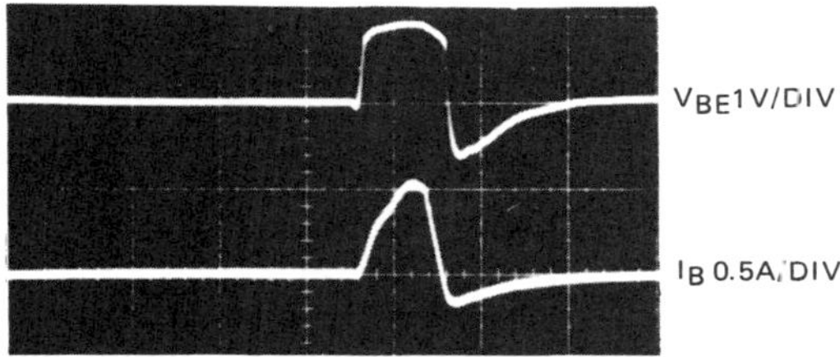

c) Output device (VT1) base-emitter waveforms (Collector open circuit)

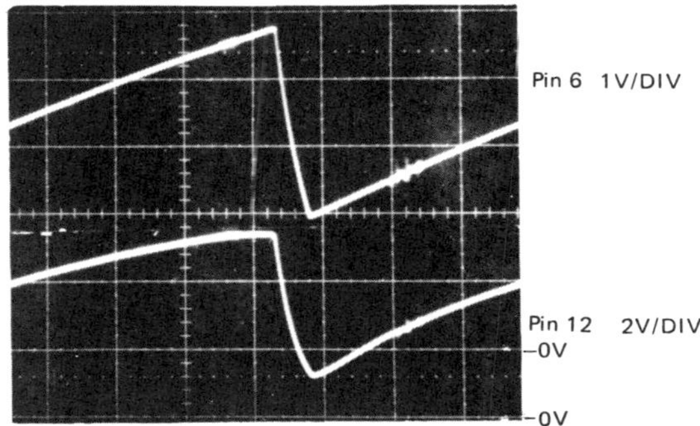

d) ICI Pin 6 Oscillator ramp waveform Pin 12 pulse width modulator ramp waveform

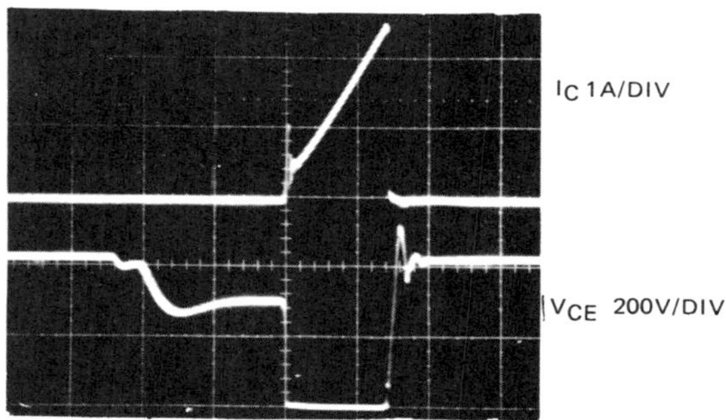

e) Output device (VT1) collector waveforms (feedback loop broken) Collector current, Collector-emitter voltage

→ 5μs/DIV

FIGURE 11. Module Setting Up Waveforms

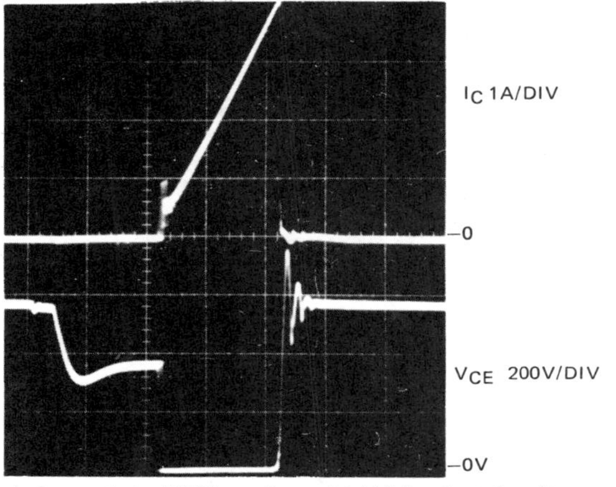

a) Output device (VT1) waveforms at a high input supply voltage

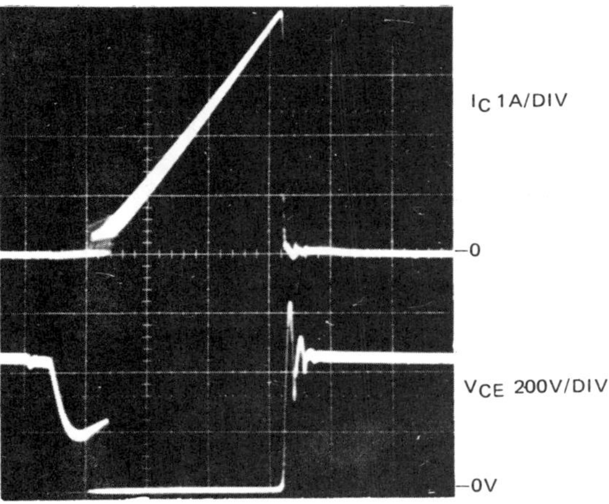

b) Ouput device (VT1) waveforms at a low input supply voltage.

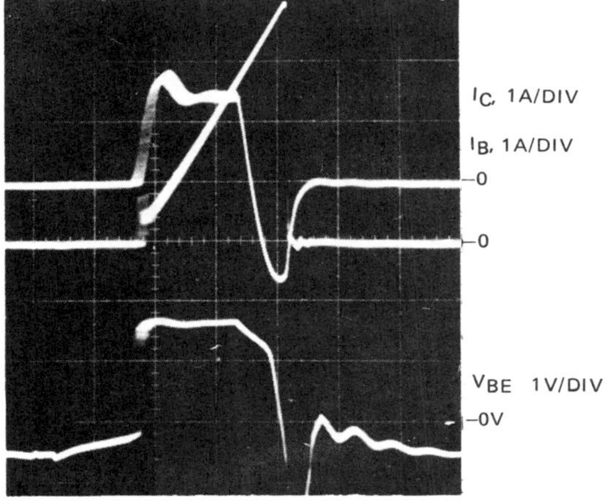

c) Output device (VT1) waveforms

Time Scale : 5μs/DIV

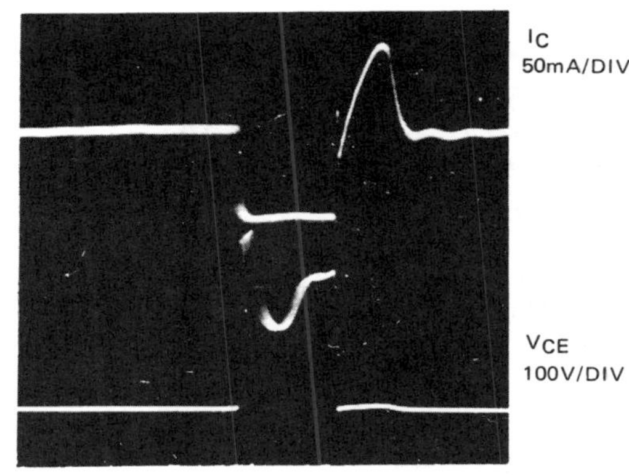

d) Driver stage (VT2) waveforms Collector voltage

5μs/DIV

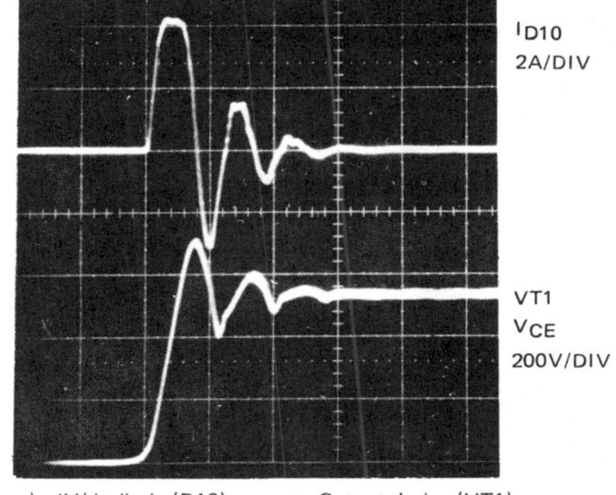

e) dV/dt diode (D10) current Output device (VT1) Collector-emitter voltage

1μs/DIV

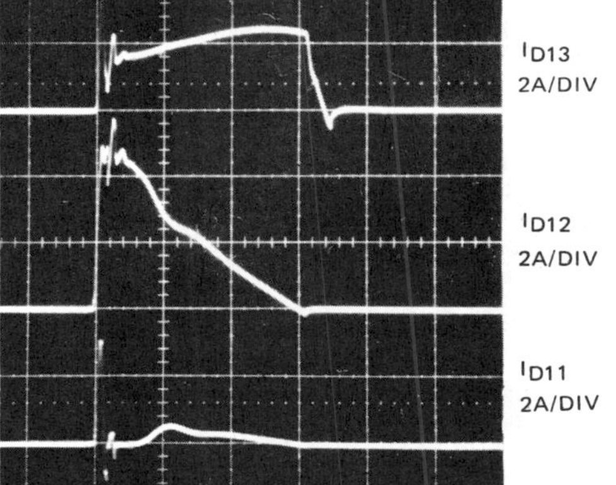

f) Rectifier current waveforms 30V rectifier (D13) 160V rectifier (D12) 220V rectifier (D11)

5μs/DIV

FIGURE 12. Normal Operating Waveforms

Power Supply Switch 'on'

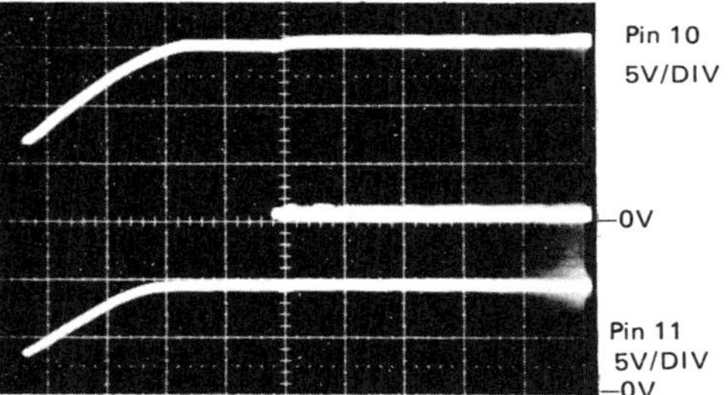

a) ICI Pin 10 output waveform, ICI Pin 11 supply rail
20ms/DIV

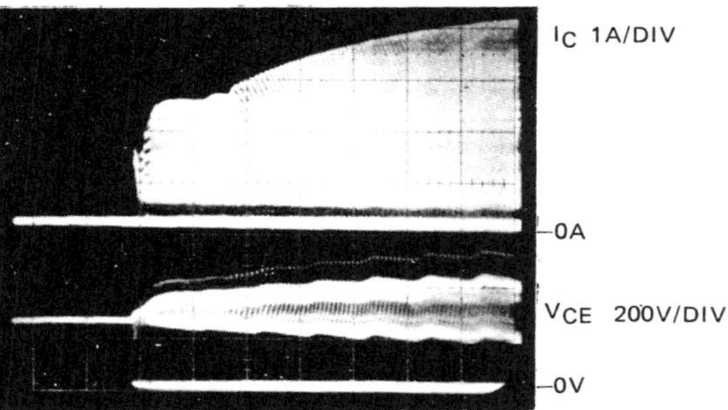

b) Output device (VT1) Collector current, Collector-emitter voltage
10ms/DIV

Power supply switch 'off'

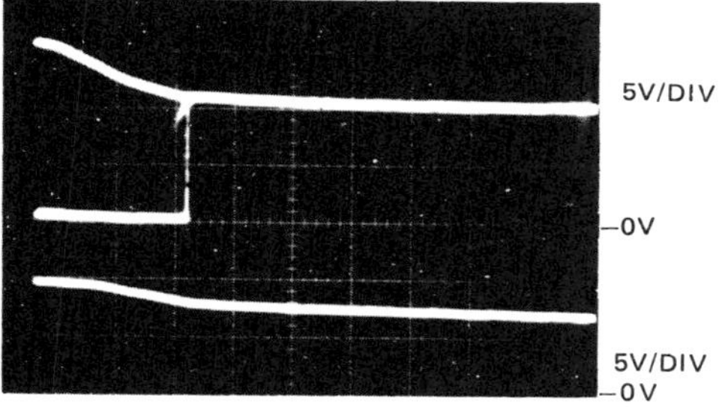

c) ICI Pin 10 output waveform, ICI Pin 11 supply rail
20ms/DIV

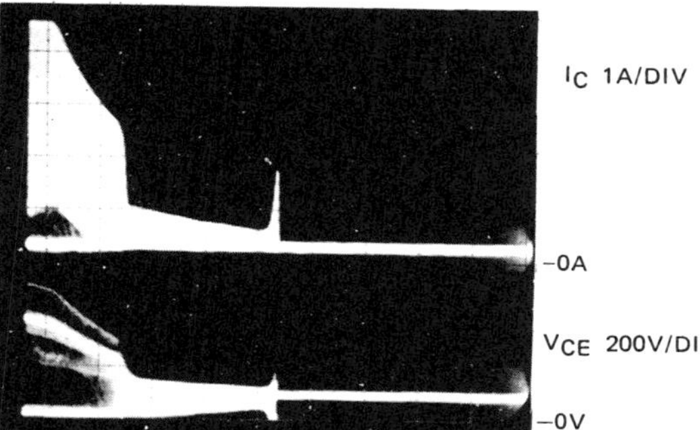

d) Output device (VT1) Collector current, Collector-emitter voltage
10ms/DIV

FIGURE 13. Switch 'on'/Switch 'off' Waveforms

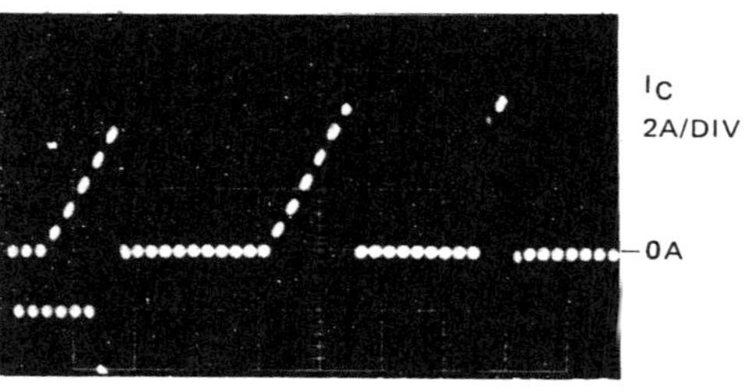

a) Output device (VT1) Collector Current
Marker at the instant of a short circuit being applied to the 160V supply.
Time scale: 10μs/DIV

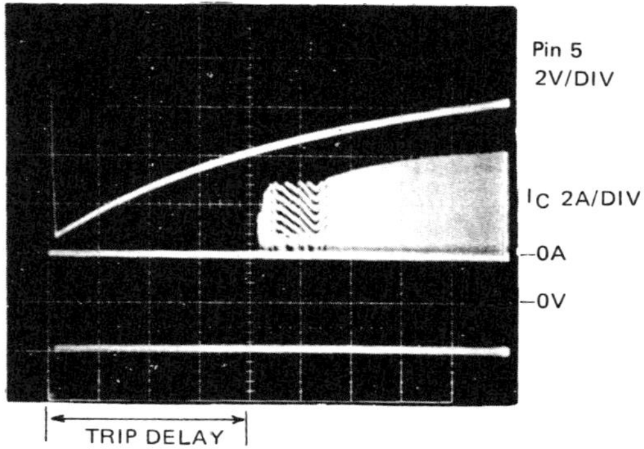

b) Protection circuit delay capacitor C_{18} voltage
Output device (VT1) collector current
Marker at the instant of a short circuit being applied.
Time scale: 20ms/DIV

FIGURE 14. Operation of the Protection Circuit Waveforms

PERFORMANCE

The performance figures given below, were obtained with a prototype module and can be taken as typical for a switching mode power supply manufactured unit.

Stability with input supply variation 180V – 265V a.c.

160V output	0.5%
30V output	0.5%
220V output	1.0%

Load regulation – input supply at 220V a.c.

160V output	140W – 50W	2.5%
30V output	30W – 10W	1.5%
220V output	24W – 5W	3.0%

100 Hz ripple content – at full load

Input supply:	180V a.c.	265V a.c.
160V output	360	80mV pk-pk
30V output	50	10mV pk-pk
220V output	400	80mV pk-pk

27kHz ripple content – at full load

160V output	180mV pk-pk
30V output	200mV pk-pk
220V output	1.4V pk-pk

Efficiency

Overall efficiency is of the order 85 per cent at full load. The main sources of powerloss being:

The dV/dt resistor, R9
The power transistor, VT1
The driver load resistor, R4 and
The power transformer, T1

REFERENCES

1. M. J. Maytum and A. Lear, 'Driver Circuit Design Considerations for High Voltage Line Scan Transistors', *I.E.E.E. Trans.* Volume BTR-19, No. 2, May 1973.
2. Applications Laboratory Staff of Texas Instruments Incorporated, *Electronic Power Control and Digital Techniques,* McGraw-Hill Book Company, New York, 1976, p. 6.
3. Applications Laboratory Staff of Texas Instruments Incorporated, *Electronic Power Control and Digital Techniques,* McGraw-Hill Book Company, New York, 1976, pp. 68-74.
4. SN76549 Data Sheet.

ACKNOWLEDGEMENTS

The author would like to thank John Bright once of Coilcraft U.K. for assistance in the design and supply of wound components, Mick Maytum once of T.I.L. for his help, and Pye TMC Components Ltd, for information on surge ratings and supply of high voltage electrolytic capacitor samples.

APPENDIX A

Design of the Power Transformer T1

Requirements:

Maximum Output Power, $P_{o(max)}$, of 200W
Primary Inductance = 926μH
Primary Leakage Inductance = 9μH
Peak Primary Current = 4A
and Isolation

The current design has been accomplished using a pair of 42mm E cores Fair-rite part No. 9477036002,

Core Properties

Magnetic Path Area	A_e	183.9mm^2
Magnetic Path Length	l_e	98.04mm
Magnetic Volume	V_e	18050mm^3
Winding Area	A_w	297.1mm^2
Exposed Surface Area	A_s	7536mm^2
Initial Permeability	μ_r	1800 typical

First consider the allowable power loss for operation with a core temperature 40°C above ambient, i.e. operation at 110°C core temperature in an ambient of 70°C (this is a realistic value for the inside of a t.v. set). Taking the heat loss from the core as 520μW/mm^2 and the exposed surface area as 7536mm^2, then the total allowable power loss is: 3.9W.

Assuming an equal power loss in the transformer core and in the windings, the allowable core loss is 1.95W. Taking the core volume, V_e as 18050mm^3, the allowable loss is 108mW/mm^3. Reference to the loss curves for the appropriate ferrite material (type 77) at 27kHz indicate a peak working flux density, $\hat{B}_w$ = 157mT. (The saturation flux density at a temperature of 100°C is quoted as 345mT).

In the mode of operation used, the magnetisation field is unidirectional so the maximum working flux density is 2 x $\hat{B}_w$ = 314mT.

Looking at the requirements of the power supply in the condition where the input supply voltage is low, and the load a maximum:

$$2\hat{B}_w = V_{in} \times \delta t/n \times A_e$$

where V_{in} = Input supply voltage = 200V
δt = Transistor VT1 conduction time = 0.5t
n = the number of primary turns

$$2 \times 157\text{mT} = 200 \times 0.5 \times 37 \times 10^{-6}/n \times 183.9 \times 10^{-6}$$
$$n = 200 \times 0.5 \times 37/183.9 \times 2 \times 157 \times 10^{-3}$$
$$n = 64 \text{ turns}$$

The required primary inductance, L_p, is 926μH. This condition indicates the need for an air gap between the E cores of the transformer:

$$L_p = \mu_o \times n^2 \times A_e/(l_g + l_e/\mu_r)$$

where l_g is the total air gap length i.e.

$$l_g + l_e/\mu_r = 4 \times 10^{-7} \times (64)^2 \times 183.9 \times 10^{-6}/926 \times 10^{-6}$$
$$= 1.02\text{mm}$$
$$l_g = 1.02 - 98.0/1.8 \times 10^3$$
$$= 0.97\text{mm}$$

The gap in each leg of the core is half this value, i.e. 0.49mm.

Winding Design: The available winding area, A_w, is 297mm^2. Assuming half the area allocated to the primary winding and half to the secondary, and allowing a winding factor of 0.5, the available winding area for the primary is $A_w/4 \simeq 74\text{mm}^2$. For 64 turns, the maximum cross sectional area of the wire, is 1.16mm^2. This is more than adequate for the rms current in the primary circuit. This statement, however, neglects the h.f. wire losses which are significant at 27kHz. Sectionalising the windings reduces the proximity effect. The use of stranded wire is also beneficial. Tables show that the penetration depth in copper at 100°C and at 27kHz is 0.45mm. To minimise wire losses, the wire diameter $d \not> 2\Delta$ where Δ is the penetration depth. Bearing in mind the fact that the 27kHz ramp waveform in the primary winding will have a frequency spectrum extending beyond 27kHz, a stranded winding of strand diameter 0.27mm (32 s.w.g.) was used.

The secondary windings (160V and 30V) were wound in similar wire. Sectionalising and close coupling of the windings results in the primary leakage inductance, and consequently the voltage overshoot at transistor switch 'off', being held within specification, i.e. L_p leakage <9μH. If the isolation requirements call up a 6mm creepage distance in air between isolated windings, currently available transformer parts would not allow a 200W design to use the 42mm E cores and the winding design mentioned above. An alternative solution to increasing the core size would be to encapsulate the transformer windings. At lower maximum power ratings, however, the winding area of the 42mm cores is sufficient to allow a 6mm creepage distance between isolated windings.

NOTE: The power transformer described has been developed in co-operation with Coilcraft i.e., their part number X3184.

APPENDIX B

Modifications to Improve Circuit Performance

Tolerance of Overvoltage Protection Circuit: To lessen the variation between different power supplies, 2% resistors can be used in the resistor R29, R14 divider chain, and a 5% zener diode used in position D14. Elimination of variable resistor VR2 will enable the overvoltage protection circuit to be set more accurately. To provide an independant overvoltage protection mechanism circuits given below can be used.

Overvoltage Protection: If the overvoltage protection provided by the circuit shown in Figure 4 is not sufficiently sensitive, then the circuit may be modified by the addition of the single transistor arrangement shown in Figure 15. Transistor VT1 conducts when the feedback voltage (pin 15) exceeds the reference input (pin 14) by a V_{BE}. The transistor discharges the trip delay capacitor (pin 5) to below the threshold voltage, turning the output (pin 10) 'off'. The power supply assumes a 'burst mode' of operation.

In order to use this amendment, the d.c. operating point of the error amplifier inputs should be lowered to ensure that the threshold voltage on pin 5 can always be reached, and typical component values are given.

Low Power Regulation: An arrangement which will give regulation down to low loads (12% of full load) by operating the circuit in a variable frequency mode is shown in Figure 16. The differential amplifier, consisting of transistors VT1 and VT2, operates the phase comparator circuit when the feedback input (pin 15) exceeds the reference input (pin 14). The phase comparator circuit modulates the oscillator ramp charging rate. The use of a third transistor is necessary to ensure that the minimum pulse width output (pin 10) is maintained as the system goes into low frequency operation.

Use of such a circuit would make the overvoltage protection circuit described previously superfluous.

Control Loop Stability: Increasing the value of capacitor C14 and C15 to 50μF will increase the control loop stability margin and provide better tracking between the main regulated output and the feedback supply. When electrolytic capacitors are used a sufficient safety margin in the voltage rating should be allowed as they are less tolerant to overvoltage than the plastic film types.

Circulating Current Paths: To reduce radiation and prevent interference in the control circuit, circulating current paths in the power stages should be minimised. A reduction was obtained by repositioning coupling capacitor C25 (Figure 4), from its original position between point w and the zero voltage side of resistor R8, to between points w and s of transformer T1. A further non electrolytic capacitor (≏ 470nF) connected in parallel with the input supply decoupling capacitor C4, but mounted close to the power transformer T1, will decouple high frequency components.

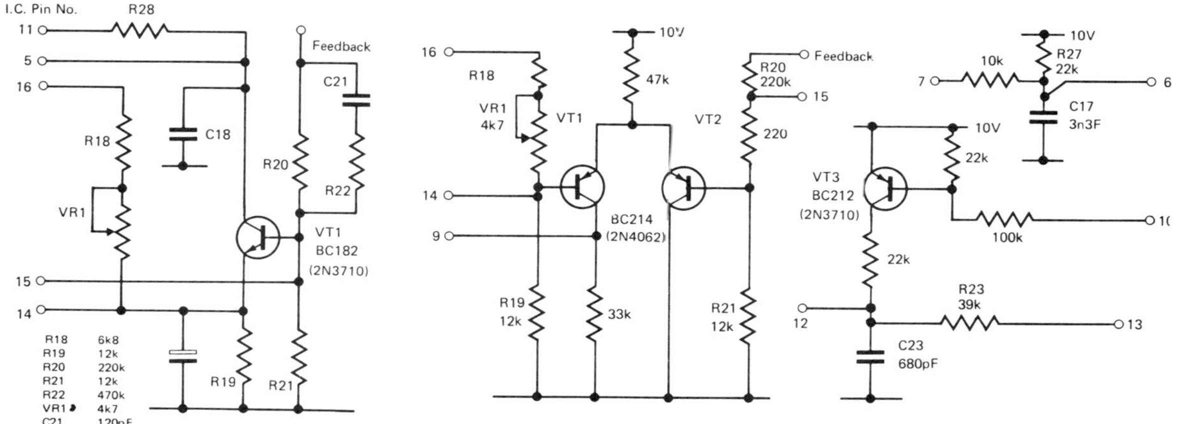

FIGURE 15. Overvoltage Protection Improvement

FIGURE 16. Low Load Regulation Circuit Additions

COMPONENTS LIST

Capacitors

C1	100nF	300V a.c.
C2	5nF	4kV
C3	5nF	4kV
C4	220μF	400V
C5	33nF	100V
C6	220pF	
C7	50μF	
C8	1μF	
C9	3n9F	800V
C10	1nF	300V a.c.
C11	470nF	100V
C12	470nF	250V
C13	1μF	250V
C14	4μ7F }	160V High
C15	4μ7F }	Ripple current
C16	470μF	40V
C17	3n3F	
C18	470nF	
C19	1μF	
C20	180pF	
C21	100pF	
C22	15 or 22μF	
C23	680pF	
C24	22μF	
C24	5nF	4kV

Integrated Circuit

IC1 SN76549

Inductors

L1	W2961	Coilcraft (2x3 mH)
L2	W2945	Coilcraft (150μH)

Diodes/Rectifiers

D1 }	BY127
D2 }	BY127
D3 }	BY127
D4 }	BY127
D5	1S921 or 1N645
D6	1S921 or 1N645
D7	1N4007 or BZX61–C15
D8	BA248 or BY403
D9	BA248 or BY403
D10	BY205–800
D11	BY205–800
D12	BY205–600 or BYW11–600
D13	BY205–200 or BYW11–200
D14	1N753 or BZX79–C6V2

Resistors

(¼W 5% unless otherwise stated)

R1	3Ω3	10W
R2	330k	½W
R3	68k	2W
R4	15k	9W
R5	6k8	
R6	4Ω7	2W
R7	10	

Resistors (continued)

R8	0.22Ω	1W
R9	1k	12W
R10	470	2W
R11	470	5W
R12	12	
R13	1k5	
R14	10k	
R15	Value to suit limitation of range adjustment	
R16	1k5	
R17	27k	
R18	5k6	
R19	18k	
R20	270k	
R21	18k	
R22	560k	
R23	39k	
R24	100k	
R25	220	
R26	270	
R27	22k	
R28	330k	
R29	120k	

Potentiometers

VR1	4k7
VR2	2k2

Transistors

VT1	BUY70B
VT2	BD410

Transformers

T1 X3184 Coilcraft (Wound on 42mm E cores) Pin configuration below.

T2 X3072 Coilcraft (Wound on 25mm E cores) Pin configuration below.

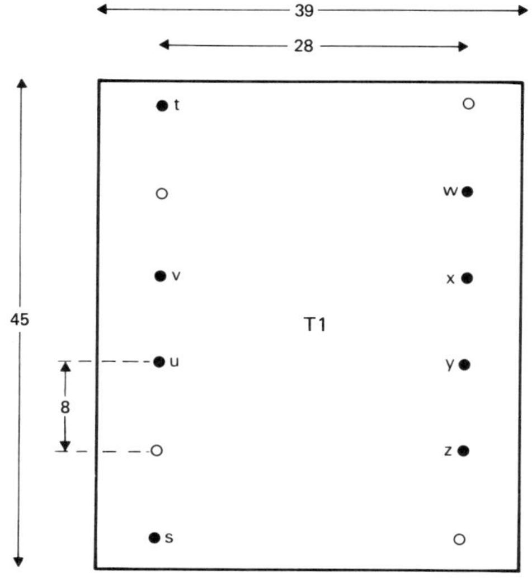

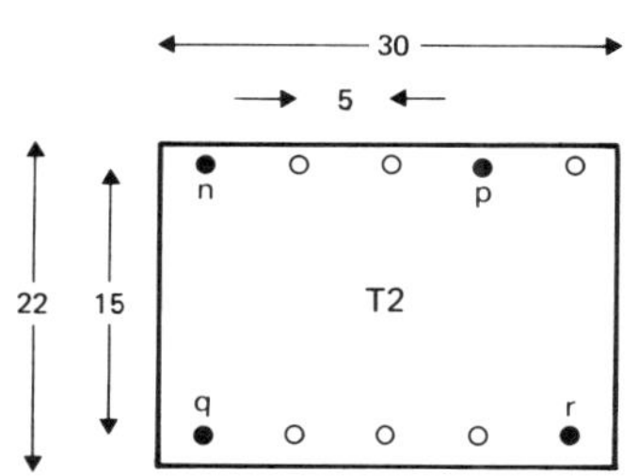

Viewed from below Dimensions in mm

III SELF OSCILLATING SWITCHING MODE SUPPLIES

by
Peter Wilson

As outlined in Chapter I, the self oscillating system is a simple, economic and efficient form of isolated switching mode power supply, and its design problems can be overcome by using a Darlington transistor. The use of a thyristor to turn the Darlington transistor 'off', and the various control systems were also extensively discussed. In this chapter the principle of operation of self-oscillating circuits is described, followed by two examples, i.e. one for use from a European 240V r.m.s. 50Hz supply and one from a 110V r.m.s. 60Hz supply.

CIRCUIT DESCRIPTION

General

A complete circuit diagram is given in Figure 1. The heart of the power supply is the high frequency transformer, T1. This transformer performs the following functions:

(i) Provides the isolation barrier. Transformers are available for this application which meet the I.E.C. 65 and B.S. Isolation Specification.

(ii) Allows energy transfer from the primary winding d-e to the secondaries f-g-h at high frequency; the primary current supplied from the rectified a.c. input supply being switched by the Darlington transistor, Q1. Multiple outputs are possible.

(iii) Provides drive for the Darlington transistor Q1 from winding b-c, eliminating high dissipation 'dropper' resistors from the input supply.

(iv) Generates a reference voltage from winding a-b which is used to control the conduction time of Q1 and thus provide the regulating action.

As is usual, the power supply operates in the shunt mode for ease of isolation, and flexibility in the choice of output voltage/voltages. When transistor Q1 is in conduction the rectifiers D14, D15 are reverse biassed and so is diode D13. Base current for Q1 is taken from winding b-c through resistor R5. The timing capacitor C9 is charged by the regulator during Q1 conduction time. Thyristor Th1 fires when C9 is charged to its gate trigger voltage. This initiates the energy transfer period. Transistor Q1 is turned 'off', reverse base current, $I_{B(off)}$, being drawn through the inductor L2 by thyristor Th1. Cessation of current flow in winding d-e causes the voltage polarity to reverse, and rectifiers D14, D15 conduct, transferring the energy stored

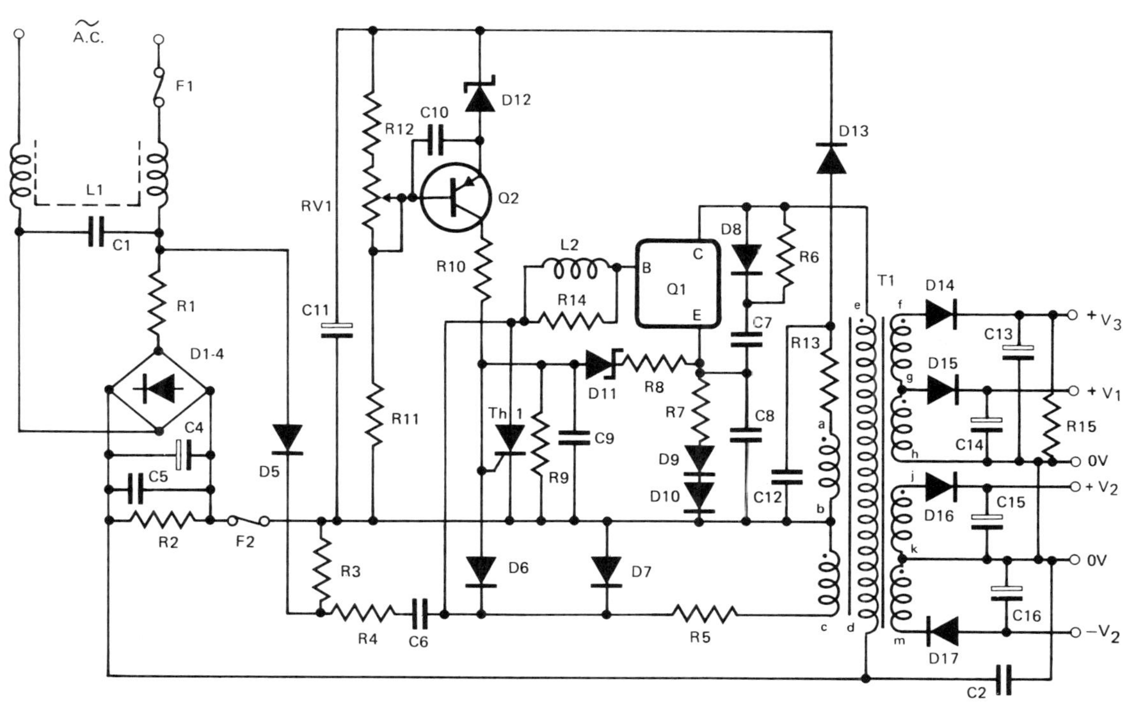

FIGURE 1. Self Oscillating Switching-Mode Power Supply

in the transformer T1 to the output circuits. Simultaneously, diode D13 conducts, replenishing the supply to the regulator circuit. When the energy transfer period is complete, the voltages sustained across the transformer windings collapse and the cycle repeats, base current to Q1 from winding b-c being restored. In normal operation, the running frequency will depend on the load, primarily; the frequency increasing with decreased load. The conduction time of Q1, i.e. the mark/space ratio will also vary with input voltage.

Principles of Operation

Normally the operating cycle comprises four distinct parts:

(a) Energy storage time, t_c, i.e. the time when the Darlington transistor Q1 is in conduction and the current in transformer T1 primary winding is increasing.

(b) The turn 'off' transition time, t_a. This is the time when transistor Q1 turns 'off' and the polarity of the voltage across the primary winding of transformer T1 reverses. The turn 'off' transition time is controlled by the dV/dt limiting circuit, components C7, D8, R6. Diode D8 will be in conduction during this time.

(c) The energy transfer time, t_d. The time when the rectifiers on the outputs conduct transferring the energy stored in transformer T1 to the output reservoir capacitors. The time ends when the energy is completely transferred. During this time a reverse voltage of nV_o is sustained across the primary winding.

(d) The relaxation time, t_b. Following energy transfer, the voltages sustained across transformer T1 windings collapse. The primary winding voltage falls to zero, the transition time being a function of the primary inductance and the dV/dt capacitor (C7) value. The falling voltage on

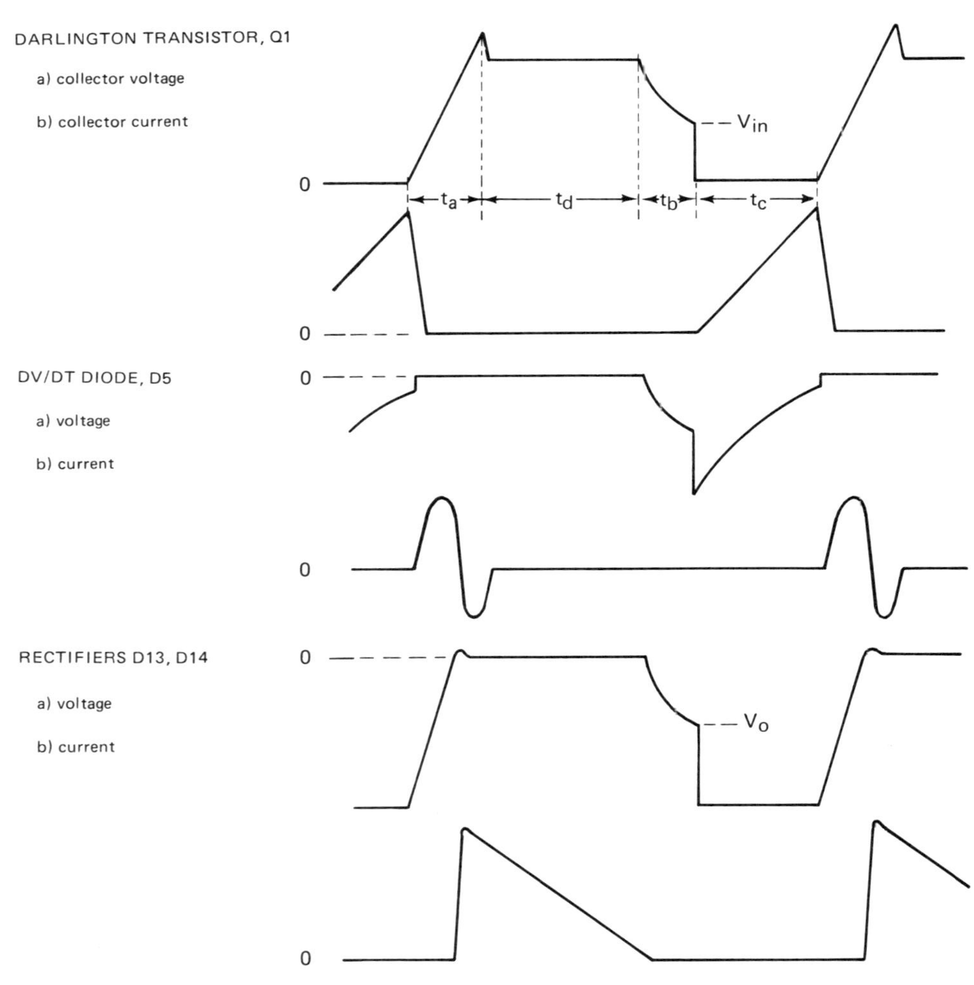

FIGURE 2. Operating Waveforms

the primary results in a positive going voltage being developed across the drive winding. This turns on transistor Q1 and starts the next cycle. Figure 2 shows the operating waveforms.

The following equations describe the circuit operation. Where:

P_o	=	Total output power, including switching losses
L_p	=	Transformer T1 primary inductance
$\hat{I}$	=	Peak current in the Darlington transistor Q1
f_o	=	The operating frequency
V_{in}	=	The rectified input supply voltage
nV_o	=	The transformer turns ratio multiplied by the output voltage
V_x	=	Voltage overshoot seen on the transformer primary at Q1 turn 'off'
C7	=	The value of the dV/dt capacitor.

I.e.

$P_o = L_p \times \hat{I}^2 \times f_o/2$		equation 1
$V_{in} = L_p \times \hat{I}/t_c$		equation 2
$f_o = 1/(t_a + t_b + t_c + t_d)$		equation 3
$V_{in} \times t_c = n \times V_o \times t_d$		equation 4
$t_a = C7 \times (V_{in} + nV_o + V_x)/\hat{I}$		equation 5
$t_b = \pi (L_p \times C7)^{1/2}$		equation 6

THE HIGH VOLTAGE DARLINGTON TRANSISTOR

General

The integrated Darlington connected power transistor is now an established product, a typical example being the TIP120 family whose layout is shown in Figure 3a. The major advantage of this connection is the high d.c. gain which, as a by product, gives very short switch 'on' times. This type of Darlington, however, has long switch 'off' times ($\approx 10\mu s$) and this restricts their use in high frequency switching applications. At switch 'off' the basic configuration allows no path for stored charge removal from the output section except through the relatively high base emitter resistors. Clearly much lower values of integrated resistor would aid charge removal at switch 'off'. There is a limit to the values of these components, since too low a value would effectively prevent the operation of the input transistor and dissipate large amounts of power in the resistors.

The elegant solution to this problem is shown in the equivalent circuit of the BU180A, Figure 3b. A diode across the input transistor base-emitter allows direct access to the output sections base for charge removal once the input section switches 'off' and its base emitter becomes reverse biassed. Obviously to provide an effective 'off' current drive, the drive voltage source should be more negative than the Darlington's emitter terminal. Switch 'on' is uneffected by the diode. The speed up diode has been a recognised technique for some time now. Established technology takes various forms, e.g. where the diode is assembled in 'piggy back' fashion across the appropriate circuit points. Another

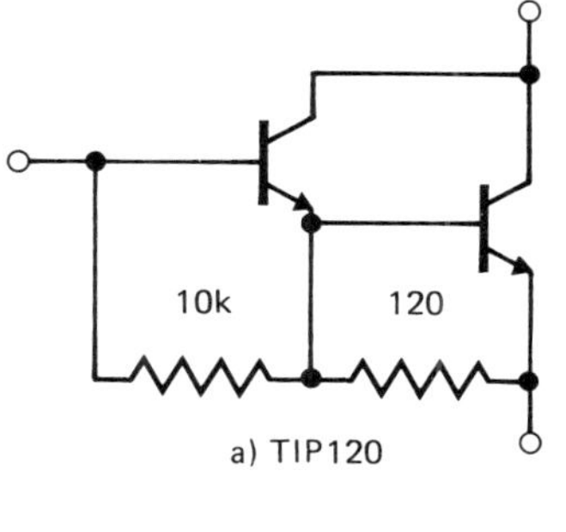

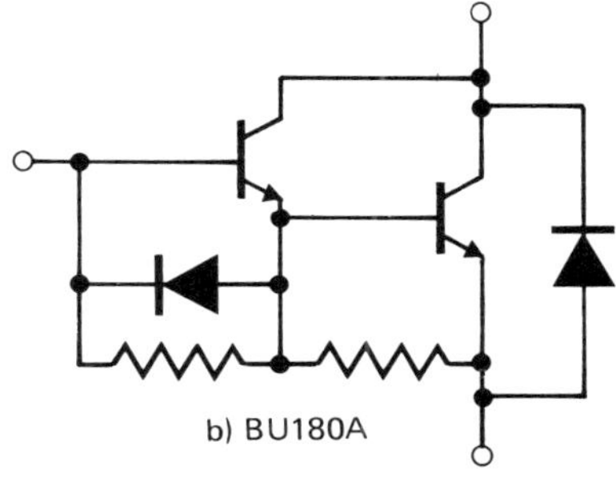

FIGURE 3. Darlington Configurations

method is to mount the diode on a ceramic substrate and wire to the main chip. A relatively new technology is the complete integration of all the resistors and diodes. The essence of the breakthrough is the integration of this 'speed up' diode. The problem overcome is the integration of a diode on a substrate which is also the collector terminal of a high voltage power device; this has been successfully achieved with a standard double diffused epitaxial glass passivated construction. The glass passivation technique allows plastic encapsulation of the chip. Thus such a Darlington features high speed, high voltage, economy, and reliability. High switch-'off' speed is achieved by making use of the speed up diode, high voltage is conventional technology, economy if plastic encapsulation can be the technology, and reliability by reducing the discrete component count in the application. When the drive has been optimised, fall times of 300ns are easily achieved, with typical storage times of the same order.

Design Details

Power Transistor 'on' Base Current, $I_{B(on)}$.

The minimum value of $I_{B(on)}$ is set by the limit conditions of minimum supply rail voltage and maximum collector current I_C (corresponding to maximum output power) to ensure the selected transistor type does not incur an excessive $V_{CE(sat)}$ power loss. Typically, the forced gain $I_C/I_{B(on)}$ required for a discrete device under these conditions will be between 5 and 10. At the other extreme, when the supply rail voltage is maximum and the collector current minimum (corresponding to minimum power

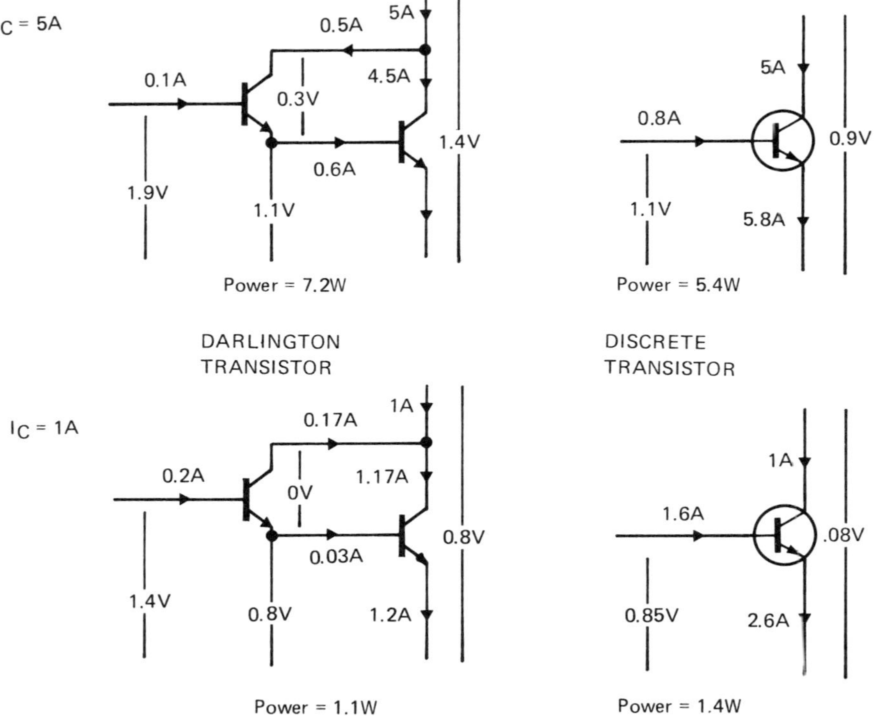

FIGURE 4. Static Saturation Conditions

output) the transistor forced gain can be below unity. This is because the base current will increase with supply rail voltage (≈2x) and the collector current will fall with reducing output power (≈5x). While this can only improve the $V_{CE(sat)}$ the collector turn 'off' can be substantially degraded leading to a high turn 'off' power loss. This comes about through excessive stored charge in the collector region – a well known effect in high voltage transistors.[1]

A comparison of the static conditions for a discrete and Darlington transistor at the operating extremes is shown in Figure 4. At 5A collector current the Darlington dissipates 30% more power while at 1A it is 20% less. Under working conditions, when the collector current is triangular, the difference between the average saturation power losses is negligable. The low $I_{B(on)}$ of the Darlington means its base drive circuit power loss is nearly an order of magnitude lower than the single transistors. This factor improves the power supplies efficiency and lowers the operating temperature. Study of the 1A collector current condition shows the discrete transistor to be 'super' saturated (V_{CE} = 80mV) whereas the Darlington's output transistor is only 'moderately' saturated (V_{CE} = 800mV). The Darlington's input transistor is 'super' saturated ($V_{CE} \approx$ OV) but as this is a much smaller size than the output transistor the amount of stored collector charge is very much reduced compared with the discrete transistor.

The point being made is that, in a Darlington, the output section is automatically held, by saturation of the driver, in a 'moderately' saturated condition giving consistent results between devices and reasonably low amounts of collector stored charge to remove at switch 'off'.

Transistor 'off' Base Current, $I_{B(off)}$.

To minimise the transistors turn 'off' power, the level of $I_{B(off)}$ should be adequate for the level of collector current involved and be maintained throughout the collector current fall time, t_f. For a Darlington, tracking of $I_{B(off)}$ with I_C can be obtained by using the circuit of Figure 5. Emitter current, I_E flowing in resistor R7 develops a voltage which varies with collector current. Over most of the operating range the voltage developed across base inductor L2 when turn 'off' switch S1 closes will approximately be I_ER7 from the emitter circuit. The slope of the turn off base current will be I_ER7/L2 A/s. When driven correctly, the transistor storage time, t_s, remains relatively constant so that $I_{B(off)} = I_E.R_7.\ t_s/L2$ A. As for a Darlington $I_E \approx I_C$ then $I_{B(off)}/I_C = R7.t_sL2$ and tracking occurs. Capacitor C8 maintains the emitter voltage particularly during the collector current fall time, t_f. Use of an inductive turn 'off' drive also helps to maintain $I_{B(off)}$ during the fall time. Practical waveforms are shown in Figure 6.

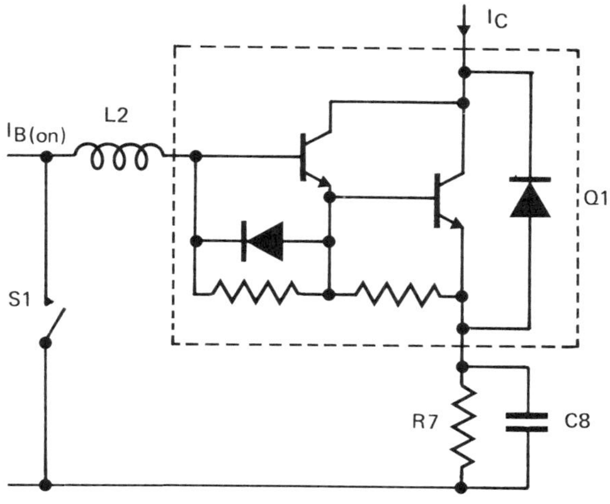

FIGURE 5. $I_{B(off)}$ Tracking Circuit

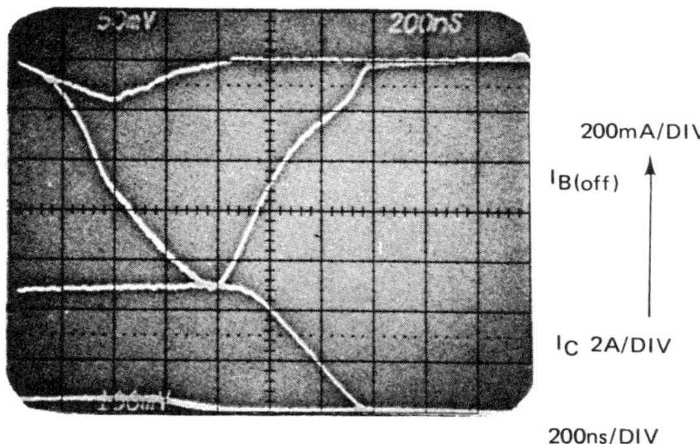

FIGURE 6. $I_{B(off)}$ Tracking at Two Levels of I_C (Using Circuit of Figure 5)

The beauty of this simple system is that the drive tracking is instantaneous and gives clean switching even at the power supply start-up when the collector current varies over a very large range. If a single transistor were used, the fall time, t_f, would tend to deteriorate at low collector currents due to the swamping effects of the relatively high level of base current.

Collector Voltage Rise (dV_{CE}/dt)

It is desirable to limit the rate of collector voltage rise for two reasons. First to allow the transistor to switch 'off' completely before its collector voltage is very high so minimising the transistor power loss. Secondly due to the unavoidable capacitive coupling in the isolation transformer the primary voltage rise time should be as slow as possible to minimise the capacitive current in the output system ($dV/dt = I/C$).

The network to control the rise rate has been discussed elsewhere,[2] and in Chapter II.

Collector Voltage Fall

In a self oscillating system the transistor turn 'on' is of special importance. The turn 'on' speed will be a direct function of the output stage loop gain. So to avoid potential forward second breakdown failure due to long turn 'on' times the gain needs to be as large as possible.[2] Here again the low drive requirement of the Darlington allows at least an order of magnitude increase in loop gain.

Fast-Soft Recovery

The output rectifiers obviously need to be fast types for high efficiency and low damping of the oscillators loop during the Darlington's switch 'on'. An additional specification of soft recovery means the rectifier recovery current will smoothly decrease to zero without any kinks or sharp transitions which can cause radiation problems. This feature is shown in Figure 7 and guaranteed in the BY205 rectifier range recommended for this position in Chapter 1.

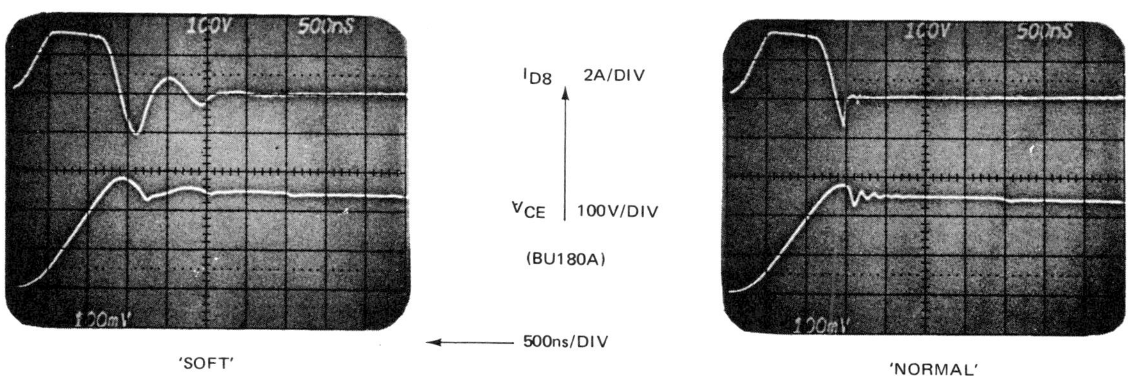

FIGURE 7. Radiation Reduction Through Use of Soft Recovery Diode

A 150W SUPPLY OPERATING FROM 240V 50Hz

Performance Summary

Output Power		150W
Input Voltage Range		180-265V a.c.
Output voltages	at 0.95A	150V
	at 0.05A	200V
Supply regulation, 150V	100% to 30% of load	1·5%
	100% to 3.5% of load	4·0%
Supply stabilisation, 150V	180-265V r.m.s. input voltage	0·4%
Output ripple voltage, 150V	at f_0	0·75V pk-pk
	at 100Hz	0·16V pk-pk
Efficiency	at full load	85%
Frequency of operation		20-78kHz

Detailed Circuit Description

The principles of the basic circuit are described at the beginning of the chapter, and a more detailed circuit description is given here. Figure 8 shows the circuit diagram of a complete 150W power supply designed to operate from a 50Hz 240V a.c. mains supply. Table 1 lists the component values.

Input and Filter Circuits: The a.c. input voltage is rectifier by the bridge D1-4. Resistor R1 is a surge limiter, and capacitor C4 the main reservoir capacitor. Resistor R2 ensures that C4 is discharged when the supply is switched off – particularly in a fault condition when the fuse F2 has been blown. The capacitor C5 provides decoupling of the high frequency switching waveforms in transformer T1 and Darlington transistor Q1. Capacitor C2 decouples high frequency switching transients between primary and secondary windings on transformer T1. Because of the isolation requirement C2 is limited to a value of 5nF and must have high voltage capability at high frequency. The input filter circuit, C1, C3, L1, is of a standard form. Its purpose is to suppress high frequency radiation both into and from the a.c. supply.

Starter Circuit. The oscillation of the system must be initiated at switch 'on' to give consistent operation. The circuit R3, C6, D5 and R4 performs this function. Negative going pulses at the input supply frequency (50Hz) are applied to the emitter of Q1. When the device Q1 emitter current exceeds the level at which the device has sufficient gain, oscillation starts and base current is then derived from the winding b-c. By injecting emitter current rather than base current to transistor Q1 at start up, variation in start up voltage is reduced. Operation of the circuit is illustrated in Figure 9. The resistor R4 is chosen to provide 3mA of emitter current at 160V a.c. Once the circuit has started the peak collector current in Q1 is limited by the overcurrent protection circuit until the outputs are established and the regulator acts. The starter circuit is also used when the power supply enters the 'burst mode' – the bursts being initiated at 20ms intervals.

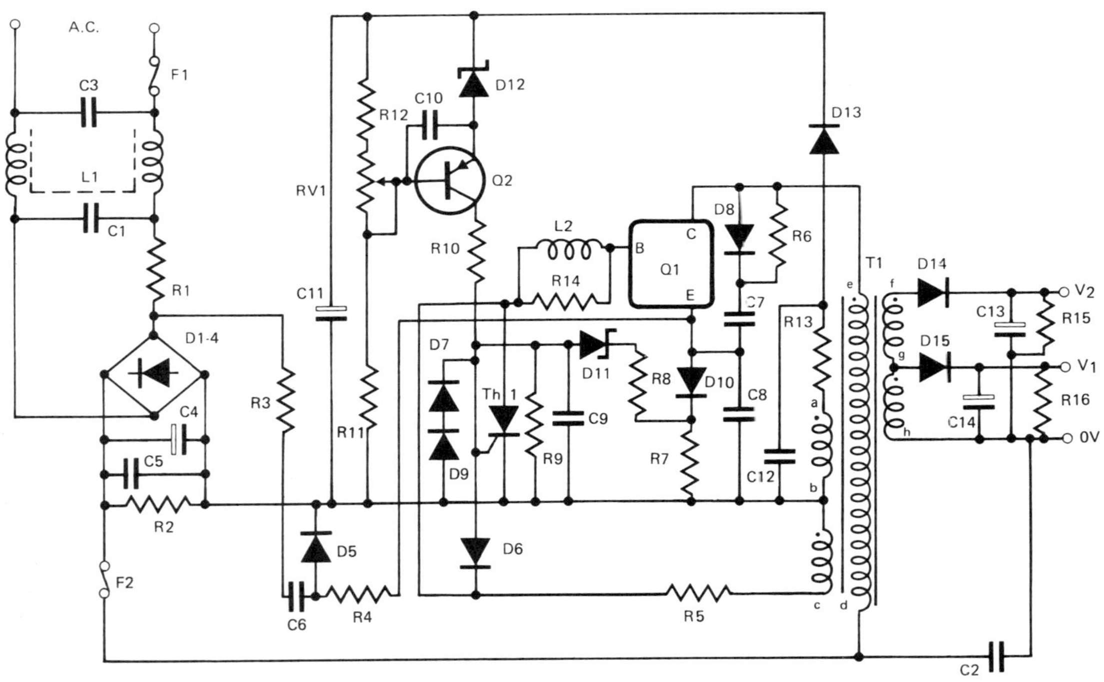

FIGURE 8. A 150W Supply Operating from 240V 50Hz.

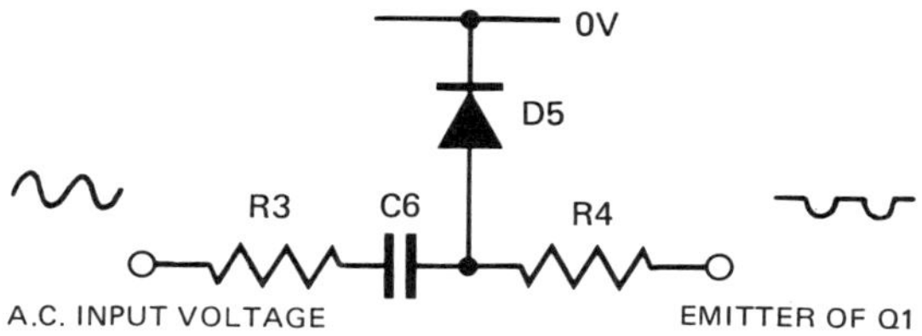

FIGURE 9. Starter Circuit

Table 1 Components List for the 150W Power Supply

C1	100nF	600V	L1	2 x 3 mH	
C2	5nF	4kV	L2	6μH at 1A	
C3	100nF	600V			
C4	220μF	400V	R1	3Ω3	11W
C5	1μF	600V	R2	330k	0.5W
C6	100nF	600 V	R3	1k	0.5W
C7	3n3F	800V (1000V/μs)	R4	68k	
C8	1μF	100V	R5	1k2	7W
C9	2n2F	160V	R6	1k	11W
C10	2n2F	160V	R7	1Ω	2.5W
C11	4μF	35V	R8	100Ω	
C12	5n6F	160V	R9	27k	
C13	10μF	250V	R10	390Ω	
C14	50μF	250V	R11	8k2	
			R12	2k7	
D1			R13	47Ω	0.5W
D2	BY127		R14	47Ω	0.5W
D3			R15	10k	5.0W
D4			R16	3k3	11.0W
D5	1N4004				
D6	BY401		Q1	BU181/BUW81	
D7	1S920		Q2	BC212	
D8	BY205-800				
D9	1S920		RV1	1k	
D10	BY127				
D11	BZY88-3V3		Th1	BRY59A	
D12	BZY88-7V5				
D13	BY402				
D14	BY205-800				
D15	BY205-600				
F1	2AT				
F2	2AF				
T1	As described in the appendix.				

The Drive Circuit. The Darlington transistor, Q1, must remain saturated during its conduction time. The value of resistor R5 is chosen to satisfy this condition when the voltage developed across winding b-c is known. Power dissipation in resistor R5 is lower than if Q1 had been a single transistor because of the higher gain of the Darlington configuration.

c.f. for I_C = 4.0A, BUY70B requires I_B = 0·8A
BU181 requires I_B = 0.04A

The effect of components L2 and R14 are neglected when Q1 is in conduction. Turn 'off' of Q1 is initiated by the firing of thyristor Th1. This is a BRY59 device with an 'on' state voltage, V_T, specified as 1·6V at 1·5A and a turn 'on' time, t_{gt}, of 1μs maximum (see Chapter I). Stored charge in Q1 is extracted through the base terminal. Inductor L2 controls the rate of charge removal and is chosen to optimise Q1 collector current fall time. A negative bias across the base emitter terminals of Q1 is achieved by the use of components C8, R7, D10 in series with the emitter terminal so that, at turn 'off', the emitter terminal is held positive. As Q1 turns 'off', the polarity of the voltage developed across the base drive winding b-c reverses. The base of Q1 is prevented from falling too far negative by the diodes, D6, D7 and D9. An excessive negative voltage at the base terminal might otherwise breakdown an internal emitter base junction. The reversed polarity across winding b-c is used to discharge the timing capacitor, C9 through diode D6. Diodes D7 and D9 clamp the discharge voltage to 2 x V_F below 0V. The timing circuit is thus reset for the next cycle. Resistor R14 damps the voltage developed across L2 during the turn 'off' cycle, preventing Q1 from being switched on again by induced voltages. The incorporation of a resistive element, R7 in the emitter series network allows tracking of the turn 'off' current with emitter current.

The Control Circuit. The function of the control circuit is to charge the timing capacitor C9 at a rate dependent on the reference voltage developed by the winding a-b. The voltage developed by winding a-b is rectified by D13 and smoothed by capacitor C11. The small signal transistor, Q2 operating in the linear mode, charges capacitor C9 through resistor R10. An increase in the reference voltage results in increased charging current. Potentiometer RV1 permits adjustment of the charging rate. The zener diode D12 connected in series with the emitter or transistor Q2 will mask variations in the emitter base forward voltage giving a more temperature stable and reproducible design. It also permits the use of a higher voltage reference supply. This allows more turns to be used on winding a-b resulting in improved transformer coupling and better regulation performance. The components C12 and R13 form a 'snubber' network which removes the chance of an erroneous reference voltage being developed by delaying the turn 'on' of Diode D13, and so preventing peak rectification.

As the load on the power supply is reduced, the operating frequency increases. It is normally advisable to fix the maximum operating frequency to avoid high dissipation in the power handling components, i.e. C4, T1, Q1. In this design the reduced power transfer at the higher frequencies reduces the losses. Maximum frequency is reached when the turn 'on' and turn 'off' transitions become the major portion of the operating period. The power supply then assumes 'burst mode' operation.

The Output Circuit. As the power supply operates in the shunt mode, isolated outputs over a range of voltages can be achieved, the restriction being in the available winding area on the transformer T1. This design provides 150V and 200V supplies as may be required, for example, in a colour t.v. receiver. The 200V winding (low current) is made as an overwind on the 150V supply thus minimising the winding area required. Fast, soft recovery diodes D14, D15 are used, as previously stated, to minimise switching losses, and radiation into the supplies. The supplies are decoupled by capacitors C13, C14 which need to be high quality components (low effective series resistance) to minimise high frequency ripply and give reliable operation. Pre-load resistors R15, R16 are added to prevent 'burst mode' operation when the external load is removed. They also limit the voltage overshoot seen at the collector of transistor Q1 in this condition.

Protection Circuits. Componts R8 and D11 together with emitter series resistor R7 provide over current protection for Q1. When the voltage developed across R7 exceeds D11 zener voltage, the timing capacitor C9 is charged rapidly and the thyristor Th1 is fired, turning transistor Q1 'off'. Over voltage protection on the output supplies is provided by the regulator action. The rate of rise of voltage across the Darlington transistor Q1, at turn 'off', is limited by the components C7, D8, R6. This limits the peak dissipation in the device to an acceptable level. No peak voltage clamp circuit is used as the transformer coupling is sufficiently good to maintain the peak voltage within the device ratings.

A 100W SUPPLY OPERATING FROM 110V 60Hz

Performance Summary

Total power output distributed as follows:	110W
225V	10W
130V	80W
±35V	20W

Outputs isolated from a.c. supply line and short circuit protected.

130V supply regulation (45W load variation)	<700mV
130V supply stabilisation (100V – 130V a.c.)	<300mV
130V supply ripple voltage	<400mV pk-pk h.f. <100mV pk-pk 60Hz
Efficiency (d.c. to d.c.)	85%
Switching frequency	20 – 30kHz
Operating a.c. input range	90 – 130V

Circuit Description

In Figure 1 the a.c. supply is rectified by bridge diodes D1-4 and smoothed by capacitor C4. Resistor R2 discharges the capacitor after the supply is switched off. Inductor L1 and capacitor C1 form a conventional radio frequency interference (r.f.i.) filter network. Surge limiting resistor R1 and fuses F1 and F2 provide circuit fault protection.

As for the 150W supply just described, since the outputs are isolated a monitoring or reference winding a-b is needed to provide a feedback signal for the error amplifier. Resistor R13 and capacitor C12 'snubs' the leading edge of the pulse from the winding removing spikes which would rectify and give a false indication of the output voltages. Diode D13 and capacitor C11 rectify and smooth the winding voltage for the error amplifier which consists of reference diode D12, transistor Q2, resistors R11, R12 and R10, stabilising capacitor C10 and output voltage setting potentiometer RV1.

The blocking oscillator loop is formed by primary (collector) winding d-e, base positive feedback winding b-c and the BU180A power switching transistor Q1. Resistor R5 limits the base current to about 100mA. The drive voltage from the winding b-c is large, about 100V peak to peak, but the power loss in resistor R5 is only 5W because of the low drive requirement of Darlington transistor Q1. This large drive voltage is used as it gives a very fast switch 'on' of Q1 ($\simeq$400ns). To attempt this with a single transistor would result in an excessive power loss in resistor R5. This is therefore a practical illustration of the Darlington giving the advantage of a faster turn-'on' and hence better inherent reliability than a single transistor.

The transistor Q1 is turned 'off' after thyristor (s.c.r.) Th1 has fired; resistor R14 and inductor L2 control the base current during turn-'off'. Emitter resistor R7 diodes D9, D10 and capacitor C8 give tracking of $I_{B(off)}$ with I_C for transistor Q1. The thyristor firing occurs when capacitor C9 has recharged to V_{GT} after being discharged by diode D6 during the power transistor Q1 'off' time when the drive from winding b-c is negative. The error amplifier provides this recharging current and hence can control the power transistor 'on' time before the thyristor fires. Under certain conditions the error amplifier would try to generate a very long 'on' period for the power transistor leading to excessive collector currents. This is avoided by the voltage developed across resistor R7 making zener D11 conduct, charging capacitor C9, firing the thyristor and so terminating the 'on' period. Peak current limiting in this design occurs at about 5A. Resistor R8 limits the zener dissipation. Diode D7 stops a destructively large negative voltage being applied to the Darlington base. The oscillator is started by a pulse method. Capacitor C6 is charged via diode D5, resistor R4 and the base circuit from the a.c. supply and discharged by resistor R3. As the capacitor is only charged for one quarter of the supply period ($\simeq$4ms), oscillator starting is only attempted during this time. This form of starting leads to less power transistor stress in the event of short circuited outputs or light loading. Note that only small start currents are needed as the use of a Darlington has made the base circuit impedance high. Resistor R9 provides a discharge path for capacitor C9 during the 'burst' starting. The collector voltage rise of the power transistor is controlled by diode D8, resistor R6 and capacitor C7 forming a conventional dV_{CE}/dt network. Output rectification is half wave, diodes D14-17 and smoothing capacitors C13-16, the power being transferred when the Darlington is 'off'. Capacitor C5 is a non-electrolytic type to decouple the power supply switching currents from the electrolytic smoothing capacitor C4.

Table 2 gives the full components list for the supply, as shown in Figure 1, to provide 100W and operate from 110V r.m.s. 60Hz.

Table 2. Component List for 100W Supply

C1	470n	200V a.c.
C2	4n7	1kV
C4	680µF	185V
C5	2µ2	200V
C6	47n	200V
C7	6n	600V
C8	1µF	100V
C9	2n2	160V
C10	4µF	40V
C12	6n9	
C13	10µF	300V
C14	47µF	150V
C15	470µF	
C16	470µF	
F1	3A Slow Blow	
F2	2A	
D1	BY127	
D2	BY127	
D3	BY127	
D4	BY127	
D5	1N4004	
D6	BA248	
D7	BA248	
D8	BY205-600	
D9	1S020	
D10	1S020	
D11	1N708A	
D12	1N711A	
D13	BA248	
D14	BY205-800	
D15	BY205-600	
D16	1SX172	
D17	1SX172	
L1	10 + 10mH Coilcraft W2961	
L2	1µH T-Form Inductor, (exact value depends on circuit layout)	
Q1	BU180A	
Q2	2N3702	

R1	2Ω	10W
R2	47k	1W
R3	470k	
R4	2k7	
R5	470Ω	10W
R6	330Ω	10W
R7	1Ω	3W
R8	220Ω	
R9	2k7	
R10	390Ω	
R11	8k2	
R12	2k2	
R13	47Ω	
R14	22Ω	
R15	22k	3W
RV1	1k	
Th1	BRY59A	
T1	Core Fair-rite 9477036002	

Winding

a-b	14t @ 30swg
b-c	23t @ 32swg
d-e	46t @ 21swg
f-g	38t @ 30swg
g-h	60t @ 24swg
j-k	17t @ 28swg
k-m	17t @ 28swg

Core gapped for L_{de} = 470µH @ 4A d.c. Leakage inductance <6µH or Coilcraft W2959

m j f g kh

d c b a e

Characteristics

This specific circuit was designed as a replacement module for a v.r.t. power supply in a particular colour television. The components replaced are the v.r.t., its tuning capacitor, the full wave rectifiers, 60Hz smoothing capacitors and filter choke. In the modified system the degauss coils were driven directly from the a.c. supply and the tube heater from a winding on the e.h.t. transformer. Supply rail requirements have been given in the performance summary.

Figure 10 shows the output voltage variation over the a.c. input range of 100-130V a.c. Two curves are shown for each voltage, i.e. the maximum and minimum brilliance conditions of a colour television which was being driven by the power supply. It is very clear from Figure 10 that the switching-mode system gives a 130V deflection supply which is better stabilised (10x) and regulated (4x) than given by the v.r.t.. The 225V supply also doubles as a peak voltage clipper circuit for the primary which explains its greater voltage variation compared with the other outputs. Even so it is comparable with the v.r.t.s and could be further improved by increasing the preload power (R15). The piece part costing for the switching-mode system is some 15% below a v.r.t.. In the longer term the potential saving on the switching-mode is greater if its production volume reaches the same level as currently enjoyed by the v.r.t..

The frequency variation with input voltage and load is given in Figure 11. Note that the frequency always remains outside the audio range.

Figure 12 shows this supply's typical current and voltage wave shapes. Points to note are the triangular collector current and the collector voltage 'relaxation' period when the voltage slowly falls to below the supply line value and initiates turn on. The turn-'on', Figure 13, is accomplished in 400ns and results in a device power loss of less than 400mW. Turn-off, Figure 14, is 'clean' and takes less than 500ns and results in a power loss of less than 500mW. Figure 15 shows the typical 130V rectifier waveforms. Use of the BY205 gives the soft recovery shown in Figure 16 and discussed earlier.

REFERENCES

1. M. J. Maytym and A. Lear. "Driver Circuit Design Considerations for High Voltage Line-Scan Transistors." *Proc I.E.E.E.* BTR19, No.2, 1972, pp 127-135.

2. M. J. Maytum. "Transistorised Self-Stabilising Horizontal Deflection." *Proc. I.E.E.E.* BTR20, No.1, 1974, pp 32-64.

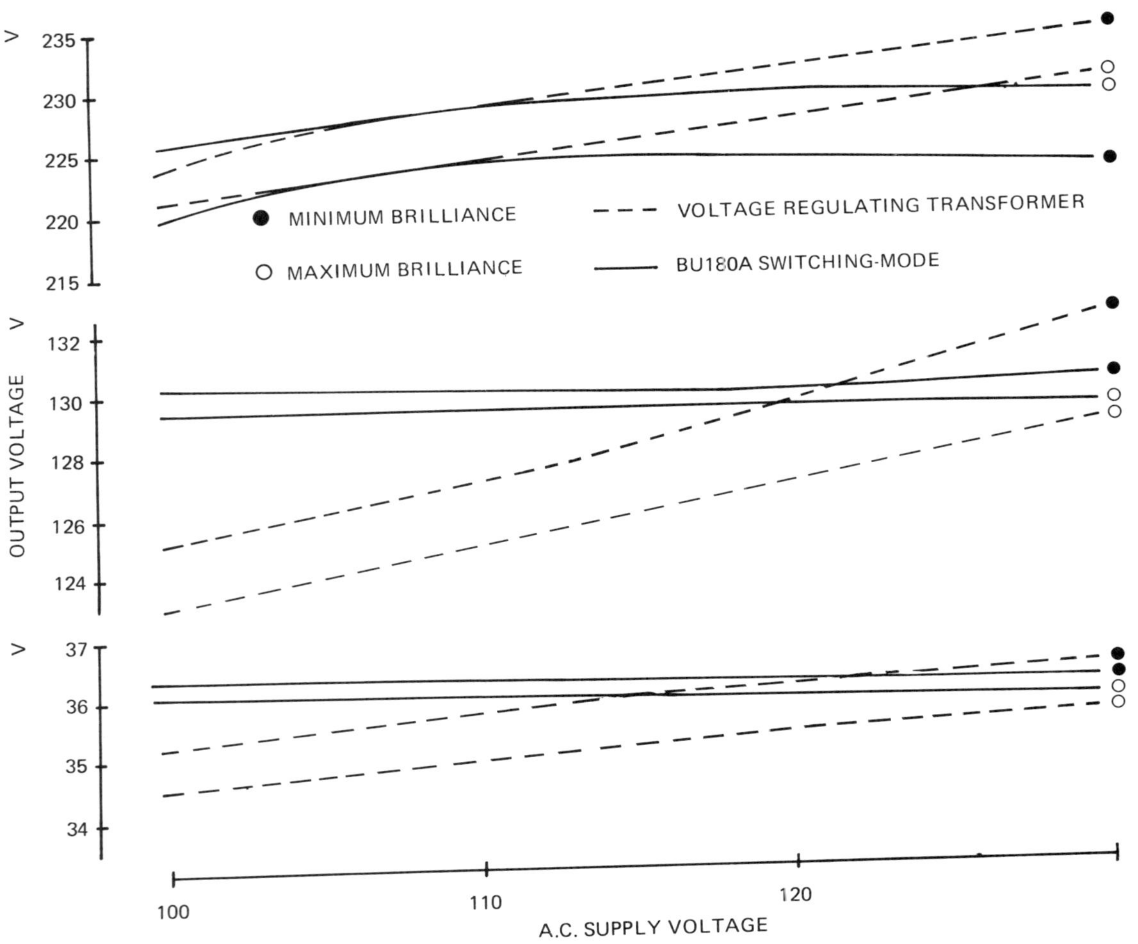

V

235
230
225
220
215

● MINIMUM BRILLIANCE
○ MAXIMUM BRILLIANCE
- - - VOLTAGE REGULATING TRANSFORMER
—— BU180A SWITCHING-MODE

OUTPUT VOLTAGE V

132
130
128
126
124

V

37
36
35
34

100
110
120
A.C. SUPPLY VOLTAGE

FIGURE 10. Performance Comparison Between Switching Mode and V.R.T. Supplies

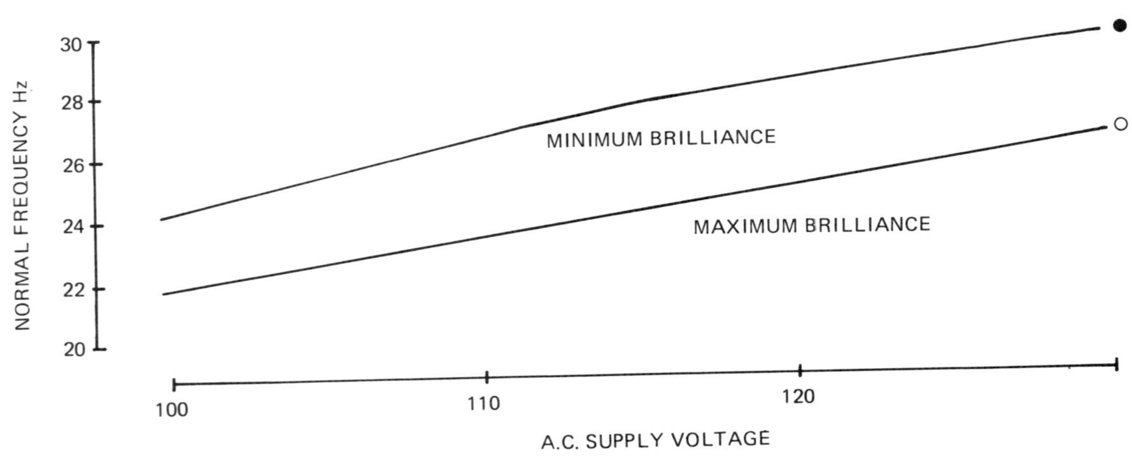

FIGURE 11. Frequency Variation of Input Voltage and Load

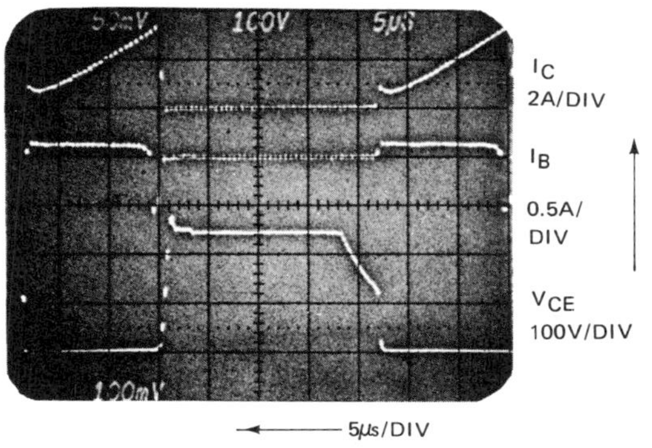

FIGURE 12. Typical Power Device (Q1) Waveforms

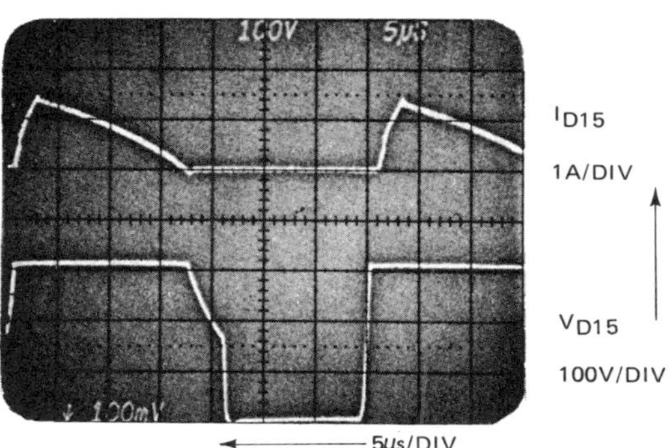

FIGURE 15. 130V Output Rail Rectifier (D15) Waveforms

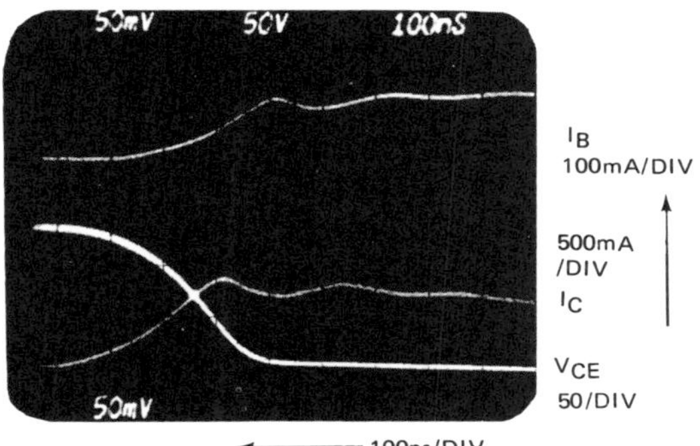

FIGURE 13. Device (Q1) Turn-'On' Behaviour

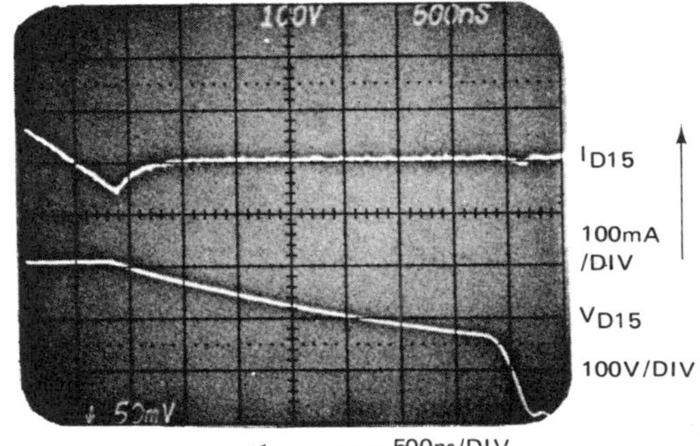

FIGURE 16. The Soft Recovery Characteristic of a BY205 When Used in D15 Position

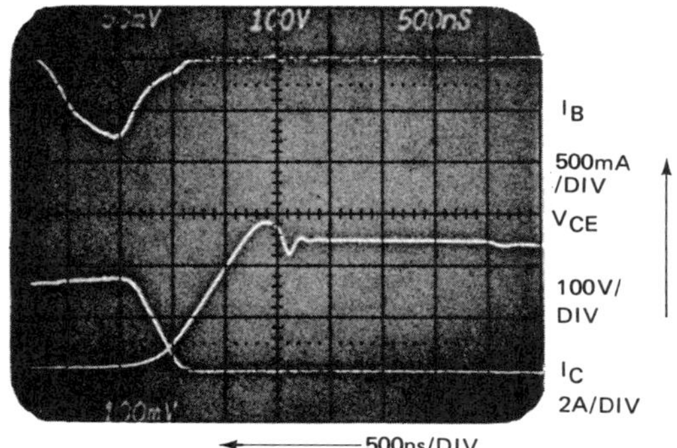

FIGURE 14. Device (Q1) Turn-'Off' Behaviour

APPENDIX

Transformer Design for the 150W Power Supply.

Specification: Input supply voltage 200-360V d.c.

Isolated outputs 150V at 0·95A

200V at 50mA

Operating frequency 20–78kHz

Close coupling between primary and secondary windings for good regulation and low primary leakage inductance.

Calculation:

(a) Primary inductance. The system operates in the complete energy transfer mode (c.e.t.). Equations 1 and 2 are used to determine the primary inductance L_p and the peak primary current, $\hat{I}$.

$\hat{I} = 2P_o/(f_o \times V_{in} \times t_c)$

$L_p = (V_{in} \times t_c)/\hat{I}$

substituting $V_{in} = 200V$, $f_o = 20kHz$, $t_c = 1/2\ f_o$, $P_o = 150W$

$\hat{I} = 3{\cdot}0A$

$L_p = 1{\cdot}66mH$

To determine Lp more accurately, recalculate putting

$t_c = \frac{1}{2}(1/f_o - t_a - t_b)$, and using equations 5 and 6,

$t_c = 23\mu s$

$\hat{I} = 3{\cdot}26A$

$L_p = 1{\cdot}41mH$

(b) Ferrite core selection. In this mode of operation, the magnetising field is unidirectional.

i.e. $\hat{\check{B}} = V_{in} \times t_c/n \times A_e$

The maximum flux density should not exceed B_{sat} at the highest operating temperature (110°C). For the Fairrite 42mm E core, (Part No. 9477036002) B_{sat} at 125°C is quoted as 305mT. Choosing to operate at 280mT $\hat{\check{B}}$ the number of primary turns is calculated: n = 89.

Core Losses: Ferrite data shows the losses at 280mT and 20kHz to be ≏ 100mW/cm³ at room ambient.

Total losses = V_e x 100mW
= 1.8W

Allowing the winding losses to equal core losses, Total power loss = 3.6W

The transformer surface area exposed for cooling, A_s is 7536mm². A power loss of 477μW/mm² is required. In practice, a transformer will radiate at 400μW-500μW/mm² with a 40°C rise in core temperature above ambient. Additional heat sinking will be required if a lower temperature gradient is required.

(c) Winding design

Winding	No. of Turns	Wire Gauge
Primary (d-e)	89	22 s.w.g.
150V secondary (g-h)	67	22 s.w.g.
200V overwind (f-g)	22	30 s.w.g.
Drive (b-c)	22	30 s.w.g.
Reference (a-b)	14	30 s.w.g.

The available winding area is 160mm². This is divided equally between primary and secondary windings. Allowing a space factor of ½, the primary 'copper' area is 40mm². Some of this area, 10% say, is taken by the reference and drive windings. Cross sectional area of one turn of the primary = .405mm², indicating 22 s.w.g. wire. For convenience, the 150V secondary can be wound in the same wire gauge. The low current windings are wound in 30 s.w.g. wire. To keep the primary leakage inductance low, the secondary windings are wound between the halves of a split primary.

IV AN I.C. SWITCHING VOLTAGE REGULATOR

by
John Spencer and Peter Wilson

Apart from in the control section, the switching mode power supplies discussed so far have employed discrete components. With the increased use of such supplies it was inevitable that an integrated circuit version would be developed. This chapter therefore, discusses such an i.c., the TL497 switching voltage regulator, and its applications. Although the principle of regulators or 'choppers', both series and shunt, has been discussed in a previous volume[1], the basic operation is again given here with, however, the bias necessary to understand how an i.c. supply functions and to develop the necessary equations for worked example calculations. A description of the TL497 i.c. follows, explaining how each of its functions operates, which leads into the practical examples given at the end of the chapter.

PRINCIPLE OF OPERATION

Series (Step-Down) Switching Voltage Regulator

The principle of operation and the method by which voltage conversion at high efficiencies can be achieved using switching regulators can be demonstrated by analysing the basic configuration of a (step-down or series) switching voltage regulator (Figure 1). As shown here device

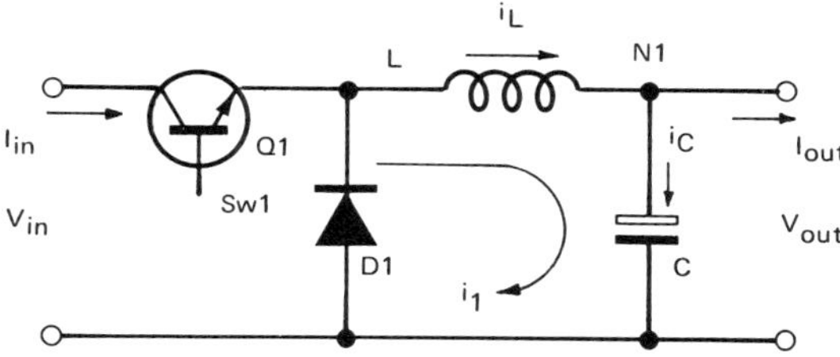

FIGURE 1. Series (Step-Down) Switching Voltage Regulator

Q1 is the switch transistor,which is turned 'on' and 'off' by the regulator's control circuit at a frequency and duty cycle required to maintain the desired output. Because this transistor is always in the saturated state when it is conducting, or otherwise completely non-conducting, the power dissipated in the switch is much lower than that dissipated in a conventional series regulator, whose series transistor is continuously operated in the linear region. The diode D1 is the catch, or efficiency, diode and provides a continuous path for the current in the inductor (L) when the switch (Q1) turns 'off'. During the time Q1 is turned 'on' (t_{on}), the input voltage V_{in} is applied to the input of the LC filter causing the current i_1 to increase. When Q1 is turned 'off' the energy stored in the inductor maintains the current flow to the load through D1. The LC filter will average the voltage seen at its input and deliver that voltage to the output load, i.e.

$$V_{out} = V_{in} \cdot t_{on}/(t_{on} + t_{off}) = V_{in} \cdot t_{on}/\tau$$

. . . . equation 1

Therefore, by controlling the duty cycle, t_{on}/τ changes can be compensated for in the input voltage. If V_{in} increases, the control circuit will cause a corresponding reduction in the duty cycle and thereby maintain a constant V_{out}. Since the inductor current is shared by the input when transistor Q1 is 'on', and goes to ground through D1 when Q1 is 'off', the average input current corresponds to the output current times the duty cycle of the switch Q1, i.e.

$$I_{in} = I_{out} \cdot t_{on}/\tau$$

Disregarding the switching losses, the ideal efficiency (η) then becomes:

$$\eta = 100.P_{out}/P_{in}$$

Since, $P_{out} = V_{out} . I_{out}$

and, $P_{in} = V_{in} . I_{in}$

$$= 100.V_{out} . I_{out}/V_{in} . I_{in}$$

Substituting for V_{out} and I_{in},

$$= (100.V_{in} . I_{out} . t_{on}/\tau)/(V_{in} . I_{out} . t_{on}/\tau)$$
$$= 1 \times 100$$
$$= 100\%$$

In an actual circuit, however, a portion of the input power is lost during the transistion as Q1 is turned 'off' and 'on'. Minimising the frequency will keep these losses low, although too low a frequency will result in an impractical inductor value. This is discussed further in the following sections.

To optimise the design of a circuit using an i.c. switching voltage regulator it is necessary to understand the operation of the basic series or step-down switching voltage regulator circuit shown in Figure 1. First, defining the initial conditions prior to the closing of switch Sw1, i.e.

$$(\text{At } t = 0-) \qquad V_C = V_{out}$$
$$i_L = 0 = i_1$$

When the switch Sw1 is closed the current in the inductor cannot change instantaneously. Therefore, at Sw1 just closed $(t = 0+)$ $V_C = V_{out}$

$i_L = 0 = i_1$

Writing a loop equation around the circuit,

$$V_{in} = R_S . i_1 + L . di_1/dt + V_C$$

where R_S is the source impedance of the input.

Substituting

$$i_1 = 0, \quad V_C = V_{out}$$

$$V_{in} = L . di_1/dt + V_{out}$$

Therefore,

$$di_1/dt = (V_{in} - V_{out})/L$$

The current through the inductor (i_L) at any given time, t, is

$$i_L = (V_{in} - V_{out}).t/L \qquad \text{equation 2}$$

For a constant V_{in}, V_{out} and L, i_L varies linearly with time.

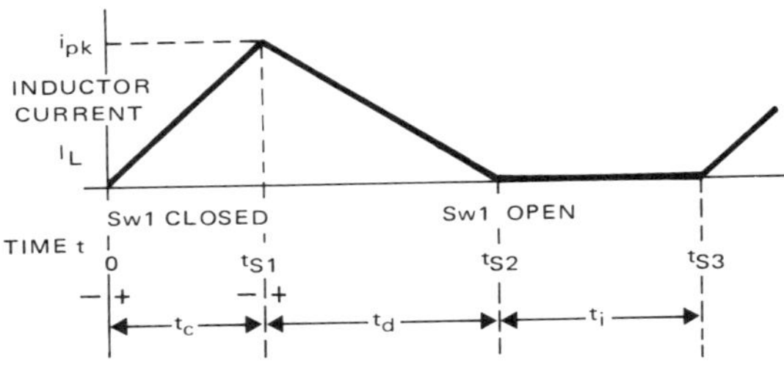

FIGURE 2. Inductor Current Waveform

The current increases while switch Sw1 is closed according to the waveform shown in Figure 2. When Sw1 is opened the voltage across the inductor inverts to maintain a constant current flow. In this state the diode D1 is forward biassed providing a current path for the discharge of the inductor into the load and filter capacitor. The peak current reached by the inductor with Sw1 closed is:

$$i_{pk} = (V_{in} - V_{out}).t_{on}/L \qquad \text{equation 3}$$

where here,

$$t_{on} \equiv t_c, \text{ the charge time}$$

When Sw1 opens the current through the inductor is i_{pk} since the current cannot change instantaneously. With switch Sw1 open and diode D1 forward biassed ($V_F = 0$) the voltage across the inductor becomes V_C which is V_{out}. To determine the discharge time of the inductor with Sw1 open:

Prior to Sw1 open $(t = t_{S1}-)$ $i_L = i_{pk}$

$V_C = V_{out}$

At Sw1 just open $(t = t_{S1}+)$ $i_L = i_{pk}$

$V_C = V_{out}$

Writing a loop equation for i_1 in Figure 1,

$$V_F + L . di_1/dt + V_C = 0$$

Substituting

$$V_F = 0 \quad V_C = V_{out}$$

$$di_1/dt = -V_{out}/L$$

The current through the inductor for $t > t_{S1}$ is:

$$i_L = i_{pk} - V_{out}(t - t_{S1})/L$$

The discharge time of the inductor then is that time required for i_L to equal zero.

Therefore, $t_{S2} - t_{S1} = t_d = i_{pk} . L/V_{out}$ equation 4

Analysing the currents at the inductor/capacitor/output node (N1)

$$i_L = i_C + i_{out}$$

where i_{out} is the output or load current.

If i_{out} is considered constant,

$$\Delta i_C = \Delta i_L = i_{pk}$$

when, $i_L = i_{out}$; $i_C = 0$

when, $i_L = 0$; $i_C = -i_{out}$

For the voltage across the capacitor to remain constant the net charge stored in the capacitor must remain constant. Therefore, the charge delivered to the capacitor from the inductor ($\Delta Q+$) must equal the charge extracted from the capacitor ($\Delta Q-$) by the load, as illustrated in Figure 3. The discharge time of the capacitor, i.e. the interval or idle time, t_i, shown in Figure 4, can then be determined.

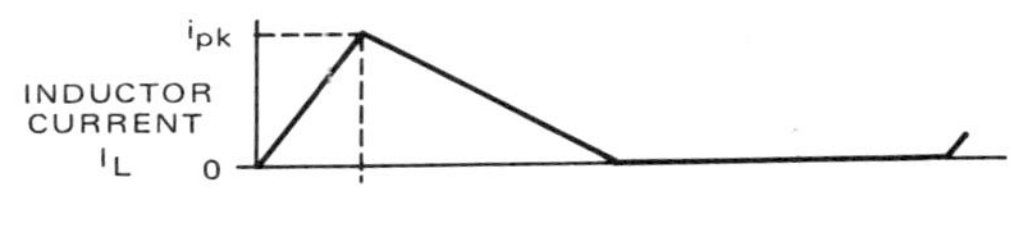

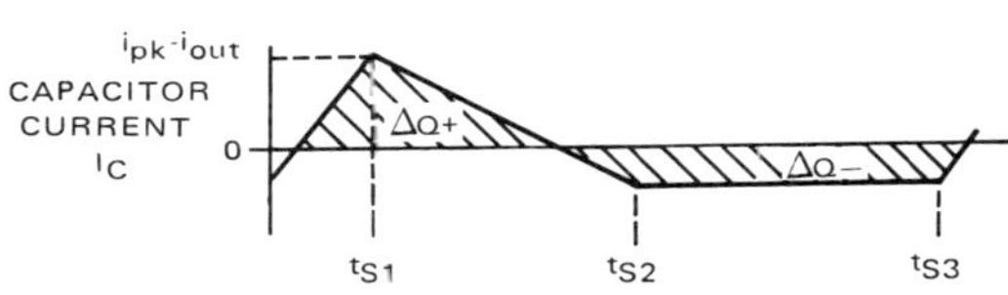

FIGURE 3. Capacitor Current Waveform

$$\Delta Q+ = \tfrac{1}{2}.\text{Base(B) x Height } (i_{pk} - i_{out})$$

$$\text{as } B = (i_{pk} - i_{out})(t_c + t_d)/i_{pk}$$

$$\Delta Q+ = (i_{pk} - i_{out})^2.(t_c + t_d)/2.i_{pk}$$

$$\Delta Q- = (i_{out}.t_i) + \tfrac{1}{2}.\{(t_c + t_d) - B\}.i_{out}$$

$$= (i_{out}.t_i) + \tfrac{1}{2}\{(t_c + t_d) - (i_{pk} - i_{out}).(t_c + t_d)/i_{pk}\}.i_{out}$$

Making $\Delta Q+$ equal to $\Delta Q-$ and solving for t_i

$$t_i = (i_{pk} - 2.i_{out})(t_c + t_d)/2.i_{out}$$

equation 5

To determine the frequency of oscillation the lengths of the various sections of the regulators cycle are added together.

$$\tau = t_c + t_d + t_i \qquad \text{equation 6}$$

The frequency $f = 1/\tau$ equation 7

Knowing the total change in current and the time, ΔV_C can be calculated.

During t_d, $\Delta i_C = i_{pk}$ (see Figure 3)

$$\Delta V_C = \frac{1}{C}\int i.dt$$

The increase in V_C during t_d is:

$$\Delta V_{C1} = i_{pk}.t_d/C$$

For $t = t_i$, the decrease in V_C during t_i is

$$\Delta V_{C2} = i_{out}.t_i/C$$

Therefore, the total

$$\Delta V_C = \Delta V_{C1} + \Delta V_{C2},$$

$\Delta V_{C(total)}$ is the output ripple voltage, ΔV_{out} say

$$\Delta V_{out} = (i_{pk}.t_d + i_{out}.t_i)/C \qquad \text{equation 8}$$

The previous derivations have been for the discontinuous mode of operation (because t_i is not zero). In the continuous mode the inductor current never settles to zero. Prior to the complete discharge of the inductor the regulator circuit initiates another charge cycle. As a result a DC idle current is passed through the inductor. By reference to Figure 2 the output current at which the circuit changes from the discontinuous to the continuous mode of operation can be determined. The point of transition occurs when the inductor current flows before the previous cycle is completed. Under these conditions the capacitor current waveform is as shown in Figure 5.

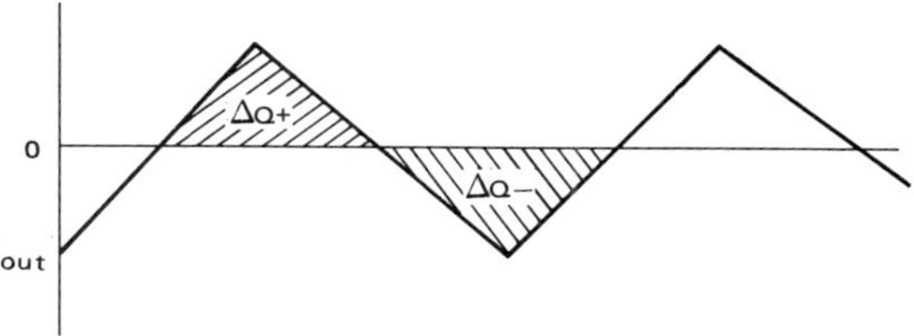

FIGURE 5. Continuous Mode Capacitor Current Waveform

As $\Delta Q+$ must equal $\Delta Q-$ this occurs when,

$$i_{out} = i_{pk}/2 = i_x \qquad \text{equation 9}$$

where i_x is the output current at which the inductor enters the continuous mode of operation.

Summarizing:

	$L =$	$(V_{in} - V_{out})t_{on}/i_{pk}$	from equation 3
	$f =$	$1/(t_c + t_d + t_i)$	from equations 6 & 7
where,	$t_c =$	t_{on}	
	$t_d =$	$i_{pk}.L/V_{out}$	from equation 4
	$t_i =$	$(i_{pk} - 2i_{out})(t_c + t_d)/2i_{out}$	equation 5
	$C =$	$(i_{pk}.t_d + i_{out}.t_i)/\Delta V_{out}$	from equation 8

and the maximum i_{out} for discontinuous mode of operation, i.e.

$$i_x = i_{pk}/2 \qquad \text{from equation 9}$$

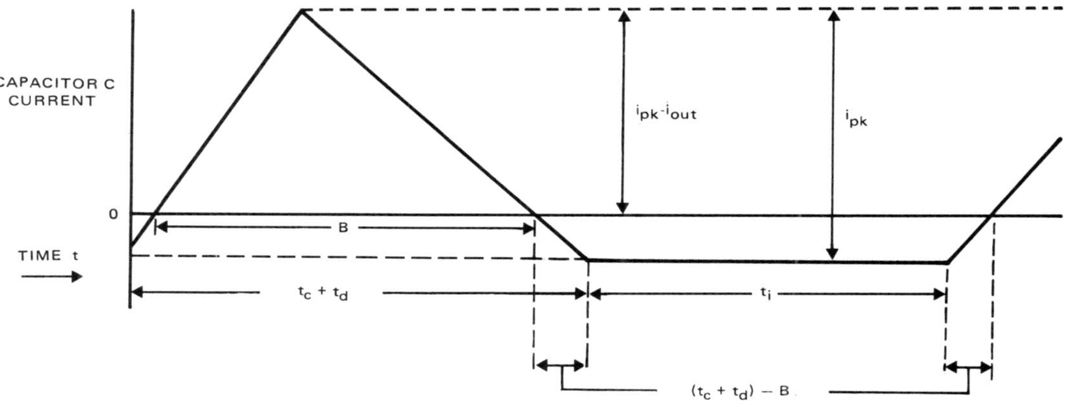

FIGURE 4. Charge Equalization Waveform

Shunt (Step-Up) Switching Voltage Regulator

In the step-up or shunt regulator the formulae change slightly. The basic circuit configuration is shown in Figure 6. During the charging cycle (switch Sw1 is closed) the inductor (L) is fed directly by the input potential.

$$i_{pk} = V_{in}.t_{on}/L \quad \text{. . . . equation 10}$$

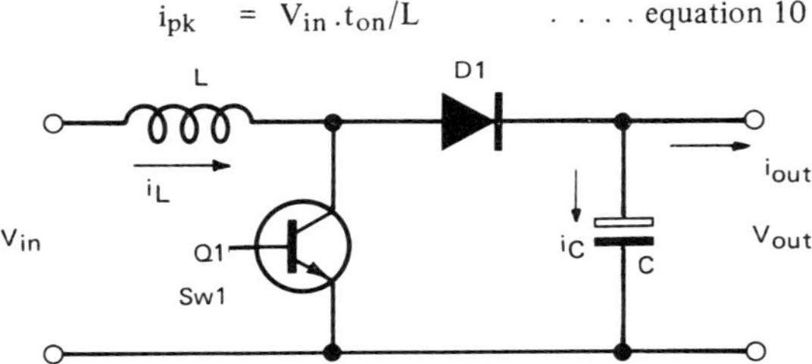

FIGURE 6. Shunt (Step-Up) Switching Voltage Regulator

During the charging cycle of the inductor in the shunt regulator, the diode D1 is reverse biassed and does not allow the current in the inductor to supply any contribution of current to the load. This results in less charge delivered to the load capacitor than in the series circuit. Peak currents in the shunt configuration are therefore considerably higher for given load currents. The shunt circuit delivers power to the load only during the discharge cycle of the inductor (when switch Sw1 is open). Diode D1 is forward biassed and the inductor discharges into the load capacitor C. The potential across the inductor during this phase of the charge/discharge cycle is $V_{out} - V_{in}$. The discharge time of the inductor then becomes:

$$t_d = i_{pk}.L/(V_{out} - V_{in}) \quad \text{. . . . equation 11}$$

Equating the charge/discharge ratio (t_c/t_d), it will be noted that as the input/output differential voltage increases, the discharge time will decrease. For conditions where the differential voltage is greater than the input voltage, the discharge time becomes less than the charging time, i.e.

$$t_c/t_d = \Delta V/V_{in}$$

Studying the current waveforms (I_L and I_C) in Figure 7 and recalling that $\Delta Q+$ must equal $\Delta Q-$ for the potential across the load capacitor to remain constant, the relation of peak

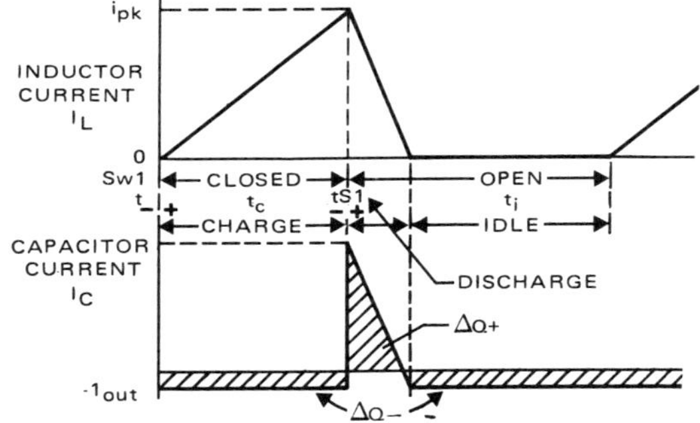

FIGURE 7. Shunt Circuit Current Waveforms

current to output current can be obtained. Defining ΔQ as the area under the respective curves, the maximum load or output current, i_x, for discontinuous operation, ($t_i = 0$), is:

$$i_x = i_{pk}.t_d/2(t_d + t_c) \quad \text{. . . . equation 12}$$

Making $\Delta Q+$ equal to $\Delta Q-$ and solving for t_i where $i_{out} < i_x$ (t_i is not 0).

$$t_i = (i_{pk}.t_d/2.i_{out}) - (t_d + t_c) \quad \text{equation 13}$$

and the output ripple voltage

$$\Delta V_{out} = \left\{ i_{pk}.t_d + i_{out}.(t_i + t_c) \right\} / C \quad \text{. . . . equation 14}$$

Summarizing for the shunt or step-up configuration

L	=	$V_{in}.t_{on}/i_{pk}$	from equation 10
t_d	=	$i_{pk}.L/(V_{out} - V_{in})$	equation 11
t_i	=	$(i_{pk}.t_d/2.i_{out}) - (t_d + t_c)$	equation 13
C	=	$\left\{ i_{pk}.t_d + i_{out}(t_i + t_c) \right\} / \Delta V_{out}$	from equation 14
i_x	=	$i_{pk}.t_d/2.(t_c + t_d)$	. . . . equation 12

Inverting Shunt Switching Voltage Regulator

Figure 8 gives the basic circuit of a regulator to obtain a negative supply. Using this the various formulae to determine the circuit components can be obtained as before.

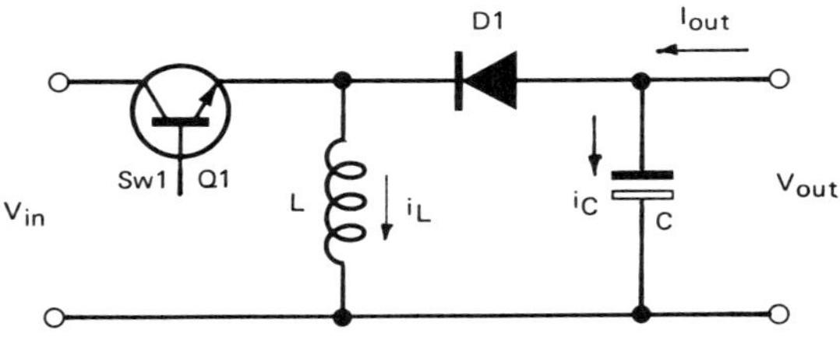

FIGURE 8. Inverting Shunt Switching Voltage Regulator

During the charging cycle (switch Sw1 closed) the inductor (L) is fed only by the input potential in a similar manner to the step-up configuration, i.e. as before:

$$i_{pk} = V_{in}.t_{on}/L \quad \text{viz equation 10}$$

Also as in the step-up configuration, here the input provides no contribution to the load or output current during the charging cycle, and thus the load current will be limited by the peak current, i.e.

$$i_x = i_{pk}.t_d/2.(t_d + t_c) \quad \text{as equation 12}$$

The current waveforms in the inverting configuration look identical to those shown for the step-up configuration. The same formulae, therefore, apply for t_i, i_x and the ripple voltage ΔV_{out}. The discharge rate (t_d) however, differs from that seen for the step-up configuration, i.e. here,

$$t_d = i_{pk}.L/V_{out} \quad \text{. . . . equation 15}$$

THE TL497 SWITCHING VOLTAGE REGULATOR I.C.

General

All the active functions required in the construction of a switching voltage regulator are contained on a single monolithic chip in the TL497 switching voltage regulator i.c. It can also be used as the control element to drive external components for high-power output applications. The i.c. was designed to offer versatility and to be useful in the various step-up, step-down and voltage inversion applications requiring high efficiency. It contains a precision 1.2V reference, a variable pulse generator, a high-gain comparator, current limit sense and shutdown circuits, a catch diode, and a switching transistor.

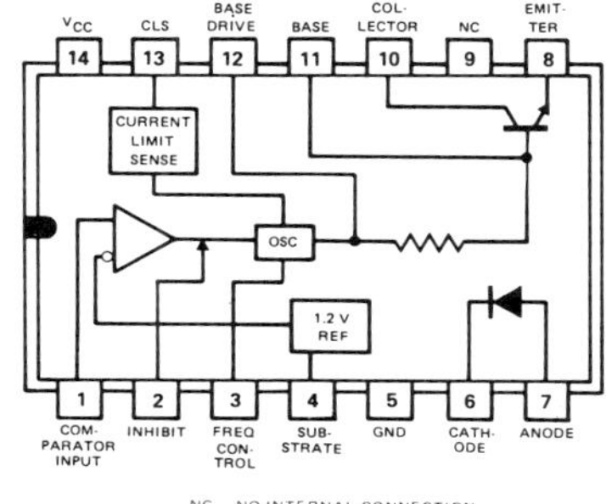

FIGURE 9. Block Diagram of the TL497 Regulator I.C.

Programming

A block diagram of the TL497 is given in Figure 9 which also shows the pinning arrangement. The internal 1.2V prevision reference is internally connected between the substrate terminal and the inverting input of the high-gain comparator. The output of the circuit is sensed through a resistor ladder network (R1–R2) by the non-inverting input of the comparator. The output voltage is programmed by the resistors R1 and R2 in accordance with

$$V_{out} = (1 + R1/R2) \times 1.2$$

For optimum performance

$$R2 = 1\text{k}2 \text{ ohm} \qquad \text{... equation 16}$$

$$R1 = (V_{out} - 1.2)\text{k ohm} \qquad \text{... equation 17}$$

Whenever the non-inverting input of the comparator is more negative than the 1.2V reference the oscillator is gated 'on'.

Oscillator

The oscillator is composed of a current pulse generator which charges and discharges the external timing capacitor C_t at linear rates. The charging rate is one-sixth that of the discharge rate which results in a maximum duty cycle of 85% during maximum frequency operation, i.e.

$$t_c = 0.85\tau \qquad \text{equation 18}$$

The total period of the charge/discharge cycle is determined by the external timing capacitor C_t and is constant for all input voltages within the TL497 recommended operating ranges. The voltage waveform at C_t is illustrated in Figure 10. The charge/discharge period varies with C_t as shown in Table 1.

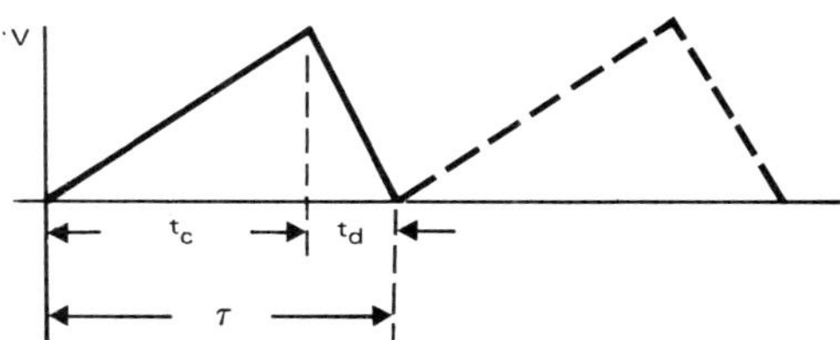

FIGURE 10. Voltage Waveform at Timing Capacitor

The dotted line of Figure 10 shows the timing capacitor waveform under maximum frequency conditions. Only under these conditions does time determine the oscillators frequency, i.e.

$$f_{max} = 1/\tau \qquad \text{equation 19}$$

These conditions exist during start up of the system or whenever the comparator indicates the output voltage is less than the desired voltage out. After the timing capacitor is discharged the oscillator control circuit will again sample the output of the comparator to determine if the output voltage is at a satisfactory level. If the comparator indicates the output is deficient, the current generator will retrigger and the oscillator will go through another charge/discharge cycle; after which it will sample the comparator again and so forth. This is the case during maximum frequency operation. If on the other hand, the comparator indicates the output voltage is satisfactory, the current generator will standby until it is triggered by the comparator when the output voltage decays below the desired level, as illustrated in Figure 11.

Table 1

C_t(pF)	22	33	47	100	150	220	270	330	470	1000
t_c (μs)	3.9	4.8	6.2	10.5	14.3	20	24	29	41	85
τ (μs)	4.5	5.6	7.0	12.4	16.7	23	27	33	47	100
f(max) (kHz)	225	180	145	80.5	60	45	36	30	21	10

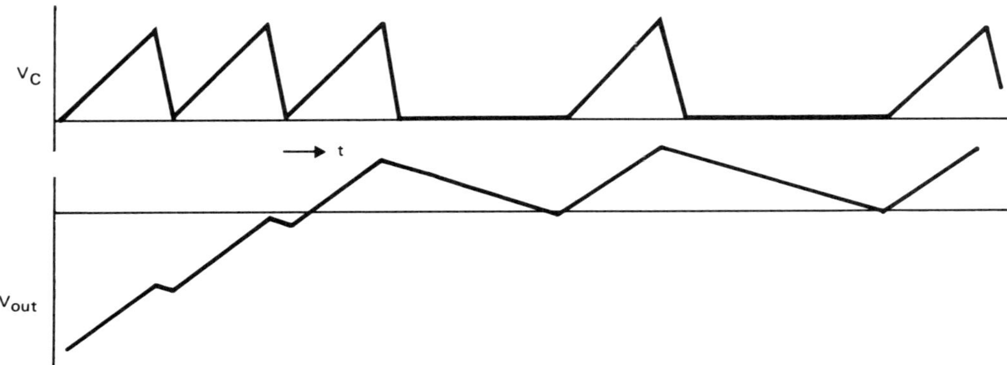

FIGURE 11. Charge/Discharge Cycle Waveform

'On' Time/'Off' Time/Frequency

The switch transistor is turned 'on' during the charging portion (t_c) and turned 'off' during the discharge portion (t_d) and any subsequent standby period after the charge/discharge cycle of capacitor C_t. The 'on' time therefore is always constant. The frequency and 'off' time vary according to load requirements. The 'on' time of the switching transistor coincides with t_c as shown in Table 1.

Current Limiting

The TL497 also provides current limit sense circuits for protecting the switching transistor and the load. With current limiting, saturation of the power inductor may be prevented and 'soft' start-up achieved. Current limiting is accomplished with the current-limit control provided. The voltage developed across the user selected series current limit resistor, R_{CL}, is sensed. When this voltage becomes greater than one V_{BE} drop (0.45 – 1V) the current limit circuitry boosts the current generators by supplying an additional current path to charge the timing capacitor. This in effect shortens the 'on' time of the switching transistor and reduces the amount of energy developed in the inductor. This can be observed as an increase in the slope of the charging portion of the charge/discharge cycle of the timing capacitor, as illustrated in Figure 12.

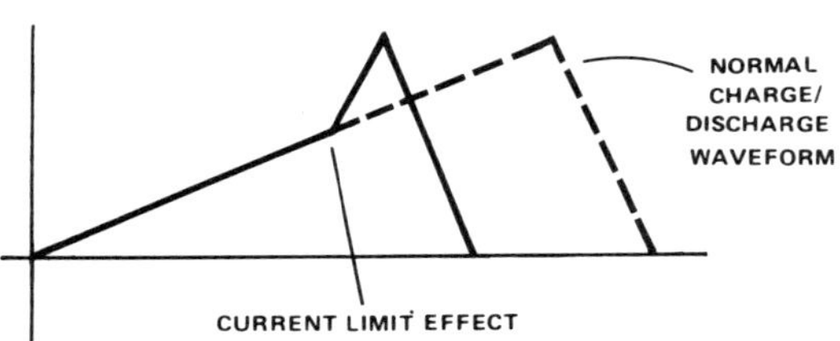

FIGURE 12. Timing Capacitor Charge/Discharge Cycle

Switching Transistor

The switching transistor provided in the TL497 is a high-gain device designed to switch up to 500mA using the base drive circuit provided by the TL497, i.e. an external transistor is required for peak currents greater than 500mA . . . . Note 1.

Access to the internal base current limiting resistor is made available, however, so that drive to the output transistor can be increased where desired. The emitter and collector are also brought out for greater versatility.

Catch Diode

An uncommitted catch diode matched to the switching transistor capable of operating at peak currents of 500mA is available for commutation or rectification.

Enable Circuitry

A shutdown circuit is also provided for external control which allows the user to enable and disable the TL497 i.c. by means of an external t.t.l. logic command. A logic 'high' disables the i.c. and turns 'off' the switching transistor. A logic 'low' enables the i.c. and allows it to operate as described previously.

WORKED EXAMPLES

For Series (Step-Down) Regulators

Input Voltages less than 15V

1. *Specification:* $V_{in} = 15V$

$V_{out} = 5V$

$I_{out} = 200mA$

Ripple voltage (or ΔV_{out}) $<0.3\%$, i.e. $<15mV$

Calculations: For best regulation the design should be for discontinuous operation,

i.e. $i_x < i_{pk}/2$. see equation 9

To use the internal transistor and diode

$i_{pk} < 500mA$ see Note 1

Therefore the maximum $i_x = 500/2 = 250mA$

As the required I_{out} is 200mA, the internal components can be used and the circuit function in the discontinuous mode.

At start up or in an overload condition allow the

maximum operating frequency to be 50kHz ($\tau_{min} = 20\mu s$).

From Table 1, the value of timing capacitor

$C_t \simeq 200pF$ (i.e. $\tau \simeq 22\mu s$) and

$t_c \simeq 19\mu s$, say

$L = t_c.(V_{in} - V_{out})/i_{pk}$ from equation 3

Note: this ignores the voltage dropped across the current limit resistor R_{CL} and the switching transistor's $V_{CE(sat)}$.

$L = 19 \times 10^{-6}.(15 - 5)/500 \times 10^{-3}$

$= 380\mu H$

$t_d = i_{pk}.L/V_{out}$ see equation 4

Note: this ignores the forward drop across the diode V_F.

$t_d = 500 \times 10^{-3}.380 \times 10^{-6}/5$

$= 38\mu s$

$t_i = (i_{pk} - 2i_{out})(t_c + t_d)/2.i_{out}$ see equation 5

$t_i = (500 \times 10^{-3} - 400 \times 10^{-3})(19 \times 10^{-6} + 38 \times 10^{-6})/400 \times 10^{-3}$

$= 14.25\mu s$

Operating frequency at nominal load

$f = 1/(t_c + t_d + t_i)$ from equations 6 & 7

$= 1/(19 + 38 + 14.25) \times 10^{-6}$

$= 14kHz$

The value of the output capacitor

$C = (i_{pk}.t_d + i_{out}.t_i)/\Delta V$ from equation 8

$= (500 \times 10^{-3}.38 \times 10^{-6} + 200 \times 10^{-3}.14.25 \times 10^{-6})/15 \times 10^{-3}$

$= (19000 + 2850)/15 \mu F$

$= 1455\mu F$

Divider chain resistors:

$R2 = 1k2$ ohm from equation 16

$R1 = (V_{out} - 1k2)k$ ohm $= 3k8$ ohm from equation 17

Current limiting resistor:

$R_{CL} = 0.6/i_{pk}$ equation 18

(Note: taking average value of V_F)

$= 1\Omega 2$

Figure 13 shows the circuit diagram of a step down (series) regulator incorporating these calculated values. The feedback capacitor C_F provides hysteresis to the comparator input in this configuration when $V_{in} < 15V$ for optimum performance. Actual values for power consumption, times, etc. are given beneath the figure.

An indication of correct operation of the circuit is given by observing the waveform on the timing capacitor C_t (Pin 3). Figure 14a shows the correct operation and

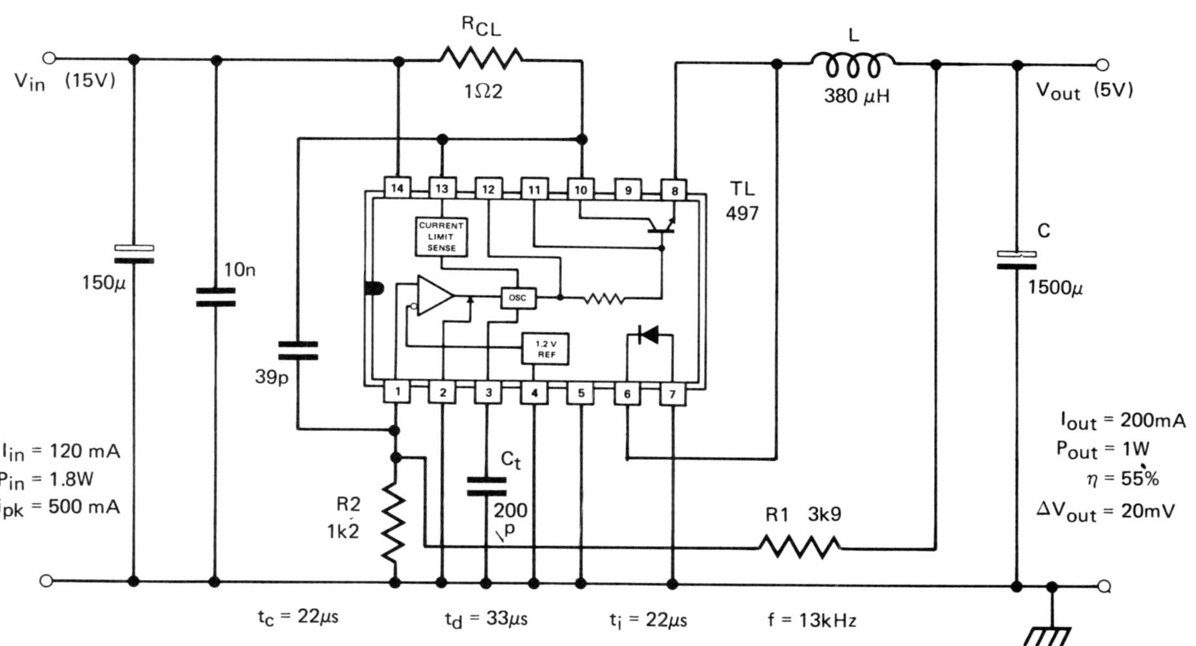

FIGURE 13. Series Regulator Circuit Diagram (V_{in}<$15V$)

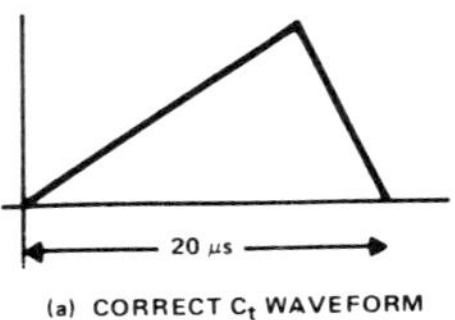

(a) CORRECT C_t WAVEFORM

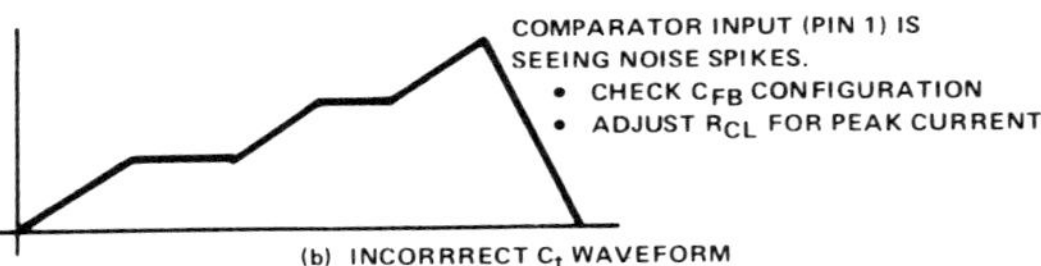

(b) INCORRRECT C_t WAVEFORM

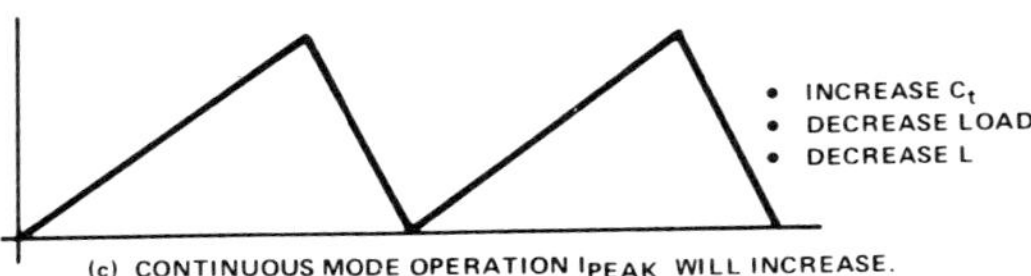

(c) CONTINUOUS MODE OPERATION I_{PEAK} WILL INCREASE.

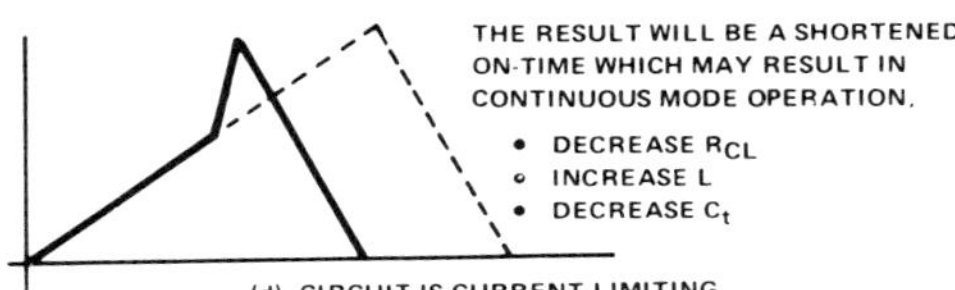

(d) CIRCUIT IS CURRENT LIMITING.

FIGURE 14. Circuit Performance Waveforms

Figures 14b to d give incorrect waveforms and the possible reasons for the malfunctions.

2. *Specification:* V_{in} = 11 to 15 (12V nominal)

V_{out} = 5V

I_{out} = 1A

$\Delta V_{out} < 100mV$, i.e. <2%

Calculations: The high output current requires the use of an external transistor and diode. To avoid operation in the continuous mode, i_x is set higher than the nominal i_{out} = 1A, i.e. 1.2A, say.

i_{pk} = 2.4A from equation 9

This figure influences the choice of the external transistor Q1 and diode D1. A BD242 transistor and a 1SX172 diode are chosen here.

Letting the maximum frequency be 35kHz, say, from Table 1 C_t = 270pF and t_c = 24µs.

A more accurate form of equation 3 is:

$$t_c = i_{pk} \cdot L/(V_{in} - V_{CE(sat)} - V_{out})$$

Hence L = 24 (11 – 1.0 – 5.0)/2.4µH using the lower limit of V_{in} and the value of $V_{CE(sat)}$ for a BD242 at 2.4A collector current, (series resistance in the inductor is ignored).

L = 50µH i.e. 56µH standard value, say,

A more accurate form of equation 4 is:

$$t_d = i_{pk} \cdot L/(V_{out} + V_F)$$

where V_F is the forward voltage drop of diode D1 at 2.4A.

Hence t_d = 2.4 x 56/5.5µs

= 25µs

When i_{out} = 1.0A,

t_i = (2.4 – 2.0) (24 + 25)/2 x 1µs from equation 5

i.e. t_i = 10µs

The operating frequency at nominal load with

V_{in} = 11V from equations 6 & 7

f = 1/(24 + 25 + 10)

= 17.2kHz

For ΔV_{out} = 100 mV at i_{out} = 1.0A

C = (2.4 x 22.4 + 1 x 10)/0.1

= 638µF

In practice a larger value capacitor is required because of the poor performance of electrolytic capacitors at high frequencies.

As in example 1 R1 = 3k8
R2 = 1k2

A 100nF capacitor between the feedback input and ground is required for optimum performance.

With a value of the current limit resistor R_{CL} equal to 0.22 ohm, when the voltage developed across it exceeds approximately 0.6V, the conduction time of the output device is terminated.

The circuit diagram of this power supply is shown in Figure 15.

Performance: Load regulation, I_{out}, 1A to 0A better than 1%
Stabilization, V_{in} 15 to 11V, better than 0.4%
Output voltage ripple, ΔV_{out}, typically 100mV pk to pk.
Efficiency 60% at V_{in} = 12V.

Input Voltages greater than 15V

3. *Specification:* V_{in} = 30V

V_{out} = 5V

I_{out} = 2.5A

$\Delta V_{out} < 200mV$ (<4%)

Calculations: The high current and voltage require the use of an external transistor and diode. A design for i_x = 2.8A will ensure that the regulator normally operates in the discontinuous mode.

SECTION 2

DEFLECTION CIRCUITS

V SELF-STABILISING HORIZONTAL DEFLECTION STAGES

by
Mick Maytum & Vikram Bose

The horizontal deflection stage consumes the largest amount of power in the television set, monitor, or visual display unit (v.d.u.). As a result the power supply design is strongly influenced by the horizontal stage's requirements. Most modern power supplies (p.s.u.s)/deflection systems use two relatively expensive active semiconductor power devices, one in the p.s.u. for stabilising its output voltage and the other acting as a switch in the horizontal deflection circuit.

The concept of a self stabilising deflection circuit is to integrate stabilisation and deflection functions using only one power transistor operating directly from a rectified a.c. supply. The system is applicable to 90° and 110° colour tubes and most large screen monochrome tubes. Although the idea is relatively new, it employs well established techniques from shunt switching mode and horizontal deflection practice. In essence the system is a parallel operated shunt switching mode p.s.u. and a horizontal deflection circuit. Use of suitable blocking diodes and circuit timing allow a single power transistor to control both functions without compromising either. Thus, as the stabilising action is based on switching mode power supply principles, all the associated benefits as discussed in the previous section are present. Namely:

> Wide operating range (150V-270V a.c.) gives excellent picture stability.
> High efficiency permits compact cabinet designs, and lower set operating temperature gives greater overall reliability.
> Light weight and simple smoothing circuit allows component economy.

However, compared with the system of a separate switching mode power supply plus conventional transistorised horizontal deflection circuit, the self-stabilising circuit gives much less switching edge radiation, as it uses only one power transistor.

The self-stabilising horizontal deflection circuits can be divided broadly into two classes[1] as illustrated in Figure 1. In the 'low voltage injection' case the current pulses, which flow out of the secondary of the shunt switching mode's transformer T1 via diode D4, are averaged by decoupling capacitor C2 to provide deflection circuits supply voltage.

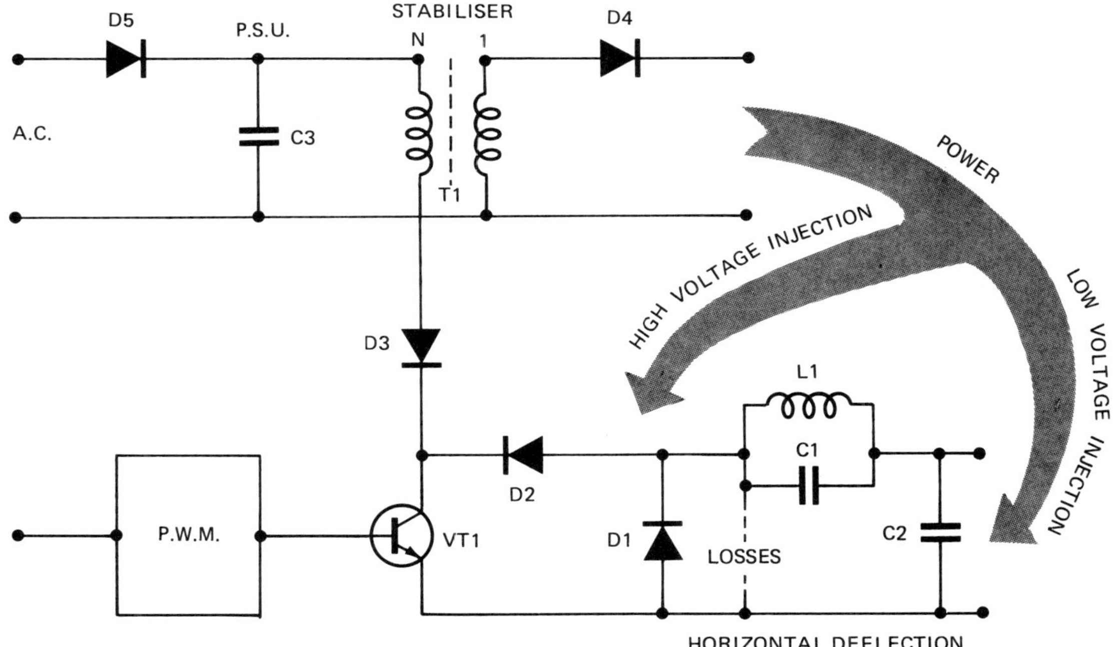

FIGURE 1. Self Stabilising Concept

In the high voltage injection case secondary diode D4 is connected to the efficiency diode D1, i.e. the high voltage or retrace end of the deflection circuit. In Europe the low voltage injection (l.v.i.) system offers the best solution for colour deflection, while large screen monochrome deflection can be equally served by both systems. In the U.S.A. the high voltage injection (h.v.i.) system is favoured for colour and monochrome deflection.

To control the stabilization function, integrated circuits are available, for example, the SN76549 as described in earlier chapters. Use of these integrated circuits allows the power transistor to be protected against excessive voltages and currents by temporarily stopping the system operation should the limits be approached. Protection can also be achieved against other faults, such as open circuits in yokes, tuning capacitors and in the feedback network, or short circuits in wound components and other parts of the set. These self protection features allow faults to be corrected without serious component damage occuring and also reduces the fire hazard. However for this application, use is also made of the '549's phase detector circuit, which was not employed in switching mode power supplies. The i.c.'s mode of operation discussed in this chapter is one of a driven pulse width modulator (p.w.m.) capable of being interconnected with most available line processors. Its use as a simple line processor cum p.w.m. is given in Appendix C.

SYSTEM OPERATION

Figure 2 shows the basics of a conventional transistorised horizontal deflection system. The a.c. supply is rectified by diode D5, and smoothed by reservoir capacitor C3, producing supply voltage, V_i. Transistor VT2 stabilises input voltage V_i to output voltage V_o, which is fed to the deflection system decoupling capacitor C2. Many variants are possible in the p.s.u. area. For example, diode D5 could be replaced by a full wave bridge to remove the d.c. component from the a.c. supply, and transistor VT2 could be replaced by a thyristor operating on the a.c. side of the p.s.u. to produce a thyristor phase controlled system. The point being made is that an active power semiconductor is required in the p.s.u. to produce a stabilised output voltage. (Note 1)

In the deflection circuit of Figure 2 inductance L represents a lumped value of the deflection yoke, e.h.t. transformer and any convergence inductance. Capacitor C1 represents the retrace tuning capacitance. It is difficult to assign where in the circuit and at what time losses occur in a simplified circuit, so it must be remembered that the losses, shown at the cathode of the efficiency diode D1, are in practice distributed throughout the deflection circuit. The losses cause the peak collector current of the deflection transistor VT1 to be larger than the peak current of the efficiency diode D1.

In practical systems the transistor VT1 conducts positive collector current for less than half of the horizontal period. As the retrace time fraction is approximately 0·2, the diode D1 could carry current from 1–0·5–0·2=0·3 of the total period. To ensure a continuous trace the transistor VT1 must be ready to conduct when the deflection circuit trace current becomes positive. This is achieved by initiating the drive to the transistor base earlier than the expected zero crossing of the deflection circuit current. As the current is negative at the initiation the transistor collector-base diode becomes forward biassed and conducts negative trace current (shown shaded in the collector current waveform). In addition, as the trace current is then flowing in the transistors collector base diode, the efficiency diodes current is reduced to zero. The removed period of efficiency diode current is shown shaded in the diode current waveform.

Stage one of the system conversion, shown in Figure 3, is achieved by the addition of a coupling diode, D2, in series with the deflection transistor's collector. This diode isolates the transistor from the efficiency action by preventing negative collector current. The efficiency diode now conducts the whole of the (negative) efficiency current and the transistor passes only the positive portion of the trace current. It will be noted that the initiation of transistor base drive can occur as early as immediately after retrace, (earlier than this would upset the retrace), or as late as the zero crossing of the trace current. Thus the operation of the deflection circuit is unaffected provided the drive pulse width is between the limits of 0·8 and 0·5 of the total period. (Note 2).

Stage two, Figure 4, is reached by the addition of load resistor R1 and the so called 'primary' diode D3 from the rectified supply V_i to the deflection transistor. The purpose of the primary diode is to prevent reverse energy flow from the deflection circuit to load R1 and V_i, when the retrace voltage rises above voltage V_i and the coupling diode, D2, becomes forward biassed. At the end of retrace when the deflection circuit voltage falls below voltage V_i the coupling diode, D2, becomes reverse biassed and the primary diode, D3, becomes forward biassed, holding the deflection transistor's collector voltage at V_i. When the transistor is driven 'on', its collector voltage falls to $V_{CE(sat)}$, and V_i (minus a diode forward voltage drop plus $V_{CE(sat)}$) is applied to the load R1. As previously noted the normalised drive pulse width can be varied from 0·5 to 0.8 and hence so can the period for which V_i is applied to the load. Thus the energy taken from the input supply V_i by the load can be varied by changing the transistor drive pulse width. The transistor's collector current will now be the sum of the positive deflection current and the current through load R1.

Stage three, Figure 1, is replacing the load R1 with transformer, T1, of turns ratio N to 1, whose secondary is connected via the deflection supply diode D4 to the

Note 1. It is possible to specify a power supply system which does not use active semiconductors. An example is the constant voltage transformer, but this has the disadvantages of cost, weight, bulk and radiation.

Note 2. This idealised example assumes a transistor of zero storage time so in practice the normalised storage time of the device should be subtracted from the 0·5 – 0·8 range of drive pulse width.

deflection circuit. The exact point of connection gives the two variants of the self-stabilising system considered. If the cathode of diode D4 is connected to the deflection supply decoupling capacitor C2, a l.v.i. system results. Joining the cathode of diode D4 to the retrace voltage end of the deflection circuit (cathode of efficiency diode D1) gives the h.v.i. system. The voltage waveform (Figure 5) and performance differences between the l.v.i. and h.v.i. systems are dramatic. In the l.v.i. system, when the transistor turns 'off', the energy stored in transformer T1 during the transistor's conduction time is released via diode D4 to the decoupling capacitor C2 clamping the transformer's secondary voltage to V_O plus the diode forward voltage drop. Thus the primary voltage is approximately NV_O *above* the input

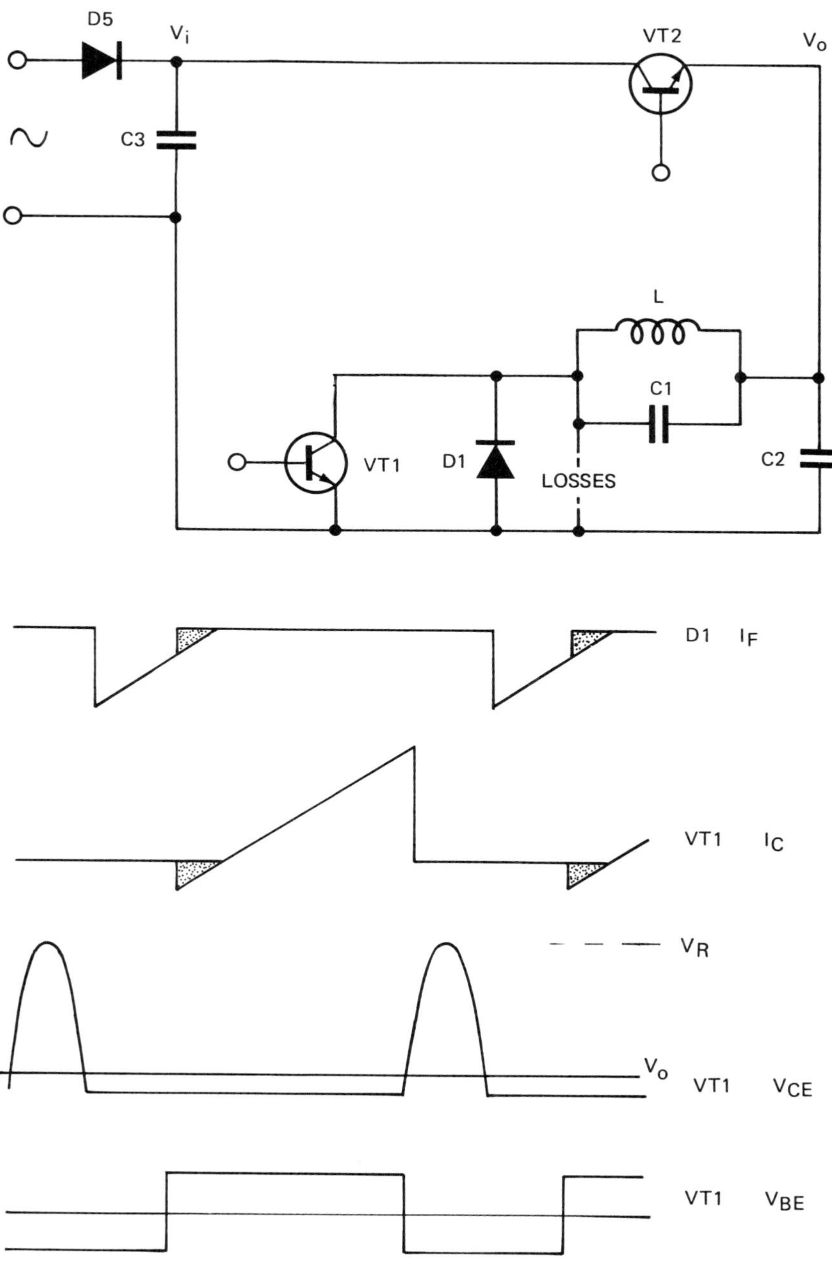

FIGURE 2. Conventional Circuit

supply V_i during the conduction of diode D4. As the drive circuitry will alter the drive pulse width, and hence the total transistor conduction time to maintain V_o constant, the peak primary voltage will always be $NV_o + V_i$ and the primary waveform a rectangular pulse. When the transistor switches 'off', its collector voltage will initially follow the faster rising edge of the transformer primary. The peak voltage will be decided by the greater of the peak primary or retrace voltages. These in turn depend on the input supply, transistor conduction time, N, and the exact ratio of V_R/V_o. If the retrace voltage, V_R, is greater than the primary voltage (low mains, N<5), then the collector voltage will follow V_R while it exceeds the primary voltage, resulting in a 'bump' corresponding to peak retrace voltage.

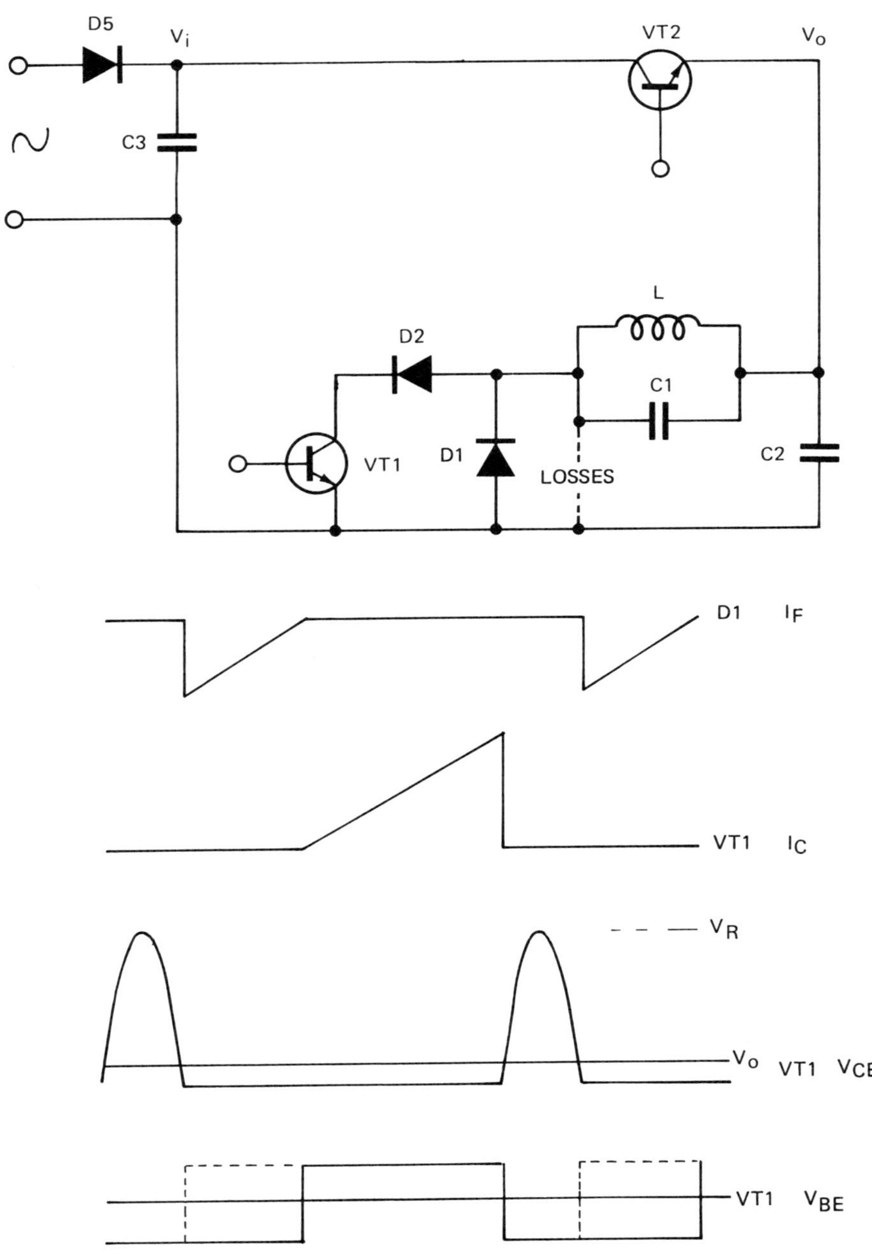

FIGURE 3. Addition of Series Collector Diode

Additional secondary windings and rectifiers on transformer T1 could produce stabilised supply rails for video output stages, low level stages and audio power amplifiers.

At transistor turn 'off' in the h.v.i. system the stored energy in transformer T1 forward biasses secondary diode D4 so that the secondary winding follows the retrace voltage pulse. The energy being injected from the secondary is relatively small compared with the total circulating energy of the deflection circuit, so that the retrace pulse waveform is not appreciably distorted. In this system, the primary voltage waveform is more complicated than the l.v.i. case.

When the deflection transistor switches 'off', the stored energy in the transformer causes the primary voltage

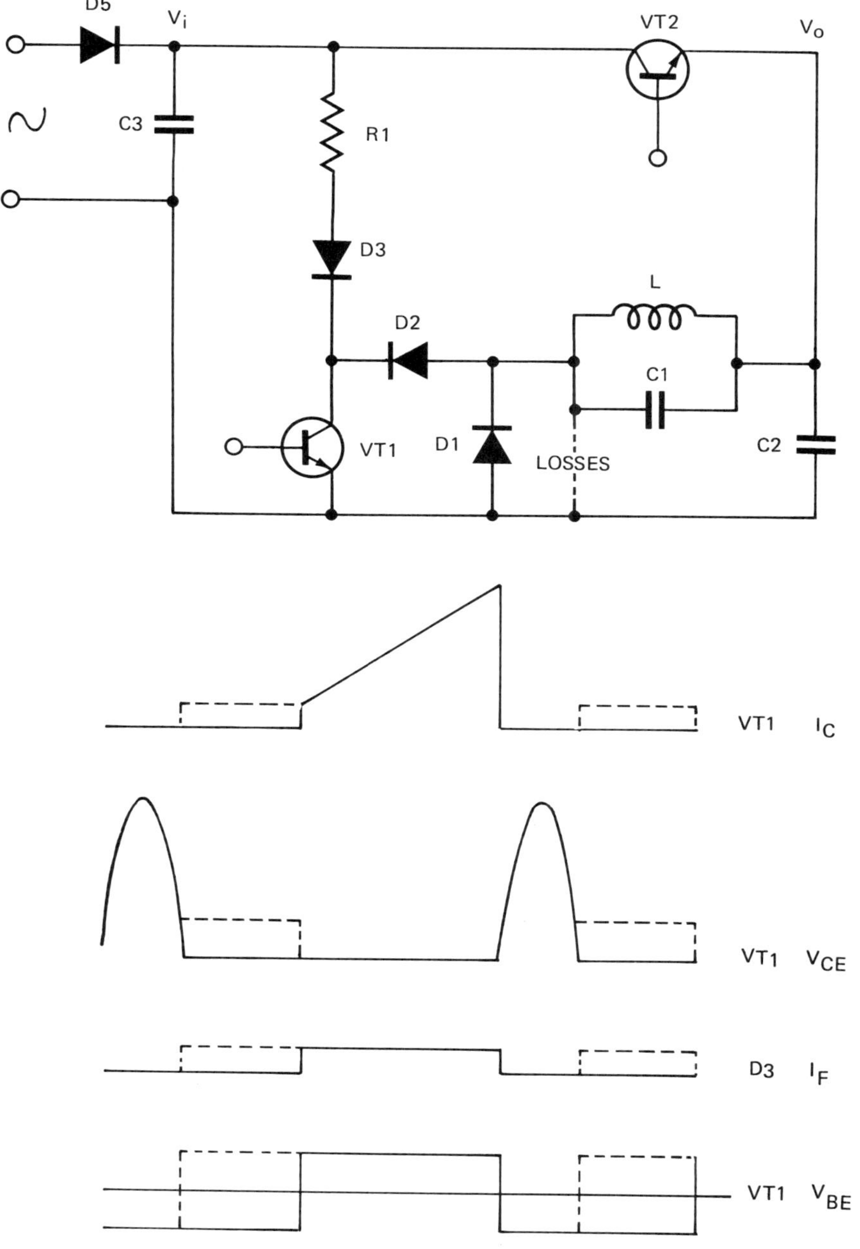

FIGURE 4. Extra Collector Loading

LOW VOLTAGE INJECTION

HIGH VOLTAGE INJECTION

V_i –

V_i –

TRANSFORMER TI PRIMARY VOLTAGE

V_o –

V_o –

DEFLECTION CIRCUIT VOLTAGE

TRANSISTOR VTI V_{CE}

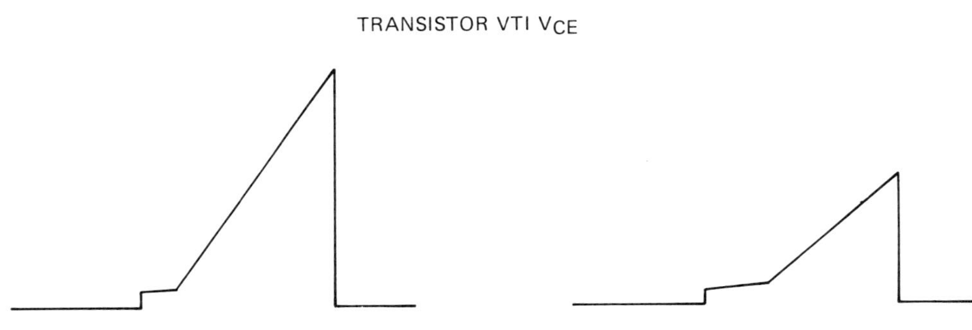

TRANSISTOR VTI I_C

FIGURE 5. Circuit Waveform Differences

to rise rapidly. Soon after the winding voltage passes zero ($V_{CE} \hat{=} V_i$), the secondary diode D4 becomes forward biassed and the primary voltage waveform is N times the retrace voltage waveform above the input supply V_i. After retrace, the deflection circuit voltage will equal the forward voltage of the efficiency diode D1 and, as diode D4 is still forward biassed, the transformer's secondary voltage will be almost zero. Similarly, the primary voltage will also be zero, resulting in a deflection transistor collector voltage of V_i. Under steady state conditions the total transistor conduction time controls the period for which the input voltage V_i is applied to the transformer primary and hence its increase in inductive energy. This energy is transferred to the deflection circuit during the transistor's 'off' period. To ensure the correct amount of energy is injected during each cycle, the operating levels in the deflection circuit are monitored. Normally just the deflection supply voltage, V_o, is used and compared against a reference, the difference signal controlling a pulse width modulator, (p.w.m.), which in turn determines the total transistor conduction time. Thus a feedback system is formed where any variation in deflection supply voltage is nullified by a change in transistor conduction time which causes a different inductive energy to be stored and transferred to the deflection circuit, thus stabilising the deflection supply voltage to the desired value.

AREAS OF APPLICATION

Factors controlling the deflection supply voltage, V_o, are normalized transistor conduction time, δ, transformer turns ratio, N, input voltage, V_i, and the system class.

Normalized Transistor Conduction Time (δ)

With the range of conduction time available (0·5 – 0·8) the l.v.i. system can stabilise V_o against a four to one change in V_i.[2] Splitting the δ range at 2/3 gives the two extremes of the l.v.i. system one with $0{\cdot}8 > \delta > 2/3$ and the other with $2/3 > \delta > 1/2$ both stabilising against a two to one V_i change. The h.v.i. system has the larger δ range of 0·8 – 0·4, but this full range is needed to stabilise against a two to one V_i change.

Input Voltage, V_i

A true European set could tolerate an a.c. voltage range of 220V – 15% to 240V + 10%. This is a maximum V_i value of 370V. The minimum V_i value at 220V – 15% should be above the 185V (=370/2) design minimum. Areas using 110V could use voltage doublers to produce the required V_i. Prime 110V designs with a V_i range of 180V to 90V will give half the V_o values of the European design for the same δ and N.

Turns Ratio, N

Figure 6 shows the variation of the deflection supply voltage, V_o, with stabiliser transformer turns ratio, N. For a desired value of V_o there will be a fixed value of N for the h.v.i. system and a range of N between $\check{\delta}$ = ½ and $\check{\delta}$ = 2/3 for the l.v.i. cases. The final choice of system and N value is usually set by the power transistor's volt-amp, VA, requirement (the product of the peak working collector voltage and current).

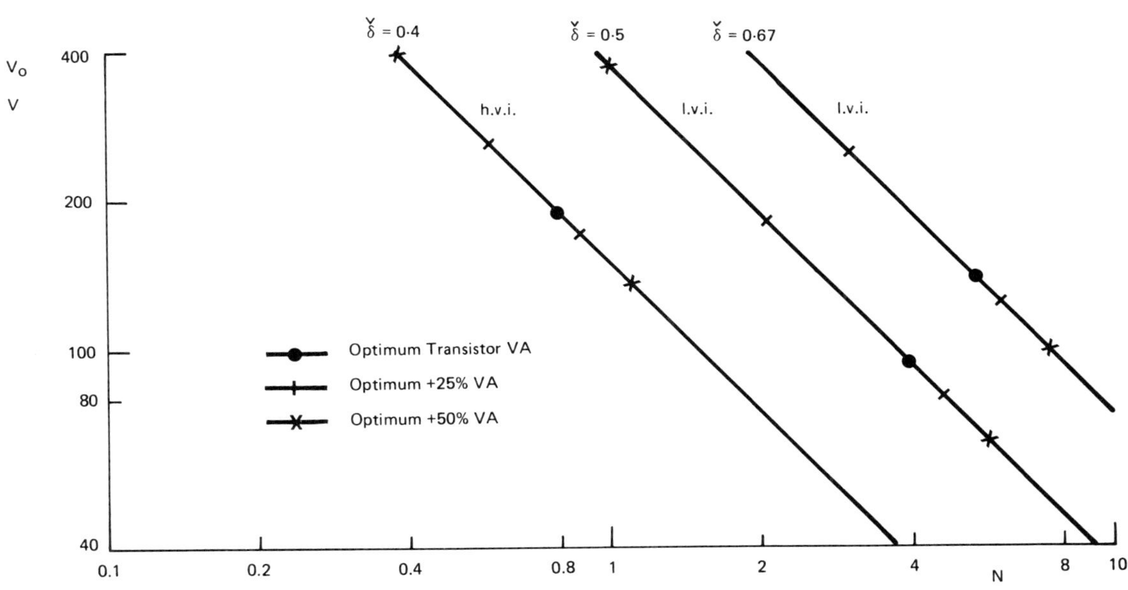

FIGURE 6. Deflection Supply Voltage, V_o, against Stabilizer Transformer Turns Ratio, N.

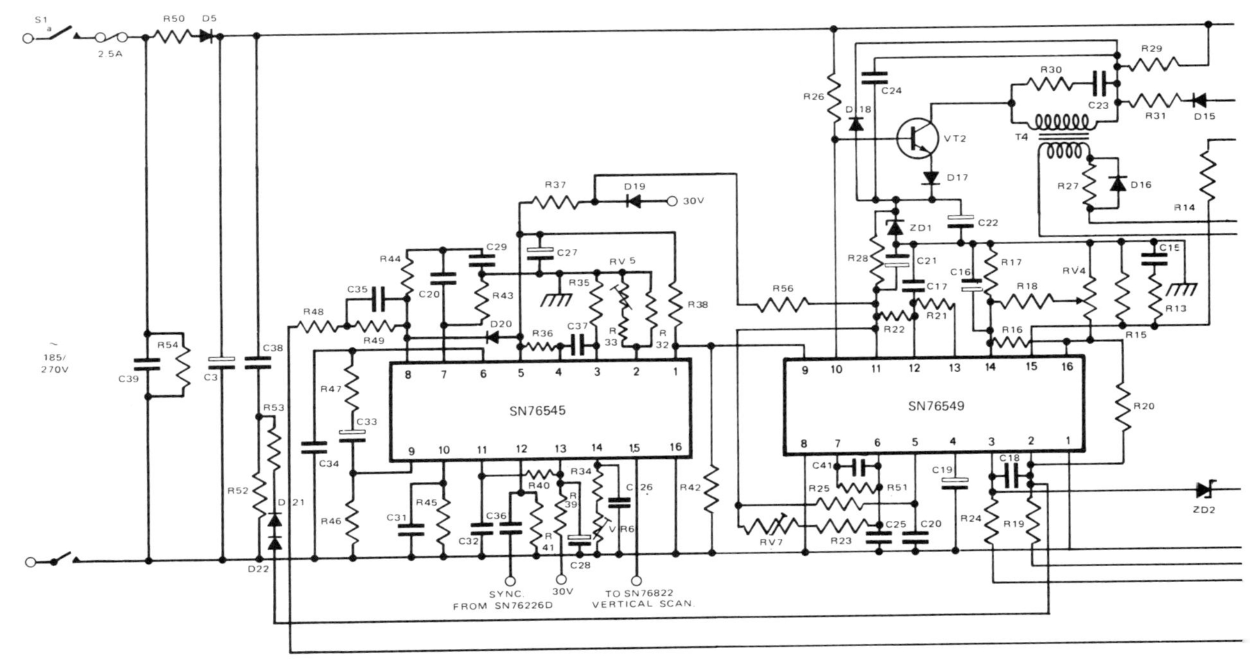

FIGURE 10. Self Stabilising System

Components List for Figure 10

R1	8Ω	16W	R24	2k2		R47	82Ω		C14	100n	750V
R2	33Ω	1W	R25	1M5		R48	15k		C15	1μ	
R3	820Ω	3W	R26	47k	6W	R49	150k		C16	16μ	10V
R4	1Ω5	2W	R27	2Ω2		R50	6Ω		C17	1n	
R5	120k		R28	180		R51	180k		C18	270p	
R6	820k		R29	10k	15W	R52	0·33Ω		C19	1μ	10V Tantalum
R7	18k		R30	10k	15W	R53	180		C20	100n	
R8	4k7		R31	4k7		R54	330k	½W	C21	22μ	35V Tantalum
R9	150k		R32	8k2		R55	12k	5W	C22	64μ	16V
R10	0·1		R33	1k5		R56	2k7		C23	3n3	
R11	2x390k	½W	R34	270k		C1	15n		C24	100n	
R12	6k8		R35	12k		C2	64μ	150V	C25	6n8	
R13	15k		R36	22k		C3	4n		C26	100n	
R14	220k		R37	820		C4	1μ5	100V	C27	250μ	12V
R15	15k		R38	10k		C5	1n	200V	C28	25μ	12V
R16	15k		R39	1k5		C6	2μ2	100V	C29	20n	
R17	47k		R40	270k		C7	1μ5	100V	C30	100n	
R18	100k		R41	27k		C8	25μ	40V	C31	20n	
R19	2k2		R42	2k2		C9	470μ	40V	C32	150p	
R20	27k		R43	390k		C10	220n		C33	32μ	12V
R21	47k		R44	3k3		C11	47n	1k5V	C34	20μ	
R22	82k		R45	56k		C12	100p	400V	C35	100p	
R23	18k		R46	3k3		C13	10μ	350V	C36	100n	

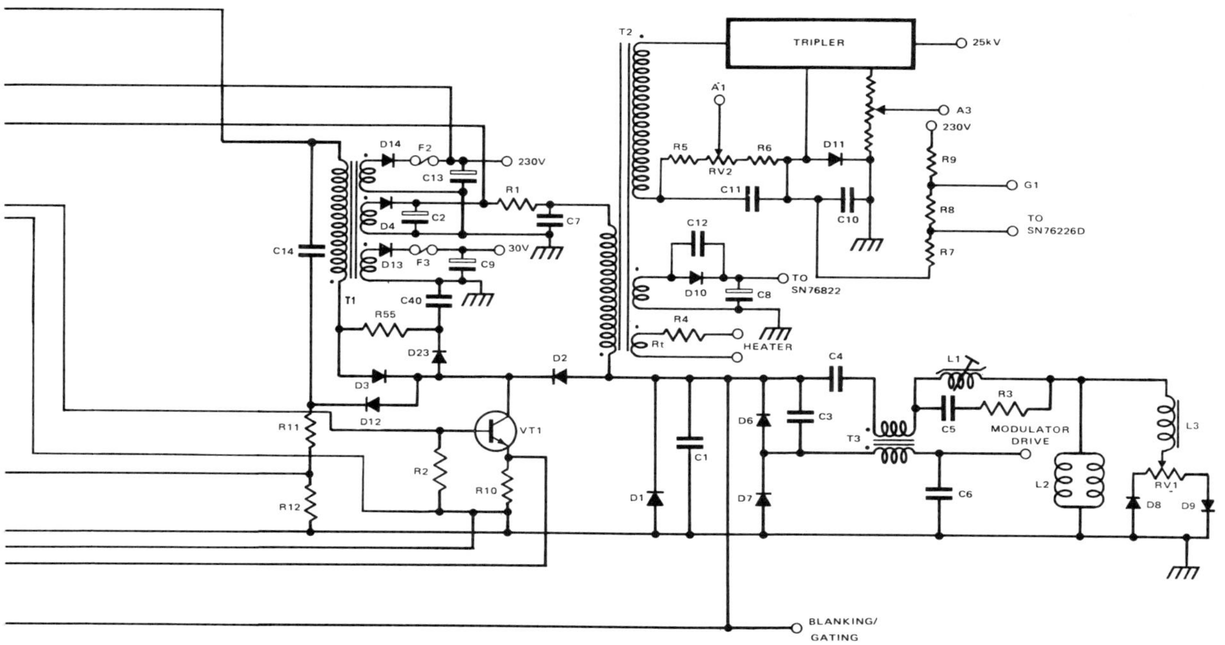

for the A51-160 P.I. Colour Tube

C37	5n6	
C38	1μ	400V
C39	220n	400V
C40	1n	1000V
C41	1n	
D1	BY127	
D2	BYW11-1000 or BY205-1000	
D2	BYW11-1000	
D3	BY205-800	
D4	BY205-400	
D5	BY127	
D6	1N4007	
D7	BY205-1000	
D8	1N4001	
D9	1N4001	
D10	BY206-400	
D11	1S921	
D12	BY127	
D13	BY205-400	
D14	BY205-800	
D15	1N4004	
D16	1N4002	

D17	1S920
D18	BY404 or 1N4004
D19	1N4148
D20	1N4148
D21	1S920
D22	1S920
D23	BY205-800
RV1	100Ω 3W Shift
RV2	1MΩ Background
RV3	Focus assembly
RV4	47kΩ Supply Adjust
RV5	470Ω Horizontal Freq.
RV6	100kΩ Vertical Freq.
RV7	2k2kΩ P.W.M. Osc. Adjust.
VT1	BU137
VT2	BD410
VT3	BC212 (2N4062)
ZD1	BZX61/12
ZD2	BZY88/8Z2

L1	Linearity coil. 50t @ 21 s.w.g. on standard assembly 12-65μH
L2	A51 – 150X Horizontal Yoke = 600μH
L3	Shift choke. 700t @ 31 s.w.g. on 5mm dia x 4cm ferrite rod, 11mH
T1	See Appendix B
T2	E.h.t. transformer. Regapped TFAT1109-61 for primary inductance = 3mH
T3	Modulator transformer 21t @ 22 s.w.g. primary 52t + 52t @ 29 s.w.g. sectioned secondary on 25mm pot core gapped primary inductance = 150μH
T4	Driver transformer 42t @ 22 s.w.g. secondary 625t + 625t @ 40 s.w.g. primary on 25mm E core gapped for L_p = 300mH

In Figure 7 the variation VA with N is shown. The VA is relative to the scan transistor VA in a conventional system. As the self-stabilising power transistor is doing two jobs – deflection and power supply, its relative VA will always be greater than one. Cost and efficiency dictate that the transistor VA should be minimised and the VA curves show there are optimum values of N to do this. Optimum (dot), 1·25 (dash), and 1·5 (cross), VA turns ratios have been marked on Figure 6. So the choice of N is now considerably restricted. Table 1 lists the ranges of N and V_o for optimum and a maximum relative VA of 1·25.

Table 1

	H.V.I.	L.V.I.	
	$\check{\delta}$ = 0·4	$\check{\delta}$ = 0·5	$\check{\delta}$ = 0·67
Optimum N	0·8	4	5·3
Optimum V_o	185	93	140
N Range	0·6 – 0·9	2 – 4·7	3 – 6
V_o range	260 – 170	180 – 80	250 – 125

Table 2 lists N and V_o for optimum and a maximum relative VA of 1·25 for 110V a.c. supply.

Table 2

	H.V.I.	L.V.I.	
	$\check{\delta}$ = 0·4	$\check{\delta}$ = 0·5	$\check{\delta}$ = 0·67
Optimum N	0·8	4	5·3
Optimum V_o	93	47	70
N range	0·6 – 0·9	2 – 4·7	3 – 6
V_o range	130 – 85	90 – 40	125 – 62

Tubes and Deflection Yokes

Table 3 shows the commonly used deflection circuit supply voltages (V_o) by application. These figures assume the deflection yoke is directly driven from the scan device, (very little tapping on the horizontal output transformer), which results in the most economic design of horizontal output transformer.

Table 3

Deflection Voltage V_o V	Application
11	Monochrome portable
24 – 30	Monochrome portable/large screen
60 – 90	Colour (especially with toroidal yokes)
110 – 125	Monochrome large screen, colour, monitors
140	Monochrome large screen, colour, ,,
200	Monochrome large screen, colour, ,,

A comparison of this table with Tables 1 and 2 shows that the l.v.i. is favoured in Europe for the majority of the colour and large screen monochrome applications. In 110V areas the situation is reversed and h.v.i. is most suitable. Portable monochrome and 30V large screen monochrome systems are so non-optimum that they are not practical with these present classes of self-stabilising system.

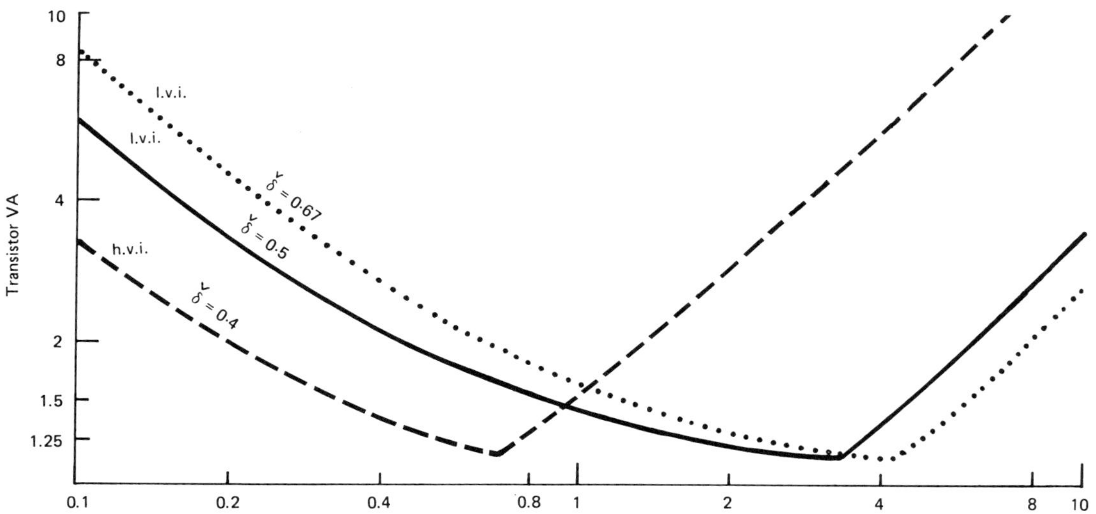

FIGURE 7. Relative Transistor VA against Stabiliser Transformer Turns. Ratio N:1

DESIGN EXAMPLE FOR A 90° P.I. COLOUR TUBE

Basic Deflection Circuit

Figure 8 shows a conventional horizontal deflection circuit with values suitable for driving the A51 – 160X 90° PI colour tube. A low voltage injection design will be used, (this is most suited for Europe). The choice of East-West pin cushion correction circuits, diodes D6, D7, transformer T3, capacitors C3 and C6 are discussed in Appendix A. Two methods of beam current limiting are employed. Both depend on the principle that current from the 230V rail via resistors R7, 8, and 9 forward biasses diode D11. Tube beam current flows in opposition to the 230V current back to the e.h.t. generation system. When the beam current exceeds the current from the 230V, diode D11 becomes reverse

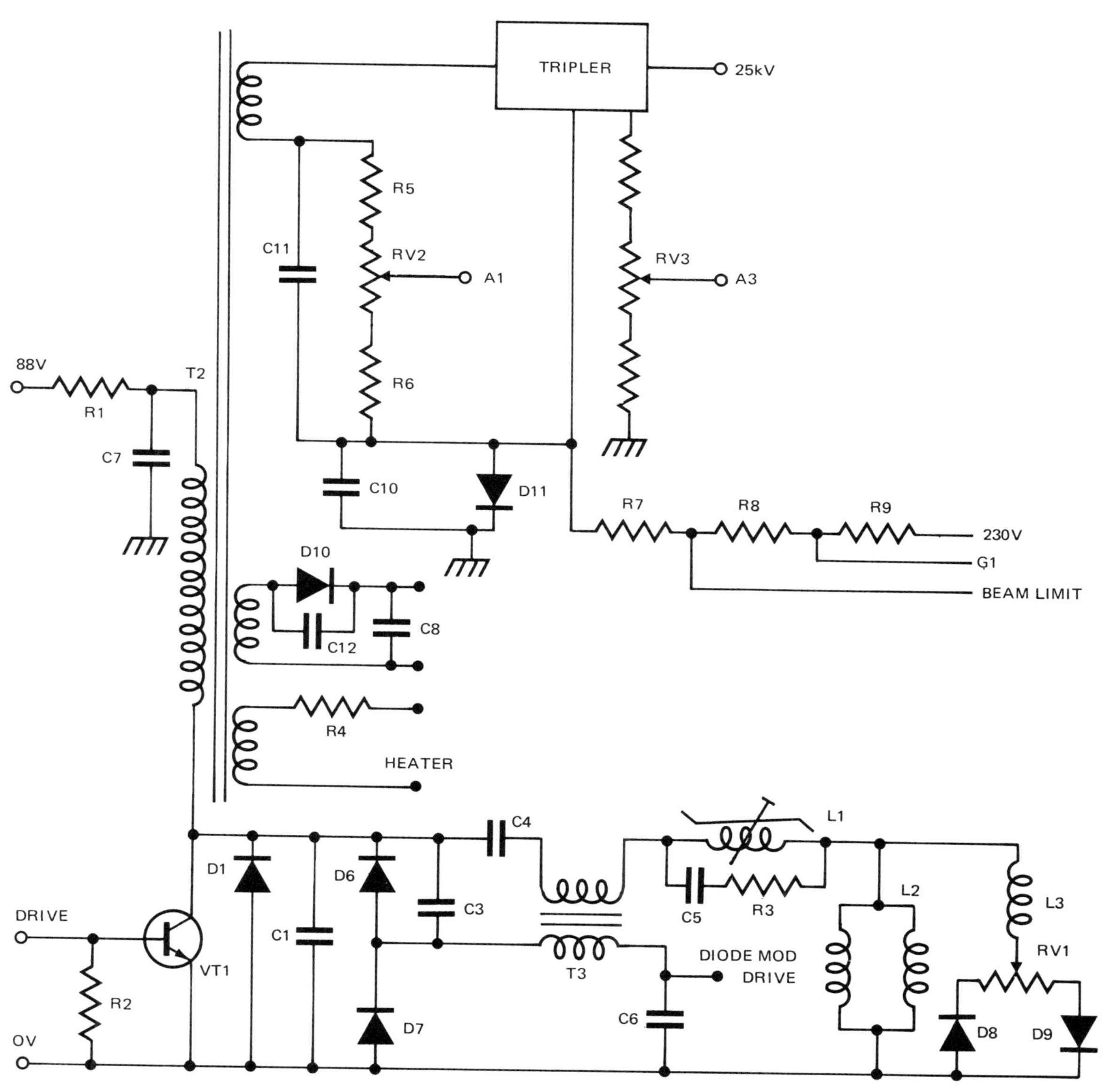

FIGURE 8. 90° P.I. Colour Tube Deflection Circuit

biassed, causing the g1 and beam limiter outputs from the divider to fall in potential. Normally the SN76226 luma i.c., which is driven from the beam limiter, would control the contrast and finally the black level in the colour system to limit the maximum average beam current to its present value. If, however, there is some malfunction in the colour system the output voltages from the divider continue to fall reducing the tubes g1 voltage to provide an overriding current limit. Capacitor, C10, protects diode D11 against tube flashover and averages the beam current. The scan rectified supply developed across capacitor C8 is used for the low level stages in the vertical output circuit to give vertical amplitude tracking with beam current.

The sequence of conversion is shown diagrammatically below. Quantities that are the result of calculations using measured or estimated values are underlined. Formulae which are used to link quantities are shown in their relative positions.

Symbols

$\hat{I}_C$ Peak collector current in self stabilizing transistor
I_S Peak positive scan current in conventional circuit
$\hat{I}3$ Maximum transformer, T1, primary current
$\bar{I}_{D2}$ Maximum average current of coupling diode D2
$\bar{I}_{D3}$ Maximum average current of primary diode D3
$\bar{I}_{D4}$ Maximum average current of deflection supply diode D4
$\check{L}$ Minimum primary inductance of transformer T1
N Transformer T1 turns ratio
$\hat{P}_D$ Maximum power demand of deflection circuit
$\hat{P}_o$ Maximum total receiver power demand
$\check{P}_o$ Minimum total receiver power demand
$\hat{V}_{CE}$ BV_{CBO} rating of self stabilizing transistor
V_{D2} Voltage rating of coupling diode D2
V_{D3} Voltage rating of primary diode D3
V_{D4} Voltage rating of deflection supply diode D4
$\hat{V}_i$ Maximum rectified input voltage
$\check{V}_i$ Minimum rectified input voltage
V_o Deflection supply rail voltage
$\hat{V}_P$ Maximum primary voltage of transformer T1, w.r.t. 0V
V_R Deflection circuit retrace voltage
δ Minimum fraction of positive scan current
$\check{\delta}$ Design value of minimum transistor conduction fraction
$\hat{\delta}$ Design value of maximum transistor conduction fraction
τ Operating period (typically 64μs)

Calculations

This calculation sequence will now be followed through using values from the conventional circuit of Figure 8.

Conventional System: $I_S, \hat{P}_o, \check{P}_o, \hat{P}_D, V_o, V_R, \delta$,

Power Supply: $\hat{V}_i, \check{V}_i$

$$V_P = V_i/(1 - \delta)$$

↓

Conduction Period

$\underline{\check{\delta}}$ $\underline{\hat{\delta}}$

↓

$$\check{L} = (V_i.\check{\delta})^2 \times \tau/2\check{P}_o$$

$$\hat{I}3 = \hat{P}_o \left(\frac{1 + \check{P}_o}{\hat{P}_o} \left\{ \frac{1 - \hat{\delta}}{1 - \check{\delta}} \right\}^2 \right) \Big/ \check{V}_i \times \hat{\delta}$$

↓

Switched Mode Transformer Primary

$\underline{L}$ $\underline{\hat{I}3}$

$$N = \frac{\hat{V}_i}{V_o} \times \frac{\check{\delta}}{1 - \check{\delta}}$$

↓

Transformer Turns Ratio

↓

$\underline{N}$

$$\hat{V}_{CE} = 1{\cdot}25\ (\hat{V}_P \text{ or } V_R)$$
$$\hat{I}_C = I_S + \hat{I}3$$
$$V_{D2} = 1{\cdot}25\hat{V}_P$$
$$\bar{I}_{D2} = I_S \times \delta/2$$
$$V_{D3} = 1.25V_R - \check{V}_i$$
$$\bar{I}_{D3} = \hat{P}_o/\check{V}_i$$
$$V_{D4} = 1{\cdot}25V_P/N$$
$$\bar{I}_{D4} = P_D/V_o$$

↓

Semiconductor Ratings

$\underline{\hat{V}_{CE}}, \underline{\hat{I}_C}, \underline{V_{D2}}, \underline{\bar{I}_{D2}}, \underline{V_{D3}}, \underline{\bar{I}_{D3}}, \underline{V_{D4}}, \underline{I_{D4}}$

Conventional Circuit

Table 4 shows how the total receiver power demand is made up.

Table 4

		Minimum	Maximum	
Horizontal Deflection, 88V (V_o)		27	59 ($\hat{P}_D$)	W
Video Output, 230V		7	21	W
Vertical Deflection, Audio Signal Processing	30V	19	27	W
Total Power		53 ($\check{P}_o$)	107 ($\hat{P}_o$)	W

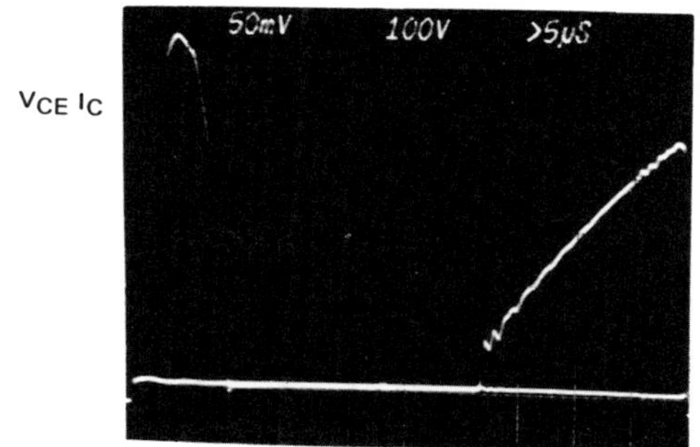

FIGURE 9. Deflection Transistor Voltage and Current

Figure 9, a photograph of the transistor collector voltage and current waveforms of a conventional circuit (measured with a series collector diode D2), enables the remaining parameters to be measured.

I_S	=	4·5A			
$\hat{P}_o$	=	107W	V_o	=	88V
$\check{P}_o$	=	53W	V_R	=	750V
$\grave{P}_D$	=	59W	δ	=	0·37

Power Supply

A design which would satisfy most of the European requirements would operate from 185V a.c. to 265V a.c. After rectification this would typically yield a d.c. supply voltage between 200V ($\check{V}_i$) and 370V ($\hat{V}_i$).

$$\check{V}_i = 200V$$

$$\hat{V}_i = 370V$$

Conduction Period

In an optimised design the maximum primary voltage of transformer T2, V_P, at $\hat{V}_i$ would equal the retrace voltage, V_R. For this condition

$$\check{\delta} = 1 - \hat{V}_i/V_R = 1 - \hat{V}_i/V_P$$
$$= 1 - 370/750$$
$$= 0·51$$

This condition can be satisfied as the inherent deflection circuit value is 0·37. The transformer winding voltage will be $\hat{V}_P - \hat{V}_i = 380V$ so that at minimum supply voltage $V_P = 380 + \check{V}_i = 580V$. Hence the maximum conduction will be

$$\hat{\delta} = 1 - \check{V}_i/V_P$$
$$= 1 - 200/580$$
$$= 0·66$$

$$\check{\delta} = 0·51$$

$$\hat{\delta} = 0·66$$

Switched Mode Transformer Primary

The primary inductance, L, can now be calculated as

$$L = (\hat{V}_i \times \check{\delta})^2 \times \tau/2\check{P}_o$$
$$= (370 \times 0.51)^2 \times 64 \times 10^{-6}/2 \times 53$$
$$= 21mH$$

This inductance must be maintained to a peak current of $\hat{I}3$

$$\hat{I}3 = \frac{\hat{P}_o}{\check{V}_i \times \hat{\delta}}\left(1 + \frac{\check{P}_o}{\hat{P}_o}\left\{\frac{1-\hat{\delta}}{1-\check{\delta}}\right\}^2\right)$$

$$= \frac{107}{200 \times 0·66}\left(1 + \frac{53}{107}\left\{\frac{1-0·66}{1-0·51}\right\}^2\right)$$

$$= 1·0A$$

Transformer Turns Ratio

This is given by

$$N = \frac{\hat{V}_i}{V_o} \times \frac{\check{\delta}}{1-\check{\delta}} = \frac{370}{88} \times \frac{0·51}{1-0·51}$$

$$= 4·4$$

The practical realisation of this transformer is further discussed in Appendix B.

Semiconductor Device Ratings

Application of the quoted formulae give the results given in Table 5.

Table 5

Device	Rating	Recommended Unit
Transistor VT1	V_{CE} = 940V I_C = 5·5A	BU137
Diode D2	V_{D2} = 940V I_{D2} = 1A	BYW11-1000 or BY205-1000
Diode D3	V_{D3} = 740 I_{D3} = 0·5A	BY205-800
Diode D4	V_{D4} = 210V I_{D4} = 0·67A	BY205-400

All the diodes specified are fast soft recovery types which generate very much less radiation than the conventional fast rectifier which tends to exhibit "snap off" during its reverse recovery time (t_{rr}). The average currents calculated have no allowance for reverse recovery losses however this has been comprehended in the device selection.

Complete System

The converted system is shown in Figure 10. Full details of the SN76545 horizontal/vertical processor i.c. and the SN76549 pulse width modulator i.c. functioning may be found in their respective data sheets. The major phase related circuit waveforms are shown in Figure 11. The power transistor VT1 'turn off' is controlled by the SN76545 i.c. which compares the synchronising pulse on pin 12 with the horizontal scan sawtooth on pin 7 to give the correct video to scan phasing. The power transistor VT1 'turn on' is controlled by the SN76549 i.c. which compares the proportion of the deflection supply voltage applied to pin 15 with the reference voltage on pin 14 to maintain a constant deflection supply voltage.

Figure 12 shows the smooth switch 'on' and switch off' characteristics of the circuit. This occurs due to transistor VT1 conduction being very short initially and then progressively increasing to reach normal operating conditions during start up and the reverse occuring during switch 'off'.

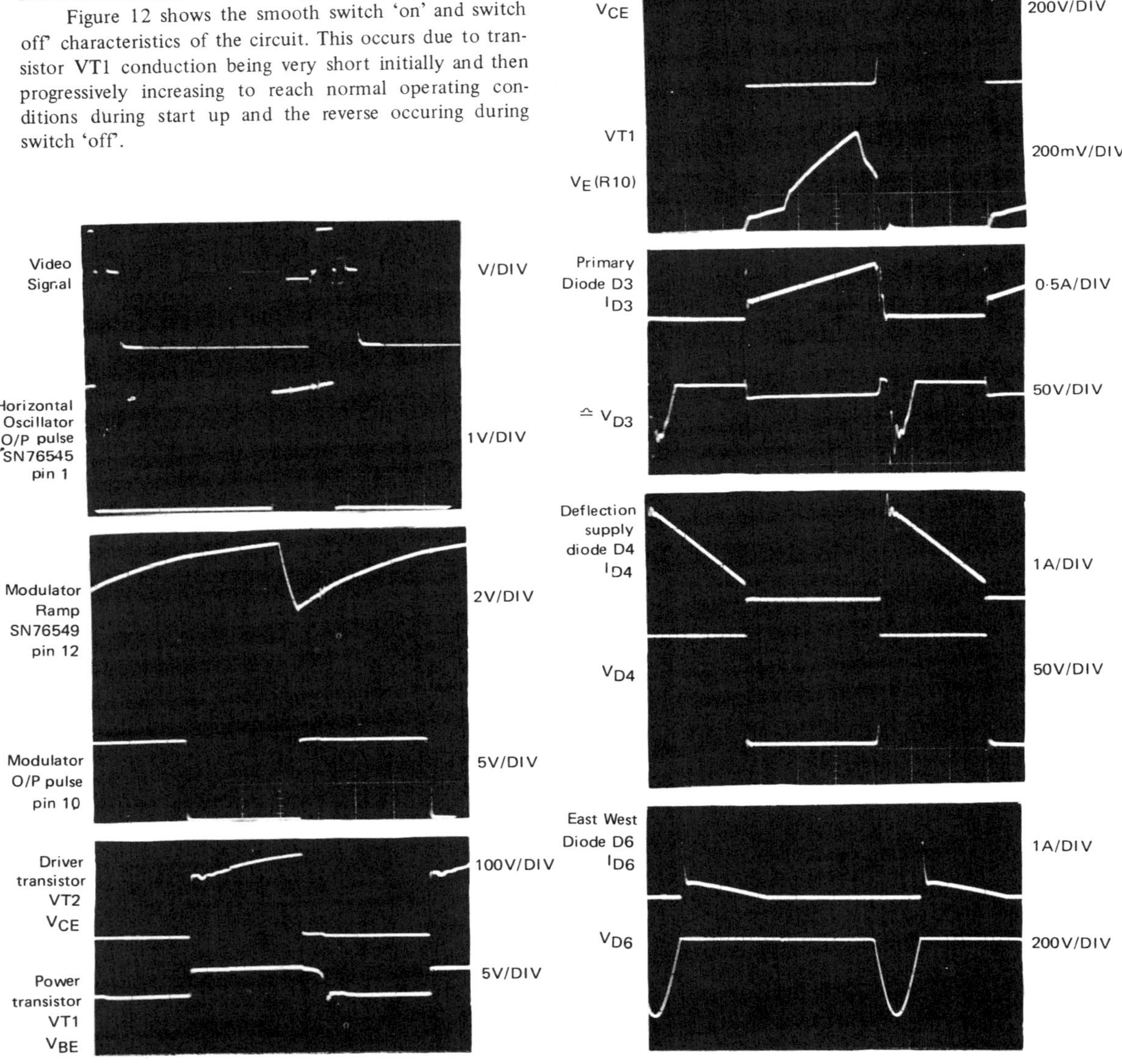

FIGURE 11. Key Circuit Waveforms at 10µs

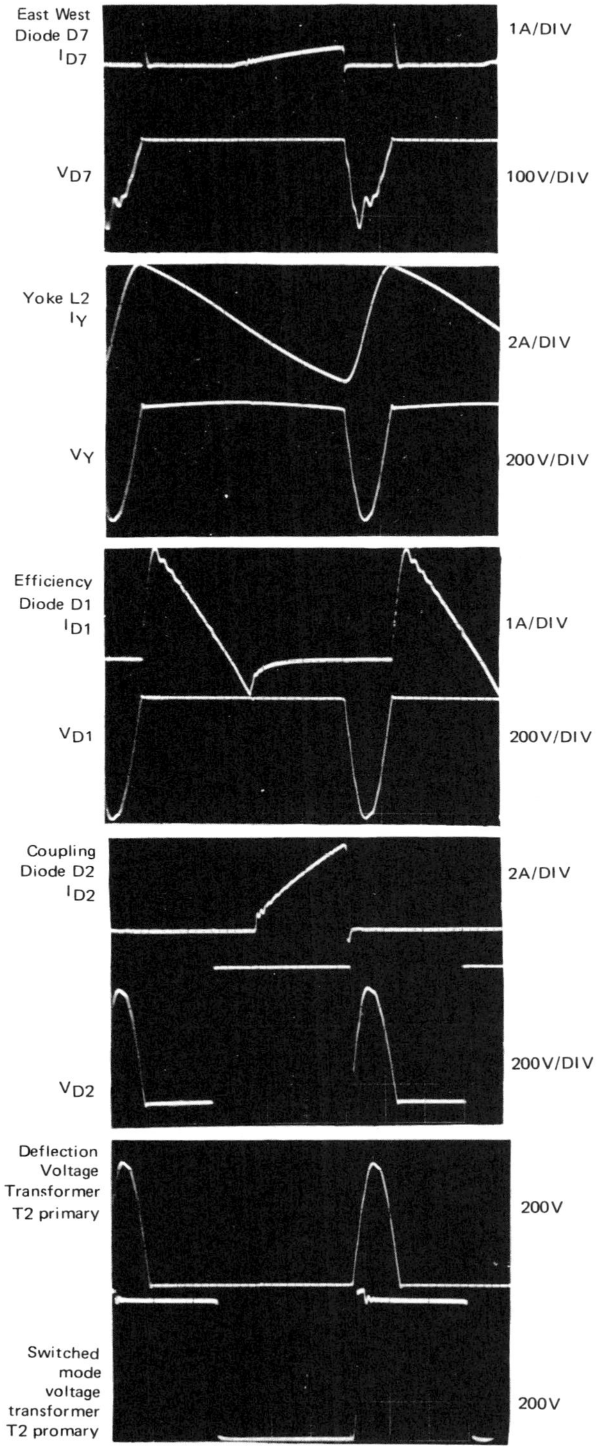

East West
Diode D7
I_{D7}
1A/DIV
V_{D7}
100V/DIV
Yoke L2
I_Y
2A/DIV
V_Y
200V/DIV
Efficiency
Diode D1
I_{D1}
1A/DIV
V_{D1}
200V/DIV
Coupling
Diode D2
I_{D2}
2A/DIV
V_{D2}
200V/DIV
Deflection
Voltage
Transformer
T2 primary
200V
Switched
mode
voltage
transformer
T2 promary
200V

Transistor
VT1
V_{CE}
500V/DI
2A/DIV
I_C
Deflection
Supply
50V/DI\
Transistor
VT1
V_{CE}
500V/DI
I_C
2A/DIV
Deflection
Supply
50V/DI\

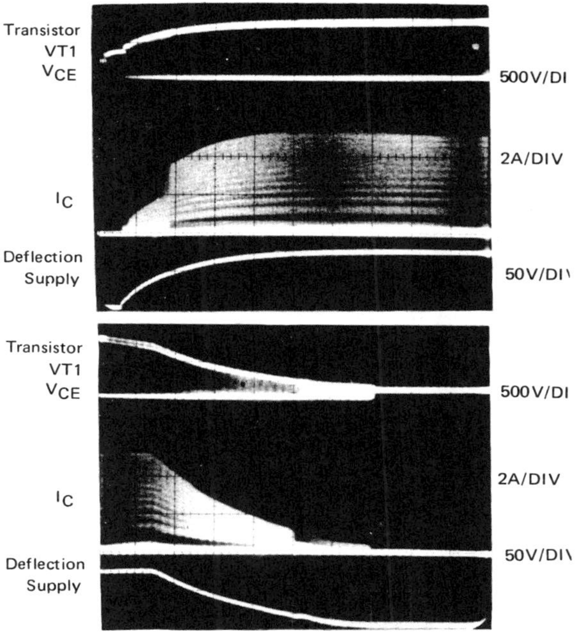

FIGURE 12. System Start Up and Shut Down Waveforms at 200ms

Performance

The deflection specification (e.h.t. regulation, picture size, etc) is equally as good as the conventional circuit, but additional full fault protection is now incorporated. The deflection supply voltage specification comprehends an a.c. voltage change of 185–270V and a beam current change of 0·1 to 1mA.

Change		< 0.5%
Peak to peak ripple	50Hz	< 0.3%
	15kHz	<0.6%

The above figures show that the system presented is capable of high performance whilst being extremely cost effective. This is combined with excellent inherent reliability from both the normal operation standpoint and the mitigation of fault conditions by the protection circuits.

REFERENCES

1. M. J. Maytum, Transistorised Self-Stabilising Horizontal Deflection Systems, *Proc I.E.E.E.*, Volume BTR20, No. 1 pp 32-64, Feb 1974.

2 M. J. Maytum, Transistorised Self-Stabilising Horizontal Deflection Systems, *Proc I.E.E.E.*, Volume BTR20, No. 1 pp 43, Feb 1974.

3 Balayage Monostandard 625L Receptance, *Videocolor* SA, France 1975.

APPENDIX A

East-West Pincushion Correction Circuit

Undoubtedly a transductor is the most economic form of pincushion correction circuit. However, its correction range and shape are limited and picture geometry changes with beam current are difficult to avoid.

It is these two drawbacks which have made many designers opt for the slightly higher cost diode modulator circuit for E-W correction. The operation of this circuit has been covered in detail elsewhere[3]. One bonus of the diode modulator is that it can easily perform the width control function and dynamic 'S' correction as well.

Figures 13 and 14 show the two main types of diode modulator. Typically about a 20% yoke current variation capability is required (this is for pincushion, width control plus a tolerance allowance). For this the primary inductance of modulator transformer T3 is 20% of the total yoke circuit inductance. The dissipative diode modulator is so called because it produces a d.c. supply rail at point A which must be loaded above a certain power level for the modulator to work. By using about a 1:2 turns ratio for transformer T3 and a 280V peak-peak winding on the e.h.t. transformer T2 a 30V d.c. supply will result which can be used for the vertical scan system. In the 90° PI system the minimum load requirement is about 12W. As the vertical scan system power requirement is 15W the loading condition is met. However, a very large amount of smoothing has to be used to reduce the varying class B vertical scan power demand to a reasonably steady value at the diode modulator. The non-dissipative diode modulator does not produce a supply rail from which power must be taken and so gives a more efficient horizontal deflection stage. If the vertical deflection power were taken from the horizontal deflection circuit the stabilising transistor's collector current is increased in two ways; one by providing the power through the switching mode transformer, the other by providing the power through the horizontal transformer. By taking the vertical deflection power directly from the switching mode transformer the stabilising transistor's collector current is minimised and the efficiency of the horizontal deflection circuit is improved. Another factor is the voltage rating of the 30V rail rectifier. Extracting the power from the switching mode transformer requires a 100V rated rectifier whilst one for horizontal scan rectification requires a 300V rectifier.

As a general principle, it is best to take as much power as possible directly from the switching mode transformer secondaries as this reduces the transistor/rectifier current ratings and the rectifier voltage ratings.

Both types of diode modulator will dissipate power in the modulator drive circuit. By virtue of its operation the dissipative version will lose more power in its modulator circuit than the non-dissipative version. It is possible to remove the efficiency diode when using the non-dissipative diode modulator as its series connected diodes can perform the efficiency action. One most contrast circuit simplicity and the cost of a fast high current diode plus a slow high current diode (when the efficiency diode is removed) against improved linearity/efficiency and the cost of a slow high current diode and two low current diodes, one fast, the other slow. Table 6 details the performance of the diode modulators discussed with regard to the 90° PI tube.

The system chosen for the 90° PI tube is the non-dissipative type with an efficiency diode. By changing the power of magnitude rating of relatively few components this total system concept is capable of being up rated to the 110° PI tube.

Table 6

Modulator	Diode D1		Diode D6		Diode D7		Maximum Modulator
	Average Current A	Voltage Rating V	Average Current A	Voltage Rating V	Average Current A	Voltage Rating V	Driver Power W
Dissipative	0·6	1000	0·8*	300	1·1*	300	3
Non-dissipative	0·6	1000	0·15	900	0·15*	900	1·5
	—	—	0·75	900	0·75*	900	1·5

*Fast

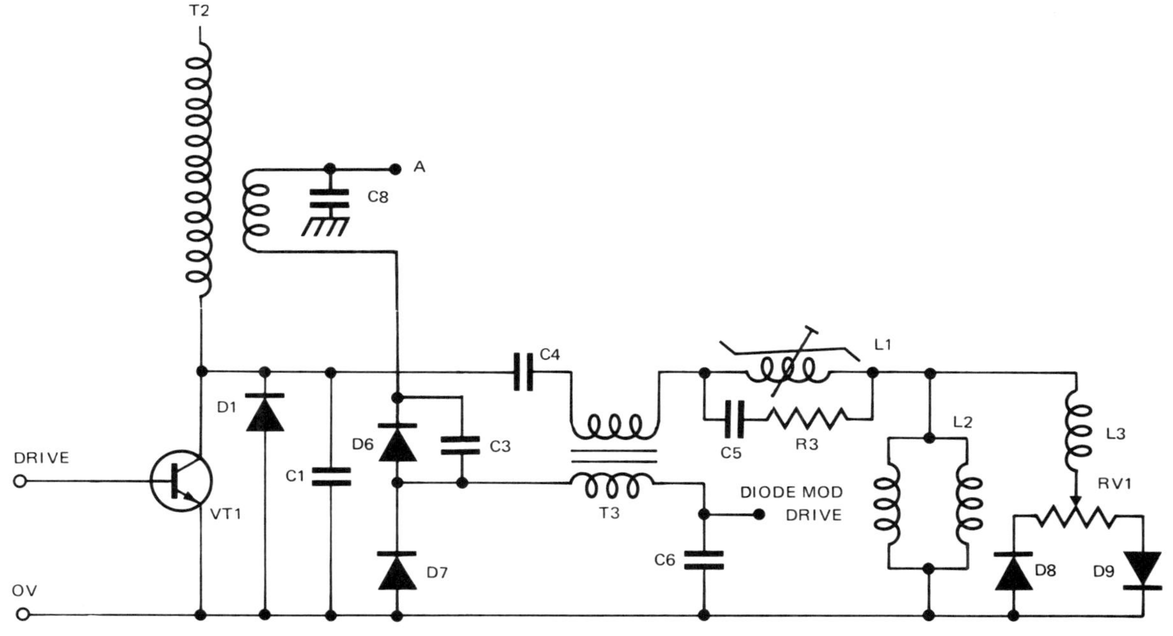

FIGURE 13. Dissipative Diode Modulator

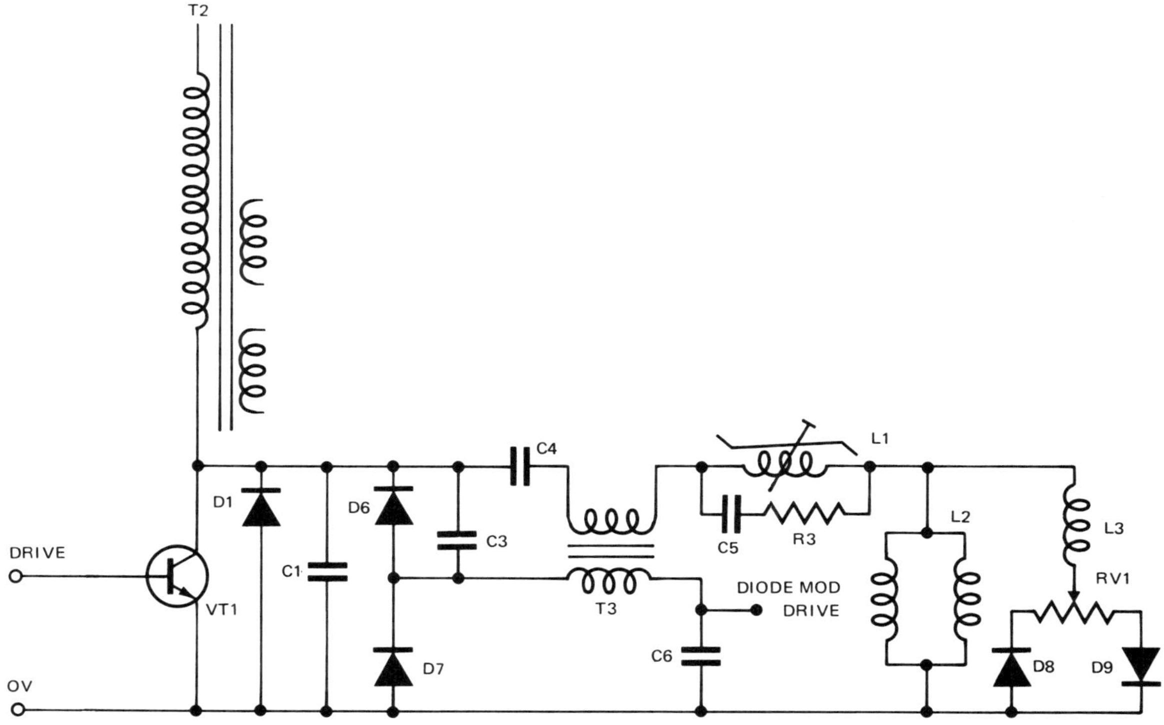

FIGURE 14. Non-Dissipative Diode Modulator

Design of Switching Mode Transformer

The calculated transformer requirements from the design example are:

Primary L = 21mH @ 1A

Secondary

Voltage V	Current A	Power W	Fraction of $\hat{P}_o$
88	0·67	59	0·55
30	0·9	27	0·25
230	0·09	21	0·20

The primary/88V winding ratio is = 4·4:1

The transformer operates with a magnetic bias and in design should be treated as a d.c. carrying choke. Modern low loss ferrite core materials make the design B_{sat} limited rather than hysteresis loss limited. The largest core flux density occurs at the lowest input voltage $\check{V}_i$ and the maximum power demand $\hat{P}_o$. Under these conditions the amplitude of the transformer current change, ΔI, during the transistor conduction time will be

$$\Delta I = \check{V}_i \times T \times \hat{\delta}/L$$

$$= 200 \times 0{\cdot}66 \times 64 \times 10^{-6}/21 \times 10^{-3}$$

$$= 0{\cdot}40A$$

The ratio alternating magneto motive force (ΔH) to peak force is given by

$$\Delta I/\hat{I}3 = 0{\cdot}4/1$$

$$= 0{\cdot}4$$

The flux density will vary in a similar manner. So if a peak flux value of 300mT is chosen the alternating flux density $\hat{\check{B}}$ will be

$$\hat{\check{B}} = 0{\cdot}4 \times B_{sat}$$

$$= 120mT$$

A suitable core for this application is the Fair-rite 94-036002 (EE42) in A77 material. The magnetic dimensions are A_e = 184mm², l_e = 94mm and winding area A_W = 297mm².

The number of primary turns n_p can be calculated from

$$n_p = \check{V}_i \times \hat{\delta} \times T/\hat{\check{B}} \times A_e$$

$$= \frac{200 \times 0{\cdot}66 \times 64 \times 10^{-6}}{120 \times 10^{-3} \times 184 \times 10^{-6}}$$

$$= 383$$

Assuming a 70% winding area usage a wire gauge is needed to give a winding density better than

$$383/0{\cdot}7 \times 297 \times 0{\cdot}5$$

$$= 3{\cdot}7t/mm^2$$

The 88V winding will require 383/4·4 = 87 turns in a space of 0·7 x 297 x 0·5 x 0·55 = 56mm² using a wire giving a winding density of 1·5t/mm². Table 8 summarises these operations for the other windings.

Table 8. Winding Details

	Area mm²	Turns	Turns/mm²	Gauge s.w.g..
primary	104	383	3·7	26
88V winding	57	87	1·5	22
30V winding	26	30	1·2	21
230V winding	21	226	11·0	32

To reduce leakage inductance the primary should be sectioned. Also checks should be made on the current density of the wire gauges finally selected. An approximate value of total air gap l_g can be calculated from the formula.

$$l_g = \mu_o \times n_p^2 \times A_e/L - l_e/\mu_r$$

$$= \frac{4\pi \times 10^{-7} \times 383^2 \times 184 \times 10^{-6}}{21 \times 10^{-3} - 94 \times 10^{-3}/2000}$$

$$= 1{\cdot}6 \times 10^{-3}m$$

$$= 1{\cdot}6mm$$

This gives some idea of the spacer sizes required for setting the primary inductance to 21mH.

SN76549 as a Line Processor cum P.W.M.

The internal oscillator and phase detector circuit of the '549 enable it to operate as a simple line processor in addition to its p.w.m. function, as shown in Figure 15.

Separate sync. pulses are fed into pin 9 and compared with the scan sawtooth waveform, obtained from the fly-back, which is fed to pin 8. The output of the phase detector (pin 7) triggers the line oscillator (pin 6) initiating turn 'off' of the line output transistor (VT1 in the earlier example), and hence maintaining correct video to scan phasing. Turn 'on' is effected normally, comprehending the scan voltage and adjusting the conduction time of the power transistor.

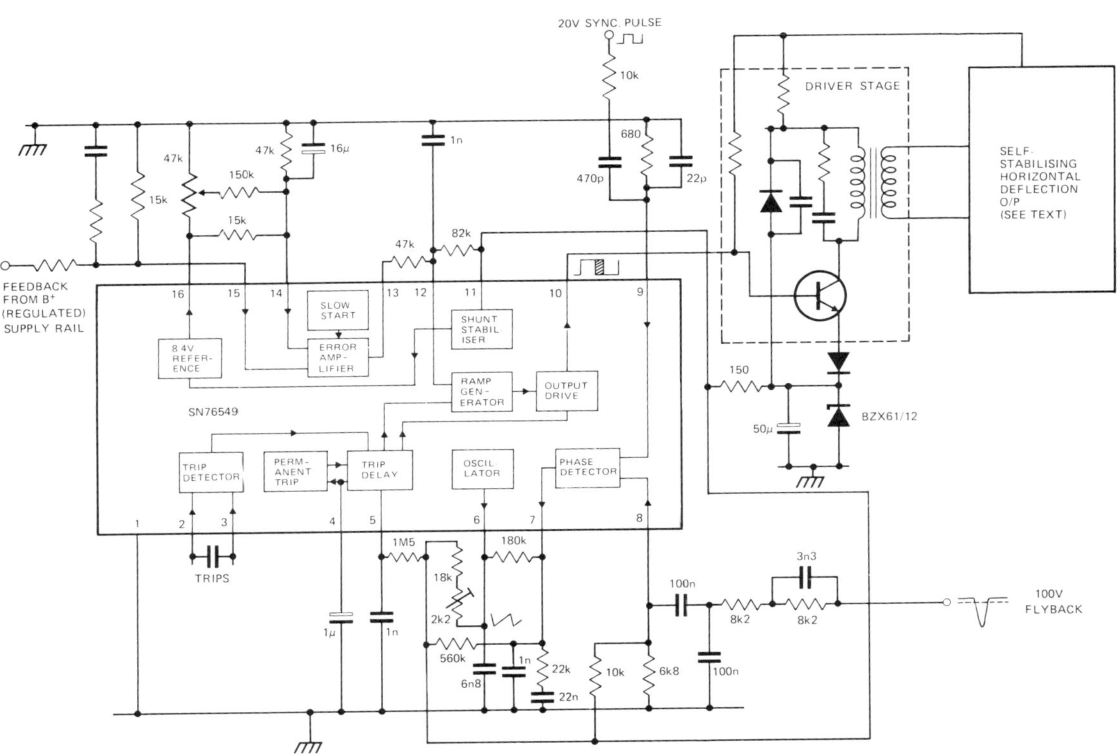

FIGURE 15. Use of '549 I.C. as Line Processor and P.W.M.

VI CONVENTIONAL HORIZONTAL DEFLECTION STAGES

By
Peter Wilson

Conventional horizontal deflection circuits are of the form shown in Figure 1. During the last part of the forward scan, transistor VT1 is in normal conduction, drawing collector current from the primary of the e.h.t. transformer and from the deflection coils, L_Y. The scan period is ended by the transistor being turned 'off' by the driver stage. The abrupt termination of collector current results in a controlled resonance occurring between inductive and capacitive elements in the collector circuit. The retrace voltage, which is seen at the collector of output transistor VT1, is stepped up by a secondary winding on transformer T1 to generate the e.h.t. supply for the tube. Retrace time is normally fixed by C_t, the timing capacitor, to approximately 12 μs. The efficiency period, during which diode D1 conducts, follows the retrace time and provides the initial forward scan current, after which transistor VT1 is again switched 'on' to provide the remaining forward scan. Typical waveforms are shown in Figure 2.

In order that the transistor operates efficiently, it must be kept in saturation during its normal conduction period, and must be turned 'off' fast in order to eliminate high transient dissipation. It is generally accepted that high voltage transistors used in switching applications must be turned 'off' in a controlled manner to minimise transient power loss.[1,2] The duration of the base current fall time approximates to the device storage time (t_s) for optimum switching – Figure 2. The negative bias maintained on the base-emitter junction throughout the retrace period ensures that the device withstands the peak collector voltage. The collector emitter breakdown voltage when the base emitter junction is reverse biassed, BV_{CEX} (where X indicates a negative voltage) approaches BV_{CBO}, and is higher than BV_{CEO} (the breakdown voltage obtained if the base was left open circuit). A reverse base-emitter voltage of 2 to 4V is generally used.

For the purpose of examination, the horizontal deflection stages considered in this chapter are applicable to small screen 12-14 inch portable t.v. receivers. However, the principles apply equally to other c.r.t. deflection stages provided suitably rated output devices are used.

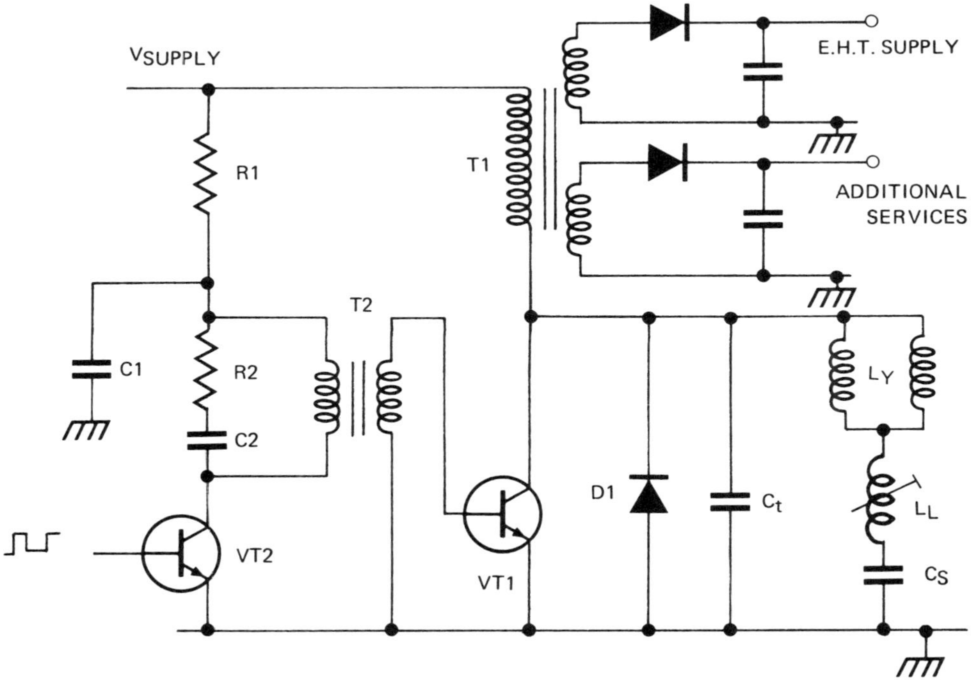

FIGURE 1. Basic Horizontal Deflection Circuit.

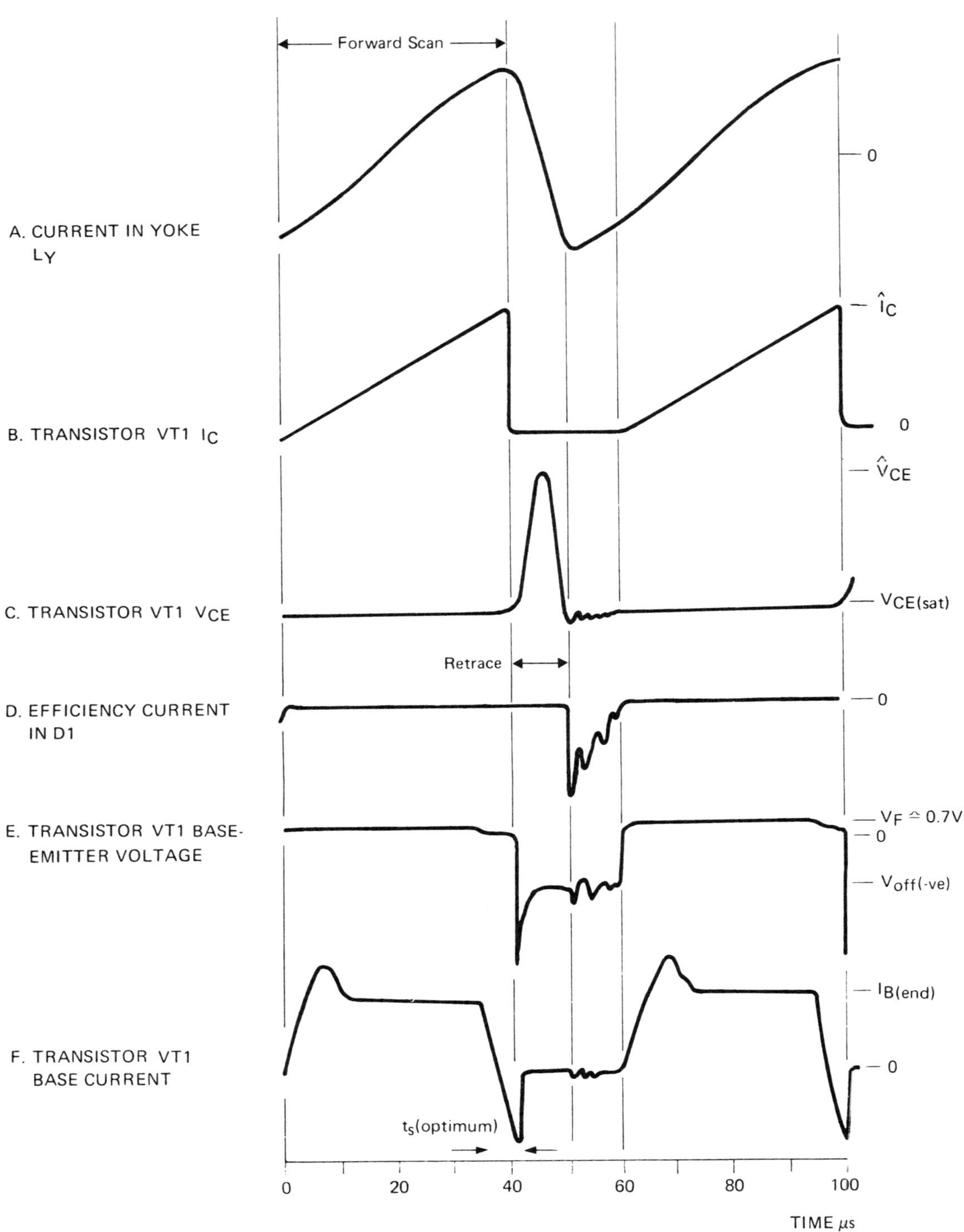

FIGURE 2. Typical Horizontal Deflection Stage Waveforms.

DRIVE CIRCUIT CONFIGURATIONS

Using an npn High Voltage Power Output Device

General: Horizontal deflection stages have in the past typically used a germanium pnp transistor for the output switch VT1 in Figure 1. A circuit showing the employment of such a device is given in Figure 3. In order to take advantage of more modern and economical transistors, such as the BU124, the driver stage must be modified as shown in Figure 4. Such modifications result in increased efficency even though a higher base current is required to the deflection device. ($I_{B(end)}$ for a germanium device is typically 250mA c.f. 500mA required for the silicon npn device). As the collector (case) of a T03 package can no longer be grounded it should be isolated from the chassis.

The Base Emitter Resistor, R_{BE}. A resistor is required in order to prevent turn 'on' of the device caused by ringing induced at the base terminal during the retrace period. The resistor is of a value which does not appreciably reduce the value of $I_{B(end)}$. A value of 68Ω was chosen in this case.

Storage Time: This is short for the BU124 under the described conditions of use ($I_{B(end)}$ = 0.5A, I_C = 4A), i.e. typically 1.3 μs, extending to 1.5 μs at 70°C case temperature. Hence, a low value of secondary leakage inductance is required of the driver transformer in order to obtain the required rate of fall of base current, dI_B/dt

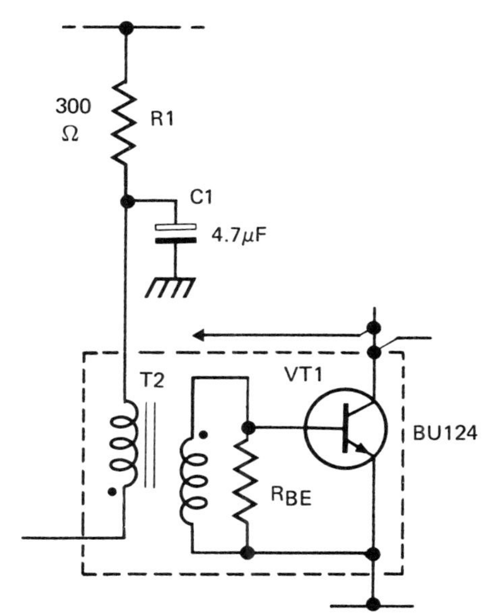

FIGURE 4. Circuit Modifications to Incorporate the BU124

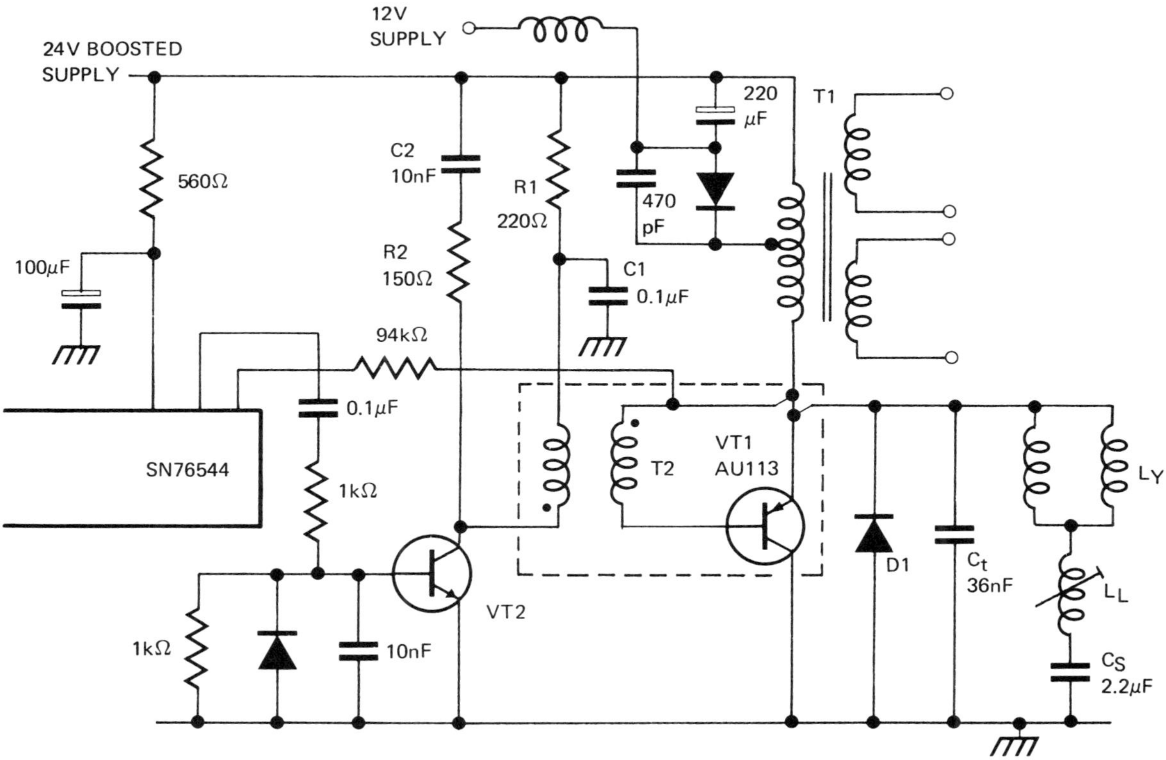

FIGURE 3. Horizontal Deflection Stage employing a Germanium pnp Output Device.

(Note 1). Low leakage inductance is not easily controlled, being strongly dependent on the winding detail of the transformer. A high value of leakage inductance causes slower, less efficient switching. Where this is unavoidable the device will still operate, since it is well within its maximum ratings under normal operation. A larger heat sink may well be required, however, to ensure that case temperature is maintained at an acceptable level. Use of a drive transformer of secondary leakage inductance 15 μH (Note 2) causes an increase in a collector current fall time. The increase shows as a 'rounding' on the peak of the collector current waveform and is a result of longer storage time. Since V_{CE} is rising during this time, dissipation is increased. In extreme cases loss of picture linearity or e.h.t. regulation could also result.

Specification: The suitability of the BU124 transistor for horizontal deflection is illustrated by a comparison of its specification with the operating conditions in a portable t.v. as detailed in Table 1.

A first order approximation to device dissipation can be made by a simple calculation, using the tabulated data:

$P_{tot} = P_{(collector\ emitter)} + P_{(base\ emitter)} + P_{(turn\ off)} + P_{(retrace)}$

a. Collector Emitter Dissipation.

$P_{(collector\ emitter)} = \hat{I}_C/3) \times V_{CE(sat)} \times (t_1/\tau)$

where t_1 = Transistor forward conduction time.

τ = scan period

= 0.46W

b. Base Emitter Dissipation

$P_{(base\ emitter)} = I_{B(end)} \times V_{BE(sat)} \times (t_1'/\tau)$

where t_1' = duration of +ve base current and

$t_1' \simeq t_1$

= 0.53W

c. Turn 'off' Dissipation

$P_{(turn\ off)} = (\hat{I}_C \times V_{CE1}/6) \times (t_f/\tau)$

where

V_{CE1} = collector emitter voltage at the end of t_f

t_f = collector current fall time = 0.5μs

= 0.13W

d. Retrace Dissipation

$P_{(retrace)} = I_{CBO} \times (2\hat{V}_{CE}/\pi) \times (t_2/\tau)$

Assuming fundamental tuning, where t_2 = retrace time

= 0.025W

Hence, total dissipation, P_{tot} is 1.15W.

While the calculation gives only an approximation of the device dissipation, measurements have verified that dissipation is typically less than 2W in this application.

Note 1. Secondary leakage inductance is the value of inductance measured across the secondary, while the primary winding is short circuit.

Note 2. Drive Transformer Ref. No. 20401 wound by Hinchley Engineering Co. Ltd. Devizes, Wiltshire, England.

Table 1. Comparison of BU124 Specification with Typical Operating Conditions in a Portable T.V.

SPECIFICATION		OPERATING CONDITION	
Max. collector base voltage (I_E = 0)	350V	Collector emitter peak voltage V_{CEX}	200V
Max. emitter base voltage V_{EBO}	8V		
Max. continuous collector current I_C	10A	Peak collector current (norm)	4A
Max. peak collector current I_C	15A	On tube flashover	9A
Max. continuous dissipation P_{tot} (25°C case temp.)	50W	Typical dissipation	2W
Operating Temperature range	65°C 150°C	Dependent on the thermal environment	≃ 70°C
Max. collector emitter Saturation voltage $V_{CE(sat.)}$ at I_C = 4.0A I_B = 0.5A	0.5V	These parameters control overall device dissipation, and are used to derive optimum drive conditions	
Max. Base emitter saturation voltage. $V_{BE(sat.)}$ I_C = 4.0A I_B = 0.5A	1.5V		
Collector current full time, t_f at I_C = 4.0A I_B = 0.5A	0.5 μs typical		

Using a Darlington Output Device

General: As seen from Figure 1, the driven transformer is normally connected so that the output stage is driven in antiphase with the driver. The mark/space on the output of the control i.c. is arranged with this in mind. Account is also taken of the storage times of the driver and horizontal output stages, as mentioned and shown in Figure 2. It can be seen that with a 64μs period, and a mark space nominally 28:36, the efficiency time is of the order 13μs, and the transistor forward conduction time of the order 39μs. The use of a direct drive Darlington output stage –as in Figure 5, results in a shortening of the output stage storage time. If the mark space of 28:36 is maintained, then the efficiency time is increased. This can lead to irregularities in the scan waveform, because the efficiency diode stops conducting before the output transistor is turned 'on' (this shows as bars on the picture tube). The situation is resolved by altering the mark space ratio. Typical waveforms for a direct drive Darlington output stage are shown in Figure 6. These show that an alteration of the mark space ratio to 24:40 compensates for the shorter storage time of the Darlington transistor. The shorter storage time is a direct result of the tran¬istor configuration, the output device saturation voltage being limited by the driver device in the Darlington. Consequently the collector emitter saturation voltage ($V_{CE(sat)}$) is higher, but is also less susceptible to production spread than a discrete output transistor.

Base Drive: The driver transistor operating conditions for the Darlington also differ from those of the transformer coupled driver, in that the peak current required to turn 'off' the Darlington is taken directly by the driver, i.e. the turn 'off' current is not reduced by the turns ratio of a

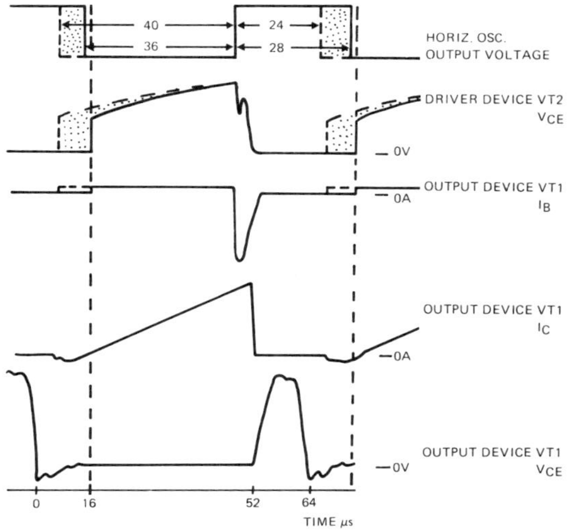

FIGURE 6. Waveforms for a Direct Drive Darlington Output Stage

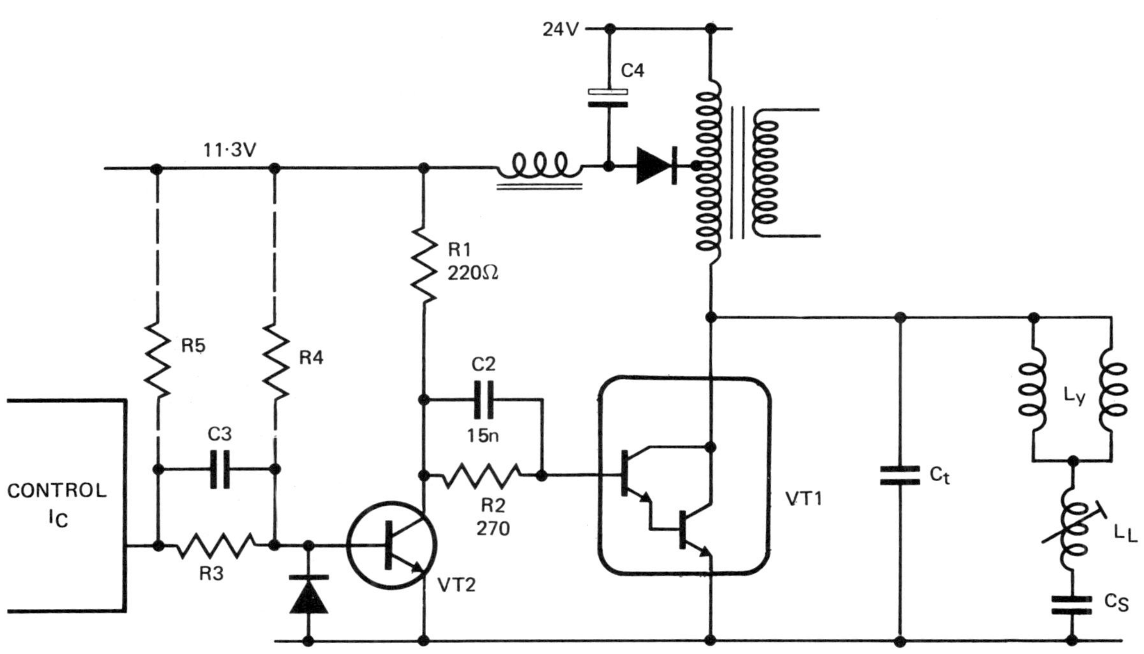

FIGURE 5. Direct Drive Darlington Output Stage

transformer. The driver transistor thus needs to have a high current gain at around 400-600mA collector current, when used in a portable t.v. where the horizontal output device reaches 4A peak collector current. The mean dissipation in the driver device need not be higher than in a transformer coupled circuit, however, as the collector current for the remainder of the conduction time is low – of the order 50mA – depending on the value of the collector series resistor (R1). Fast switching of the driver transistor at turn 'on' will not necessarily give optimum performance as peak current will increase with switching speed –and the resulting faster switching of the Darlington output device could cause unwanted radiation.

In the circuit shown in Figure 5, resistors R1 and R2 fix the end value of base current, $I_{B(end)}$, for a BU180 Darlington device to 20mA at low supply voltage (10.4V). Capacitor C2 ensures that the stored charge is extracted from it at turn 'off' and maintains a negative bias during the flyback time.

Driver Device Specification: A suitable driver device is:

BFT84		min	max
h_{FE}	@ I_C = 100mA, V_{CE} = 10V	100	
Max peak I_C	@ 25°C		2A
$V_{CE(sat)}$	@ I_C = 500mA, I_C/I_B = 10		500mV

Interfacing with the Control I.C.:

(a) Using the SN76544 Line and Frame Processor.

The output stage of the '544 is a totem pole, with a nominal 220Ω resistor in series with the upper transistor. Maximum peak current is 50mA which is sufficient to drive the BFT84. Use of resistor R4 (10kΩ) ensures that the driver device is held 'on' when the horizontal oscillator is 'off'. This is particularly important at start up, as otherwise the output stage may turn 'on' and 'latch-up' the power supply, so preventing the horizontal oscillator from starting. Capacitor C3 (15nF) across the series limiting resistor R3 (220Ω) provides positive and negative base current to the drive device at switch 'on' and switch 'off' respectively. The diode D3 across the base emitter of the driver transistor prevents the BV_{EBO} of the device being exceeded.

Alteration of the horizontal oscillator mark/space ratio is accomplished by putting a 10kΩ resistor from pin 5 of the i.c. to ground. Figure 7 shows waveforms obtained in the circuit. Operation of the driver stage from the boosted supply rail (24V) can be accommodated by changing some component values, i.e. R1 to 680Ω, 1W; R2 to 330Ω and R4 to 27kΩ. The principle of operation remains the same.

(b) Using the SN76545 Line and Frame Processor.

The '545 differs from the '544 in that there is no active pull-up on the output. The speed up capacitor C3 (now 3n3F) assists in turning 'on' the driver transistor, resistors R5 (1kΩ) and R3 (now 1k2Ω) providing sufficient base current to saturate the BFT84 during the remainder of the driver 'on' time. The 50mA maximum current capability of the '545 output stage is sufficient to turn 'off' the driver stage. As with the '544, altering the output mark/space ratio compensates for the shorter storage time of the output stage, eliminating discontinuities in the scan waveform caused by the lengthened efficiency time.

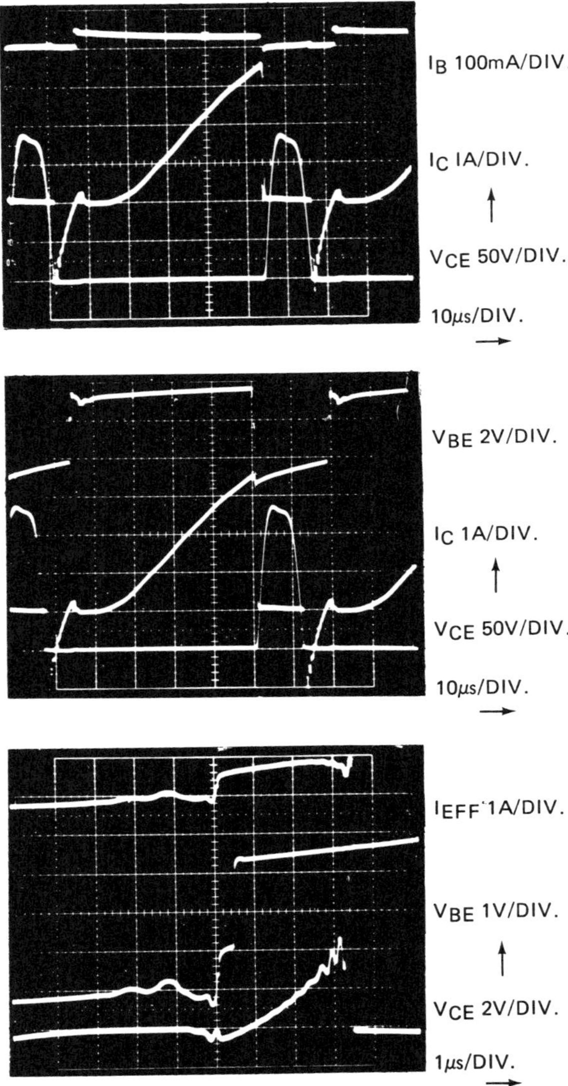

FIGURE 7. Output Stage Waveforms (Using Darlington Device)

(c) Using the SN76920 Line Oscillator Combination.

The SN76920 has a totempole output stage, a protection diode being in series with the lower half. This indicates that capacitive coupling to the driver stage is needed in order to switch 'off' the driver transistor. The capacitor C3 (here 330pF) also provides an initial current pulse required to turn 'on' the driver (this being a more important parameter than turn 'off' of the driver). Resistor R3 (here 1k2Ω) provides sufficient current to saturate the driver transistor for the remainder of the 'on' time. Peak current from the SN76920 is kept well below the maximum rated 200mA. The '920 circuit compensates automatically for pulse width variation, the rising edge of the output pulse occurring approximately 2.0μs after the end of the shaped flyback pulse. This removes the problem with scan irregularities due to the shorter storage time of the output stage.

Self Driving Horizontal Output Stages: Some recent developments have favoured elimination of the driver transformer by deriving base current for the output stage from the line output transformer (by scan rectification), as shown in Figure 8. In a similar manner to the advantages offered in power supply circuits, the use of a Darlington output stage could offer some distinct advantages over a single transistor, i.e.

(a) The base current requirement is lower and so the power loss in the limiting resistor (R1) will be less.

(b) During the storage time of the output stage, the driver stage must take the full base drive current as well as the turn 'off' current ($I_{B(end)} + I_{B(off)}$). The driver transistor current handling and gain requirements are consequently lower when a Darlington output stage is used.

(c) The scan rectified base current to the output stage is available immediately following flyback, so the output stage conduction times do not cause any problems.

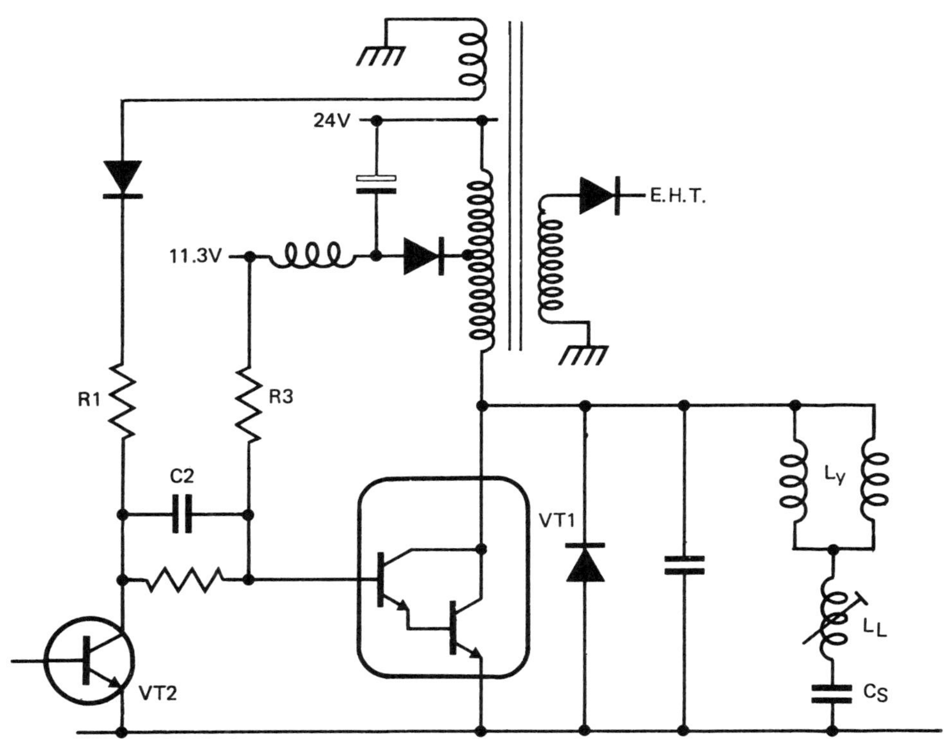

FIGURE 8. Self Driving Horizontal Output Stage

OTHER CIRCUIT CONSIDERATIONS

Picture Tube Flashover

High voltage transistors used in deflection applications must be sufficiently robust to withstand transient power dissipation under fault conditions many times more severe than experienced under normal operation. Picture tube flashover causes a severe loading of the e.h.t. transformer. This can cause saturation of the transformer core, resulting in the deflection device passing collector current limited only by its current gain (h_{FE}) at the supply voltage and the base drive. (Tube flashover was simulated by the use of test equipment which had facilities for selecting the instant of flashover, and for triggering an oscilloscope used to record the relevant waveforms. The flashover simulation was believed to be accurate – certainly over the period when the e.h.t. supply was recovering, and when the transistor is most heavily loaded. Worst case device dissipation occurred when flashover was initiated at the end of the scan period). Figures 9, 10 and 11 show collector current and voltage waveforms of the scan periods immediately following flashover. The collector current reached peak values approaching 10A during the third and fourth cycles, and the collector voltage reached a peak of 260V on the third cycle. Under such conditions one might expect reverse second breakdown to occur when the device is turned 'off'. Use of the 'multiply' facility on a Philips PM3253 oscilloscope enabled peak power (I_C x V_{CE}) to be estimated, (Figures 12 and 13). Peak power was found to be as high as 300W, during the third and fourth cycles following flashover, for a high gain unit. Low gain units exhibited lower peak powers under flashover, since the peak current was gain limited. Figures 14 and 15 show peak power measurements made under normal running conditions for comparison purposes.

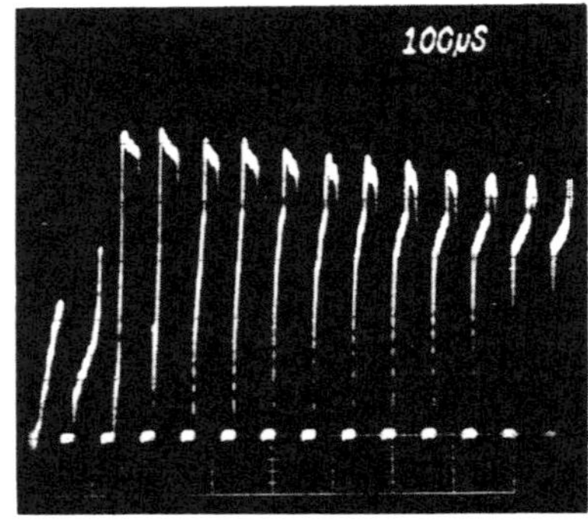

FIGURE 9. Collector Current at Flashover

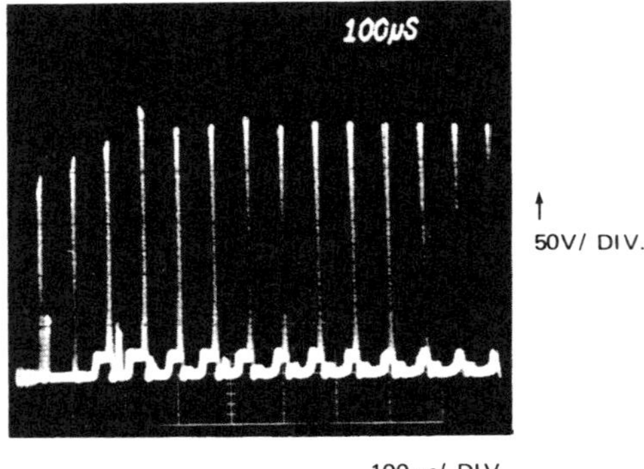

FIGURE 10. Collector Emitter Voltage at Flashover

Thermal Considerations

For long-term reliability of semiconductor devices the thermal environment in which the device is used must be considered. Adequate heat sink area and ventilation must be provided to maintain the device junction temperature below the maximum rated value, even under worst case operating conditions. Devices such as the BU124, although in a plastic T03 package, have a $\theta_{C\text{-}A}$ in free air of 39°C/W, because a nickel plated copper mounting base is used in their construction. A typical value of $T_{ambient}$ inside a portable t.v. set is 65°C – this of course being dependent on the set design. If no heat sink were available, these factors would indicate a case temperature of 143°C at 2W dissipation. For reliable operation in this application a heat sink is required and the case temperature not allowed to rise above 120°C in worst case operating conditions. A heat sink design chart is shown in Figure 16.

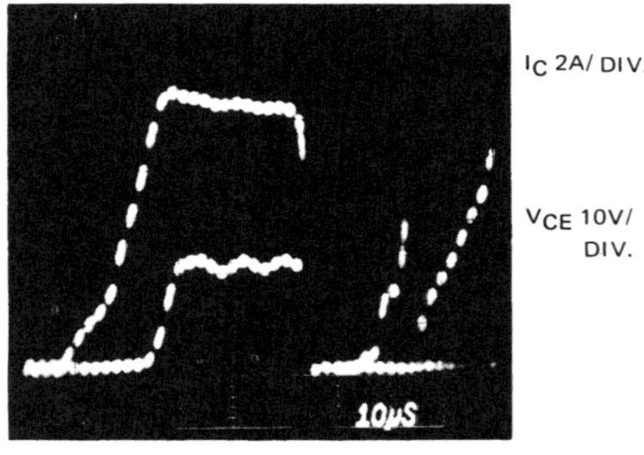

FIGURE 11. Simultaneous Voltage and Current Waveforms at Flashover

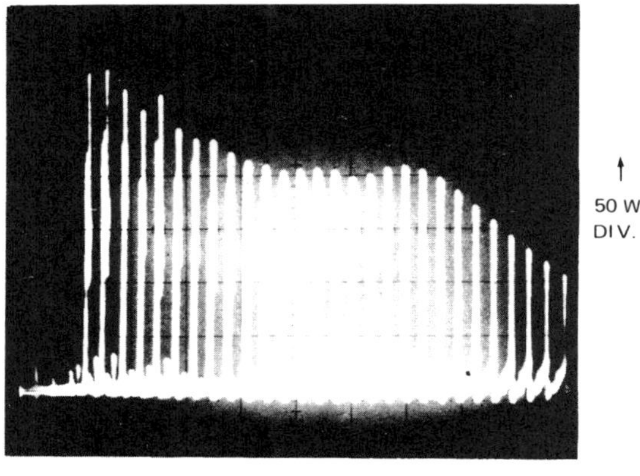

FIGURE 12. Power Dissipation of a High Gain Unit under Flashover

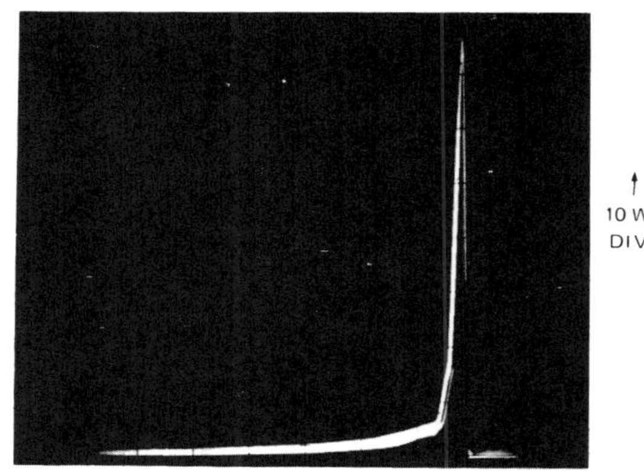

FIGURE 15. Power Dissipation of a Low Gain Unit under Normal Operation

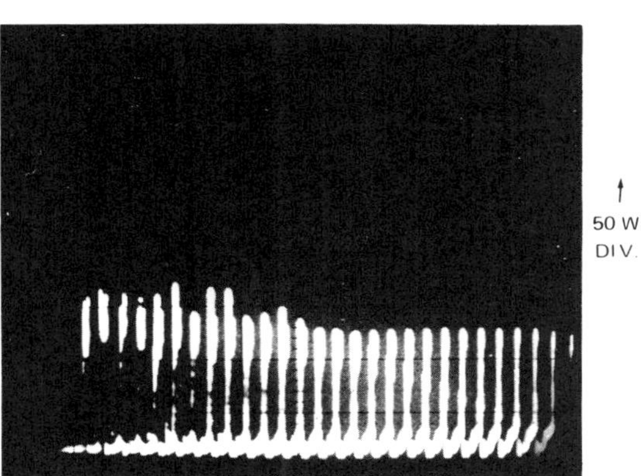

FIGURE 13. Power Dissipation of a Low Gain Unit under Flashover

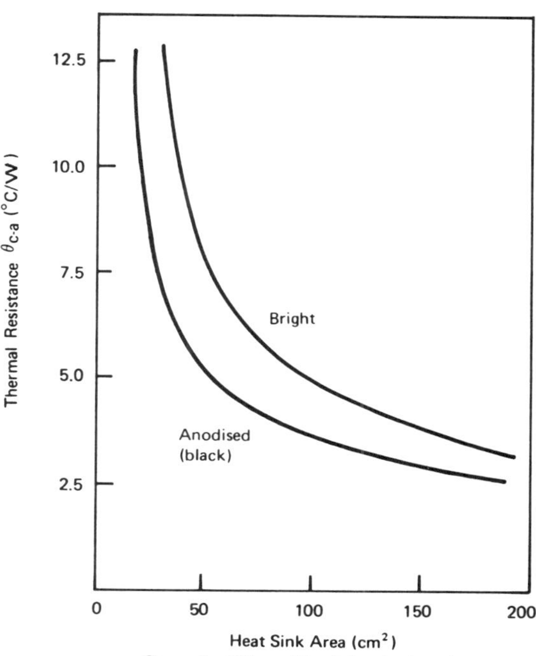

FIGURE 16. Heat Sink Design Chart.

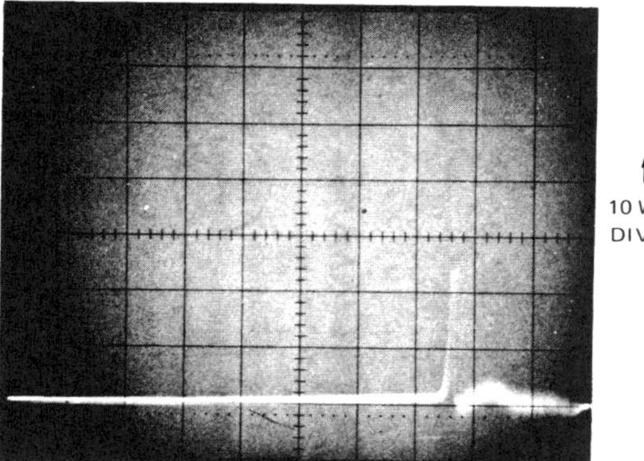

FIGURE 14. Power Dissipation of a High Gain Unit under Normal Operation

REFERENCES

1. M. Maytum and T. Lear *Driver Circuit Design Considerations for High Voltage Line Scan Transistors,* I.E.E.E. Transactions May '73, Volume BTR-19, Number 2.
2. Applications Laboratory Staff of Texas Instruments Incorporated, *Electronic Power Control and Digital Techniques,* McGraw-Hill Book Company, New York, 1976, pp. 23-34.

VII VERTICAL DEFLECTION SYSTEMS USING INTEGRATED CIRCUITS

By
Jonathan A. Dell

The generation of a raster on an electromagnetically deflected cathode-ray tube is achieved by driving the deflector coils with current waveforms of sawtooth shape, where the Frame scan circuit is responsible for the vertical component of deflection.

Formerly valves have been extensively used for this circuit, often with transformer coupling between the valve and the deflector coils.

More recently, push-pull transistor amplifiers, capable of driving the coils directly, have been introduced with consequent saving of a transformer but with increased circuit complexity and cost.

Integrated circuits designed for Audio amplifier applications and capable of handling sufficient voltage and current for direct drive may be used. The transformerless circuits, which are described in this chapter, offer the advantages of transistor circuits and also greater simplicity and reduced cost.

Before the configurations of practical circuits are described, a detailed analysis of the signals which must be generated at the deflector coils is provided.

DRIVE REQUIREMENTS

First considerations must determine the drive requirements of the deflection assembly, the characteristics of some typical systems are shown in Table 1. These characteristics are for parallel connected frame coils.

Table 1

System	13 Inch, 90° Colour	20 Inch, 110° Monochrome
Deflection assembly type	Integral	AT 1040
Manufacturer	Mitsubishi Diatron SSS ITC-370BHB22	Phillips
Frame coil resistance	12.0Ω	7.5Ω ± 8%
Frame coil inductance	22.5mH	16mH ± 10%
Peak-to-peak frame scan current	0.9A	1.1A ± 5%

The general shape of the current and voltage waveforms developed at the deflector coils is shown in Figure 1(a), (b), (c), and (d) and the equivalent circuit for the deflector coils is shown in Figure 2.

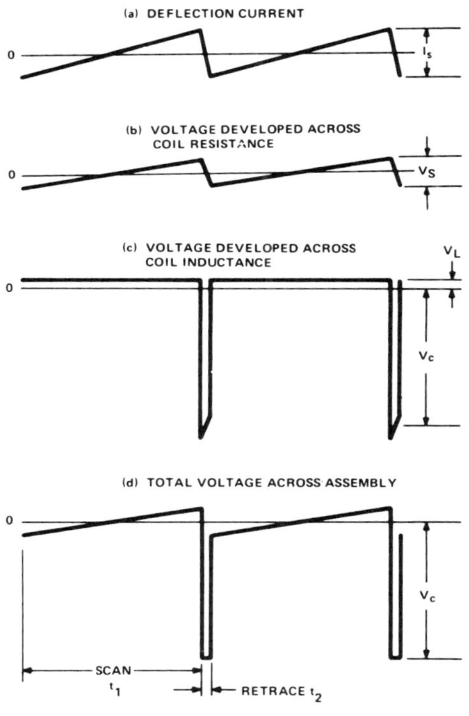

FIGURE 1. Current and Voltage Waveforms Developed at Deflector Coils

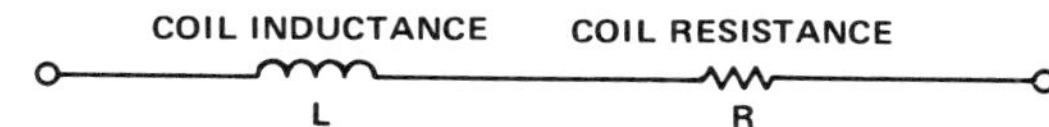

FIGURE 2. Equivalent Circuit of Deflection Assembly

The voltage, V_S, developed across the coils during the scan period, t_1, is due to the scan current flowing in the coil resistance; a small voltage developed across the inductor due to the changing current can be neglected.

$$V_S = I_S . R \tag{1}$$

R = coil resistance

I_S = peak-to-peak scan current

During flyback, the current in the deflector coils is required to return to its initial value in a time, t_2. For this to happen, the total change in flux density during the two parts of the cycle must be equal. As the flux density change is related to the volt-time product for the inductor, this parameter, equivalent to the area on either side of the x-axis in Figure 1(c), can be equated for the two parts of the cycle.

The deflector coil drive circuits, discussed later in this report, are so arranged that during flyback, the voltage across the assembly is limited by a clamping voltage, V_C.

To establish the voltage which can be developed across the inductor during flyback, it is necessary to take into account the effect of the coil resistance, because current is still flowing through it during this time. Thus, at any instant, the maximum voltage, v, across the inductor can only be the clamping voltage, V_C, plus the instantaneous voltage across the resistance, v_s.

$$v = V_C + v_s$$

The current is assumed to change linearly with time during flyback, as the coil time constant, L/R, is sufficiently greater than the flyback time.

An equation defining v_s can now be written:

$$v_s = V_S\left(\frac{1}{2} - \frac{t}{t_2}\right)$$

where t can have values between 0 and t_2

$$\therefore v = V_C + V_S\left(\frac{1}{2} - \frac{t}{t_2}\right)$$

Thus the area A_2 under the x-axis in Figure 1(c) is:

$$A_2 = \int_0^{t_2} v.dt$$

$$= \int_0^{t_2} V_C + V_S\left(\frac{1}{2} - \frac{t}{t_2}\right).dt$$

$$= \int_0^{t_2} V_C + \frac{V_S}{2} - \frac{V_S.t}{t_2}.dt$$

$$= \left[V_C.t + \frac{V_S.t}{2} - \frac{V_S.t^2}{2t_2}\right]_0^{t_2}$$

$$= V_C.t_2 + \frac{V_S.t_2}{2} - \frac{V_S.t_2}{2}$$

$$A_2 = V_C.t_2 \qquad (2)$$

During the scan period, t_1, the voltage, V_L, across the inductor is constant as the rate of change of current is linear.

$$V_L = L.\frac{di}{dt}$$

where

$$\frac{di}{dt} = \frac{I_S}{t_1}$$

So the area A_1 above the x-axis in Figure 1(c), is simply

$$A_1 = V_L.t_1 \qquad (3)$$

$$= L.\left(\frac{di}{dt}\right).t_1 = L.\left(\frac{I_S}{t_1}\right).t_1$$

$$= L.I_S$$

Equating (2) and (3), the flyback time, t_2, can be found.

$$A_1 = A_2$$

$$L.I_S = V_C.t_2$$

$$t_2 = \frac{L.I_S}{V_C}$$

Calculations of the scan voltage, current and flyback time, taking into account the deflector coil tolerances, are shown in Appendices A and B In these calculations, the European 625 line standard scan and retrace times, of 19 ms and 1 ms, respectively, are used. It is a simple matter to use other standards when these apply.

CIRCUIT DESCRIPTION

General

A basic configuration using the operational amplifier to provide current drive to the deflection assembly is shown in Figure 3.

A sawtooth signal is applied to the non inverting input of the amplifier and current from the output of the amplifier flows through the deflector coils and the current monitoring resistor, R1, to ground.

The voltage developed across this resistor is fed back to the inverting input of the amplifier. The high gain of the amplifier maintains a very small differential voltage between its inputs ensuring that the output current is a direct function of the input signal.

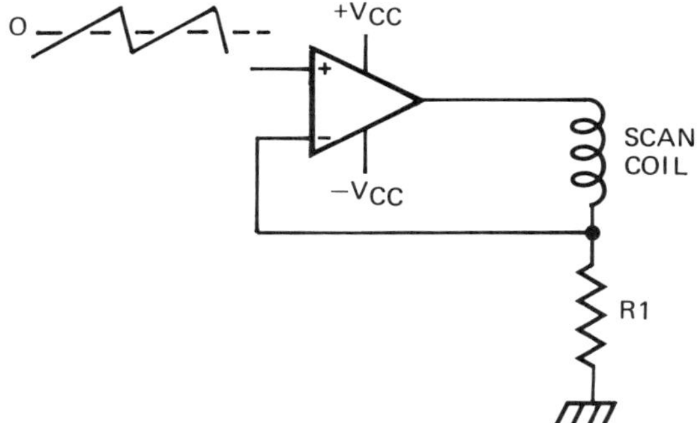

FIGURE 3. Operational Amplifier

In an alternative system often referred to as voltage drive, the feedback signal is taken directly from the deflection coils, the resistance of which now monitors the current. Although this eliminates the need for R1 and is capable of driving deflector coils with a large parallel capacity, a thermistor must be included to compensate thermal changes in the deflector coil resistance.

The current drive approach is therefore preferred.

Figure 1(d) shows that the voltage at the output of the amplifier in Figure 3 is required to swing up to $+V_S/2$ and down to V_C. To accommodate this, the positive and negative power supplies must slightly exceed these values.

$$+V_{CC} > V_S/2$$
$$V_{CC} > V_C$$

A more economical method is to ac couple the output of the amplifier to the deflector coils as shown in Figure 4, so that a single-ended power supply can be used.

The mean voltage, V_M, at the output of the amplifier must now be set to V_C [see Figure 1(d)] so that the voltage swing can be accommodated.

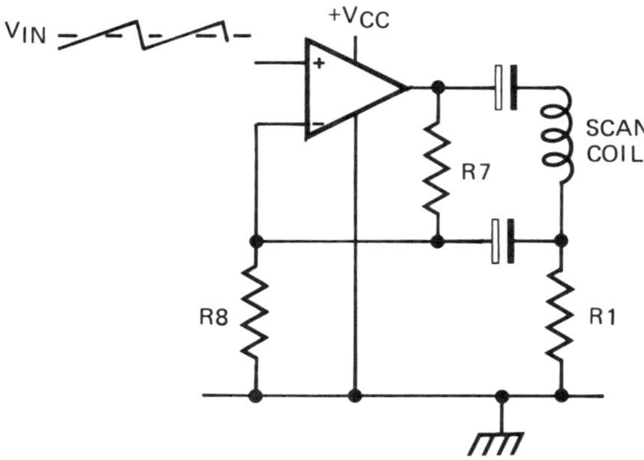

FIGURE 4. Operational Amplifier – AC Coupled Output to Deflector Coils

A more detailed study of the output voltage swing, shown in Figure 6, indicates that the maximum value of V_M is determined by the equation:

$$V_M \leqslant V_{CC} - \frac{V_S}{2} - V_b \qquad (5)$$

If R8 (Figure 4) is omitted, the mean output voltage follows the mean input voltage. If an offset is required, R8 is introduced. The voltages are then related by the equation:

$$\frac{R8}{R7 + R8} V_{out(mean)} = V_{in(mean)} \qquad (6)$$

Power Dissipation

Before further sections of the circuit are discussed, it is necessary to evaluate the power dissipation in the integrated amplifier. This can easily be derived from a knowledge of the voltage and current waveforms.

The output circuit of the amplifier, in simplified form, is shown in Figure 5 and an expanded diagram of the output voltage, current and power dissipation is shown in Figure 6. The key to the abbreviations on this diagram are shown below:

V_M = mean output voltage
V_S = peak-to-peak scan voltage
I_S = peak-to-peak scan current
V_{CC} = supply voltage
V_a = limiting voltage during flyback
V_b = end of Scan voltage for top transistor

During the first part of the scan cycle (A to B in Figure 6), the bottom output transistor VT3 is conducting and the power dissipated in it during this part of the cycle is given by:

$$P_1 = \frac{I_S}{4} \cdot \left(V_M - \frac{V_S}{3}\right) \qquad (7)$$

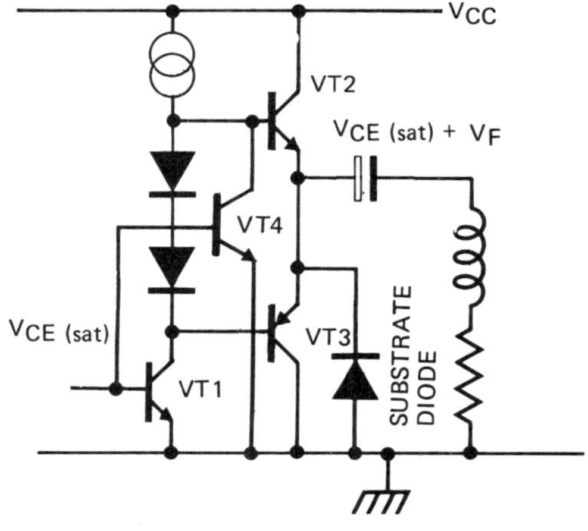

FIGURE 5. Amplifier Output Circuit

The power dissipation during the second part of the scan cycle (B to C in Figure 6), while the top output transistor VT2 is conducting, is given by:

$$P_2 = \frac{I_S}{4}\left(V_{CC} - V_M - \frac{V_S}{3}\right) \qquad (8)$$

At the start of flyback (C) the driver transistor VT1, and clamp transistor VT4, are turned hard 'on'. The voltage at the base of transistor VT2 is held at $V_{CE(sat)}$ above ground. Current must still flow into the deflector coil, however, so the voltage at the emitter of transistor VT2 falls (CD) until the output can source current once again. This occurs when the voltage reaches $-V_F$ i.e. when the substrate diode comes into conduction. So, for the first part of the flyback cycle, (DE), the substrate diode still carries current, as shown in Figure 6. The power dissipation during this part of the cycle is negligible.

Power dissipated in the second half of flyback is very small and can be neglected.

Appendix C shows the derivation of Equations (7)

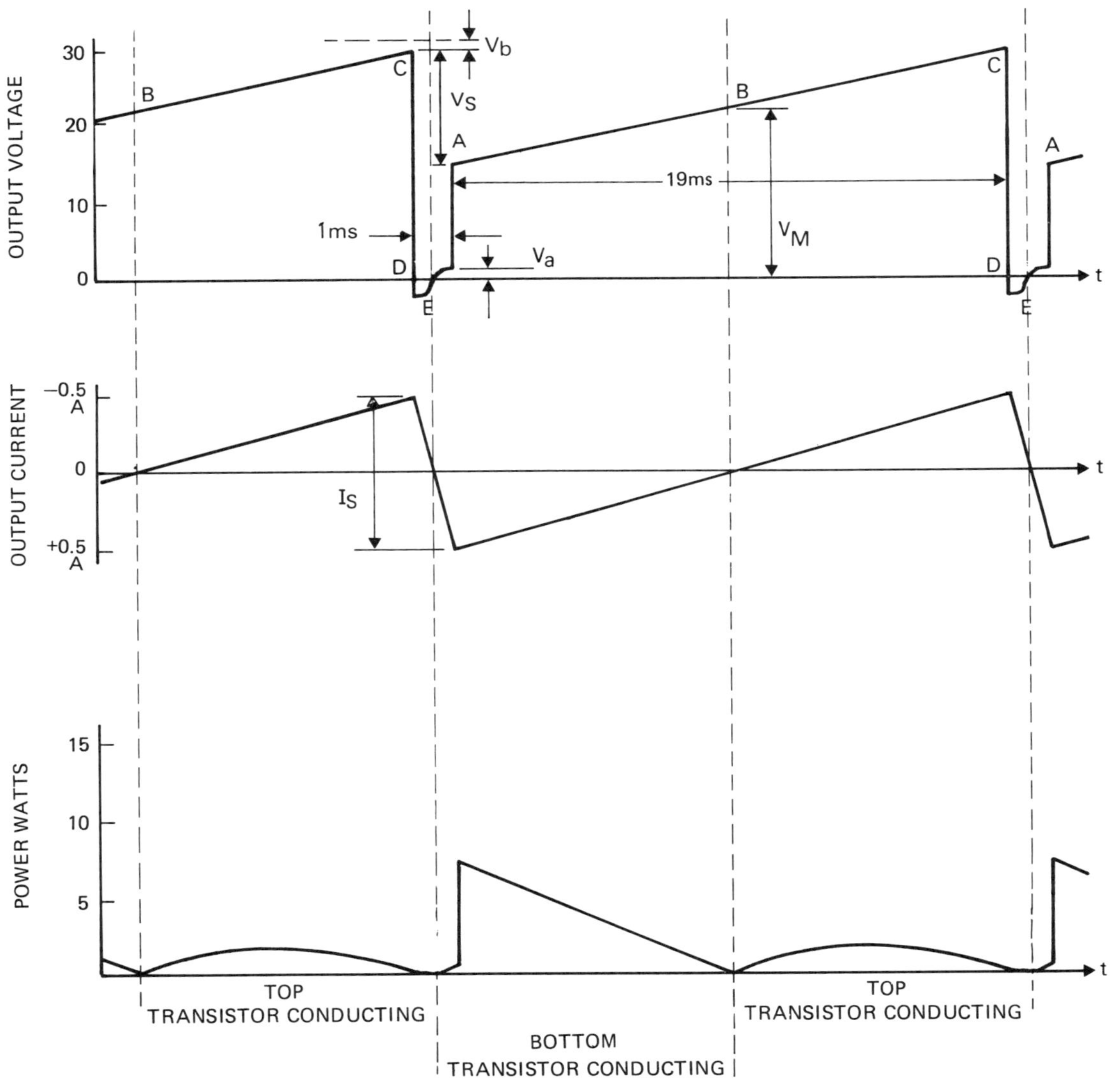

FIGURE 6. Idealised Output Waveforms and Power Dissipation

and (8). The average power dissipation over the whole cycle can be calculated from P_1, and P_2.

$$P = (P_1 + P_2)\ 9.5/20 \qquad (10)$$

The power calculations for the two practical circuits are shown in Appendices A and B and it should be noted that two components contribute to the peak-to-peak scan voltage, V_S. One component is the voltage developed across the scan coils, V_S, the other is the voltage developed across the current monitoring resistor, R1.

When the power dissipation has been calculated, a check should be made to see that the integrated amplifier can withstand the dissipation over the required operating temperature range. The calculations relevant to this consideration are also shown in Appendices A and B.

Input Waveform Generation

In the preceding circuit discussion, the availability of a suitable sawtooth drive waveform has been assumed. Generation of this signal can be achieved by one of two methods: the simple integrator (Figure 7) and the Miller integrator (Figure 8). The former was chosen as it leads to greater simplicity and simpler waveform correction circuitry. It also gives greater immunity to spurious pulses, which helps to maintain good interlace.

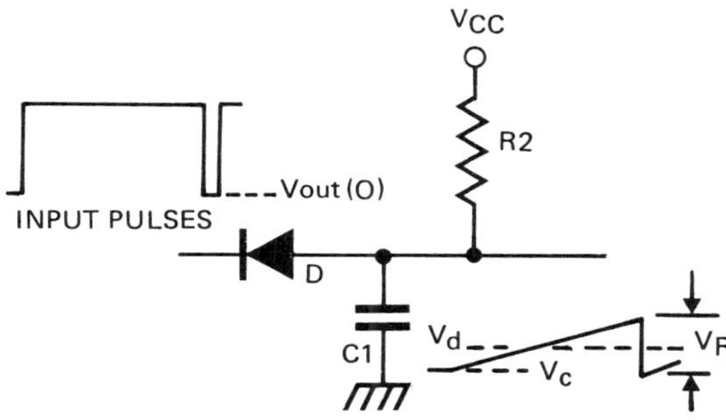

FIGURE 7. Simple Integrator

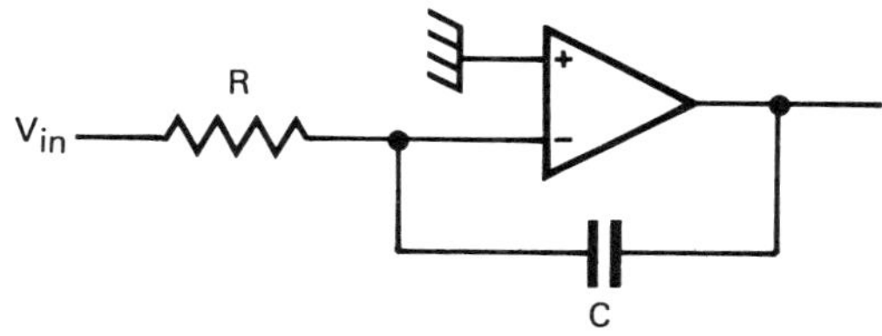

FIGURE 8. Miller Integrator

The pulses initiated during the flyback period can be generated by a separate oscillator or directly by a sync processing integrated circuit, such as the SN76544.

During the scan period, the capacitor is charged by the resistor R2 and during the flyback period, the capacitor is discharged through the diode, D. If the voltage to which the capacitor charges during the scan, V_R, is small compared with V_{CC}, the ramp generated will be reasonably linear.

The finite forward voltage, V_F, of the diode D, together with the fact that the clamping pulse may not go down to zero, means that the ramp will be clamped to a voltage:

$$V_c = V_F + V_{out(0)}$$

and thus the mean level of the signal will be offset by this amount:

$$V_d = \frac{V_R}{2} + V_F + V_{out(0)}$$

S-Correction

To achieve picture linearity when high deflection angles are used, it is necessary to drive the scan coil, with a nonlinear current waveform. If the amplifier is driven with the appropriate input waveform, the current in the deflector coils will follow. The development of this waveform is achieved by the network, consisting of R2, R3, R4, C1, and C2 (Figure 9). The associated waveforms are shown in Figure 10.

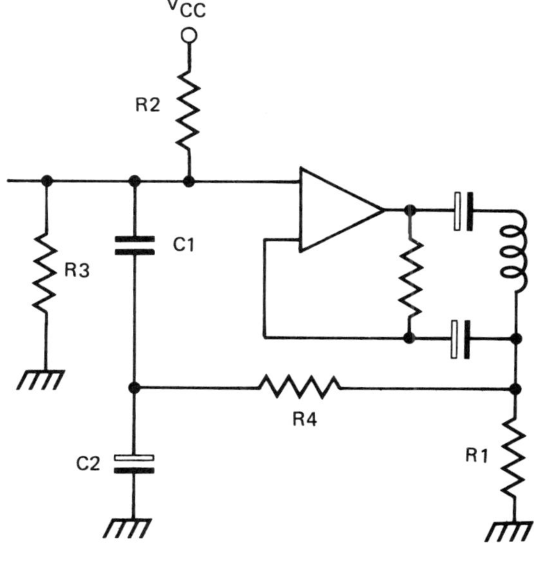

FIGURE 9. Waveform Network

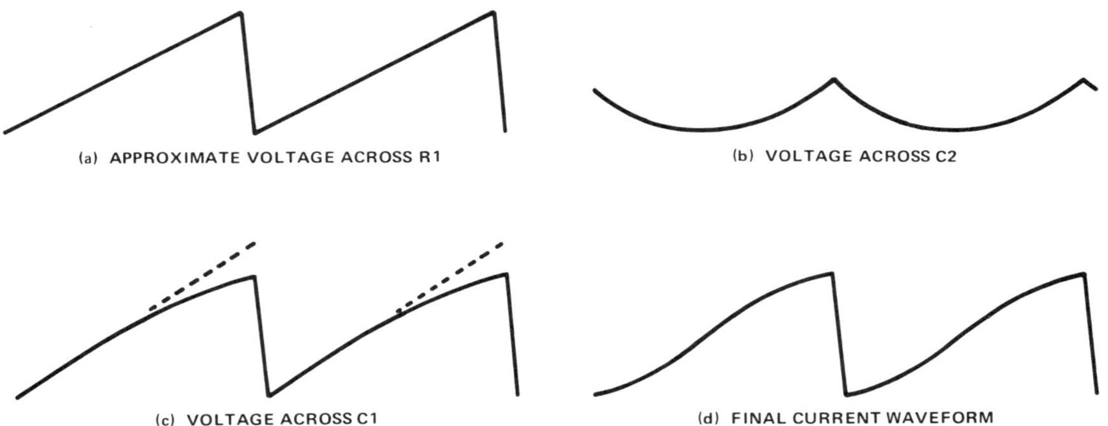

FIGURE 10. Associated Waveforms of Network

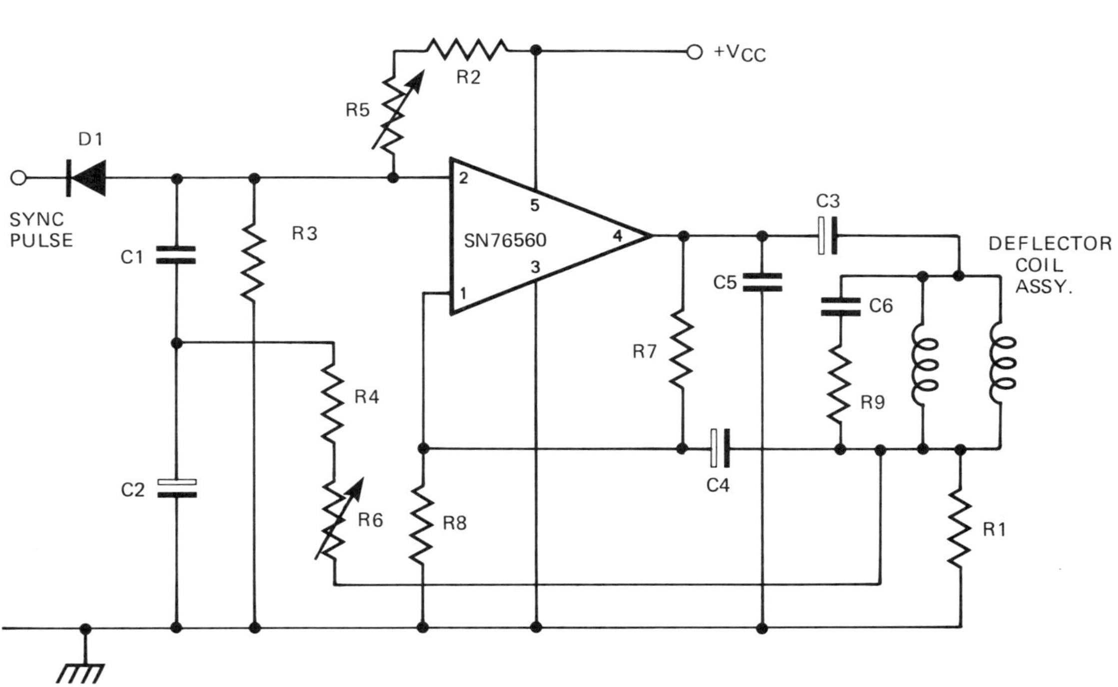

FIGURE 11. Complete Frame Output Stage

The sawtooth signal, Figure 10(a), developed across the current monitoring resistor R1, charges C2 through R4, generating a waveform of parabolic shape, shown at Figure 10(b).

The sum of the ramp signal developed across C1, Figure 10(c), and the parabolic signal is applied to the amplifier input. The value of C1 is made much smaller than C2 so that the charging current in C1 does not significantly contribute to the charging of C2. The resulting ramp gradient is reduced at the beginning of scan and increased at the end.

As the ramp gradient has to be reduced at both ends of scan, further shaping of the input signal is required. A resistor, R3, is connected in parallel with the capacitors, effectively reducing the aiming voltage of the ramp generating network, so that towards the end of scan the charging rate is reduced. This effect is shown at Figure 10(c), and now the sum of this signal and the parabolic waveform yield the required S-shape, Figure 10(d).

PRACTICAL CIRCUITS

The circuit principles discussed can be combined into a practical deflection system. Two circuits, aimed at the requirements of 20-inch 110° monochrome and 12-inch 90° colour tubes are discussed.

Figure 11 shows the circuit diagram of a complete frame output stage. The component values are chosen according to the application, Table 2 listing these for the monochrome deflection system and Table 3 for the colour system. The component layout is not critical except for the capacitor C5 (330nF) which must be placed as close to the integrated circuit as possible. This capacitor ensures stability of the composite pnp output transistor. It is also recommended, to avoid stray feedback, that the wiring is kept as short as possible and that a low inductance ground track is provided. A satisfactory printed circuit layout is shown in Figure 12. The damping components C6 and R9 prevent overshoot at the amplifier output at the start of scan and reduce the amplitude of line flyback ripple injection. The supply voltage, V_{CC}, should come directly from a decoupling capacitor, which is usually between 100μF and 1000μF depending on the source and degree of decoupling required. The circuit was designed to operate from the negative going sync pulses provided by an SN 76544, line and frame processing integrated circuit.* The flyback time is controlled primarily by the output stage, but it can be influenced by the width of the sync pulse if this is longer than about 800ns.

Table 2

R1	1Ω
R2	100kΩ
R3	47kΩ
R4	120Ω
R5	470kΩ
R6	470Ω
R7	27kΩ
R8	3.3kΩ
R9	1kΩ
C1	330nF
C2	33μF
C3	100μF
C4	47μF
C5	330nF
C6	330nF
D1	1S44
V_{CC}	26.5V to 29V

Table 3

R1	1Ω
R2	270kΩ
R3	56kΩ
R4	120Ω
R5	470kΩ
R6	470Ω
R7	39kΩ
R8	3.6kΩ
R9	1.8kΩ
C1	330nF
C2	47μF
C3	1000μF
C4	47μF
C5	330nF
C6	330nF
D1	1S44
V_{CC}	29.5V to 32V

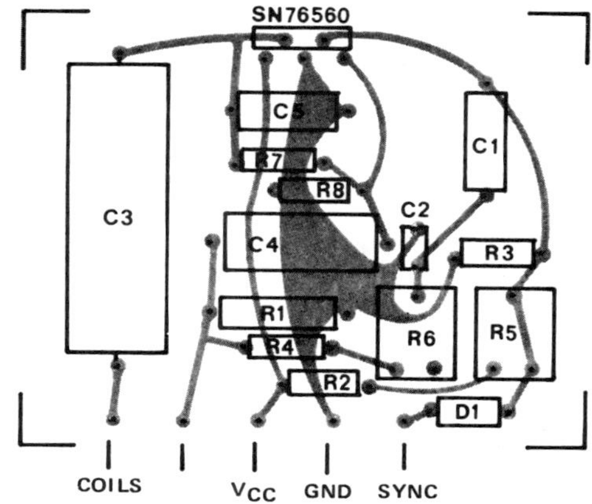

FIGURE 12. Printed Circuit and Layout

Appendices A and B show in detail the calculations relating to the two systems. For a complete analysis the deflector coil tolerances must be taken into account. Figure 13 shows a set of oscillographs of typical voltage waveforms at various points in a circuit driving the monochrome scan coils (AT1040).

The junction temperature of the device must not exceed 150°C so an adequate heatsink must be provided. It is recommended that the heatsink thermal resistance (Θ_{CA}) is low enough to maintain the junction temperature below 120°C to give an adequate design margin and extend the operating life of the device.

*With alternative source $V_{out(O)}$ should not be less than 1V

CONCLUSION

Use of integrated circuits for the frame deflection function can lead to a simple circuit design with considerable cost saving over a discrete system. The high gain of the integrated amplifiers ensures a large degree of feedback to stabilize the performance of the system against variations in the amplifier and deflector coil parameters.

Although the practical circuits have been designed for a specific application, they can easily be altered for other requirements.

The internal power dissipation for the clamped flyback technique is high, but the devices run well within their limiting conditions.

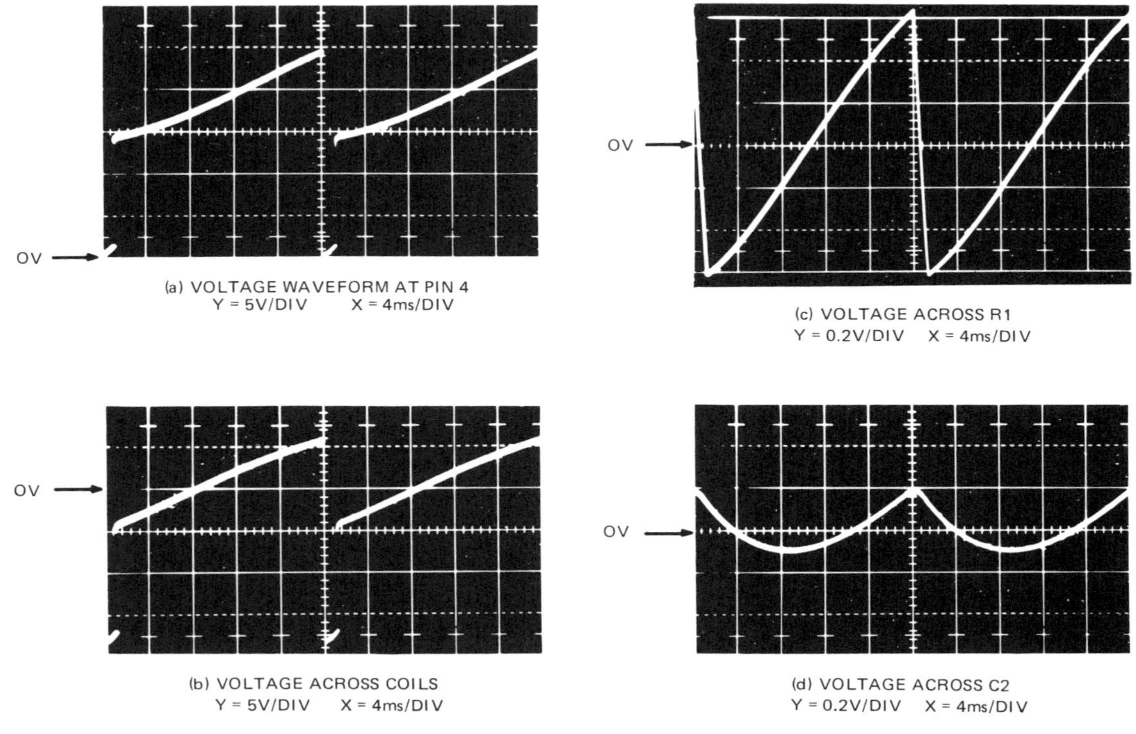

(a) VOLTAGE WAVEFORM AT PIN 4
Y = 5V/DIV X = 4ms/DIV

(c) VOLTAGE ACROSS R1
Y = 0.2V/DIV X = 4ms/DIV

(b) VOLTAGE ACROSS COILS
Y = 5V/DIV X = 4ms/DIV

(d) VOLTAGE ACROSS C2
Y = 0.2V/DIV X = 4ms/DIV

FIGURE 13. Typical Voltage Waveforms

APPENDIX A

CALCULATION ON MONOCHROME DEFLECTION SYSTEM

Effect of tolerance on values of resistance inductance and current given in Table I	$R_{max} (R_{nom} + 8\%) = 7.5 + \frac{7.5 \times 8}{100}$ $= 8.1\ \Omega$ $L_{max} (L_{nom} + 10\%) = 16 + \frac{16 \times 10}{100}$ $= 17.6$ mH	$R_{min} (R_{nom} - 8\%) = 7.5 - \frac{7.5 \times 8.}{100}$ $= 6.9\ \Omega$ $L_{min} (R_{nom} - 10\%) = 16 - \frac{16 \times 10}{100}$ $= 14.4$ mH
*$I_{S\ min}$ and R_{max} are associated as the 'Ampere-turns' for deflection will be roughly constant	*$I_{S\ min} (I_{nom} - 5\%) = 1.1 - \frac{1.1 \times 5}{100}$ $= 1.045$ A	$I_{S\ max} (I_{nom} + 5\%) = 1.1 + \frac{1.1 \times 5}{100}$ $= 1.155$ A
Scan voltage $V_S = I_S R$ . . . . (1)	$R_{max} \times I_{S\ min} = 8.46$ V	$R_{min} \times I_{S\ max} = 7.96$ V
Voltage developed across current monitoring resistor R1 (1 Ω)	$R1 \times I_{S\ min} = 1.045$ V	$R1 \times I_{S\ max} = 1.155$ V
Total scan voltage V_S'	8.46 + 1.045 = 9.505 V	7.96 + 1.155 = 9.115 V

For a flyback time of 1ms $V_M = L.I_S/t_2 + V_a$ ....from (4) $V_a = 1.2$ V	1.2 + 17.6 x 1.045/1 = 19.6 V	1.2 + 14.4 x 1.155/1 = 17.8 V
Mean output voltage set to	19.6 V	
$V_b = V_{CE(sat)}$ for top output transistor at $I_C = 0.55A$	2 V	2 V
To accommodate scan, V_{CC} must exceed $V_M + V_s/2 + V_b$ ....from (5)	19.6 + 9.505/2 + 2 = 26.35 V	19.6 + 9.115/2 + 2 = 26.17 V
Minimum V_{CC}	26.5 V	26.5 V
V_{CC} (max) = V_{CC} (min) + 10%	29 V	29 V
To calculate power dissipation $P_1 = I_S (V_M - V_{S/3})/4$....(7)	1.045 (19.6 – 9.505/3)/4 = 4.29 W	1.155 (19.6 – 9.115/3)/4 = 4.78 W
$P_2 = I_S (V_{CC(max)} - V_M - V_{S/3})/4$ ....(8)	1.045(29 – 19.6 – 9505/3)/4 = 1.63 W	1.155 (29 – 19.6 – 9.115/3)/4 = 1.84 W
Total Power $P = (P_1 + P_2) \times 9.5/20$ ....(10)	(4.29 + 1.63)9.5/20 + 7.26 x 0.5/20 = 2.81W	(4.78 + 1.84)9.5/20 + 8.03 x 0.5/20 = 3.14W

Heat sinking

The maximum θ_{JC} for the SN76560 is 6°C/W. Therefore, for a maximum operating junction temperature of 120°C and a specified maximum ambient temperature, the heat-sink thermal resistance, θ_{CA}, can be calculated from:

$$120 = \theta_{JC}.P + \theta_{CA}.P + T_{amb}$$
$$\theta_{CA} = (120 - T_{amb} - \theta_{JC}.P)/P$$
$$= (120 - 50)3.14 - 6$$
$$= 16.3°C/W$$

APPENDIX B
CALCULATIONS ON COLOUR DEFLECTION SYSTEM

$R = 12.0\Omega$ $L = 22.5mH$ $I_S = 0.9A$	Taking typical values from Table 1
Scan Voltage $V_S = I_SR$ (1)	$12 \times 0.9 = 10.8V$
Voltage drop across R1 $R1 \times I_S$	$1 \times 0.9 = 0.9V$
Total Scan voltage V_S	$10.8 + 0.9 = 11.7V$
For a flyback time of 1ms $V_M = LI_S/2 + V_a$ . . . from (4) $V_a = 1.2$ V	$(22.5 \times 0.9)/1 + 1.2 = 20.25V$
Mean Output voltage set to	20.5V
$V_b = V_{CE(sat)}$ for top output device at $I_C = 0.55A$	2V
To accommodate scan, V_{CC} must exceed $V_M + V_S/2 + V_b$ . . . from (5)	$20.5 + 11.7/2 + 2 = 28.35V$
Minimum V_{CC}	28.5V
If $V_{CC\,(max)} = V_{CC\,(min)}$ +10%	$V_{CC\,(max)} = 31$ V
To calculate power dissipation $P_1 = I_S\,(V_M - V_S/3)/4$ ....(7)	$0.9 \times (20.5 - 11.7/3)/4 = 3.73$ W
$P_2 = I_S\,(V_{CC(max)} - V_M - V_S/3)/4$ ....(8)	$0.9\,(31 - 20.5 - 11.7/3)/4 = 1.48$ W
Total Power $P = (P_1 + P_2) \times 9.5/20$ . . . (10)	$(3.73 + 1.48) \times 9.5/20 = 2.47W$

Heat Sinking

The maximum θ_{JC} for the SN76560 is 6°C/W. Therefore, for a maximum operating junction temperature of 120°C and a specified maximum ambient temperature, the heat-sink thermal resistance, θ_{CA}, can be calculated from:

$$120 = \theta_{JC}.P + \theta_{CA}.P + T_{amb}$$

$$\theta_{CA} = (120 - T_{amb} = \theta_{JC}.P)/P$$

$$= (120 - 50)/2.47 - 6$$

$$= 22.3°C/W$$

APPENDIX C

CALCULATION OF POWER DISSIPATION

Derivation of power dissipation in output transistors: Figure 6 shows the relationship of current and voltage in the output stage. During the first part of the cycle (A → B), only the bottom output transistor is conducting, and the power dissipated in it is calculated as follows:

The instantaneous voltage across the device

$$v_c = V_M \quad \frac{V_S}{2}(1 - t)$$

(t can vary between 0 and 1)

The instantaneous current in the device

$$i_c = \frac{I_S}{2}(1 - t)$$

∴ the instantaneous power

$$p_c = v_c \times i_c = \left[V_M - \frac{V_S}{2}(1 - t)\right]\left[\frac{I_S}{2}(1 - t)\right]$$

The total power dissipated in the first half cycle is simply

$$P_1 = \int_o^1 p_c . dt$$

$$P_1 = \frac{I_S}{2}\int_o^1 (1 - t)\left[V_M - \frac{V_S}{2}(1 - t)\right] dt$$

$$= \frac{I_S}{2}\int_o^1 V_M - \frac{V_S}{2} + (V_S - V_M)\, t$$

$$- \frac{V_S}{2} . t^2 . dt$$

$$= \frac{I_S}{2}\left[V_M - \frac{V_S}{2}\; t + (V_S - V_M)\frac{t^2}{2} - \frac{V_S}{2} . \frac{t^3}{3}\right]_o^1$$

$$= \frac{I_S}{2}\left[V_M - \frac{V_S}{2} + \frac{V_S}{2} - \frac{V_M}{2} - \frac{V_S}{2} \times \frac{1}{3}\right]$$

$$P_1 = \frac{I_S}{2}\left[\frac{V_M}{2} - \frac{V_S}{6}\right] = \frac{I_S}{4}\left[V_M - \frac{V_S}{3}\right] \quad ..(6)$$

For the second half cycle (B → C), the top output transistor only is conducting, and the power dissipation can be calculated in a similar way:

The instantaneous voltage across the device

$$v_c = V_{CC} - V_M - \frac{V_S}{2} . t$$

(t can vary between 0 and 1)

The instantaneous current in the device

$$i_c = \frac{I_S}{2} \cdot t$$

∴ the instantaneous power

$$p_c = v_c \cdot i_c = \frac{I_S}{2}\left[(V_{CC} - V_M)\, t - \frac{V_S}{2} . t^2\right]$$

The power dissipated in the second half cycle

$$P_2 = \int_o^1 p_c . dt$$

$$= \frac{I_S}{2}\int_o^1 \left[(V_{CC} - V_M)\, t - \frac{V_S}{2} . t^2\right] dt$$

$$= \frac{I_S}{2}\left[(V_{CC} - V_M)\frac{t^2}{2} \quad \frac{V_S}{2} . \frac{t^3}{3}\right]_o^1$$

$$= \frac{I_S}{2}\left(\frac{1}{2}(V_{CC} - V_M) - \frac{1}{3} . \frac{V_S}{2}\right)$$

$$P_2 = \frac{I_S}{4}\left(V_{CC} \quad V_M - \frac{V_S}{3}\right) \quad \ldots\ldots\ldots\ldots (7)$$

SECTION 3

NEW CONSUMER SYSTEMS

VIII INTEGRATED CIRCUIT AUDIO POWER AMPLIFIERS

by
Jonathan Dell

In previous volumes various audio amplifiers have been described ranging from completely discrete designs[1], through designs where integrated linear operational amplifiers were used as drivers to the power stage[2], to one of the first completely integrated audio power stages[3]. The SN76008 and SN76018 described in this chapter were the first of a new series of integrated circuit power amplifiers designed to give good performance with the minimum number of external components. In order to give robust performance special attention was paid to the design of the output transistors, ensuring even current distribution over their large area. The amplifiers are encapsulated in a five pin power package, which was specially designed for audio products, allowing their attachment to an external heatsink. Every amplifier passes a rigorous series of tests in production, including a safe area test on the output transistors. These features, together with the amplifiers good stability margin, ensure a product with very high reliability.

The SN76018 is specified for 8 ohm load applications whereas the SN76008 is optimised for 4 ohm loads. Both devices will give more than 7W output power and less than 1% total harmonic distortion (t.h.d.) at this output power. An application of the special version of these amplifiers, made for driving highly inductive loads in non-audio applications, the SN76560, was described in the previous chapter.

INTERNAL CIRCUIT DESCRIPTION

Figure 1 shows the schematic diagram for the SN76008 and '018. A conventional design approach is followed: the differential input stage drives a class A amplifier which is followed by a complementary output stage proving high current gain. The pnp transistors VT1 and VT2 form the differential input stage, their tail current is provided by the current source transistor VT27. The differential current at their collectors is combined by the current mirror network of transistors VT3 and VT4 to provide a single ended drive current for the base of the Darlington connected, class A stage formed by transistors

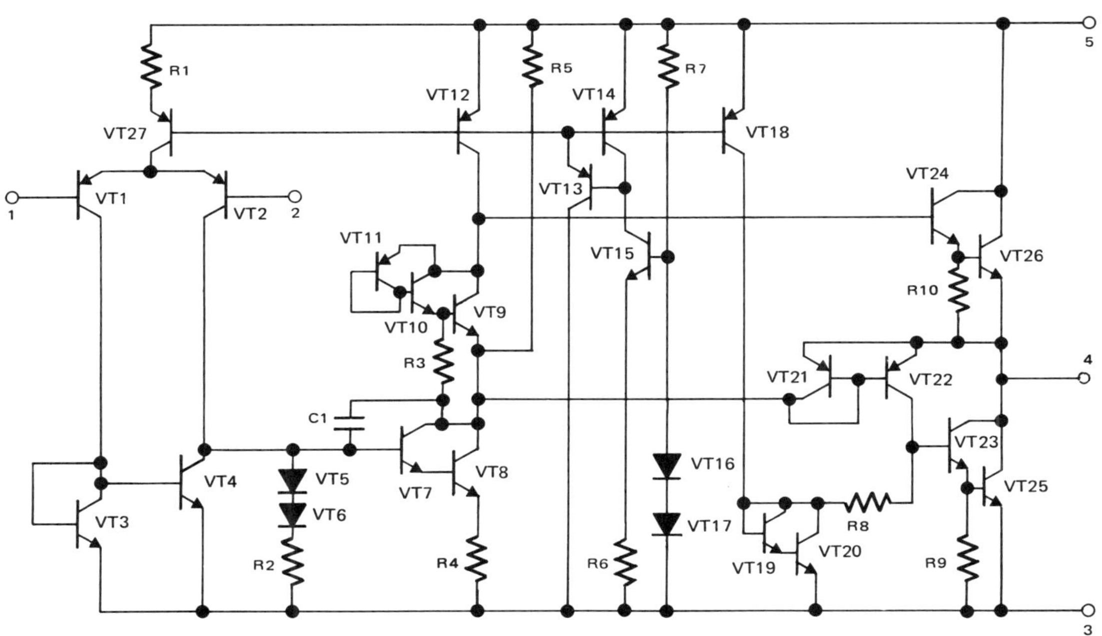

FIGURE 1. Internal Circuit Diagram

VT7 and VT8. This arrangement provides a high source impedance at the base ensuring the correct operation of the Miller capacitor, C1, which controls the open loop frequency response of the amplifier. The voltage gain of the Darlington connected, class A stage is maximised by the use of a dynamic load; current source transistor VT12. The high current gain complementary output stage is formed by a Darlington connected npn transistor (VT24 and VT26) and a composite pnp transistor formed by VT21, 22, 23 and 25. This complicated configuration is designed to overcome the poor performance of pnp transistors on a process optimised for npn transistors. The pnp current mirror VT21 and 22 drives a conventional npn Darlington, transistors VT23 and 25. The base of the Darlington is prevented from falling much below its normal operating point, as it would when the Darlington npn output transistor is turned fully 'on', by the voltage developed across transistors VT19 and 20. This helps the recovery of the composite pnp after the cross-over when current transfers between the two halves of the output stage. The quiescent current in the output stage is set by the network of VT9, 10 and 11. The voltage across this network is dependent only on the current flowing through it. The biasing of the current source transistors is carefully arranged to be independent of the supply voltage to the i.c., consequently the performance is maintained for a wide range of operating conditions.

APPLICATIONS

Simple Amplifier

Figure 2 shows the circuit of a simple amplifier using the SN76008 or SN76018. The non-inverting input, pin 2, is biased to half the supply rail by the voltage divider network R1 and R2 and the input load resistor R3. The bias point is decoupled to ground to prevent the injection of supply ripple at the input. The value of resistor R3 determines the input impedance of the amplifier and can be chosen according to the requirements. If it is likely that the input terminal will be open circuited, while the amplifier is in use, a capacitor, C7, should be connected to prevent stray feedback and oscillation at high frequencies. The inverting input, pin 1, receives a feedback signal from the output, pin 4, via the gain setting divider network, R4, R5 and C3. Capacitor C3 determines the low frequency roll-off and a gain of unity at d.c. The output, pin 4, is coupled to the load via capacitor C4. Resistor R6 should be included if it is possible to disconnect the load. This will ensure that capacitor C4 is always charged up to the correct potential, which prevents a large current pulse when the load is connected. Capacitor C5, also connected to the output, prevents instability in the composite pnp output transistor. The power supply is connected to pin 5 and a decoupling capacitor, C6, is required if the supply is connected by long leads. It is not advisable to apply high frequency decoupling at this point or high frequency circulating currents can

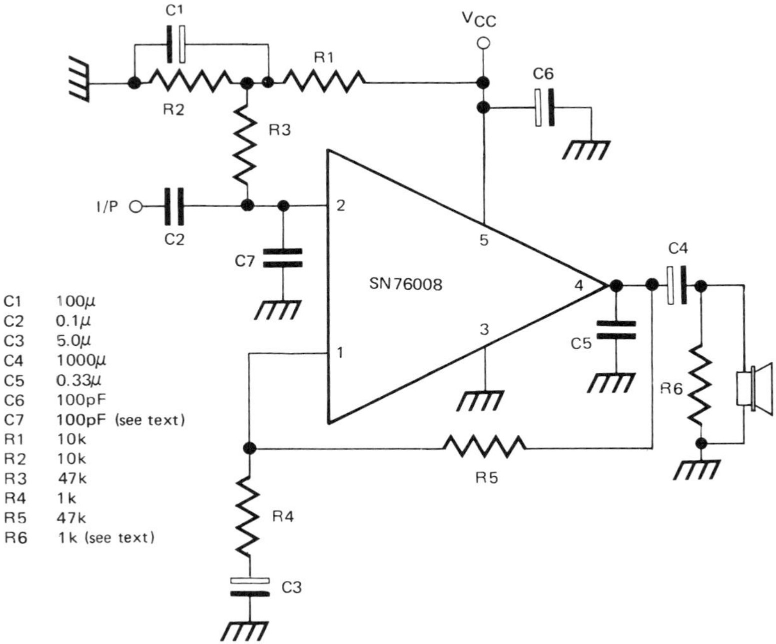

FIGURE 2. A Simple Amplifier

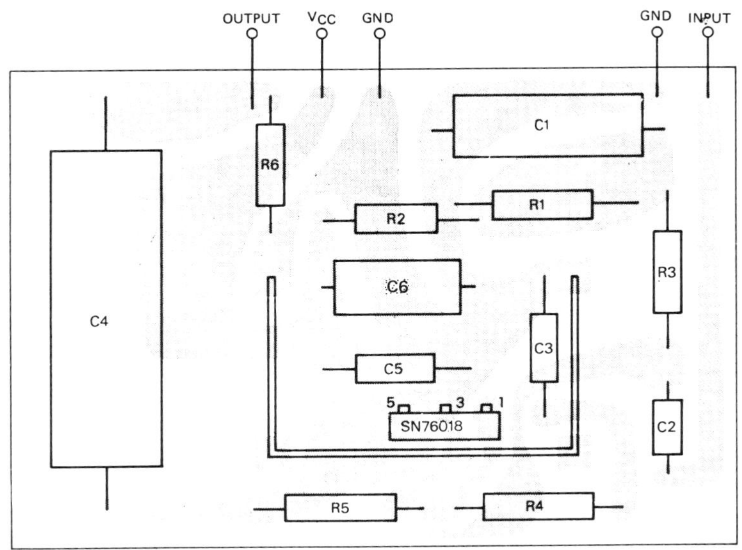

FIGURE 3. Printed Circuit and Component Layout (from component side)

result giving rise to instability. The ground connection, pin 3, is also connected to the heat sink so the heat sink will be 'live' if anything other than a single ended supply is used. The gain of the amplifier at mid frequencies is determined by the value of resistors R4 and R5 according to

$$A_V = (R4 + R5)/R4$$
$$= 20.\log_{10}(R4 + R5)/R4 \quad \text{dB}$$

The 6dB point on the low frequency roll off occurs when the reactance of capacitor C3 is equal to R4, or:

$$f = 1/2.\pi.(C3.R4) \quad \text{Hz}$$

A large value of bias decoupling capacitor, C1, is normally used, but a value can be chosen to improve the power supply ripple rejection. Ripple on the output is in phase with the supply ripple, so an antiphase signal applied at the non-inverting input via the bias network will tend to cancel any ripple injected from the supply line. The value of the capacitor C1 and the bias resistors R1, R2 and R3 for optimised ripple rejection at a particular frequency, will depend on the exact configuration of the amplifier. A printed circuit design for the basic amplifier described above is shown in Figure 3. The layout of the components is not very critical, but the capacitor C5 should be connected by the shortest possible path and the grounding should have low inductance. A two channel stereo amplifier p.c.b. design is shown in Figure 4, a common bias network being used for economy.

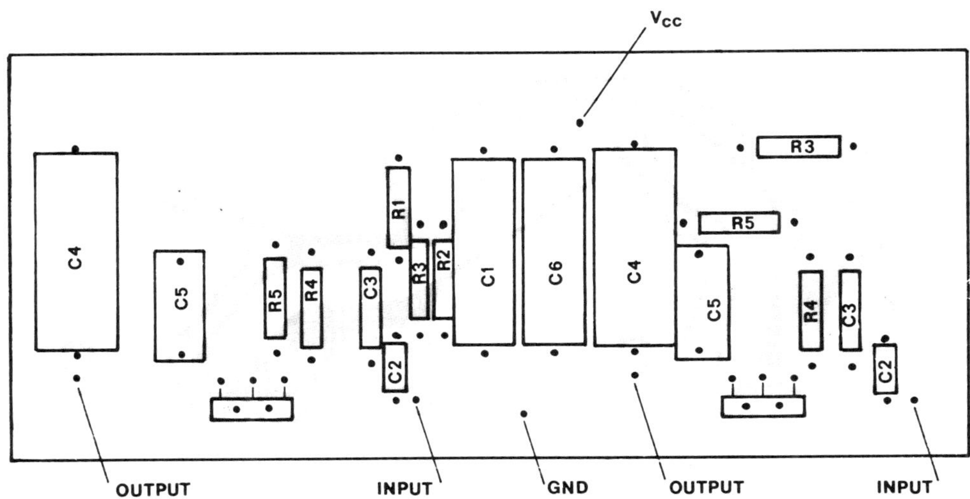

FIGURE 4. Stereo p.c.b. and Component Layout (from component side)

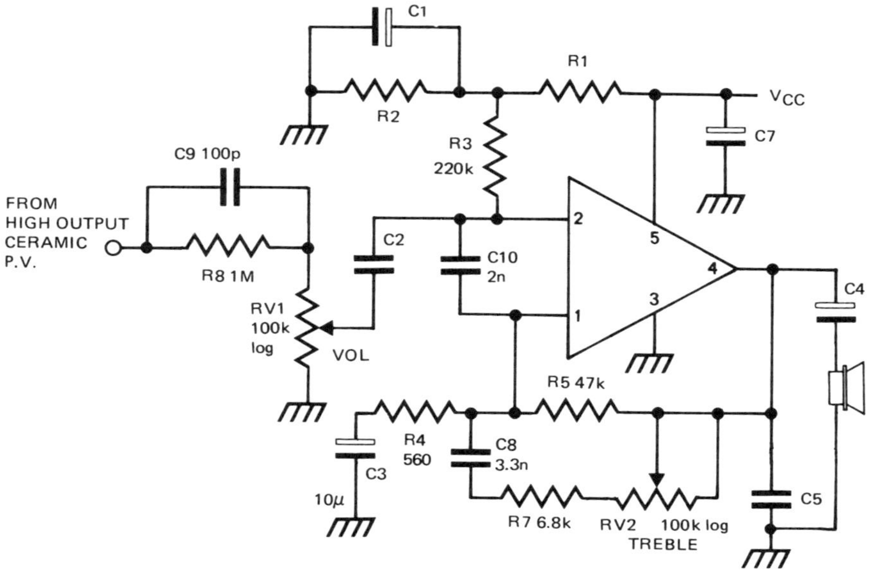

FIGURE 5. Simple Record Player Circuit

Simple Record Player

Figure 5 shows the circuit of an amplifier for a very simple record player application, which has just volume and treble controls. Capacitor C9 compensates for loss of high frequency performance due to the loading effect of the volume control, RV1, on the pick-up. Components VR2, C8 and R7 form a frequency selective phase advance network which reduces the gain of the amplifier at high frequencies – providing treble cut. The frequency response of the complete amplifier is shown in Figure 6.

Amplifier with Simple Treble and Bass Controls

Figure 7 shows the circuit diagram of another simple amplifier having passive bass and treble controls with both boost and cut. Transistor VT1 acts as a buffer pre-amplifier providing a sufficiently low impendance to drive the passive tone control network and enough gain to compensate its loss. The biasing resistor R18 is bootstrapped by capacitor C16 so that the highest possible input impendance is achieved.

This circuit is intended for use with high output crystal pick-ups. The frequency response of the overall circuit is shown in Figure 8.

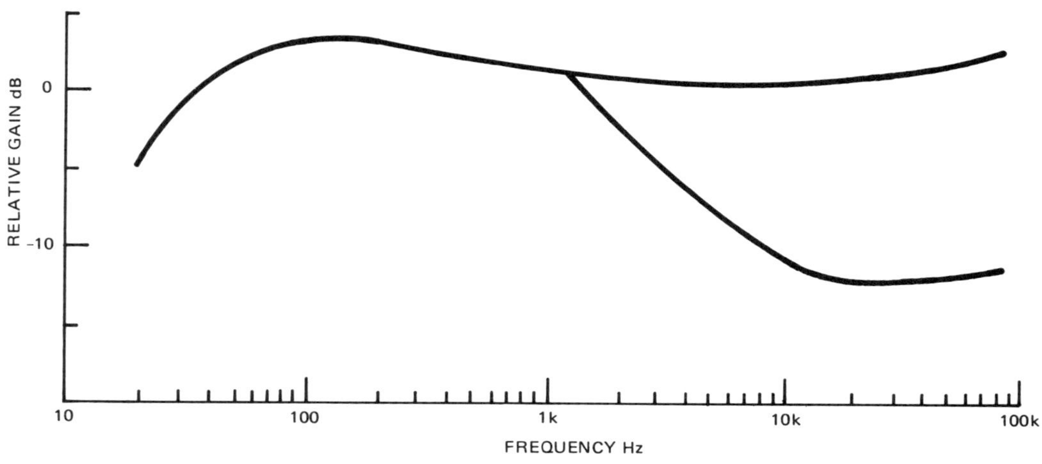

FIGURE 6. Tone Control Characteristic

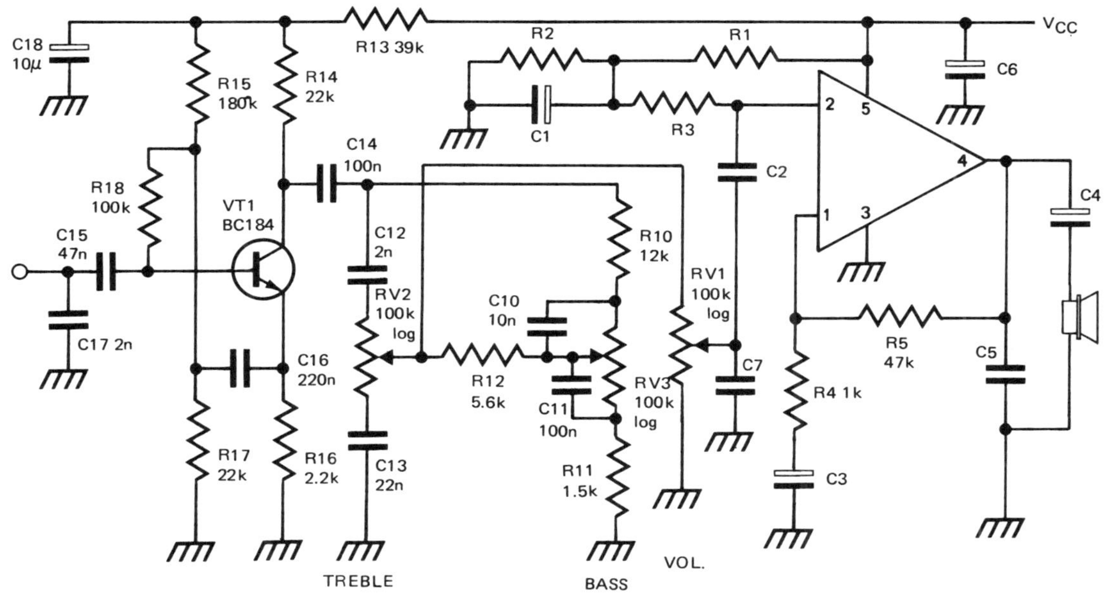

FIGURE 7. Amplifier with Simple Bass and Treble Controls

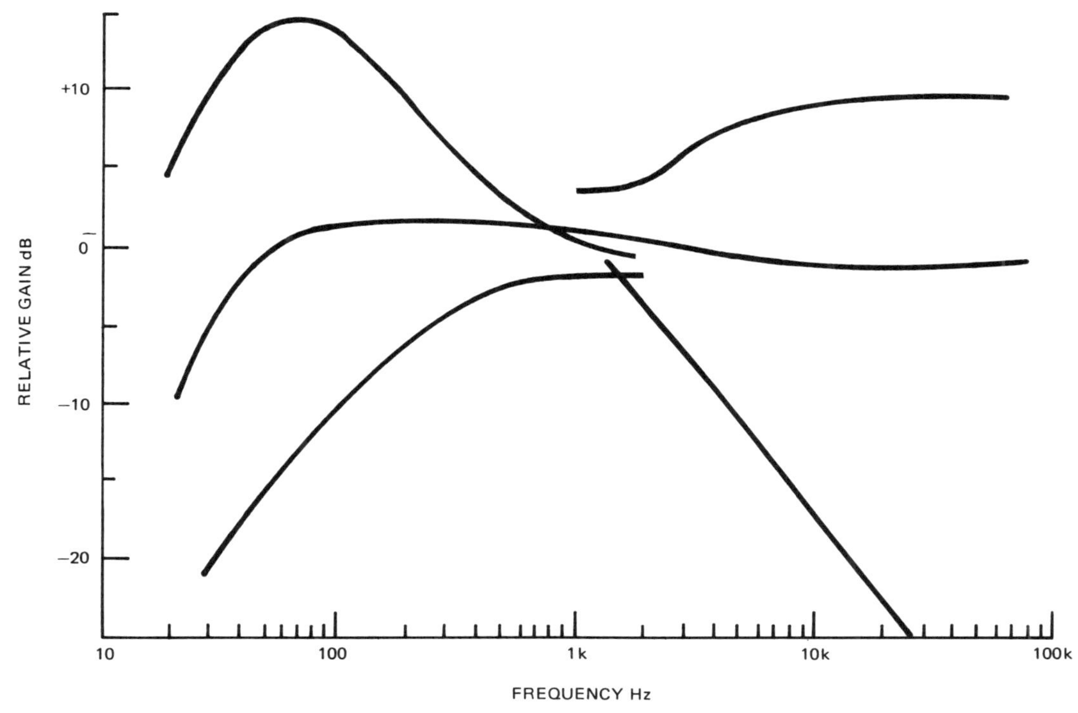

FIGURE 8. Frequency Response

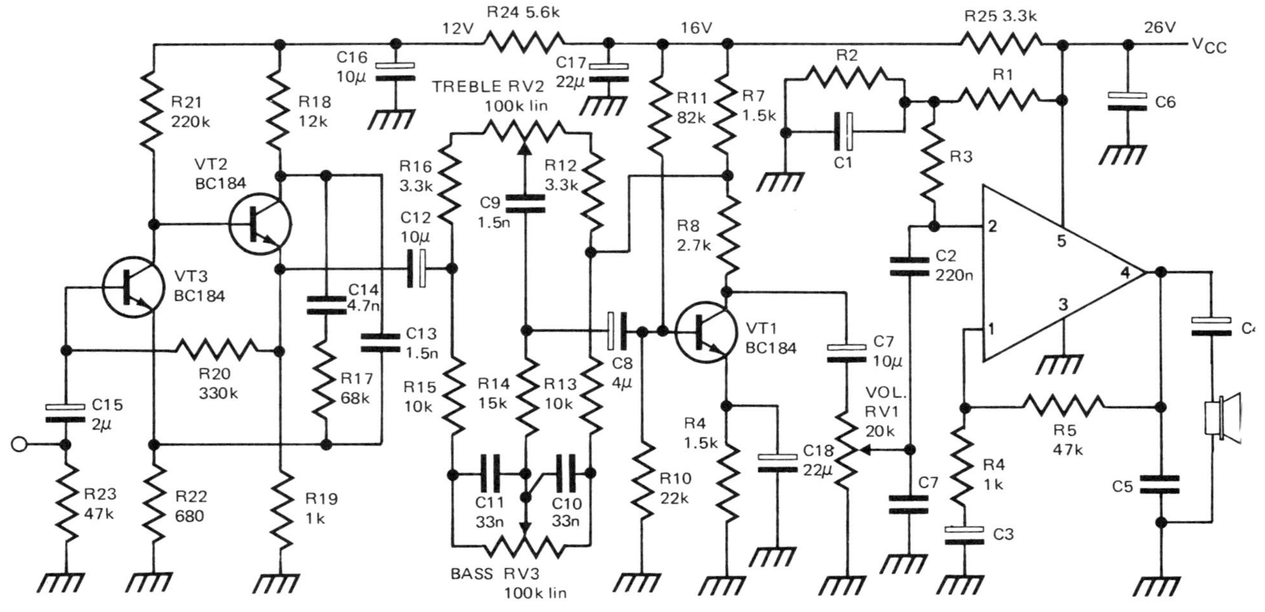

FIGURE 9. Active Tone Control Amplifier

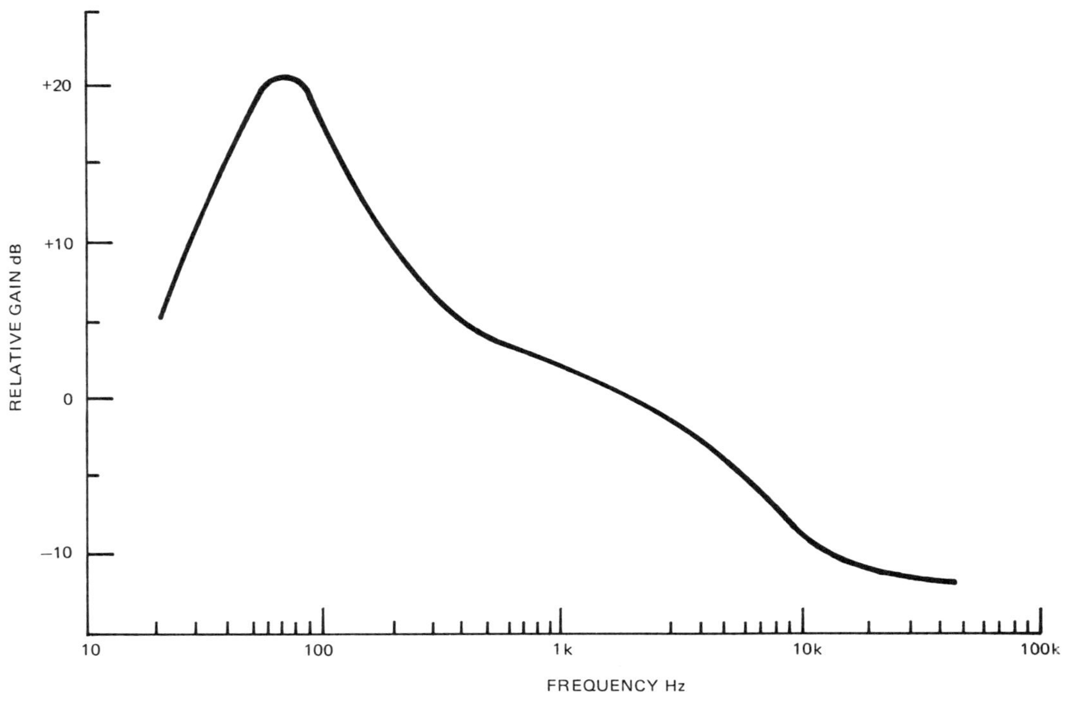

FIGURE 10. Pre-Amplifier Frequency Response

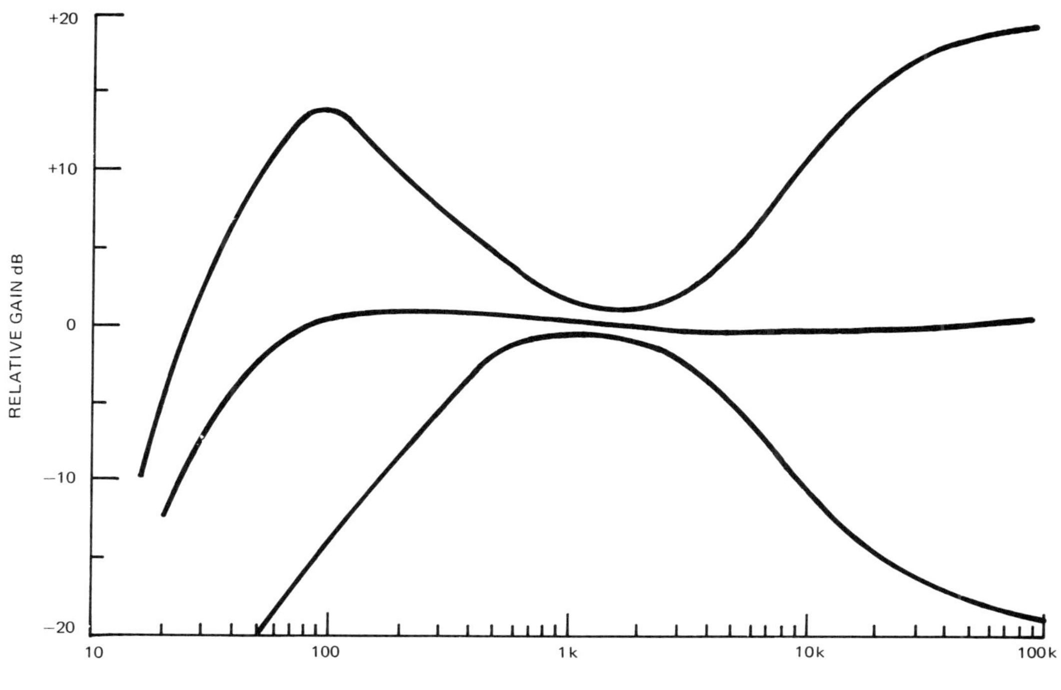

FIGURE 11. Active Tone Control Characteristic

Circuit With Active Tone Control

The power amplifiers, '018 and '008 have insufficient open loop gain to allow the connection of an active tone control network in the feedback loop while maintaining a low t.h.d. under full treble boost. An amplifier circuit incorporating an active tone control is shown in Figure 9. The low noise pre-amplifier, transistors VT2 and VT3 in this application, has the correct gain and frequency response to obtain satisfactory performance with a magnetic pick-up. The overall frequency response of this circuit can be ascertained from Figures 10 and 11.

Unity Gain Compensation

The open loop frequency response, Figure 18, shows that the internal compensation rolls off at about 5kHz and that for closed loop gains less than about 20dB extra compensation must be included to ensure stability. A circuit which allows the use of these power amplifiers under unity gain is shown in Figure 12 where the extra components for compensation are C9, R8 and R9.

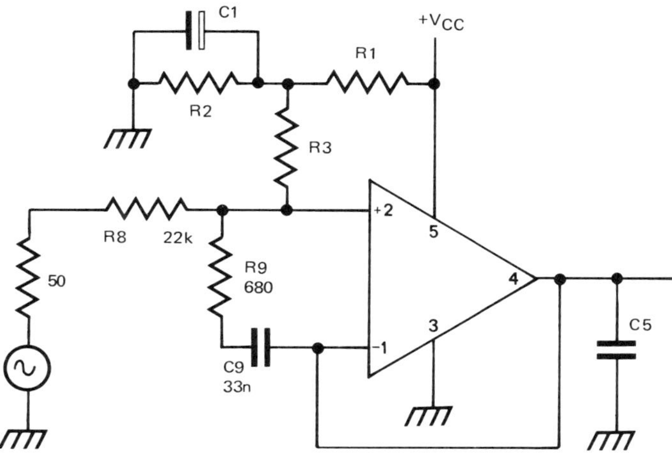

FIGURE 12. Circuit for Unity Gain Application

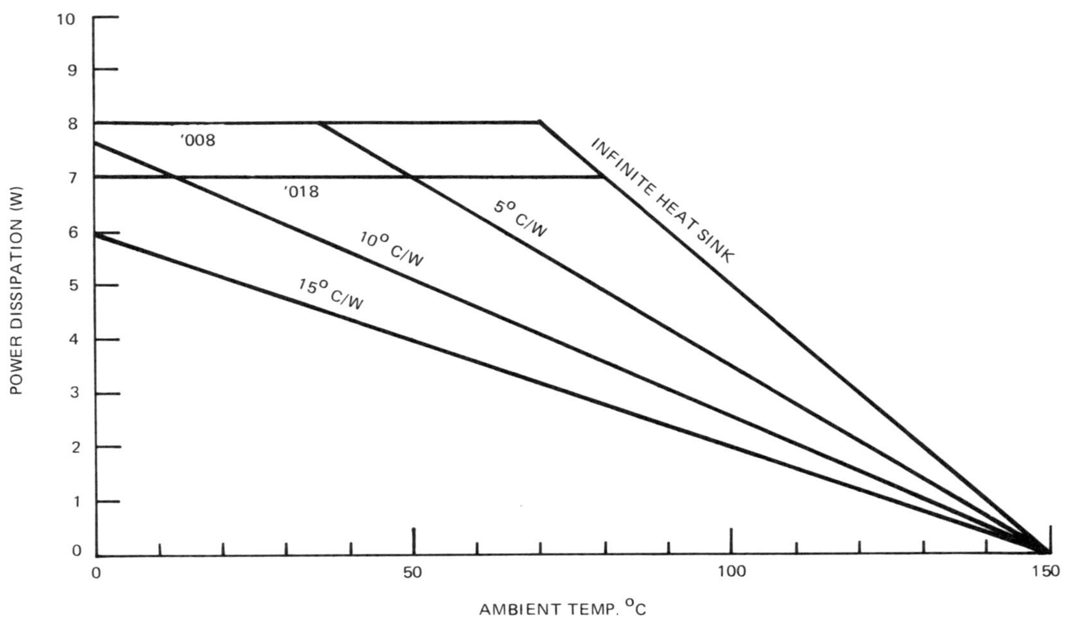

FIGURE 13. Derating Curves

PERFORMANCE

In all the applications described the power amplifiers, SN76008 and '018, have been operated with a closed loop gain of 35dB. This ensures adequate loop gain at the higher audio frequencies to maintain low t.h.d. The performance of the output stage in this respect can be judged from the curves now shown.

Dissipation

The applications of the SN76008 and '018 are governed by the limits on output current, supply voltage, and internal dissipation which are shown in Table 1 and the derating curve Figure 13.

For any load impedance and supply voltage the internal dissipation, P_{int}, for a sinewave signal can be calculated from the Equation 1.

$$P_{int} = (2^{1/2}. V_{CC}.V/R_L) - (V^2/R_L) \qquad - 1$$

V_{CC} = Supply Voltage

V = r.m.s. output voltage

R_L = load impedance

For a fixed supply voltage, V_{CC}, and load the maximum internal dissipation is given by Equation 2.

$$P_{int\,(max)} = V_{CC}{}^2/2.\,\pi^2.R_L \qquad - 2$$

Table 1. Absolute Maximum Ratings

Absolute maximum ratings at 25°C except when otherwise stated	SN76008	SN76018
Supply voltage, V_S (Note 3)	26V	32V
Output peak current <100μs (see Note 1)	4.0A	3.0A
Output peak current (repetitive)	2.5A	2.0A
Power dissipation	8W (T_C = 70°C)	7W (T_C = 80°C)
Storage temperature range	−55 to + 150°C	
Operating temperature range (see also derating curve)	0 to 70°C	
Maximum allowable junction temperature (Note 2)	150°C	

Note 1: Ensure that this value is not exceeded under transient or switch-on conditions
Note 2: This determines maximum allowable ambient temperature for a given heatsink.
Note 3: Ensure that this value is not exceeded even under no load and high mains voltage conditions.

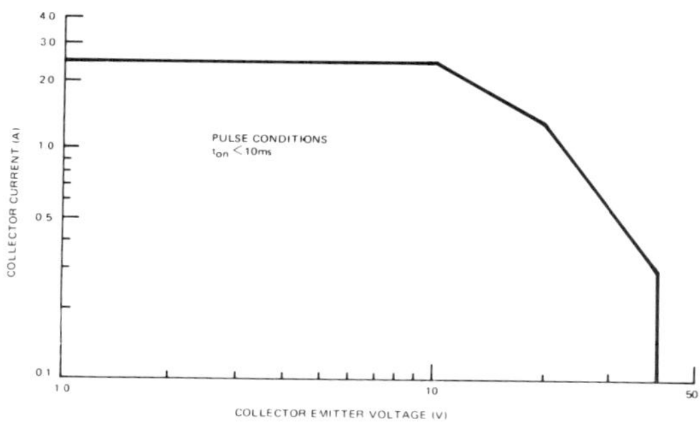

FIGURE 14. Safe Operating Area

When a power supply of unknown source impedance is employed, a series of measurements of V_{CC} and output power should be fed into Equation 1 and the maximum internal dissipation found by inspection.

Adequate heat sinking must be provided to maintain the chip temperature under worst case conditions below 150°C. It is recommended that a maximum chip temperature of 120°C is used in design to allow a safety margin and extend the working life of the device. It is also recommended that a silicone grease is used to improve the thermal contact between device and heatsinks. By measuring the temperature of the heatsink, close to the device, when it is operated under the conditions for maximum internal dissipation and maximum ambient, the chip temperature can be calculated by adding the temperature rise (T_{JC}) due to the chip to case thermal resistance (θ_{JC}), i.e.

$$T_{JC} = \theta_{JC} \cdot P_{int}$$

Safe Operating Area

An important parameter which is often overlooked in the design of audio amplifiers is the safe operating area of the output devices. For the '76018 and '76008 output devices this is shown in Figure 14. The output devices can be stressed towards their safe area limit if a sufficiently large input transient has a significant duration compared with the time constant of the speaker and its coupling capacitor. Such a pulse will change the potential across the coupling capacitor and, when the output of the amplifier returns to its quiescent voltage, a large pulse of current will flow to recharge the capacitor. This current pulse is limited by the d.c. resistance of the speaker which can be lower than 6 ohm for an 8 ohm speaker, and the effective series resistance of the coupling capacitor, usually about 1 ohm. The SN76008 and 76018 i.c.s are designed to withstand the transients encountered in a system under normal conditions and every device passes a test in production to ensure its capabilities in this respect. Care should be taken, in the design of pre-amplifiers and input switching circuits, to minimise the number of transients which occur in operation.

Power

Figure 15 shows the maximum output power which can be obtained according to load and supply voltage V_{CC}.

Distortion

Figure 16 shows the typical relationship between output power and distortion for various loads.

Figure 17 shows the effect of closed loop gain on the distortion versus frequency curve. The effect of decreasing loop gain with frequency can be seen in the curve for a closed loop gain of 45dB.

Frequency Response

Figure 18 shows the frequency response of the

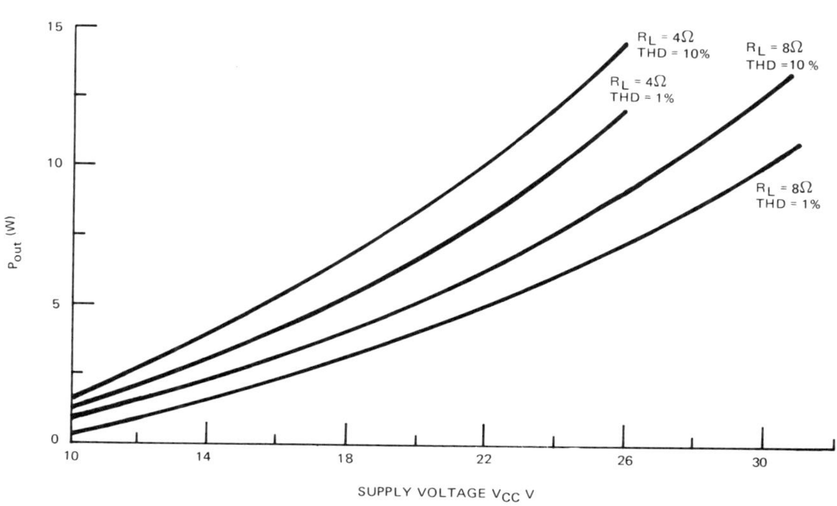

FIGURE 15. Output Power Versus Supply Voltage

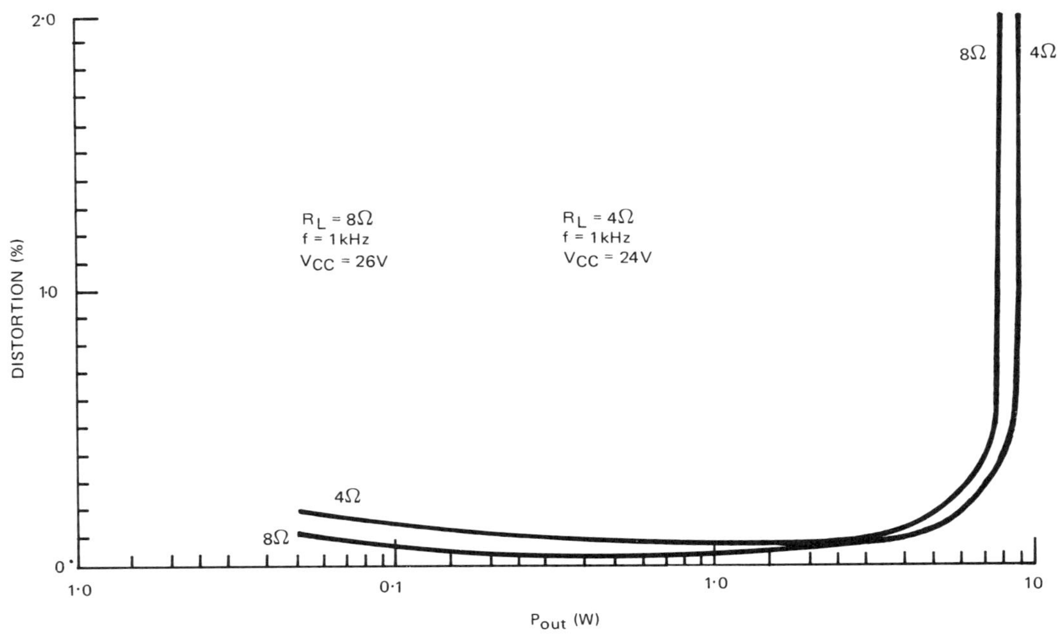

FIGURE 16. Typical Power Output Versus Distortion

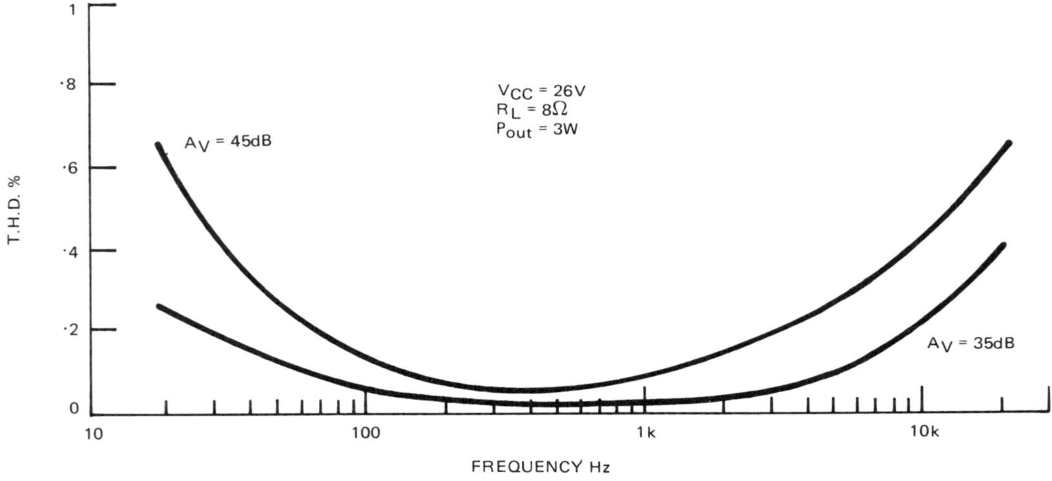

FIGURE 17. Distortion Versus Frequency

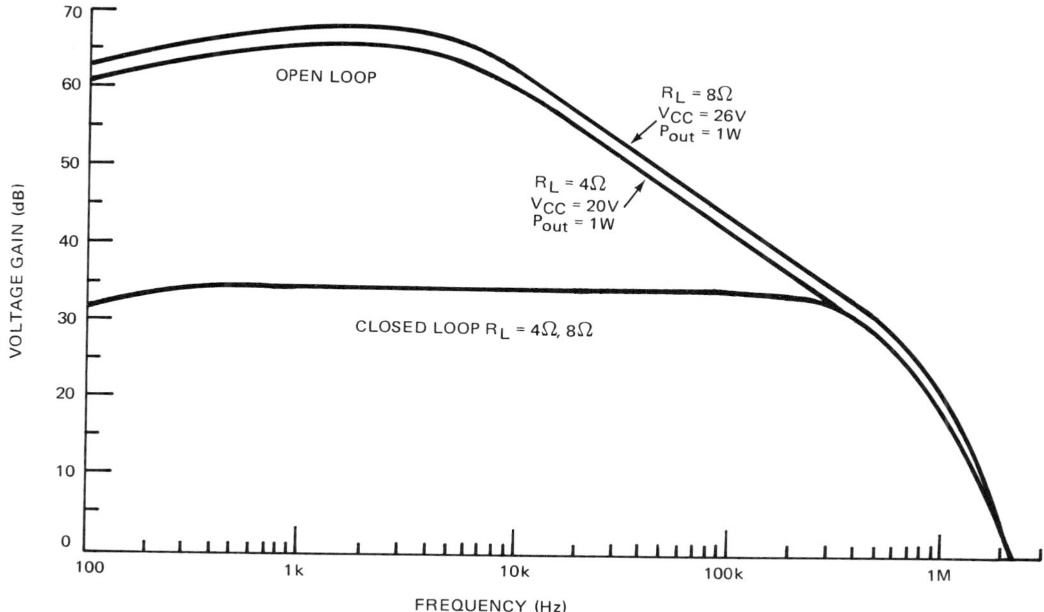

FIGURE 18. Frequency Response

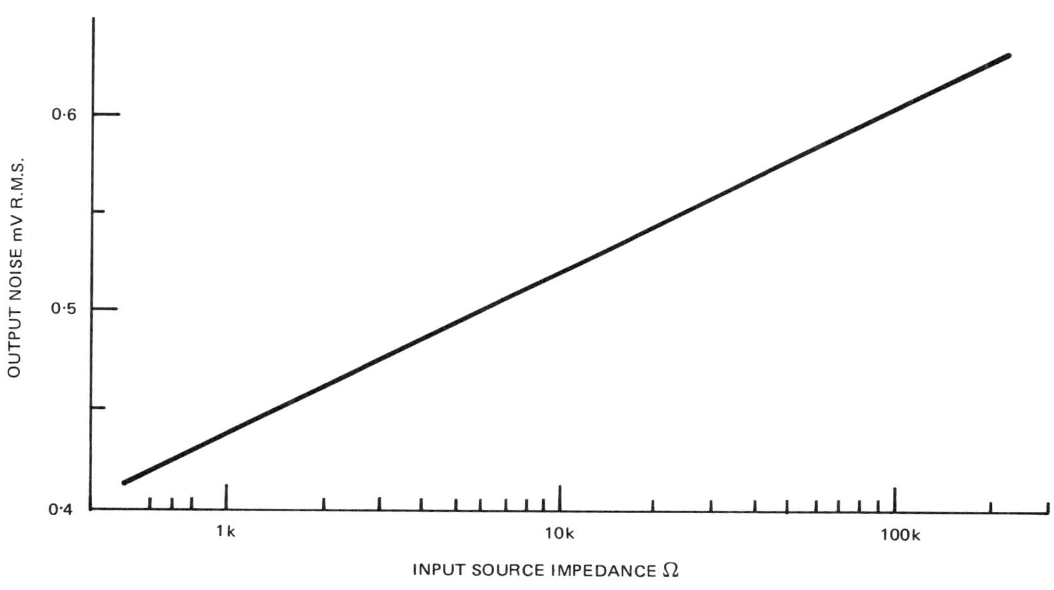

FIGURE 19. Output Noise Versus Source Impedance

amplifier under open loop and closed loop conditions.

Noise

The good noise performance of the amplifiers, promoted by the use of pnp input transistors, is dependent on the input source impedance, typically in the way shown by Figure 19. So for good noise performance it is best to keep the input source impedance as low as possible.

REFERENCES

1. Applications Laboratory Staff of Texas Instruments Incorporated, *Power-Transistor and TTL Integrated-Circuit Applications,* McGraw-Hill Book Company, New York, 1977, pp. 141-189.
2. Applications Laboratory Staff of Texas Instruments Incorporated, *Digital Integrated Circuits and Operational-Amplifier and Optoelectronic Circuit Design,* McGraw-Hill Book Company New York, 1976, pp. 159-172.
3. Applications Laboratory Staff of Texas Instruments Incorporated, *MOS and Special-Purpose Bipolar Integrated Circuits and R-F Power Transistor Circuit Design,* McGraw-Hill Book Company, New York, 1976, pp. 127-132.

IX AN L.S.I. TELETEXT DECODER

by

Bryan Norris & Garry Garrard

For a number of years both the BBC and the IBA have been working on a system of transmitting in the field blanking period, digitally encoded written material through conventional television transmitting equipment, and receiving, decoding and displaying this material on a domestic television receiver. More recently, since 1974, they have actually been transmitting information, known under its generic name of Teletext, but by the BBC and IBA as CEEFAX and ORACLE respectively. Currently the coded digital information is added to lines 17 and 18 in one field, and 330 and 331 in the other, at the program source or transmitter. The Teletext specification covers both the transmission and reception aspects[1,2]. On reception the information is decoded to give a display of 24 rows each with 40 characters. The data is transmitted at approximately 7M bits per second and each line contains sufficient information for one row of display. Thus a full page takes approximately one quarter of a second to transmit. (Access time to a particular page may be reduced by allocating additional lines or by editorial techniques). The system has the capability of an 800 page magazine. Although this chapter is devoted to the description and application in a t.v. of a Teletext decoder, the TIFAX XM-11; the development and availability of such a product, having minicomputer complexity at a consumer use price, opens the door to a far wider range of applications. Already an interactive communication (retrieval) system with a host computer or other terminals, being developed by the British Post Office (Viewdata), uses the same display format. Use of an associated product, the DM-11 direct memory access module, effects a complete changeover from a Teletext mode to an external data mode of operation. Thus current developments will allow a continued expansion of a data receiving, computing, learning, playing, recording, monitoring, controlling, etc., systems into industry and the home.

A number of factors were considered during the conception of a decoder design. The first and most important of these was the intention that, as the product was destined for the consumer market, it must be low cost and simple to use. This could have involved a trade-off between cost and features, and certainly meant that the number of integrated circuits (i.c.s) used would be optimized so that the overall function cost was a minimum. Related to this latter fact was the early decision to supply a complete fully functional module rather than individual i.c.s. This speeds the introduction of the whole Teletext System, does not involve the equipment manufacturer in expensive involved i.c. incoming inspection equipment, and, provided the module interfacing is designed for simple insertion, does not involve him in lengthy design time. Another important consideration was the decision to use processes, after a detailed review of the whole of the company's technologies, which were standard at the time of first production units. For example, charge coupled devices (c.c.d.s) will probably be an ideal process for the Teletext decoder of the future, but, without volume production experience, they would almost certainly introduce complications into the product manufacture and impose unjustified risks.

Another deliberation was whether or not to use a standard microprocessor in the system. Use of such a microprocessor would have required a minimum development investment and would have provided flexibility by means of its program read-only-memories (r.o.m.s). More functions could be easily added, it requires little buffering and will store many logic states. However, Teletext needs none of the latter features but requires a large number of functions to be performed in a fast throughput time and requires additional peripheral dedicated parts, e.g. data slicer, error correction, character rounding logic. Thus the microprocessor is first, not fast enough, and secondly, with the necessary special peripherals, is not economic when compared with a dedicated i.c. design for high volume consumer usage. Therefore the dedicated large scale integrated (l.s.i.) approach was taken for the decoder.

L.s.i. is implemented by gates interconnected to perform functions. Thus a breakdown of the system into speed required per gate level was required and an examination made of all the possible processes available to give the rudimentary divisions for the dedicated i.c.s. Further constraints in the equation for i.c. partitioning are; the minimum acceptable yield relating to maximum bar size, the number of package pins available; and the necessary interconnections between and on i.c.s. All these factors, combined with the desire to have an electrically compatible system, resulted in the use in the module of the low power Schottky transistor-transistor logic (l.p.S.t.t.l.) process extensively, but combined with integrated injection logic (i^2l), n-channel MOS (n.m.o.s.), and special bipolar linear processes.

SPECIFICATION

The TIFAX XM-11 is a sub-assembly module, designed to perform full teletext decoding from a composite video signal,[1] and to provide decoded signals suitable for driving the video output stages of t.v. receivers. The decoder is programmed using a scanning matrix keyboard, and may be interfaced with remote control circuitry.

It features:-

★ A full alphanumeric character set, upper and lower case letters,
★ 64 Graphics characters,
★ Six colours plus white display,
★ Flashing characters,
★ Boxed characters,
★ Concealed/unconcealed display,
★ Newsflash and subtitle facilities,
★ Update capability,
★ Time accessed page acquisition,
★ Suppress header and page capability.

Also for added legibility and ease of use, it has:

+ Character rounding,
+ Picture, text, and text-superimposed on picture, modes of display,
+ Keyboard entered page and time displayed on the screen,
+ Rolling page number displayed,
+ Freeze display.

It is designed to:

○ Employ only a 5V power supply (typical consumption ≏ 800mA)
○ Allow for an increase in the number of data lines,
○ Require the minimum number of connections with the t.v., (The open collector output stages have sufficient voltage and current capability to directly drive t.v. video output stages),
○ Allow additional keyboards by simply wiring in parallel,
○ Perform all code checking and correcting.

Brief Data

V_{CC}	+5V
Composite video input	1.0-2.7V pk to pk
Line flyback pulse input	–30 to –100V w.r.t. earth
Keyboard entry	4 x 5 scanning matrix
Outputs (R,G,B, Monochrome and Blanking)	0 to 15V 20mA maximum sink source.

SYSTEM DESCRIPTION

Figure 1 shows a block diagram of the complete system.

In the Data Slicer the digital information is extracted from the video signal and fed to the Clock Sync to provide synchronisation of the 6.9375MHz internal clock and to the Serial to Parallel Converter. Video is taken to the Sync. Separator where the composite sync. signal is extracted and fed to the Field Sync. The Line Flyback pulse is passed through a Monostable and taken to both Field Sync. and Line Sync. which provide their appropriate timing signals, i.e. Field Sync., Odd and Even Field pulses and Line Sync. pulses. The data, now in parallel form, is passed from the Serial to Parallel block to the Framing Code Detect, where,

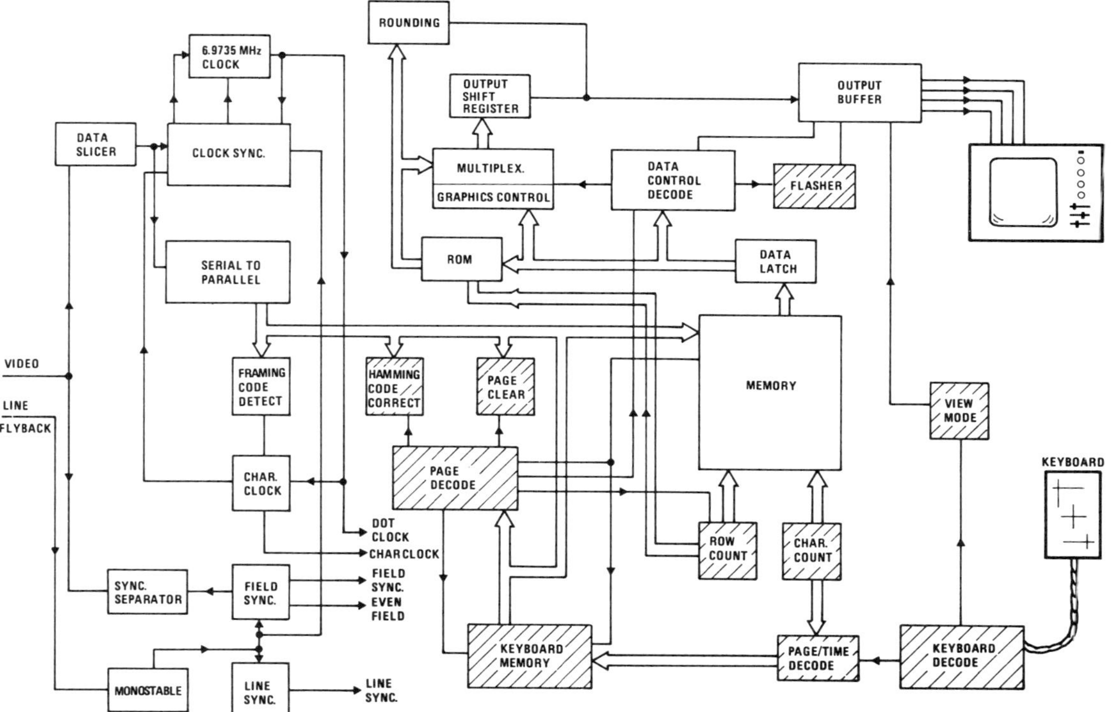

FIGURE 1. Decoder Block Diagram

if Teletext information is detected, a signal is passed to Character Clock for it to generate timing signals mainly for character control. 8-bit byte information is passed through and corrected in Hamming Code Correct to the Page Decode.

User commands are given to the decoder via a keyboard (either cable connected or remote control) and decoded in Keyboard Decode. Page/Time decoder ascertains whether the requested page is to be selected by Time code or page number only, and the relevant Page and (optional) time are stored in the Keyboard Memory. When the incoming data matches the information in the Keyboard Memory, Page Decode generates a 'write enable' signal from Page Clear allowing the page to be written into the Memory at addresses generated by Row Count and Character Count.

All information is written into the memory during the frame blanking period. For its read out and display during the active video time, the required page passes line by line through the data latch, which stores it for sufficient time for previous commands to be acted upon, to the Data Control Decode. This allows it to go into Graphics Control if graphics or address the R.O.M. for alpha-numeric information stored there. Under direction of Row Count, letters or characters come from the R.O.M., the former passing through Rounding, and the latter through Graphics Control, via the Multiplexer and Output Shift Register to the Output Buffer. Under command of Data Control Decode, which also controls the Flasher, and View Mode, which ensures the called for display mode, the Output Buffer gives the correct information to the video drivers of the t.v. set.

I.C. DESCRIPTIONS

Linear I.C. (TX005, IC1)

A block diagram of the linear i.c. is shown in Figure 2. Although the input data spectrum only extends to 5.5MHz, the gain bandwidth product of the linear section needs to be in excess of 500MHz in order to obtain t.t.l. compatible waveforms. This dictated a non saturating low impedance circuit design, made with a special bipolar linear process, which together with power dissipation limitations resulted in an optimum supply rail of 5V. The i.c. performs three functions, i.e. data slicing, sync separation, and clock generation.

The Data slicer section extracts the digital information from the composite video signal and provides t.t.l. compatible signals. Using Dual Time Constant Peak Detectors black and peak white are picked out with a long time constants

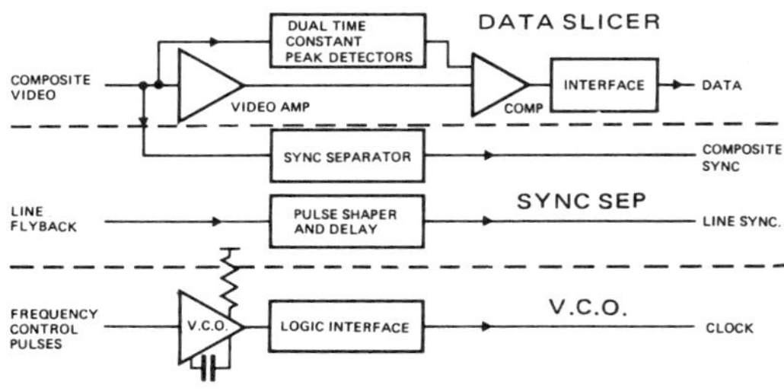

FIGURE 2. Linear I.C. Block Schematic

and the overall slicing level is adjusted to a mean level. Using a short time constant the peak 'one' and 'zero' levels are detected and the slicing level further adjusted over this short period to an optimum slicing level. Thus, when the video signal from the amplifier is compared with this continually updated slicing level in the Comparator, the most accurate signal output is obtained. The use of a level adaptive to changes in signal amplitude and distortion results in an excellent system error performance when compared with a non adaptive slicer. In the interface block the data is squared up and converted to t.t.l. levels.

The Sync Separator section removes from the composite video signal the composite sync. signal and converts it to t.t.l. compatible levels for use in the module. In this section also the line flyback pulse is passed through a pulse Shaper and Delay circuit and converted to provide Line Sync at system compatible t.t.l. levels.

The third section generates the Clock signal using a VCO (voltage controlled oscillator). In the display mode the ≏ 7M Bit signal is counted down by 444 in IC3, the Clock Control I.C., and compared there with Line Sync. Pulses giving the frequency error are fed back to this section of IC1. Here they are integrated and the appropriate error signal voltage controls the V.C.O., whose output is again made t.t.l. compatible, and used as the system Clock. Locking thus to line flyback pulse results in a jitter free display. During the field blanking interval, the clock runs at the same frequency but is phase locked to incoming data.

Serial/Parallel Converter I.C. (X904, IC2)

This i.c. accepts the serial 6.9375 M Bit, now squared up, digital signal from ICI and clocks it sequentially into a shift register. When it finds a match to the 'hard wired' Framing Code signal (11100100) it recognises Teletext information and synchronises the byte clock to the incoming data by counting thereafter each 8 bits. Each byte or 8-bit word is then read out of the register in parallel form. The i.c. is made using the l.p.S.t.t.l. process.

Clock Control I.C. (X905, IC3)

The clock control i.c. (also in l.p.S.t.t.l.) counts down the data clock to provide the byte clock and the line rate for the system. (For byte clock this involves counting by 8 for the incoming data words, and by 7 for displaying the R.O.M. information.) It also produces all clocks required in the rest of the module. As mentioned in the description of the Linear i.c. (IC1), after counting down by 444 this i.c. also performs a comparison with Line Sync to provide frequency error pulses for the V.C.O. in IC1.

Computational Logic I.C. (TX004, IC4)

This i.c. performs all the housekeeping functions of the system. The areas which it controls are shown hatched in Figure 1, and cover both data acquisition and display, As can be seen, it Hamming checks and corrects control information and parity checks display data bytes. It decodes the keyboard entered information, page number and time code, stores this in a keyboard memory and compares it with the incoming information. Once a match is made with the requested page it forwards this page into the memory, defining both the positioning in there and giving the addresses for later displaying of the page. In it also is the generated character blanking to define the display margins. Other miscellaneous functions controlled by it are the view mode and flashing facility.

In order to contain such a complex amount of circuitry and meet the speed requirements of the system this i.c. is fabricated in i.[2]1. Production n.m.o.s. could not meet such stringent requirements. The chip size is relatively large, considerable area being taken up by the necessary complex of interconnections.

Memory ICs (TX009s IC5 to 11)

A Teletext fully populated page of text requires a storage of 40 x 24 x 7 bit words i.e. 6720 bits. Although the display character rate is 1μs, random access to any location is required within 350ns to allow for delays in the system. Reading and writing operations are mutually exclusive. The ideal memory implementation[3] would be a row addressable store, i.e. one that has random access to any of the 24 displayed rows and serial access to the 40 words by 7 bits data in each row. This, with a 1 out of 24 decoder, 5-bit Row Address and 7-Bit data input/output bus, would minimise the number of package pins and have the best possible organization. Such an organization and the best technology to implement it, i.e. c.c.d., was not available as a production item. Random Access Memories (r.a.m.s) were being developed with 4k and the more ideal 8k-bit storage capacity. To position 40 characters by 24 rows, i.e. 960 positions, a 10-bit address word is required (2^{10} = 1024). This word address must be derived from the display row and 'position along a row' addresses. The number of package pins is further minimized by the system using a 7-bit data input/output bus. The 4k and 8k r.a.m.s. being developed, mainly for the computer market, did not have this organization suitable for a Teletext i.c., and also operated from a number of supplies. By using, selected for speed, standard 1k static n.m.o.s. r.a.m.s. for the memory the required organization (1k words by 7 bits) is achieved; only a single 5V supply being necessary. Also the cost of such volume production devices is well down the 'learning curve' and long term cost reduction is likely.

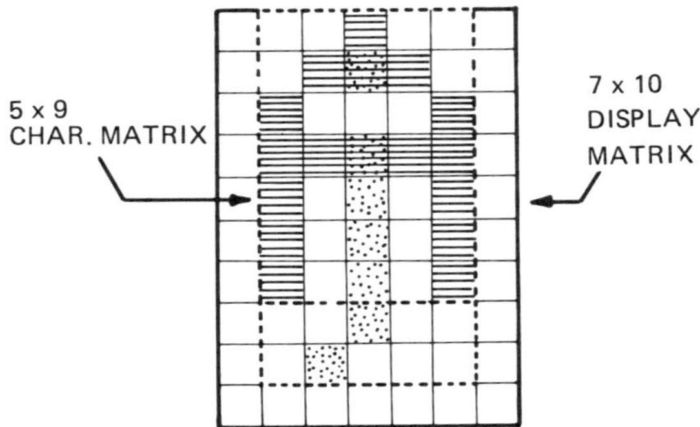

FIGURE 3. Alphanumenics Cell

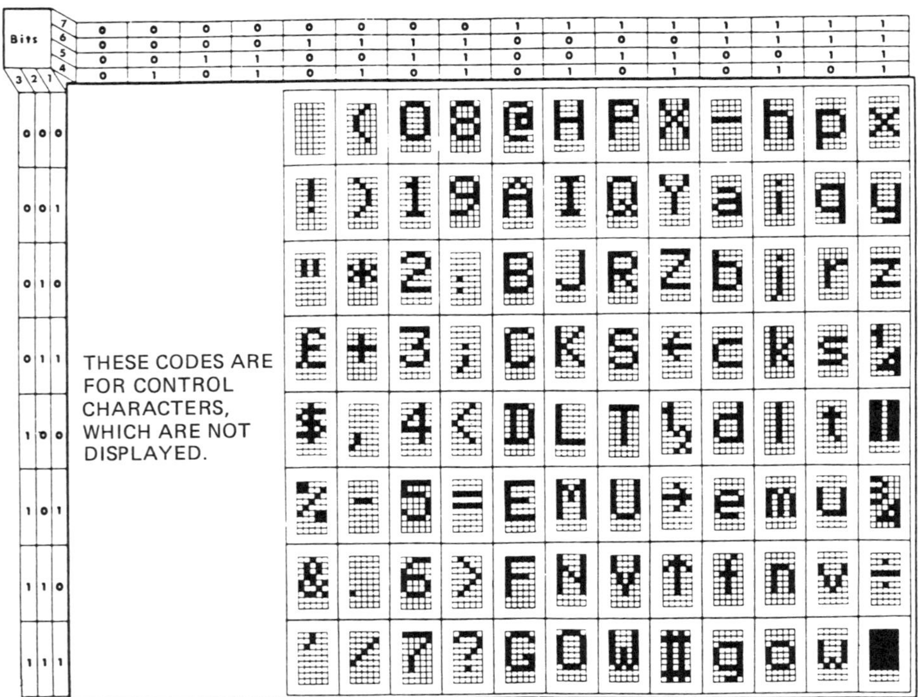

FIGURE 4. R.O.M. English Fount

R.O.M. (SN74S262 IC14)

In order to give good legibility of the alphanumeric characters, they are stored in the r.o.m. in a 5 by 9 matrix, as illustrated by the letters A and j in Figure 3, rather than the more common 5 by 7 matrix. Using the 5 x 9 format gives more design flexibility, particularly with characters whose 'tail' will normally come beneath the line, e.g. j, no repositioning in the matrix being necessary. Characters such as ¾ can also be more easily formed and legibly displayed. Thus to store 128 characters (96 of which are displayed and 32 used as control characters) the r.o.m. must be capable of storing 128 x 5 x 9 = 5760 bits. The characters in the r.o.m. can be easily changed, to be suitable for another language for example, by using a different mask during the last stage of the i.c. manufacture, viz. the SN74S263 with Swedish character fount. The English fount in the '262 is shown in Figure 4.

The organization of the r.o.m. is shown in Figure 5. It features static operation, not requiring any clocks, i.e. the output data remains valid as long as the 7-bit character input address (plus chip enable) remains unchanged. Through the 128 to 1 decoder, the correct character word (of 45 bits) is chosen from the memory. Under control of the row address (4 bits/lines) the output character appears as a 9 word sequence on each of the 5 character row outputs. The device can operate with the row address fixed while the character address changes (scanned display) as in the TIFAX module, or the character address may remain fixed while the row address changes (x-y or character scan).

In the module the sequence for a page display is as follows: The first character of the first display row A, say, has its address presented to the r.o.m. The character row address will be calling for the first (or top) of the 9 character rows. The 5 output lines will therefore provide the top line of the letter (A) which will be displayed as the first t.v. line (both odd and even field) scans across the screen at the correct position. After 5 dot positions plus two blanks for character separation, the computational logic i.c. (IC4) calls for the next display row letter address, B say, to be set up at the r.o.m.s. input. Display of the top row of this letter will then occur as the t.v. lines (odd and even) continue their scan of the screen, the row address not having changed. This sequence continues until the whole 40 character positions have been scanned and displayed. Then IC4 calls for a character row address change to the next one

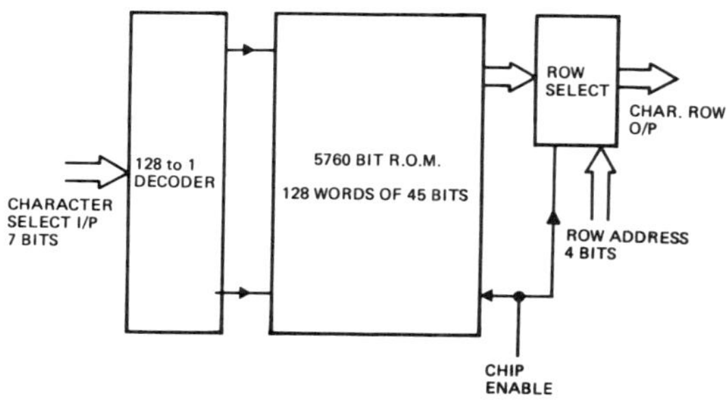

FIGURE 5. Organization of the R.O.M.

down, recalls character A for the r.o.m. input select, and the scan of the next t.v. line (odd and even) displays the next character row of A,B, etc. The scanning is continued for all nine character rows and a tenth is scanned blank for spacing between display rows. IC4 then calls up the next display row of characters and the sequence is continued for all 24 display rows.

The outputs of the Teletext r.o.m. are of the totem-pole configuration. (As they are mask programmable, they could be made open-collector or tri-state making it possible to wire-OR the outputs of several r.o.m.s. The facility of two chip enables provides for the possibility of selecting one out of four r.o.m.s.) Invalid row addresses (—4 bits gives 16 possibilities, only 10 of which are used) are automatically blocked out in the r.o.m. generating a blank on the screen.

In a scanned display system using line interlacing a repeat of the display pattern is given on alternate t.v. lines, as explained. This results in coarsely stepped diagonals which appear fainter than verticals or horizontals. A system which looks at the preceding or succeeding character row and interpolates intermediate extensions to the display by reducing the coarseness of diagonals, known as character rounding, makes the display more legible and acceptable. This is illustrated with the letter K in Figure 6.

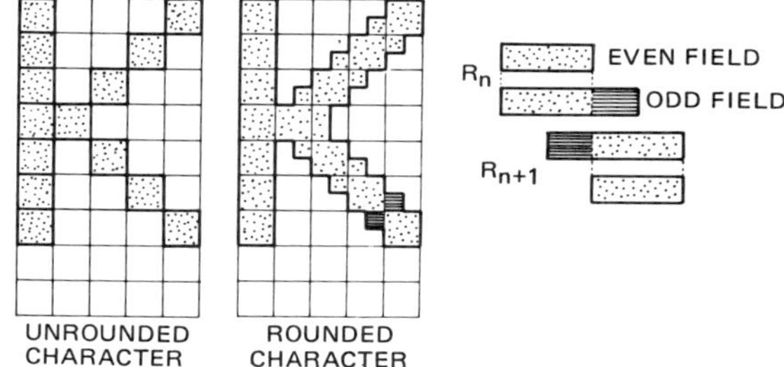

FIGURE 6. Rounding Characters

Practically this can be achieved by comparing the two character rows by using (i) two r.o.m.s, one generating the row being displayed and the other the row above or below; (ii) a single display r.o.m. with a single line store; or (iii) a single fast r.o.m. that can be accessed twice per character interval. The latter is used in the TIFAX module as it results in the minimum amount of storage and package pins required, and reduces circuit complexity and component cost. Thus the '262 has a typical character access time of 180ns which allows access twice per character row. Using a l.p.S t.t.l. process allows its power consumption to be kept down to 250mW.

Output Logic IC (X908 IC13)

The output logic i.c. performs a number of functions concerned with the decoding, routing and display of information. A block diagram of its internal arrangement is shown in Figure 7.

Under control of the computational i.c. (IC4) the data from the memory comes into the output logic i.c. and

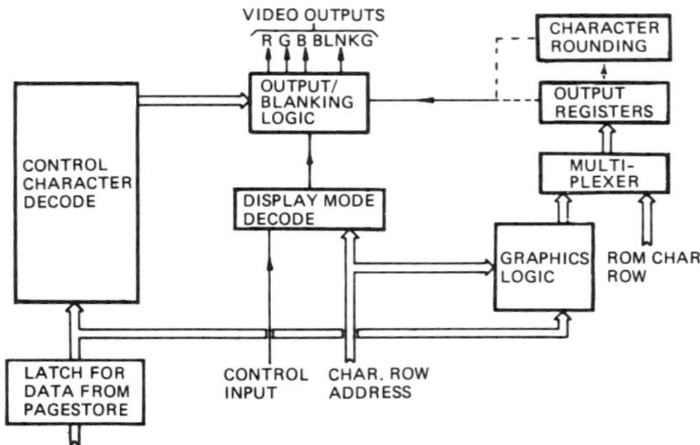

FIGURE 7. Display Logic

is stored in a latch. Seven-bit character select address information is fed from here out of the i.c. to the r.o.m. and, internally, to the graphics generator logic and to the control character decode. The latter determines whether the information in the latch is a control character or not. If not, it next determines whether the system at that time is in a graphics mode or not. The specification calls for the information to be in alphanumerics white unless directed to the contrary. Thus, assuming no previous control characters, the i.c. will not be calling for a graphics mode and the character row outputs from the r.o.m. will be allowed to pass through the multiplexer into the output registers. If the next character is a control character, say, the control decode determines what type of control, e.g. graphics, colour, flash, box, etc. If graphics it will call for the correct symbols to be passed through the multiplexer to the output registers.

The 7 by 10 (including isolation borders) matrix size is also used for displaying the graphics characters by dividing it into six separately controlled sections, as denoted by B1, B2, B3, B4, B5 and B7 in Figure 8. The illumination of any particular section(s) is determined by using 6 bits of the 7-bit character select address. One bit is assigned to each section and if it is a 'one' its section will be illuminated in a scanning fashion similar to the character scanning.

The information from the multiplexer to the output registers is in parallel form and it is converted to a serial output form in the parallel-in serial out (p.i.s.o.) register. The serial information is passed to the character rounding i.c. (X909) to be rounded, although this operation can be omitted if required. Adjusted information then goes into the output/blanking section of the i.c.

A control input from IC4 informs the display mode decode section of the type of information required, e.g. picture, text, or text on picture. After decoding, the correct signals are applied to instruct the output/blanking logic, where t.v. compatible video outputs (R,G,B and blanking) are generated. Other functions, such as flashing, will also be carried out in this latter section, under direction of the control character decode.

Rounding I.C. (X909 IC12)

In this device are a parallel-in parallel-out (p.i.p.o.) register 1, a p.i.s.o. register 2, and rounding logic gates, as shown in the boxed section of Figure 9. At the start of character clock, character line address R_{n-1} on an even field and R_{n+1} on an odd field is presented to the r.o.m. Approximately half way through this period on a positive going edge the r.o.m. output passes to the p.i.p.o. register in the X909 rounding i.c., and the p.i.s.o. register in the X908 output logic i.c. A little later the line address R_n is presented to the r.o.m. Just prior to the end of the character clock period, line R_{n+1} is transferred from the p.i.p.o. register to the p.i.s.o. register on the X909, and line R_n dot output from the r.o.m. goes to the p.i.p.o. register in the X909 and the p.i.s.o. register in the X908. The latter can then be compared with the information in the p.i.s.o. register of the rounding i.c. in the rounding logic gates, amended if necessary, and fed back to the output stages of the X908.

Delay I.C. (IC15)

In order to ensure the correct propogation delays in the system a further i.c. (IC15) is added in the module. This device may become redundant with further development of the other i.c.s.

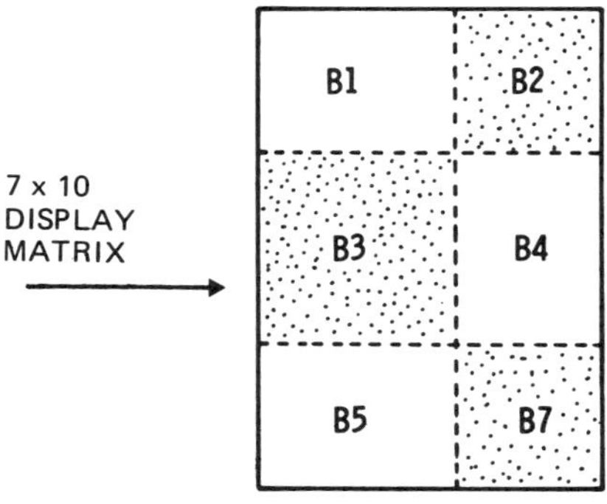

FIGURE 8. Graphics Cell

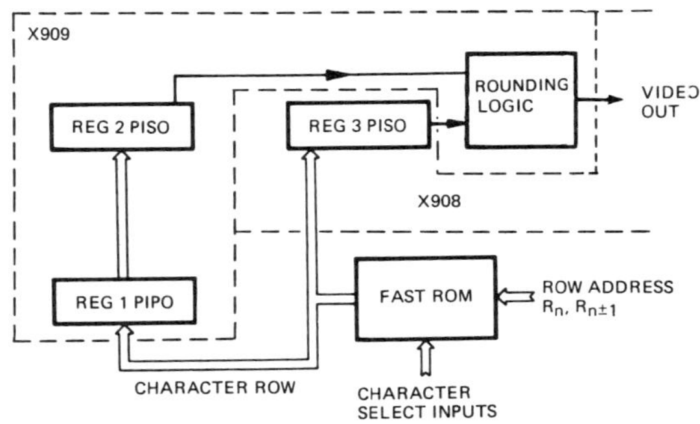

FIGURE 9. Character Rounding with a fast R.O.M.

MODULE

A block diagram of the complete module is given in Figure 10.

Summarizing, the i.c.s and all necessary passive components fit on a 160 x 100mm Eurosize printed circuit board. The only connections necessary are the two inputs, composite video and line flyback; eight connections to the keyboard; fives outputs R,G,B, Blanking and Monochrome (not required with a colour receiver); and the 5V power supply.

INCORPORATION IN A T.V. RECEIVER

General

The XM-11 module is designed to reduce to a minimum the amount of redesign necessary in order to incorporate a Teletext facility into a standard t.v. receiver. However, certain areas of existing t.v. designs may need attention on the part of the t.v. manufacturer, viz mechanical design, video output amplifiers, i.f. amplifier, keyboard design, and power supply.

Figure 11 shows the pin connections to the TIFAX XM-11 module and Table 1 gives the connections. Figure 12 shows a block diagram of a colour t.v. receiver incorporating the decoder.

Table 1. External Connections to Module

PL1		PL2	
Pin No.		Pin No.	
1	Keyboard I/P 1	13	Ground
2	Keyboard I/P 4	14	Polarising Key
3	Keyboard I/P 3	15	Line F/B Input
4	Keyboard I/P 2	16	Video Input
5	Keyboard Strobe 1	17	Blue Output
6	Keyboard Strobe 2	18	Green Output
7	Keyboard Strobe 3	19	Red Output
8	Keyboard Strobe 4	20	Monochrome Output
9	No connection	21	Blanking Output
10	Power Supply 1 (+5V)	22	Power Supply 2 (+5V)
11	Polarising Key		
12	Ground		

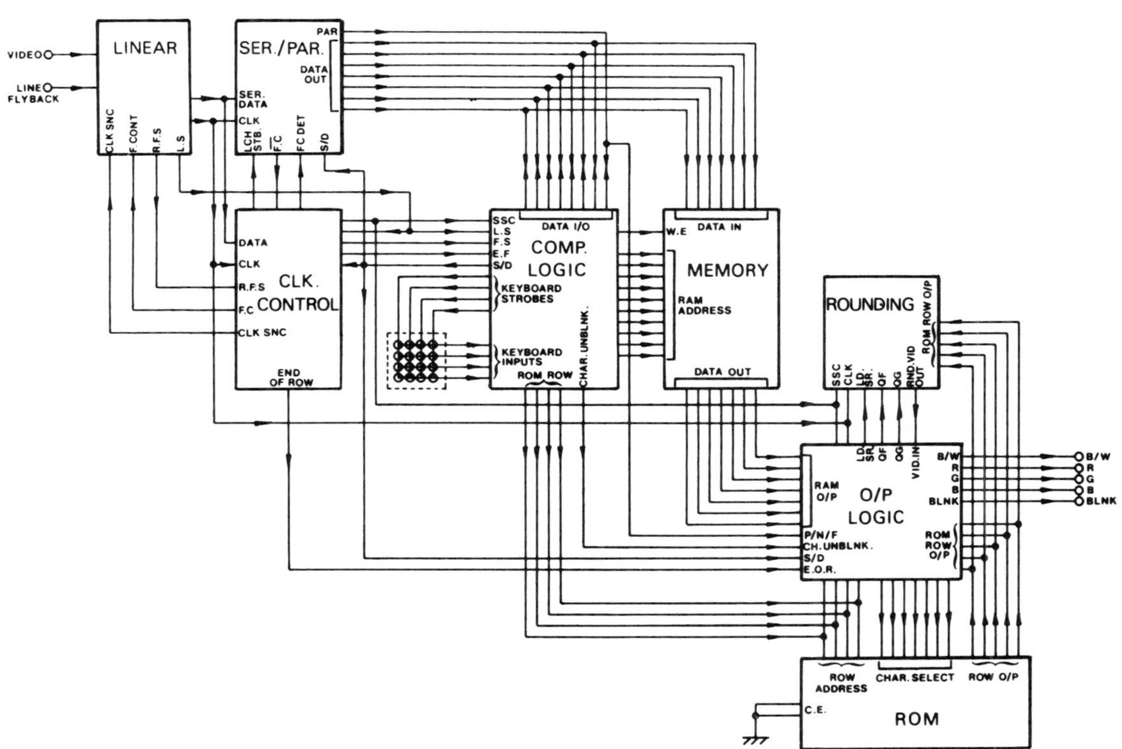

FIGURE 10. Block Diagram of Complete Module

R12
R15
IC11
C12
IC15
TP7
TP6
D2
D1
Q1
Q2
D22N700 ISSUE4
TP8
C20
R9
IC 13
C24
R8
IC1
C10
IC12
C9
C8
PL1
1
12
PL2
13
22

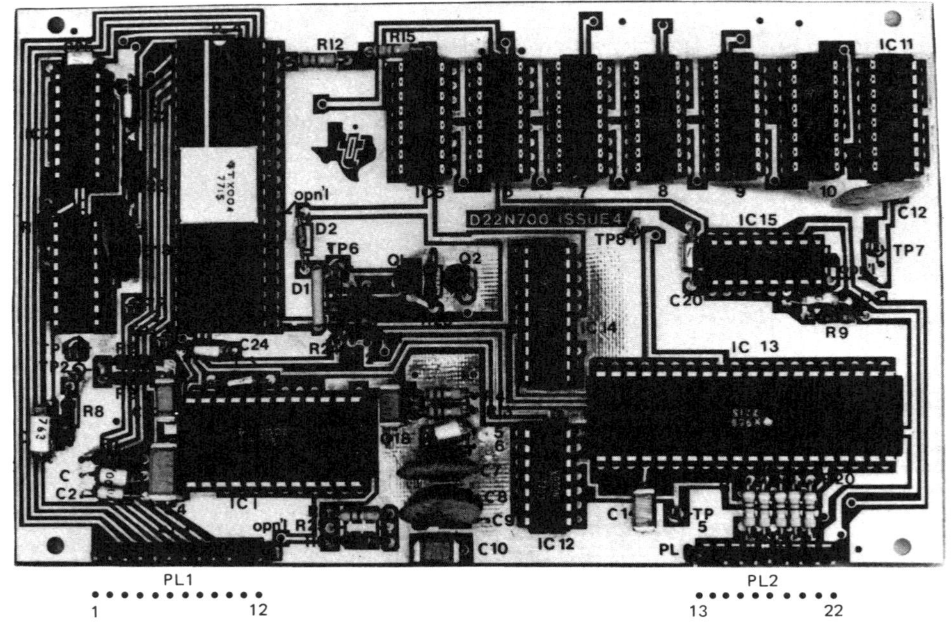

FIGURE 11. Pin Connections to TIFAX XM-11 Module

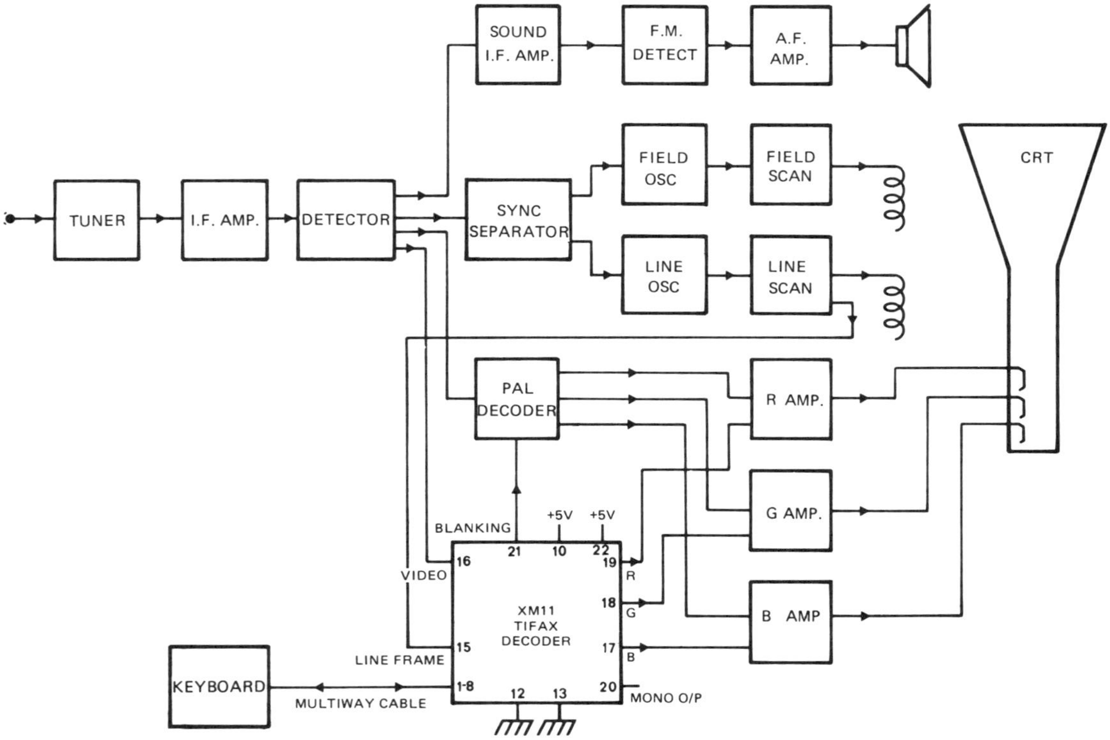

SOUND I.F. AMP.
F.M. DETECT
A.F. AMP.
TUNER
I.F. AMP.
DETECTOR
SYNC SEPARATOR
FIELD OSC
FIELD SCAN
LINE OSC
LINE SCAN
CRT
PAL DECODER
R AMP.
G AMP.
B AMP
BLANKING
+5V
+5V
21
10
22
16
19
R
VIDEO
XM11
TIFAX
DECODER
18
G
15
17
B
LINE FRAME
KEYBOARD
1-8
12
13
20
MULTIWAY CABLE
MONO O/P

FIGURE 12. Block Diagram of Colour T.V. Receiver Incorporating XM-11 TIFAX Decoder

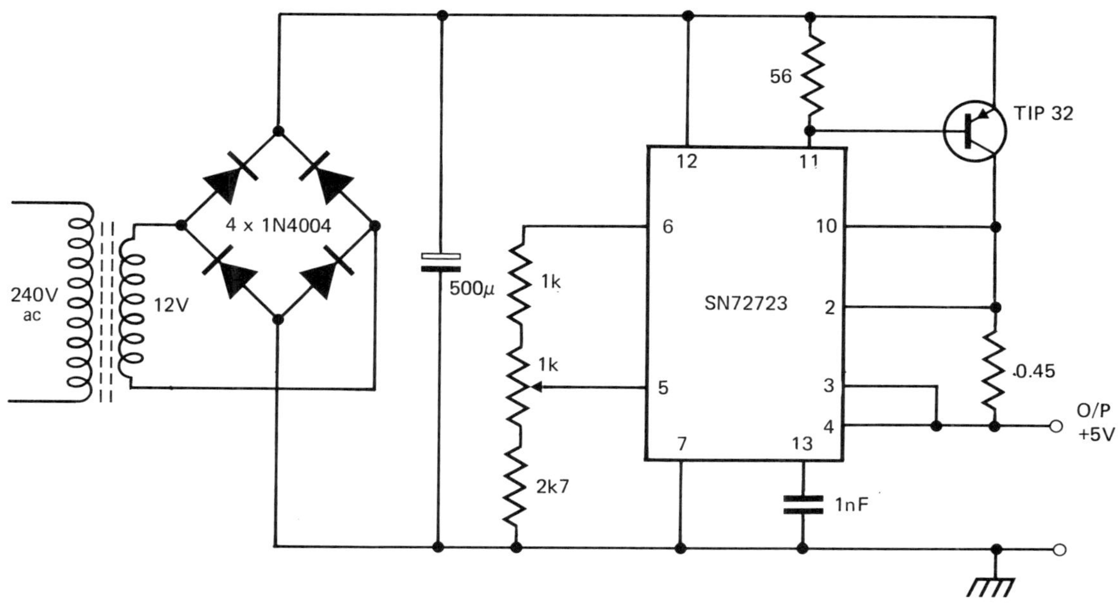

FIGURE 13. 5V Regulated Power Supply

Power Supply

Requirements: The decoder requires only a +5V supply, but this is brought out on two pins (plug 1 pin 10, and plug 2 pin 22) supplying different parts of the circuit. The main supply to the decoder is via plug 2 pin 22, which will draw a current of 900mA maximum (750mA typical). This supply may be to a standard t.t.l. specification, i.e. ±0.25V and ripple less than 100mV. The other +5V connection, via plug 1 pin 10, feeds the linear portion of the decoder circuits. These circuits are more sensitive to ripple, which must be kept less than 10mV. Nominal tolerance on this supply voltage is the same as the main supply (±0.25V).

A suitable power supply is shown in Figure 13. Alternatively the supply can be generated from the line output transformer.

Precautions: The maximum supply voltage is 6.5V. While the circuits will probably not function correctly under this condition, no permanent damage will be caused by the application of voltages up to 6.5V. Voltages in excess of 6.5V may cause permanent damage, and it is recommended that protection be provided to guard against excess d.c. voltage caused, for example, by the failure of the voltage regulator. Damage may also be caused by voltage spikes on the supply line, and it is recommended that some protection be provided against transients which cause the supply to exceed 6.5V, even for a very short time.

A possible protection circuit is shown in Figure 14. Voltage transients are shorted to earth through transistor VT2, which should have a sufficient large dissipation rating to be able to withstand the energy from the suppressed spikes. Under normal operation there is no dissipation at all. This circuit should be mounted as close to the TIFAX unit as possible with a minimum length of connection to the module. Other configurations are possible, and any circuit which will act in less than 0.5μs may be used.

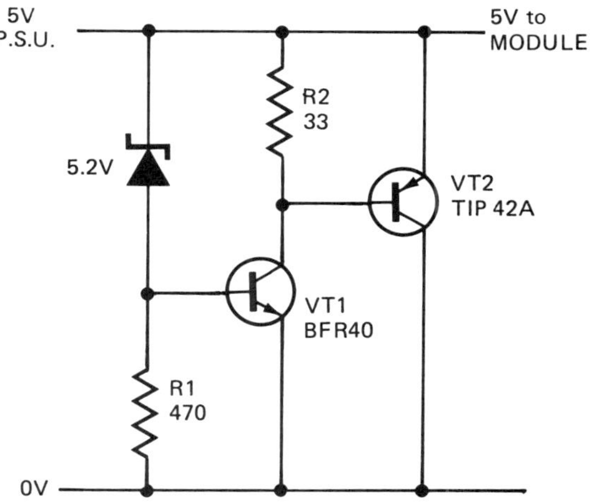

FIGURE 14. Transient Protection Circuit

Composite Video Signal Input & I.F. Requirements

General: The nominal input level required is 1-2.7V peak to peak with negative going synchronising pulse, as shown in Figure 15. It is essential that the sync pulses are retained in the video signal, since the decoder uses these pulses for an internal clock. Care should be taken not to crush the sync. pulses.

An i.f. amplifier and filter designed for good teletext performance will give excellent picture quality, but the converse is not necessarily true. The required response of the video signal, which will be defined mainly by the i.f. circuitry is a complex subject but the following brief explanation summarises the critical parameters.

I.F. Amplitude Response: To obtain good picture quality, amplitude response is of prime importance, and an i.f. amplifier designed for good picture quality will probably have adequate amplitude performance for teletext. The response should ideally be flat over a video bandwidth of 5.5MHz. However, teletext components above 4MHz are of less significance and a slight roll-off in response between 4MHz and 5.5MHz will probably not be detrimental.

I.F. Phase Response: An amplitude response as described above will not give error-free teletext reception if the phase response is not good enough. The phase requirements for teletext are compatible with normal video, but are often neglected in i.f. amplifier design, since the requirements for good picture quality are less critical.

When the signal passes through the i.f. filter and amplifier, it is delayed by a time t_d where:

$t_d = d\phi/df$ with ϕ = phase
and f = frequency

For a narrow bandwidth, the value of t_d is given in Figure 16 by the expression

$t_d = 2.778 \times (\phi_2 - \phi_1) / (f_2 - f_1)$

where

t_d is in ns
ϕ is in degrees
f is in MHz

The actual value of delay time t_d is not important if it is constant over the whole bandwidth. In order to achieve this the phase/frequency characteristic must be linear over the bandwidth in question. Non-linearities in this characteristic will result in a varying group delay, degrading the data and possibly introducing errors after decoding. The effects of phase and amplitude distortion on a data signal may be seen in Figure 17.

Measurement of Group Delay: In Figure 18 a low frequency signal f_1 is used to modulate a carrier frequency f_2 that is variable over the i.f. bandwidth. The low frequency is chosen as a compromise between the bandwidth over which group delay may be regarded as constant, and the resolution of the phase comparator (100kHz is probably suitable in most cases). Group delay is measured as a phase difference between the 100kHz reference and the detected 100kHz output. By taking measurements with the carrier frequency varied over the i.f. pass band, the group delay characteristic may be plotted.

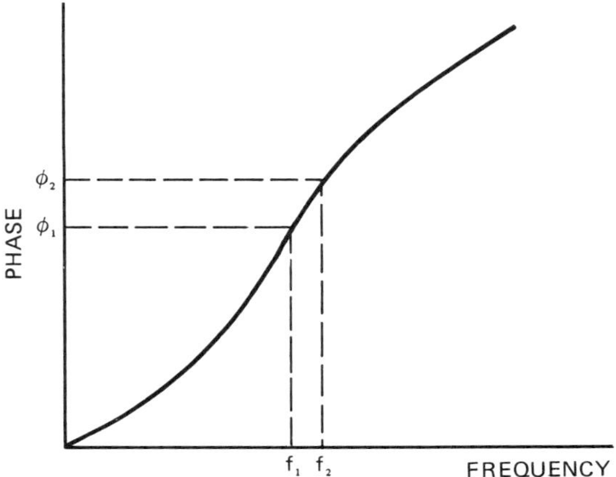

FIGURE 16. Group Delay Definition

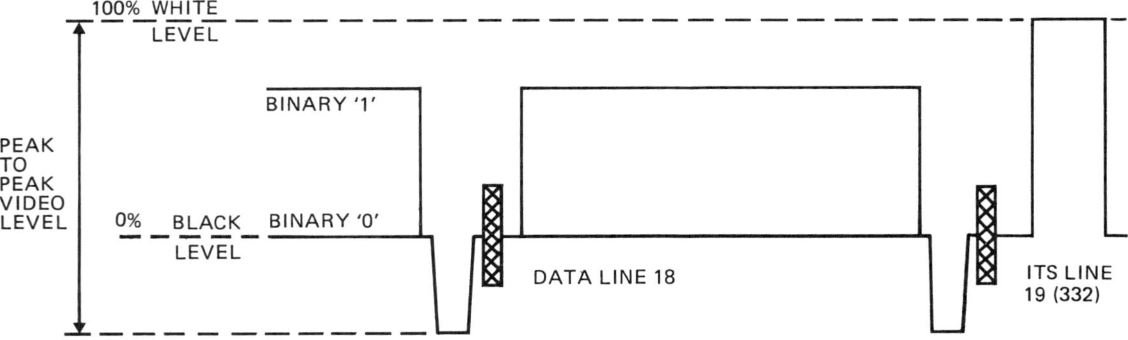

FIGURE 15. Video Input Waveforms

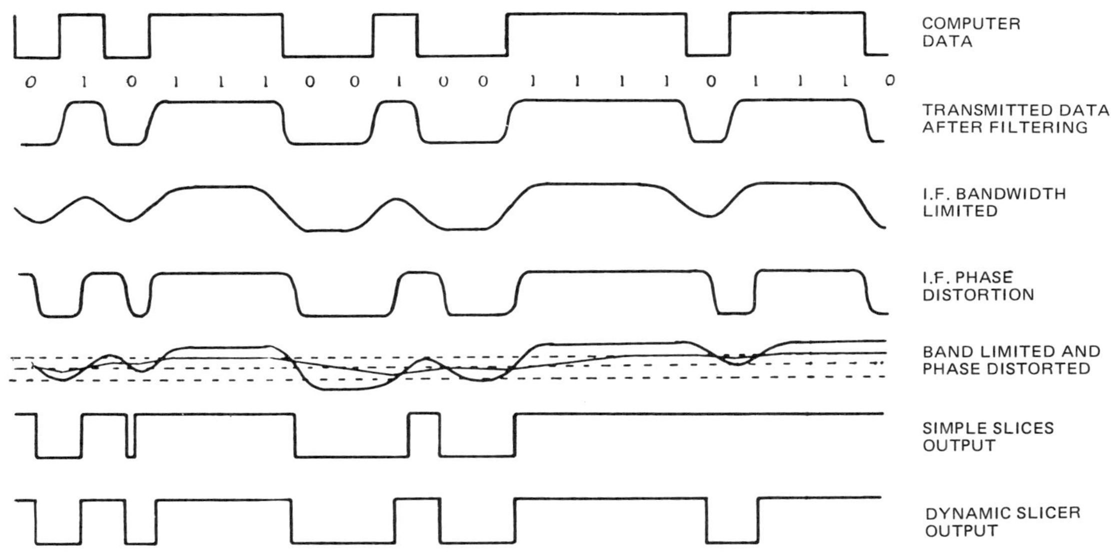

FIGURE 17. Effect of Phase and Amplitude Distortion

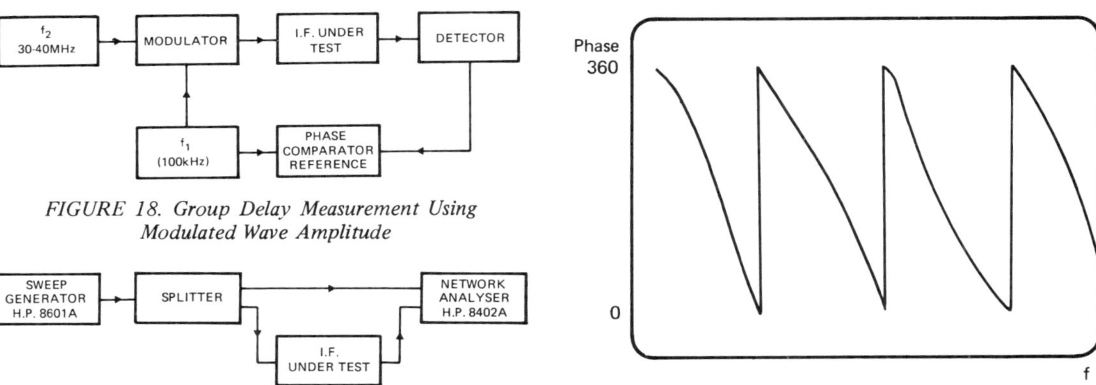

FIGURE 18. Group Delay Measurement Using Modulated Wave Amplitude

FIGURE 19. Group Delay Measurement Using Network Analyser

FIGURE 20. Network Analyser Display

At any given value of f_2:

$$t_d = (10^9/f_1) \times (\phi/360) \quad \text{ns}$$

The method may be extended to include modulation up to u.h.f.

Figure 19 shows an alternative method of measuring group delay using a Hewlett Packard Network Analyser. This method is extremely simple to set up but suffers from the disadvantage that phase distortion in the demodulator and video circuits of the television is not included. The network analyser displays the phase/frequency characteristic of the i.f., a typical display is shown in Figure 20. Group delay is calculated from the slope of the phase/frequency curve.

Practical Receivers: A number of different television receivers have been evaluated for group delay characteristics and the teletext error rates compared for a given signal level. The receivers tested had group delay variations of 100-400ns. The error rate is dependent not only on the magnitude of the variation, but also on its characteristics with frequency. For example, two receivers had similar variations of group delay magnitude, but one had a peak at low video frequencies and the other a peak at high frequencies. Distortion at the low frequency end of the video spectrum produces considerably more errors than distortion at high frequencies, due to the fact that the data energy content is higher at low frequencies.

It is not possible at this time to give absolute rules for i.f. group delay performance. Experience at this stage indicates that a very low error rate can be achieved with t_d varying up to 100ns, with relatively little dependence on the shape of the t_d versus frequency graph. With variations in t_d of up to 250ns, error rate will be dependent on the shape of the graph of t_d against frequency as previously described. If the variation in group delay exceeds 250ns, a significant number of errors will almost certainly be produced. The levels of group delay variation quoted above are those in the presence of a good signal/noise ratio and amplitude response. In poor signal strength areas, or if the amplitude response is not sufficiently flat, significant errors may be produced by lower values of group delay variation, and it is felt that a group delay variation of 50ns should be regarded as a target specification.

Methods of Improving IF Phase Response: If measurements on the i.f. show that the characteristics will result in poor teletext reception, several different approaches are possible to improve the signal.

1. Redesign of LC filter network.
   It may be possible to improve the i.f. group delay by modification of the filter networks. It is quite possible to design an LC block filter with excellent group delay characteristics – providing that group delay is considered as a design parameter. The problem is usually that there is little need to consider group delay for colour television receivers and it therefore is neglected in the design.
2. Video Correction of Phase Response.
   It is, in theory, possible to synthesise any desired phase response by the use of all-pass filters, derived from lattice sections (Figure 21). The phase-shift introduced by this network is given by
   $$\tan\beta/2 = -j\sqrt{(Z_a/Z_b)}$$
   Phase response of this network configuration with varying LC ratios are shown in Figure 22. However, the network in Figure 21 requires a balanced input and is complex in terms of components.
   If $\omega . L_a > R_o$, it is possible to transform the lattice network of Figure 21 to a bridged T as shown in Figure 23. Details of this transformation can be obtained along with much other valuable information on phase correcting networks.[4]
3. SWF Filter.
   Another possible way to provide a phase-linear i.f. is by use of a surface-wave filter. This type of device has the advantage that its phase

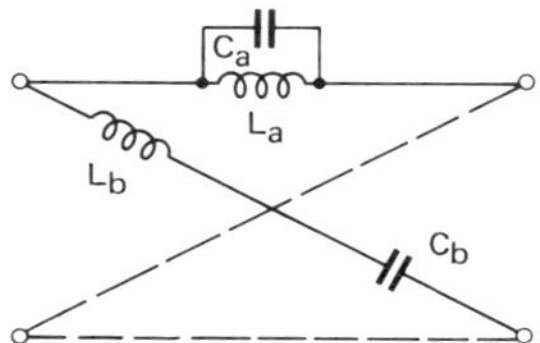

L_aC_a and L_bC_b are reciprocal impedances

i.e. $L_a = R_o^2 C_b$

$C_a = L_b/R_o^2$

where R_o = characteristic impedance.

FIGURE 21. Lattice Filter Section

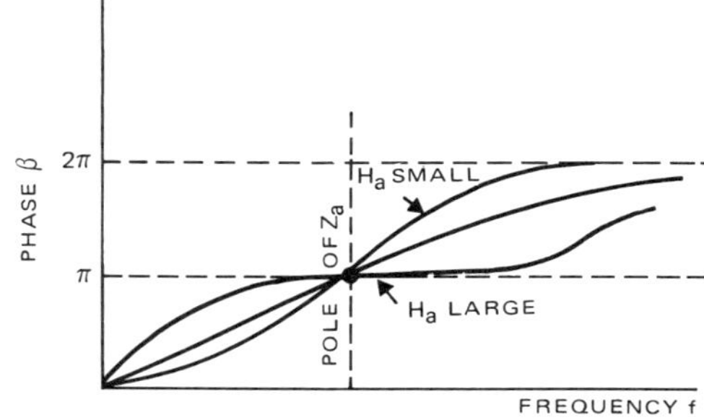

FIGURE 22. Phase Response of All-pass Lattice Network

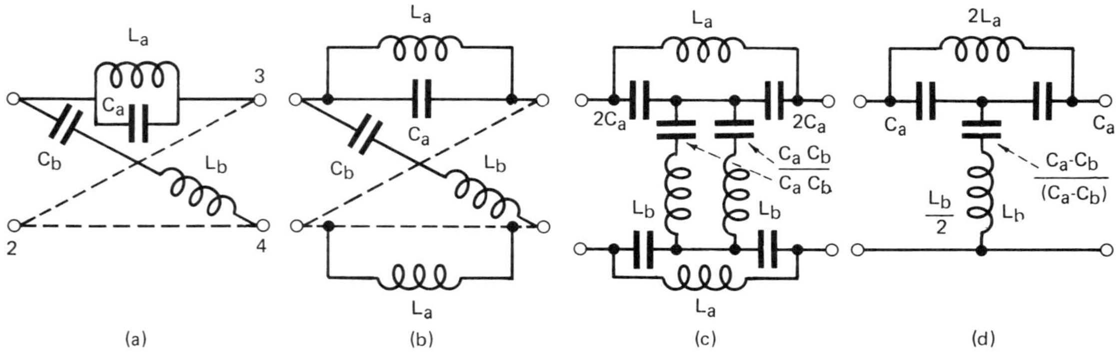

FIGURE 23. Transformation of Lattice Network to Bridged-T Network

response. can be tailored separately to the amplitude response. It is probably, however, only to be considered for use in new designs. It will give a response that is not only superior but also much more reproducable, and cannot be mis-aligned by service engineers with inadequate equipment.

Eye Height. The most useful indication of data quality is given by 'eye height'. A basic system diagram for eye-height measurement is shown in Figure 24.

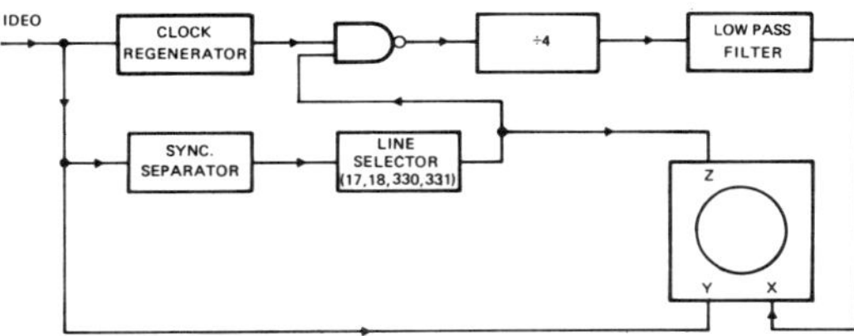

FIGURE 24. Measurement of Eye Height

It is necessary to regenerate the clock from the incoming data. This clock frequency is divided by four, and harmonics removed by a low pass filter to give a sinusoidal waveform. The latter is used as the timebase for the oscilloscope. Four clock periods are displayed. Video is applied to the Y input, and the display is gated on the oscilloscope Z input to ensure display only during data. The display is of the form shown in Figure 25.

The Eye Height is expressed as the percentage (h/H) x 100. The name 'eye height' for this percentage is derived from the fact that the shape of the hole in the middle of the display, which gives the difference between the highest level of a logic '0' and the lowest level of a logic '1', approximates to the shape of an eye. Distortion of the signal will reduce the difference between these two levels. In order to measure eye height it is necessary to integrate the display to include all possible combinations of data. This may be done either with a storage oscilloscope or a scope camera.

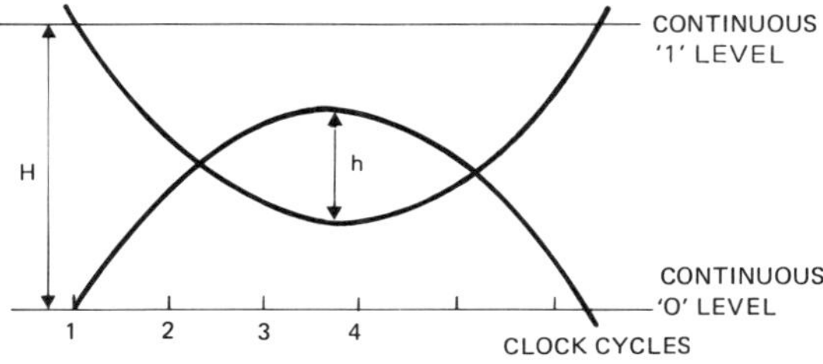

FIGURE 25. 'Eye Height' Display Form

Demodulator. The type of demodulator used will also affect data quality. T.v. signals are transmitted using a vestigial sideband signal. At high modulation frequencies this behaves like a single sideband signal, and has an envelope given by

$$E = (1 + m \sin pt + m^2/4)^{½}$$

where m = modulation depth

p = angular frequency of video sinewave

$$= 1 + ½m (\sin pt + m^4/4) - \tfrac{1}{8}m^2 (\sin pt + m/4)^2 \ldots$$

As long as m<<1 this is close to the original video waveform. However, Teletext is modulated to 40% (m = 0.4) and t.v. receivers contain filters that reduce the carrier level by 6dB making the effective modulation index 80% (m = 0.8). The effect of this on the demodulated waveform may be seen in Figure 26, where there is a change in instantaneous level of up to 10%. The effective modulation depth is reduced by adding a large carrier component to the signal, as is done in a synchronous demodulator.

Thus is it advisable to use a synchronous demodulator if at all possible. Receivers using envelope detectors may give reasonable results with good signal conditions but immunity to signal degradation of any sort will be reduced.

Connection to Module. The video signal may be taken from any suitable point after the detector, preferably using a buffer to avoid loading the existing receiver circuits. The video connection should be made using a screened cable, which should be reverse terminated to reduce reflections as shown in Figure 27. Use of the 56 ohm resistor may not be necessary if the connecting cable is short.

The video input level to the XM-11 should be capable of adjustment over the range 1.0 to 2.7V. At any one power supply voltage there is a wide range of video input level over which the module will give acceptable performance, but this range differs for different power supply voltages and for different modules. The extent of the range will be dependant on the quality (eye-height) of the data signal.

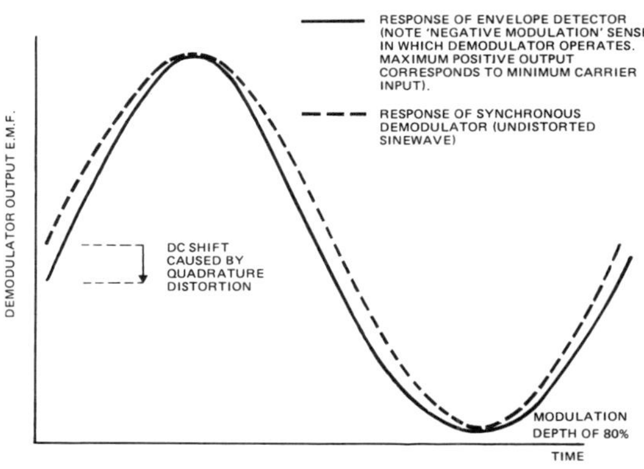

FIGURE 26. Response of Envelope and Synchronous Demodulators to a Sinusoidally – Modulated Single-Sideband Signal.

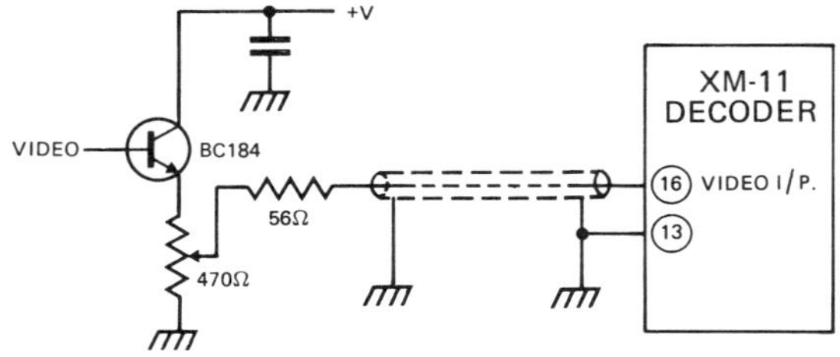

FIGURE 27. Video Input Interface Circuit

For operation at severely degraded eye heights each module will have an optimum video input level which will be dependant on the power supply voltage, the module itself and the characteristics of the video and i.f. circuits of the t.v.

Line Flyback Pulse

The line flyback pulse may be conveniently taken from a low voltage supply winding on the line transformer. A 20-30V supply winding will have a negative pulse of about 200V on it (see Figure 28). The actual value is not

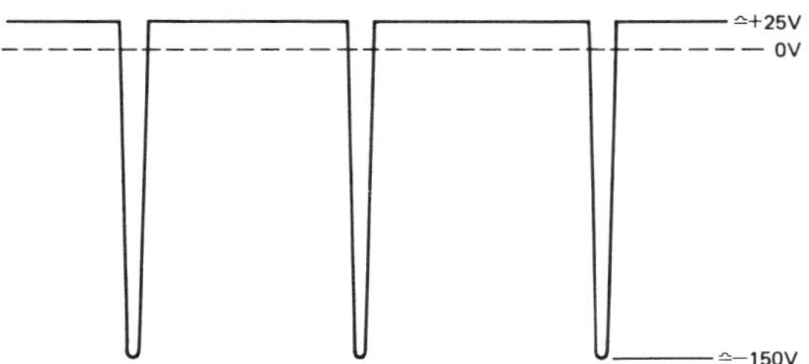

FIGURE 28. Line Flyback Pulse Waveform

critical, but the pulse must be negative with respect to ground, and an external resistor must be used to limit the pulse current to about 3mA. The pulse should be fed to the module using a screened cable, which is earthed only at the receiver end, to avoid earth loops with the video earth. This cable will capacitively load the output resulting in a CR time constant which will delay the pulse, resulting in a displacement of the display on the screen. This problem may be overcome by putting half the resistance at each end of the cable and using a speed-up capacitor as shown in Figure 29. The value of the speed up capacitor may be optimised by viewing the position of the text on the screen. The module line flyback input has an input resistance of about 22kΩ, and calculations of series resistance should allow for this.

The line flyback pulse is used to synchronise the teletext display as this results in less jitter than a system which generates a line pulse from the video input signal.

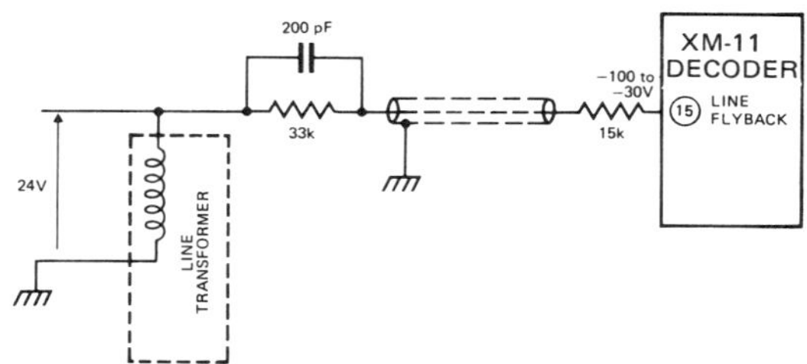

FIGURE 29. Line Flyback Pulse Interface

However, in some applications of the decoder, line flyback may not be available. In this situation, a line pulse must be generated separately. The decoder acts only on the first falling edge of the negative pulse, which should occur within 0.5μs of the end of the active video signal. Mark/space ratio is not critical provided that the negative pulse is at least 8μs wide. If the line flyback input is generated in this fashion, it is possible that a large negative pulse is not easily obtained (a pulse of at least −25V w.r.t. earth is required). Provision is made on the board for the addition of a resistor (R25) which may be used to reduce the input resistance by shunting the 22kΩ input resistor, and hence the required voltage.

The line flyback input must be provided even if the module is used to capture data only. This is possible if a 'standby' mode of operation is incorporated for the capture of time coded pages when the user is not actually watching television, and only the small signal circuits are under power.

Keyboard Connections

Control instructions are given to the decoder by using the 4 input wires and 4 output wires in a scanning matrix, as shown in Figure 30, and decoded according to the

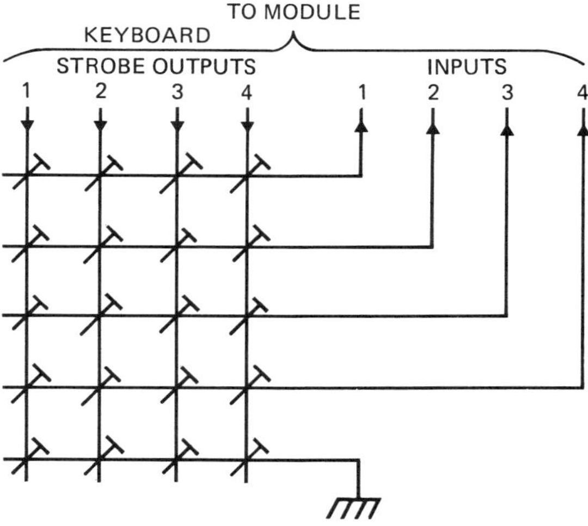

FIGURE 30. Keyboard Matrix

Table 2. Keyboard Matrix Decoding

Lines	Outputs 1	2	3	4
Inputs 1	0	4	8	Text
2	1	5	9	Mix
3	2	6	Page	Pict.
4	3	7	Time	Update
E	Reveal	N/A	N/A	N/A

matrix in Table 2. All strobe outputs, and inputs are normally held at a t.t.l. high level by means of 5kΩ internal pull up resistors. During one t.v. line in each field, each output has a negative pulse approximately 12ns in duration. These pulses are time-shared, as shown in Figure 31.

The pulses in Figure 31 are repeated on each output at field rate, i.e. every 20μs. In order to give a command to the decoder, one of the output pulses must be transferred to one of the input lines for at least 2 and preferably 3 field periods in order to allow the internal 'de-bounce' circuitry to function correctly. Similarly there should be a time interval of 2 or 3 field periods between instructions.

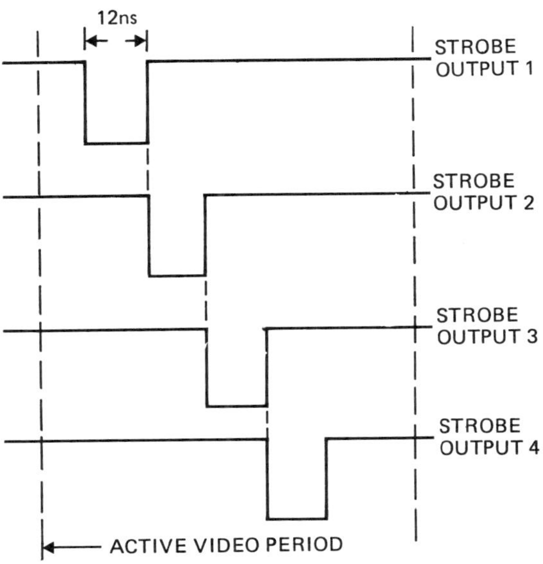

FIGURE 31. Keyboard Strobe Pulses

The 'Reveal concealed display' command operates in a different manner however. Instead of transferring a pulse from an output to an input, strobe output 1 must be held at a t.t.l. 'low' level for 3 fields.

The simplest way of controlling the keyboard matrix is by use of a hardwired keyboard using mechanical switches.

It may also be possible to use solid state analogue switches instead of mechanical switches. However, the maximum allowable series resistance in the keyboard lines is 100Ω and many devices of this type do not achieve this. The switches should be connected to the module using an 8 cored screened cable. Up to 1nF of capacity may be connected to each of the keyboard connections corresponding to about 6m of typical multiway cable. Care should be taken to insulate the connections from the possibility of static discharge. (With the prevalence of synthetic carpets nowadays, it is quite possible for the operator to charge to –25kV and if applied to the keyboard connections this voltage is likely to cause failure of the module.)

Many available keyboards do not have a matrix arrangement, but instead each contact connects one line to a common terminal, thus the keyboard has (n+1) connections, where n = number of keys). This arrangement can be used with a transistor at each matrix point as shown in Figure 32 for one of the keyboard strobe outputs.

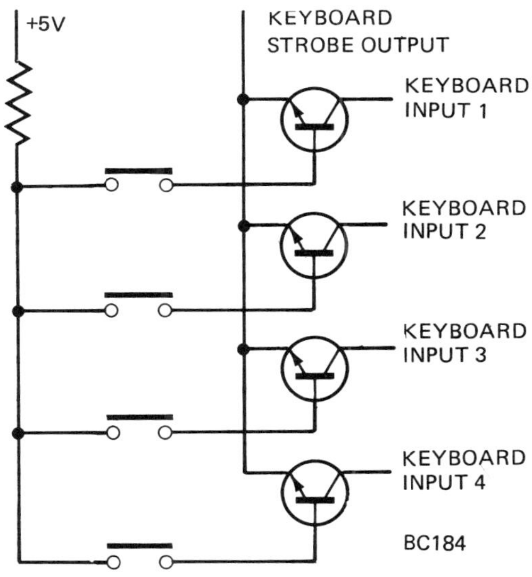

FIGURE 32. Use of n-Line to Common Keyboard

A similar arrangement can be used for initialization at switch-on. When first switched on the decoder may start in either picture or mix modes. In order to ensure initialization in the picture mode the circuit in Figure 33 may be used.

Remote Control. The keyboard connections to the TIFAX XM-11 module have operating conditions compatible with standard t.t.l. making it relatively straightforward

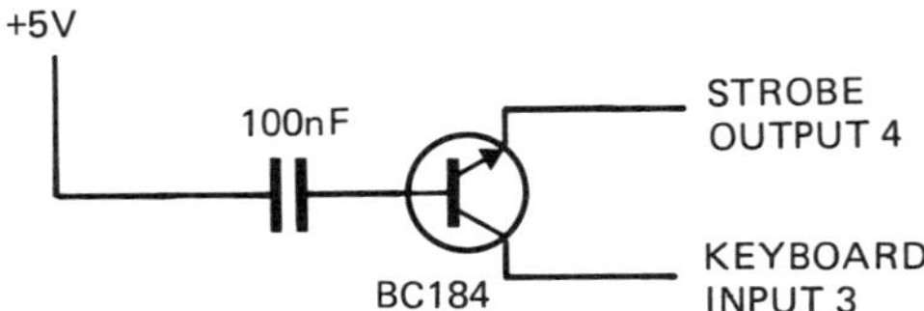

FIGURE 33. Picture Initialization Circuit

to interface with any remote control system, either ultrasonic or infra-red. Most remote control systems generate a 5 bit word for each control function; this must be decoded to transfer strobe output pulses to the keyboard inputs. The first 6 ns of the strobe output pulse are not active, giving a margin for propagation delays of external circuitry.

If remote control is used, it will probably be combined with the normal t.v. functions. In order to keep the number of buttons on the keyboard to a minimum, and also since many remote control systems have only 30 channels, some multiplexing will be necessary. The number keys 0-9 will probably be used for teletext control and channel change with an inhibit circuit to prevent channel change during teletext control. Many arrangements are possible and choice is very much up to individual preference.

Blanking Output

The blanking output must inhibit the picture drive to the video output stages. When operating in the 'Text' mode, the blanking output is 'high' at all times during display of a full page of text. If the page selected consists of a boxed display, such as a newsflash, or subtitles, the decoder automatically switches to a picture display and the blanking signal is 'high' only during that part of the scan necessary to produce the box.

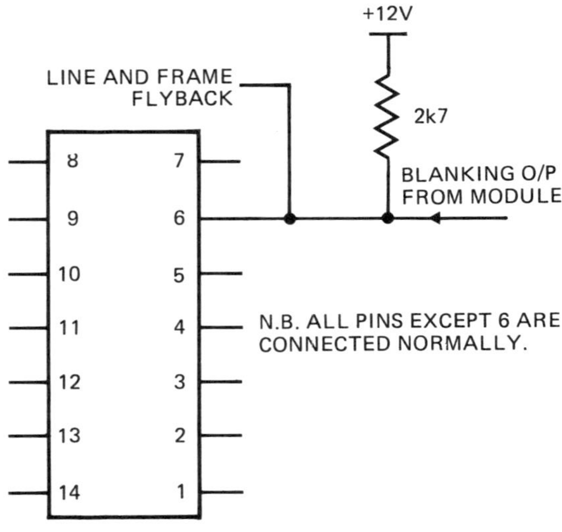

FIGURE 34. SN76227 Blanking Interface

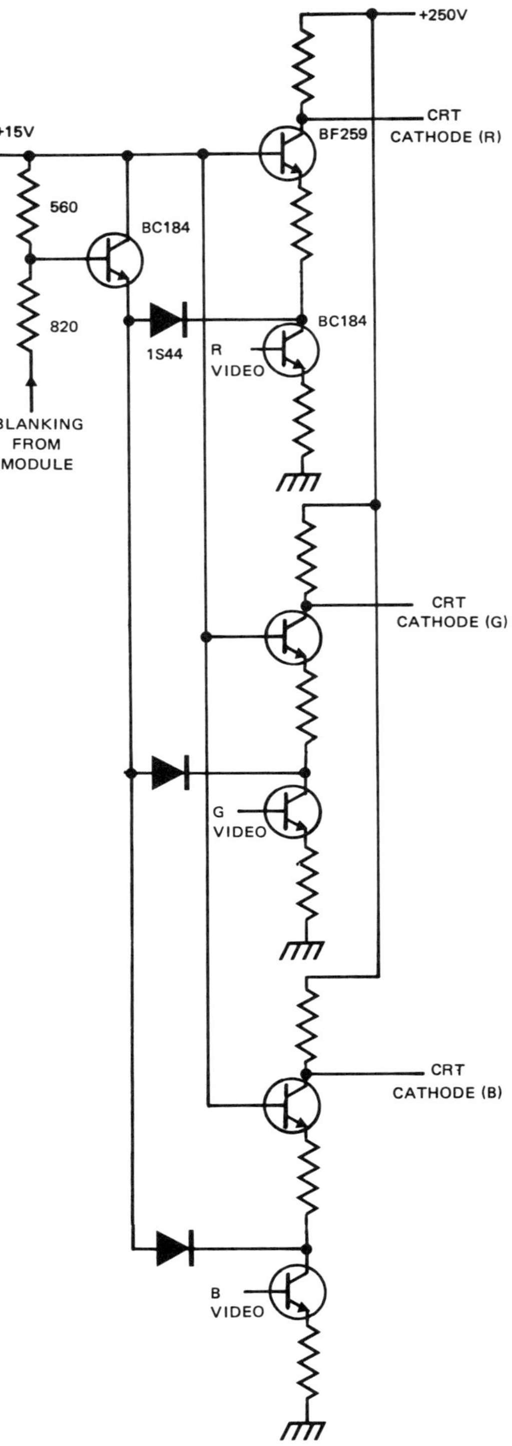

FIGURE 35. Blanking Interface with Cascode Video Output Stages

The blanking output of the module consists of an open collector transistor with a 470Ω resistor in series with it. The resistor is included to protect the output transistor. In some applications (e.g. driving standard t.t.l.) the resistor may make circuit design difficult. Provision is made on the board for the addition of a shorting link across the output resistor (R20). However, it is recommended that the resistor is left in circuit if possible.

In receivers using the SN76227 i.c. (double balanced chroma demodulator) the blanking signal may be applied to the blanking input on the i.c. (pin 6). A suitable interface circuit is shown in Figure 34. In receivers that do not use the SN76227 it may be necessary to blank each of the R.G.B. video amplifiers separately. If this is done, the three blanking signals must be fed through diodes to avoid interconnecting the video amplifiers. An example of blanking interface circuitry into a cascode output stage is shown in Figure 35.

Receivers with colour difference outputs will probably need the luminance signal blanked in addition to the difference signals. This is a particularly suitable application for the use of analogue switches which are another popular method of blanking.

An extension of the blanking function may be used to facilitate the 'Mix' mode of operation. This mode of display has two problems associated with it. The first is that circuit design can become complicated in order to avoid saturation when text and normal video are summed together. The second problem concerns the legibility of the display being very dependent on the picture content. The Teletext characters, which are all white in the 'Mix' mode, cannot be seen against a light background.

The blanking output of the XM-11 may be summed with the Monochrome output, and presented to the t.v. as a composite blanking signal. In the 'Mix' mode, this will create character shaped 'holes' in the picture. This avoids the problem of saturation, and also, provided that circuit timing is correct, gives a black 'shadow' to the characters which considerably improves the legibility.

Video Output Interface

Colour Receivers. The RGB outputs of the module consist of open collector transistors with 470Ω series resistors. Provision is made on the board for the addition of wire links to short out the resistors (R16, R17, R18) for applications where their inclusion presents design problems. However, as with the blanking output, it is recommended that the resistors are left in circuit where possible.

The RGB outputs may be very easily interfaced into cascode video amplifiers. The configuration shown in Figure 36, shows the simple modification necessary for each video amplifier in this arrangement. Blanking may be achieved as described earlier.

The open collector outputs of the TIFAX module give an extremely flexible configuration capable of driving a variety of different circuits. A simple method of interfacing with a common emitter output stage is shown in Figure 37. The video input must be blanked as described earlier. In Figure 37, transistor VT2 must be a high voltage video transistor. This method does add some extra capacity at the c.r.t. cathode drive point, but in practice does not give any visible degradation of picture quality on receivers with good h.f. response that are modified in this way.

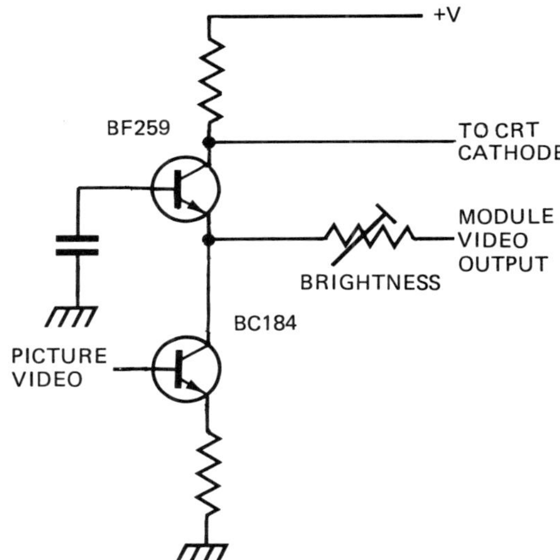

FIGURE 36. RGB Cascode Video Output Interface

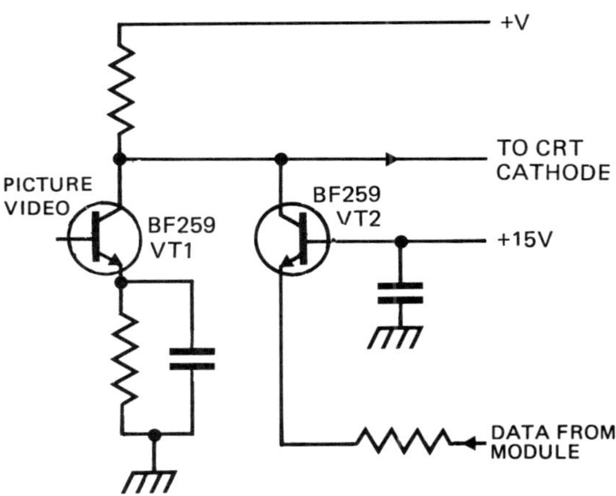

FIGURE 37. Common Emitter Output Interface

As mentioned earlier, long wires and earth returns in the video output interface can give problems in sensitive parts of the receiver due to pickup of radiation at video frequencies. This problem can be overcome at the expense of circuit complexity by using separate logic and video earth paths as shown in Figure 38. In this circuit the logic earth and thus the logic circulating current is separated from the video current, substantially reducing the effect of the long earth path. An additional feature of this circuit is the use of feedback via resistor R_F to define the full white level in the Mix mode.

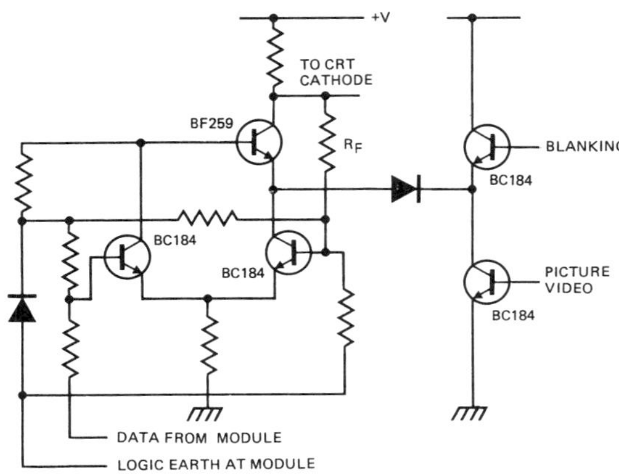

FIGURE 38. Cascode Video Output Interface (Separate Video and Logic Earth Paths)

Monochrome Receivers. A separate output is available for feeding the video output stages of monochrome receivers, which operates in a similar manner to the RGB outputs. All colour information is removed, however, and all characters and graphics will be displayed in white against a black background. Black characters on a white background can be achieved with simple additional circuit. Blanking of the picture video is still required, and will probably need applying to the output stage. A typical monochrome video output interface is shown in Figure 39.

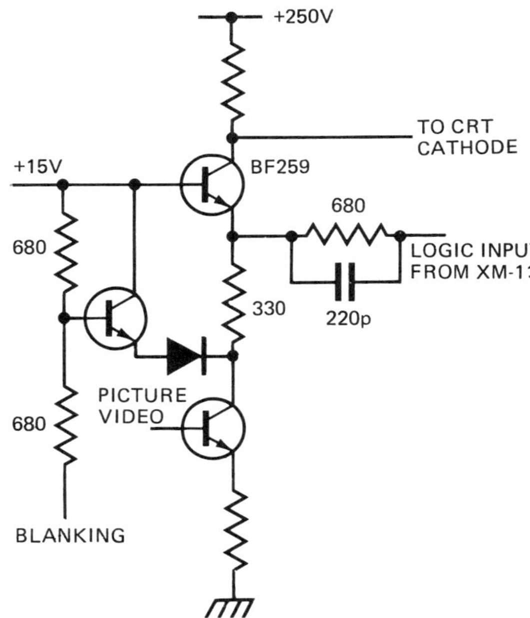

FIGURE 39. Monochrome Output Interface

Sound Muting

It may be considered desirable to mute the t.v. sound signal during display of teletext. This may be conveniently achieved by deriving a muting voltage from the XM-11 decoder blanking output. Other methods are possible (e.g. use of the keyboard 'Text' instruction) but use of the blanking signal has the advantage that it is easy to retain sound during boxed displays such as newsflash or subtitles.

A simple RC time constant as shown in Figure 40 will give a d.c. output proportional to the blanking signal mark/space ratio. During display of picture, or when text is superimposed on picture, there is no blanking output.

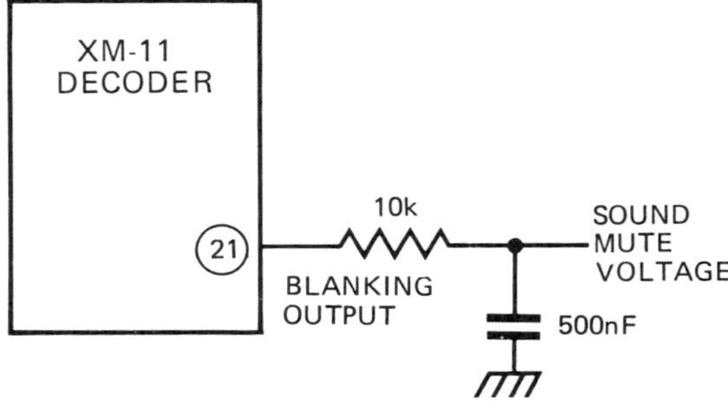

FIGURE 40. Sound Muting

During display of a full page of text the blanking output is 'high' for approximately 80% of the time. If a boxed display is present when in the 'Text' mode, the blanking output will be high only during that part of the scan necessary to produce the box. Thus if the box is $\frac{2}{3}$ of the picture width and $\frac{1}{6}$ of the picture height, the blanking voltage will be high for a percentage of time given by:

$$80 \times \frac{1}{6} \times \frac{2}{3} \simeq 9\%$$

A simple level sensitive switch may be used to ensure that sound is muted only when a full page of text is displayed.

REFERENCES

1. *Specification of Standard for Broadcast Teletext Signals;* BBC, IBA and BREMA; January 13, 1976.
2. *Broadcast Teletext Specification;* BBC, IBA and BREMA; September 1976.
3. B. Norris & R. Parsons; "Teletext Data Decoding – The L.S.I. Approach"; *IEE Transactions on Consumer Electronics,* August 1976, Vol. CE/22 No. 3. pp. 247-252.
4. F. E. Terman, *Radio Engineers Handbook,* McGraw-Hill Book Co., New York & London, Section 3, pp. 135- , 1943.

ASSOCIATED PRODUCTS

The DM-11 Direct Memory Access Module

The DM-11 module provides all the facilities of the XM-11, but has the additional feature that a signal on a single control pin effects a complete changeover from the Teletext mode to an external data mode of operation. The page memory is then made directly accessible to seven bit parallel data. Memory addressing is in the form of a six bit column address and a five bit row address. External data may be written into the memory and stored data may be read out. In addition status signals are provided to enable proper timing of read/write operations and cursor generation/insertion.

This module may be used to display from Viewdata, data from cassette recorders, microprocessors, games etc.

The XM-11 DH TIFAX Module with Double Height Character Facility

Since the design of the XM-11, several new control characters have been added to the Teletext specification,[2] including the facility for displaying double height characters. In most applications this feature is not essential, particularly since the change in the specification is made in such a way as to ensure compatibility with decoders not reacting to the double height control. However, where the Teletext system is used primarily for sub-titling, the use of double height characters becomes more important. For this type of application, the XM-11 DH module has the ability to decode the double height control character when transmitted. The subsequent letters/numbers or graphics are then displayed in double height format until the normal height control character is received or until the end of the row.

Alternative Character Founts

As stated, the r.o.m. used in the TIFAX range of products is mask programmable to allow for alternative character founts for use in countries other than the U.K. A version of the r.o.m. which generates a Swedish set of characters is available (SN74S263) and others will be produced when required.

Remote Control Interface I.C.

A mask-programmable i.[2]l. i.c. is available, development number TX010, which is designed as a remote control interface for the XM-11 module. This will allow operation with any system using a 5 bit control word. It operates from a 5V supply, has a low power consumption – typically 40mW, and is available in a 16 or 18 pin d.i.l. package. Its open collector outputs allow the device to be wired in parallel with an existing keypad if required. A latched output (Channel Change Enable), is provided to ensure that channel changes are avoided during the selection of pages of text. The output is set to a logic 'low' when either 'Text' or 'Mix' is selected. The latch is reset to logic 'high' by either 'Picture' or 'Update' and the i.c. incorporates a power-on reset circuit.

Microprocessor Control of T.V. Peripheral Circuits

It is apparent that microprocessors now present a viable and economic solution for the control of t.v. peripherals. For example, the TMS 1100 microprocessor can be programmed to remotely perform the following functions:

- ★ Channel selection
- ★ Band select
- ★ Programmed viewing
- ★ Channel Tune Up/Down
- ★ Display time and channel number
- ★ Clock set
- ★ Colour Up/Down
- ★ Volume Up/Down
- ★ Brightness Up/Down
- ★ Reset
- ★ Sound Mute
- ★ Cancel program

The XM-11 module may be combined with such a system using the remote control interface i.c.

X SYSTEM 7 TOUCH CONTROL INTEGRATED CIRCUITS

by
Giuseppe D'Elia

The use of integrated circuits to perform controlling functions instead of mechanical switches is becoming more common mainly owing to their greater reliability, smaller maintenance, and overall costs. Touch tune i.c. applications have been described previously[1], but this chapter deals with a more recently introduced set of touch control i.c.s., known as System Seven, and their use in various circuits. This includes showing how the number of external components in previously described circuits is reduced. The System Seven touch control i.c.s. consist of the SN76707 Six Channel Selector, Latch and Driver; the SN76708 ten channel Decoder Driver; and the SN76709 eight channel selector, Latch and Driver. By using a '707 and '709 a six or eight channel selector system can be built with a minimum of external circuitry. The '707 and '708 , in combination enable a 16 channel selector system to be built. The devices can be used to drive either high voltage neon indicators, or medium current light emitting diodes (l.e.d.s.) in an individual channel indicator or 'tab' display. Alternatively, the binary input/output lines can be used to drive a SN29764 one-and-a-half digit decoder driver to give a numerical indication of channel selection, as explained later.

These devices may be used with either touch pads or light action switches and, if used with the latter, the high value isolating resistors on the inputs can be eliminated.

FUNCTIONAL DESCRIPTIONS

The '707 and '709 Channel Selector, Latch and Driver I.C.s.

The Centre of the device is a four stage programmable counter, (see Figure 1), which can either be driven serially for touch selection of an output, or in parallel by the binary address inputs when an output is to be selected by remote control command. The counter feeds a four line to ten line decoder, driving the high voltage open-collector output transistor. The latter must then be connected to the tuning voltage supply rail via the tuning potentiometer. Only the output which is selected is pulled 'low', consequently, the remaining outputs will be at the supply rail potential, which is normally 33V in t.v. tuning application. When a channel in the 'off' state is 'touch activated' a current is applied to the clock input, via the tuning potentiometer, a 4M7Ω resistor and resistor R_A (as shown in Figure 2), producing a series of clock pulses. These pulses make the counter count down and consequently each output is turned 'on', in sequence, for a single clock period until the channel activated is reached.

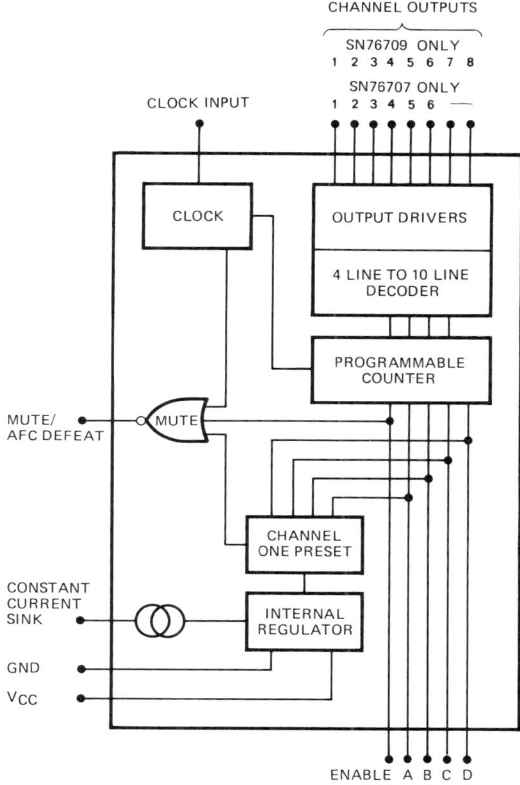

FIGURE 1. SN76707/9 Block Diagram

This output, having been turned 'on' causes the current being fed to the clock input to be shunted to ground, thus stopping the clock. The output is then held low and the voltage preset on its potentiometer is applied to the tuner. The information in the counter is automatically transferred to the data input pins, unless parallel information is being loaded, in which case the inputs are not latched until the enabling signal is removed. This feature enables data to be received and held on the same pins and thus facilitates seven segment display driving. The channel one preset circuit loads a zero on all the data lines at 'switch on' ensuring that channel 1 is called up. The channel one preset circuit relies on its supply voltage ramping up to its final value.

The clock frequency is approximately determined by the time taken to charge capacitor C by 400mV, although the initial pulse of any train is always longer

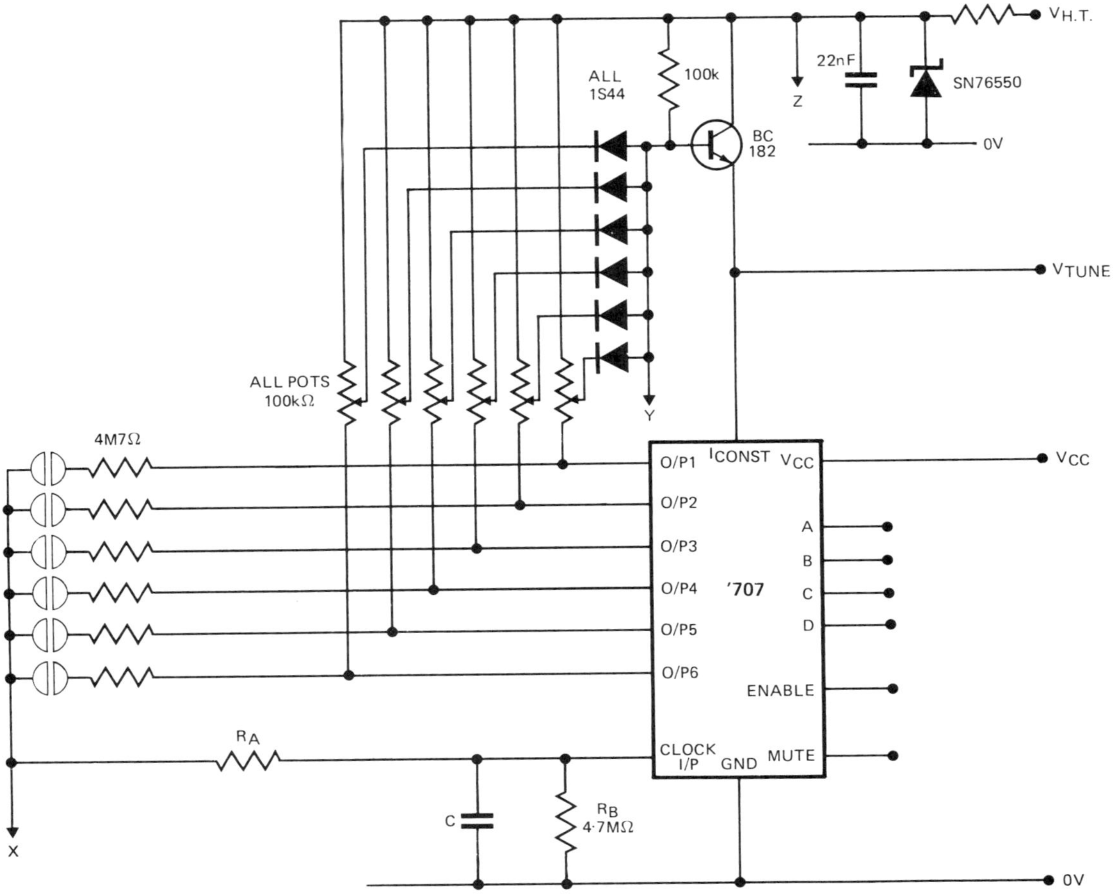

FIGURE 2. SN76707 6 Channel Selection System

because the input has to reach 4.2V before the clocking starts, as illustrated in Figure 3. The d.c. component of the clock input signal is used to drive the sound mute output. The sound mute output is also activated by the enable input or the channel one preset circuit. Resistor R_B ensures that capacitor C is discharged to below the sound mute activations threshold when the clock stops. Clock pulses may be applied to the clock input from an external source when a channel facility is required.

The '707 and '709 have an internal constant current load to maintain reasonable linearity at lower end of the tuning voltage range. The switching of the tuning voltage is accomplished using diodes in series with the sliders of the tuning potentiometers. The temperature coefficient of the diode voltage drops is compensated by the V_{BE} of the n.p.n. transistor used as the emitter follower for the constant current load in the '707 or '709.

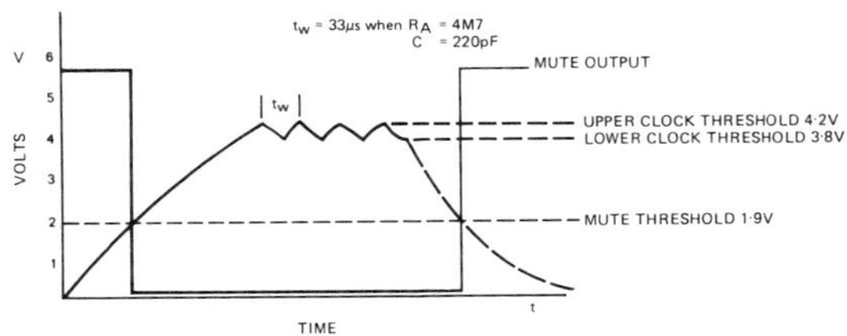

FIGURE 3. Clock and Mute Thresholds

The '708 Channel Decoder Driver I.C.

The SN76708 is a ten channel expander device for use in conjunction with the '707 to allow the implementation of a 16 channel system. Basically, the device is the same wafer as the '707, as is the '709, but has a different metallisation mask which makes only the counter, decoder and drivers externally available, as shown in Figure 4. The decoder is programmed to recognise binary states 0110 to 1111 instead of 0000 to 1001 as in the decoder of the '707/709 devices.

The counter in the '708 is permanently enabled internally and therefore acts as a transparent parallel-in parallel-out register. The mode of operation of the device is given in Figure 5. Here the binary address lines of the '707 are paralleled with those of the slave device. The common end of the touch input pads of the '707 are commoned with those of the '708 so as to provide a current path for the oscillator input from both sides.

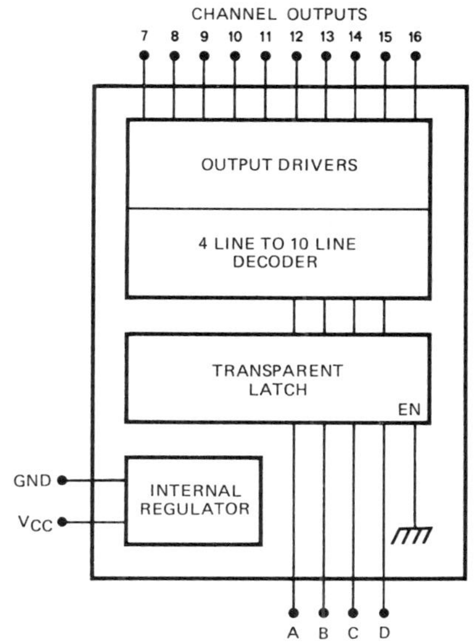

FIGURE 4. SN76708 Block Diagram

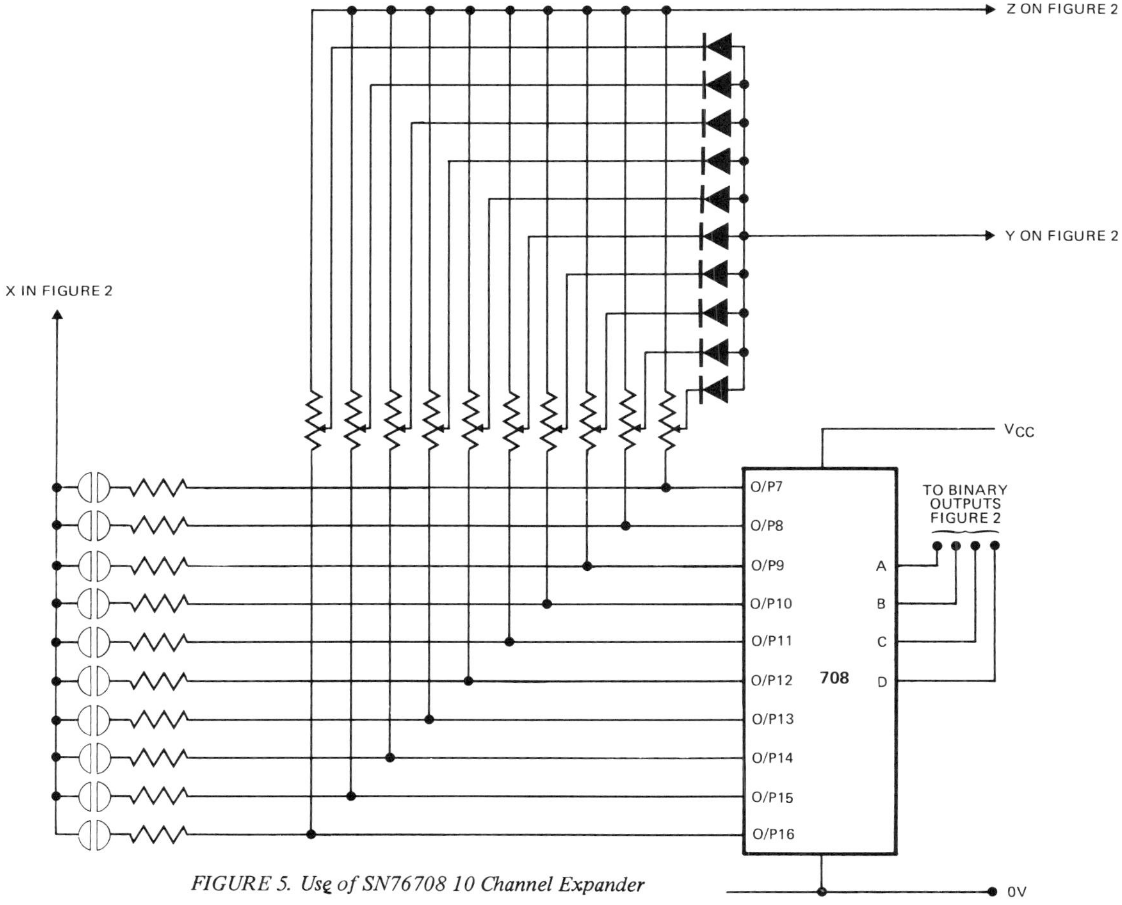

FIGURE 5. Use of SN76708 10 Channel Expander

OPERATION

Methods of Indicating Channel Selected

Due to the nature of the SN76707/8/9 outputs, there are two main categories in which the method of channel indication can be grouped, those using the channel output lines and those using the binary address lines.

Channel Output Methods: As the channel output drivers have a guaranteed breakdown of 55V they can be used to drive high voltage devices such as neons and numerical indicators displays, as illustrated in Figures 6 and 7.

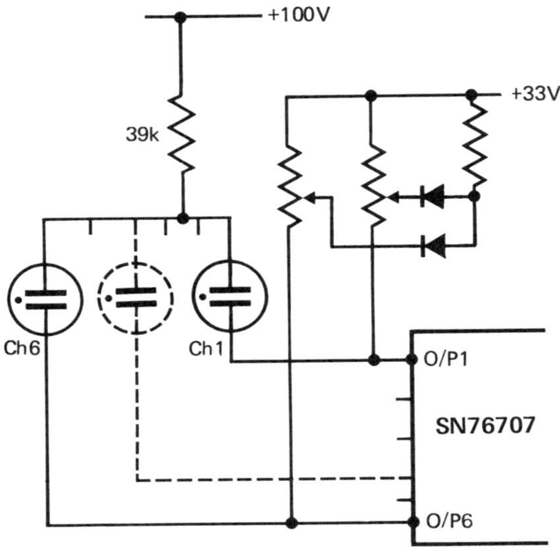

FIGURE 6. Neon Tab Display

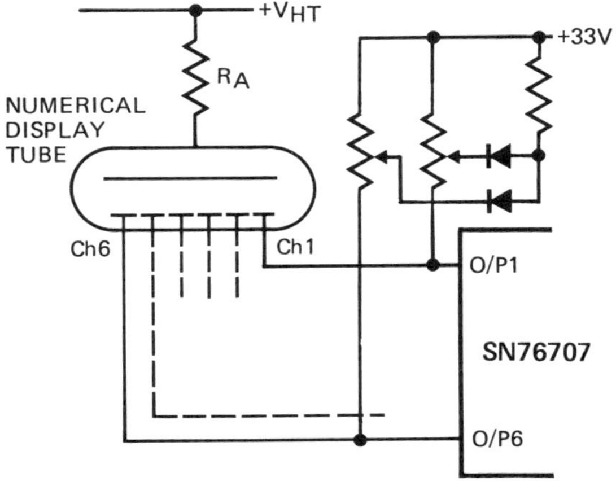

FIGURE 7. High Voltage Numerical Channel Display

This makes possible either a 'tab' type display or, in the case of a 6 or 8 channel system, the use of numerical identification.

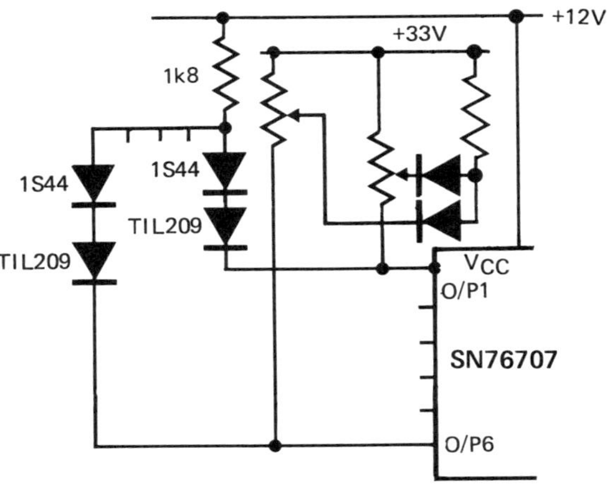

FIGURE 8. LED Tab Display

Alternatively, the channel outputs can be used to drive an l.e.d. 'tab' display as shown in Figure 8. However, due to the low reverse breakdown of typical l.e.d. indicators, a diode must be used in series with the l.e.d., as shown, to ensure that all l.e.d.s., apart from the one selected, remain non-conducting.

Address Line Methods: The address outputs of the '707/9 follow a natural binary progression from 0000 to 1111 and, as the outputs are capable of driving a t.t.l. load, can be used to drive t.t.l. decoder drivers of the SN7414N or SN7446N variety. However, if this is done, the first channel number will be zero rather than one. Also, these devices can only be used for a maximum of ten channels unless external interfacing is used to derive the correct b.c.d. code for outputs 10 to 15 to drive a second decoder. An SN29764N 4 bit binary to 1½ digit 7 segment decoder driver can be used as shown in Figure 9. This device has an 'excess one' decoder and therefore decodes binary 0000 to 1111 as 1 to 16 rather than 0 to 15. Also included are variable constant current source outputs making possible simple control of display brightness.

Use of '707/8/9 in Remote Control Systems

There are two methods of channel address available for use in remote control systems. The first is channel access via the address lines and the enable input which allows any channel to be accessed directly. It does, however, require the use of a remote control that has binary address lines and an enable pulse available.

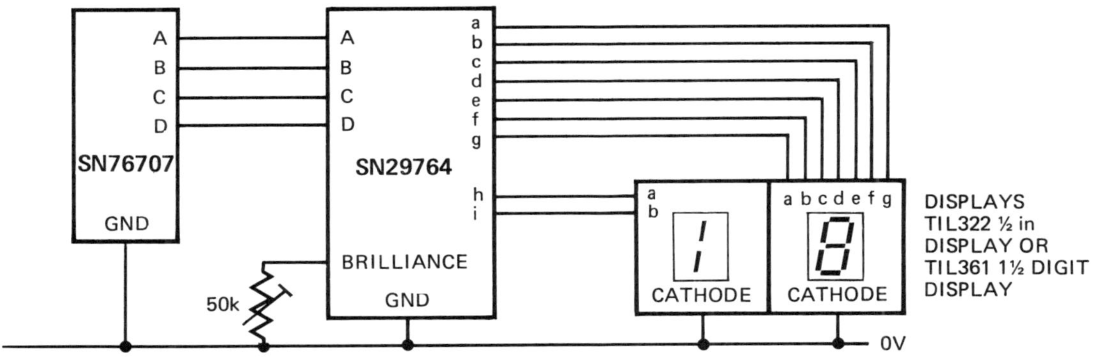

FIGURE 9. Use of SN29764 to give numerical LED display

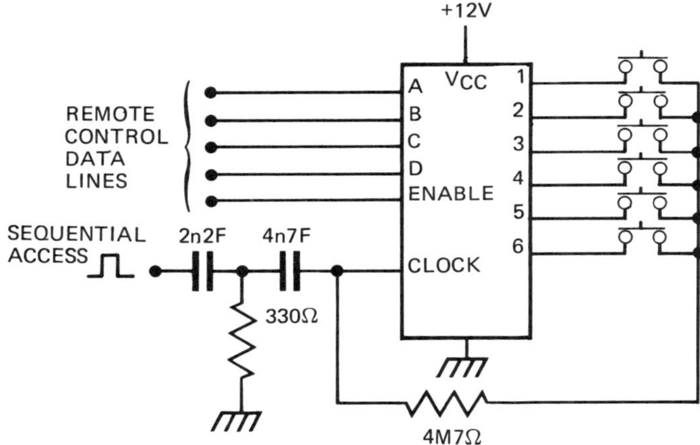

FIGURE 10. Parallel and Sequential Channel Access Method

A second method for channel access is given in Figure 10 where the clock input is activated with a series of externally derived pulses and each output accessed sequentially. There is one main problem associated with this method of access, i.e. the counter in the '707/9 always counts through 16 states irrespective of how many channels are in use. This means that an external means of resetting the counter has to be used to avoid cycling through unwanted states. A method for 6 channel use is shown in Figure 11. In this method a negative going pulse has to be derived from the remote control circuits. This pulse is fed to a SN7492 divide-by-twelve counter i.c. and to enable input of the SN76707. Thus the counter is advanced and the channel select i.c. enabled at the same time. Only the ABC outputs of the counter are used as the counter resets back to 0000 every sixth clock pulse. Therefore, the whole tuning system will reset every sixth input pulse, as the internal counter of the '707 is only being used as a latch for the data of the external counter. Similarly, by substituting an SN7493 i.c. the same method can be used to reset the '709 every eigth pulse.

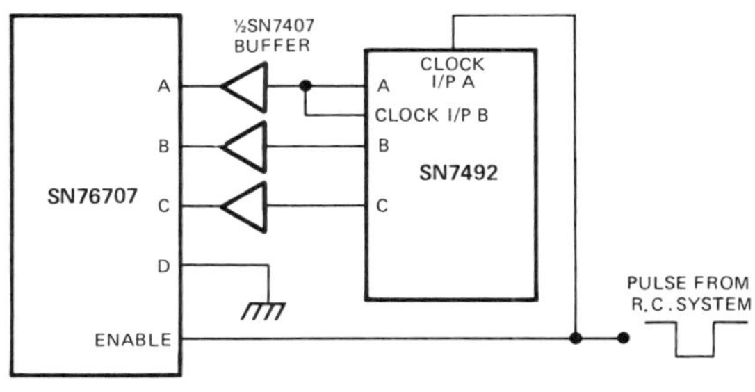

FIGURE 11. External Counter Reseting

Band Switching

Band switching, if required, can be achieved by the use of external discrete transistor switches coupled to the appropriate outputs as given in Figure 12. The use of external transistors allows the band switching to be allocated according to the individual application. Thus on an a.m./f.m. tuner system using the '709, 4 channels could be assigned to a.m. and 4 to f.m. or any combination utilising up to 8 presets. If a 'tab' l.e.d. display is used, the l.e.d. and diode can be used instead of the isolating diodes in the band switching circuits.

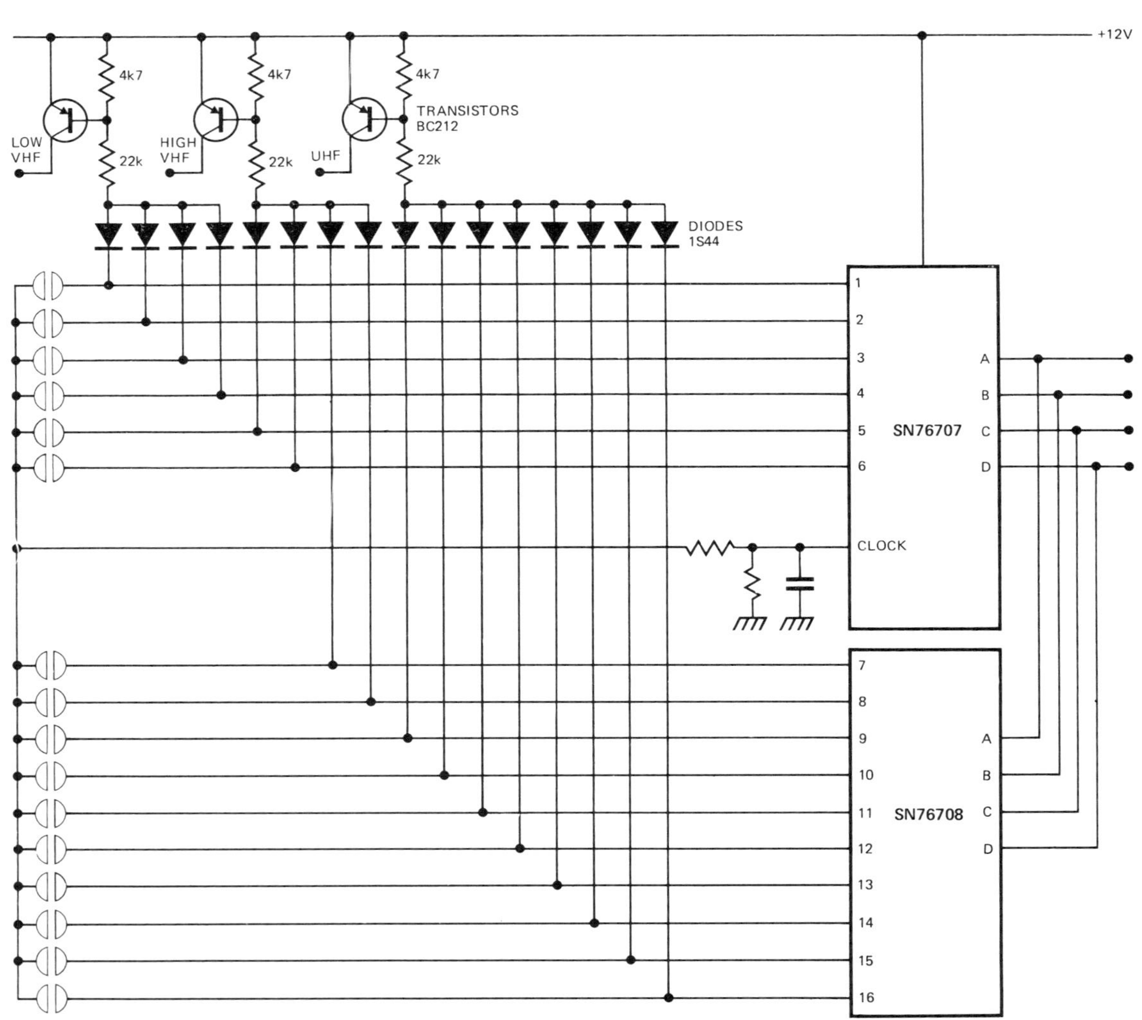

FIGURE 12. External Band Switching

APPLICATIONS

Use of '708 as a Channel Switch

By disregarding the A input, the '708 i.c. can be used in conjunction with any eight station channel select system that has latched binary outputs. In this use, only outputs 9 to 16 are used to drive the presets and display devices Figure 13 shows the '708 being used for this purpose in conjunction with the TMS3720 in a television receiver application. The system as shown has provision for remote control of sequential station access and the three analogue functions of colour, brightness and volume. At the receiver end there is provision for direct touch access to eight channels and the analogue functions. The digital to analogue converters are contained in the TMS3720, resulting in a very compact remote control and touch system.

If a channel switch device is required for a remote control system that has unlatched binary outputs, then the '709 can be used for this function, provided that an enable pulse is available.

Hexadecimal Keyboard

The '706 and '707 i.c.s. can be used in conjunction with an SN74221 t.t.l. dual monostable i.c. to make a cheap hexadecimal keyboard with strobe. The '706/7 are used in a standard configuration, apart from the replacement of the tuning potentiometer by a 100kΩ resistor. The mute

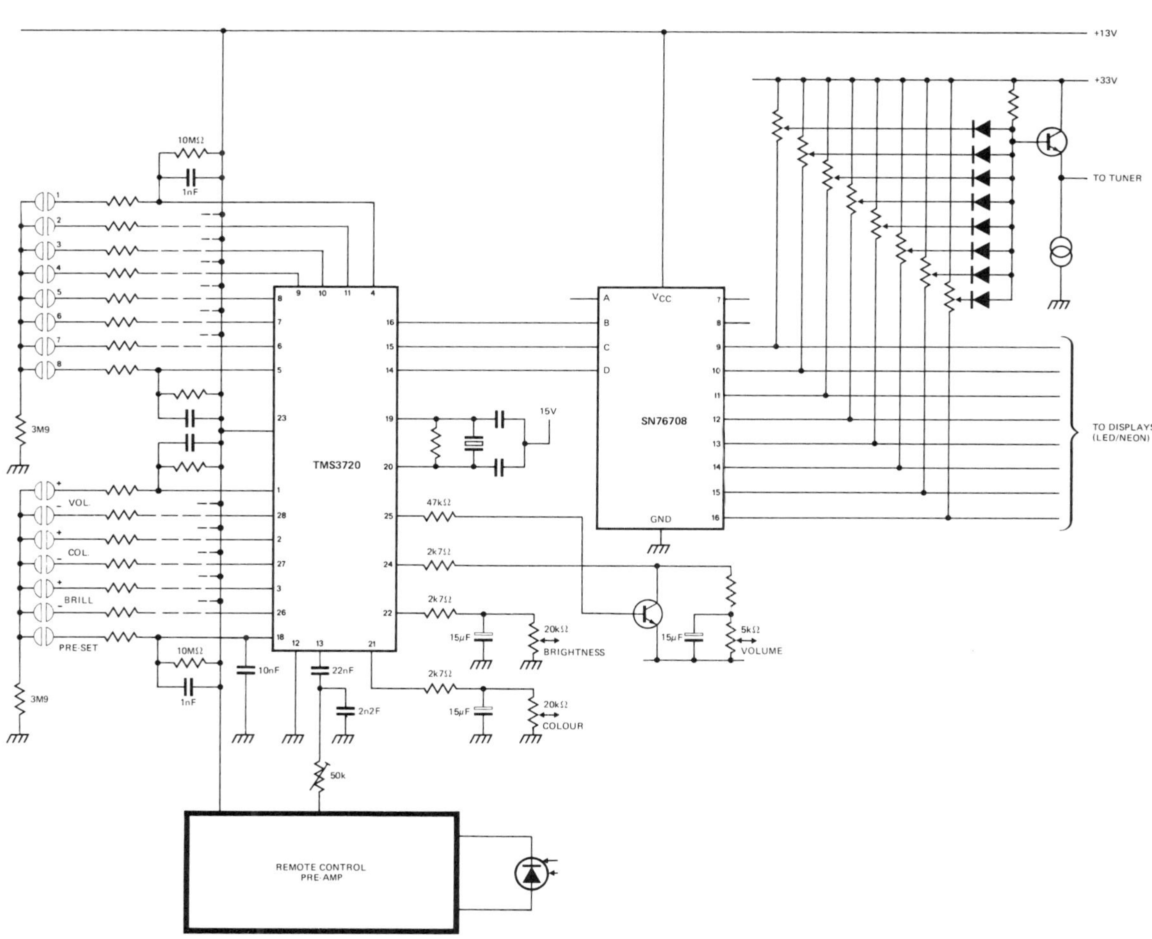

FIGURE 13. Use of SN76708 as a Channel Switch

output is used to trigger the first monostable in the '221, thereby providing a delay before triggering the second monostable, whose output is used as the actual 'data ready' pulse. Without output beffering the keyboard outputs can only drive one standard t.t.l. load. In some applications the data outputs may need to be buffeted by an SN7407 non-inverting buffer. In this case a TIL 311 hexadecimal decoder/driver display device may be used to indicate the character selected as illustrated in Figure 14.

Touch Control of a Record Turntable

The functions of a two or three speed record turntable can be touch controlled by using the 706/9 i.c.s. For such an application, the circuit functions must be such that only one function is operational at one time or they must be capable of being switched on sequentially. In the case of a manual turntable, where only motor start/speed selection or motor stop are required, then it is a straightforward matter to arrange for the output activated by a touch command to switch in the reference voltage needed for the motor servo control system to run at the desired speed The stop command is arranged so as to take the reference voltage above a preset value whereupon the supply to the motor is removed by a comparator. In such a case the number of commands used will be the number of speeds plus stop.

Figure 15 shoes the touch circuitry relevant to a two speed semi-automatic turntable which includes arm lift/lower and end of side stop. Here two outputs per speed are used, one to make the turntable run at the required speed, and a second to run at the required speed and lower the arm. This is done to enable the cleaning of records on the turntable prior to playing. When the end of side is sensed the '707 is enabled and the binary address lines are forced 'low' so as to reset the system to output 1, i.e. stop. As output 1 is used as the stop command the turntable will always turn 'on' in the stop mode.

Heating Element Control

In a previous volume a method of touch control of a heating element is given, which uses the SN16861NG and SN16862N i.c.s. in conjunction with an SN72440 zero crossing switch i.c. and a suitable Triac[2]. The use of the '709 makes this circuit more elegant as the number of i.c. packages is reduced from three to two, and a simpler numerical indication of power selected is possible using an SN7447 t.t.l. b.c.d.-to seven-segment decoder driver i.c. as indicated in Figure 16. No modification is needed to the

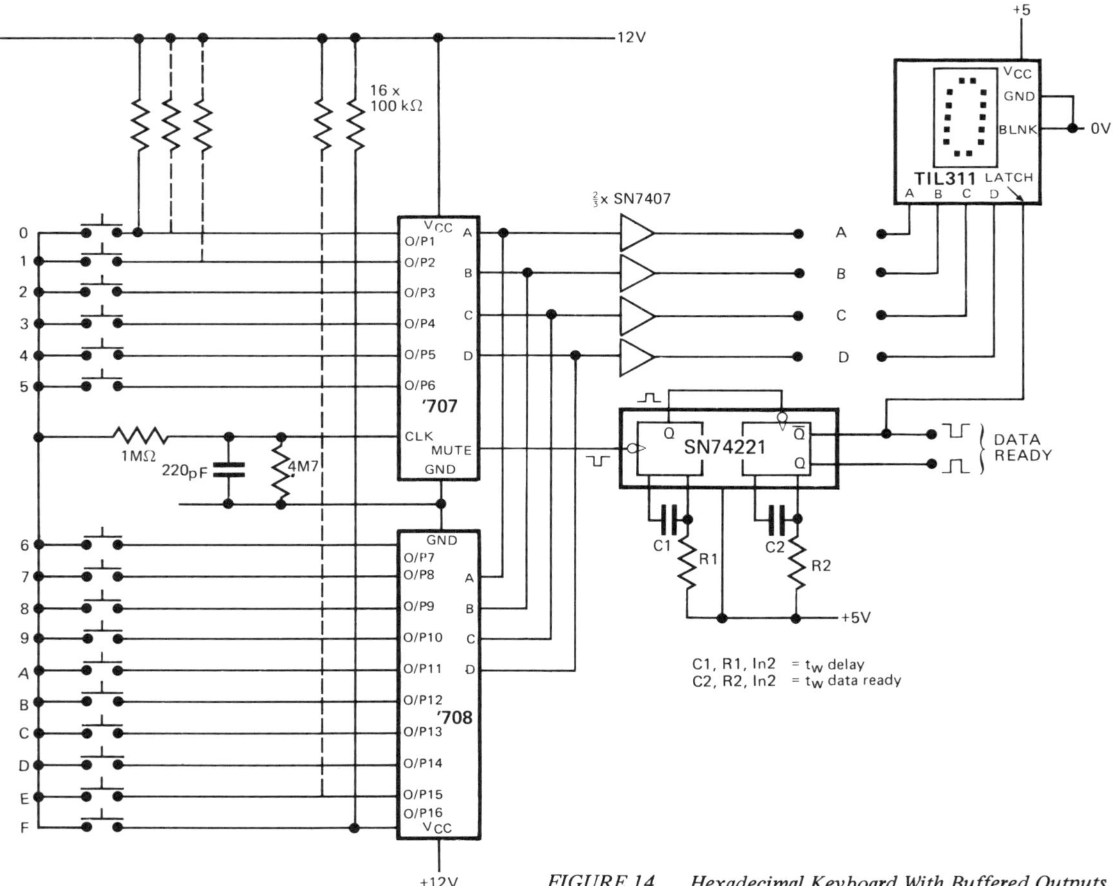

FIGURE 14. Hexadecimal Keyboard With Buffered Outputs

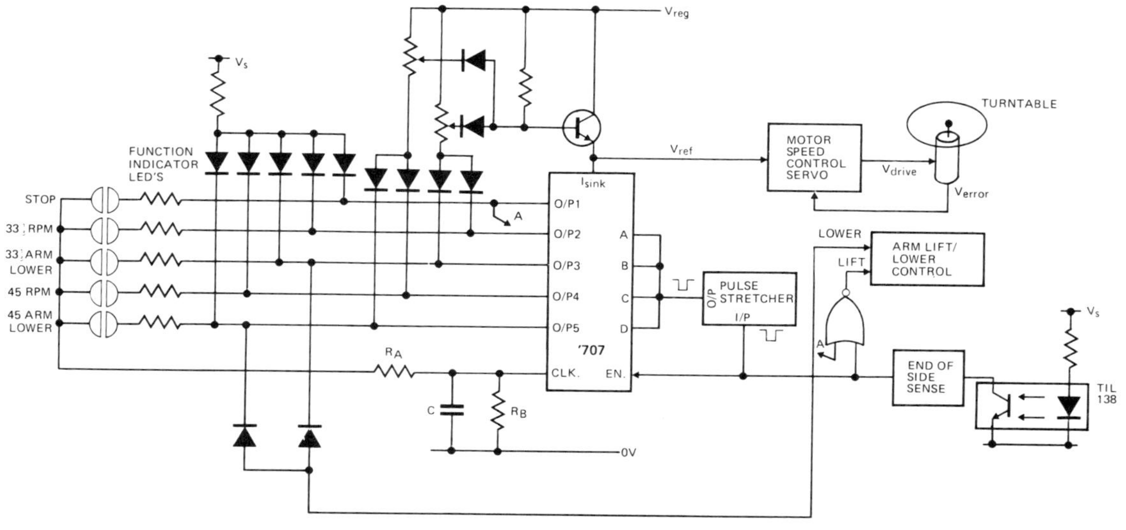

FIGURE 15. Two Speed Semi-Automatic Turntable

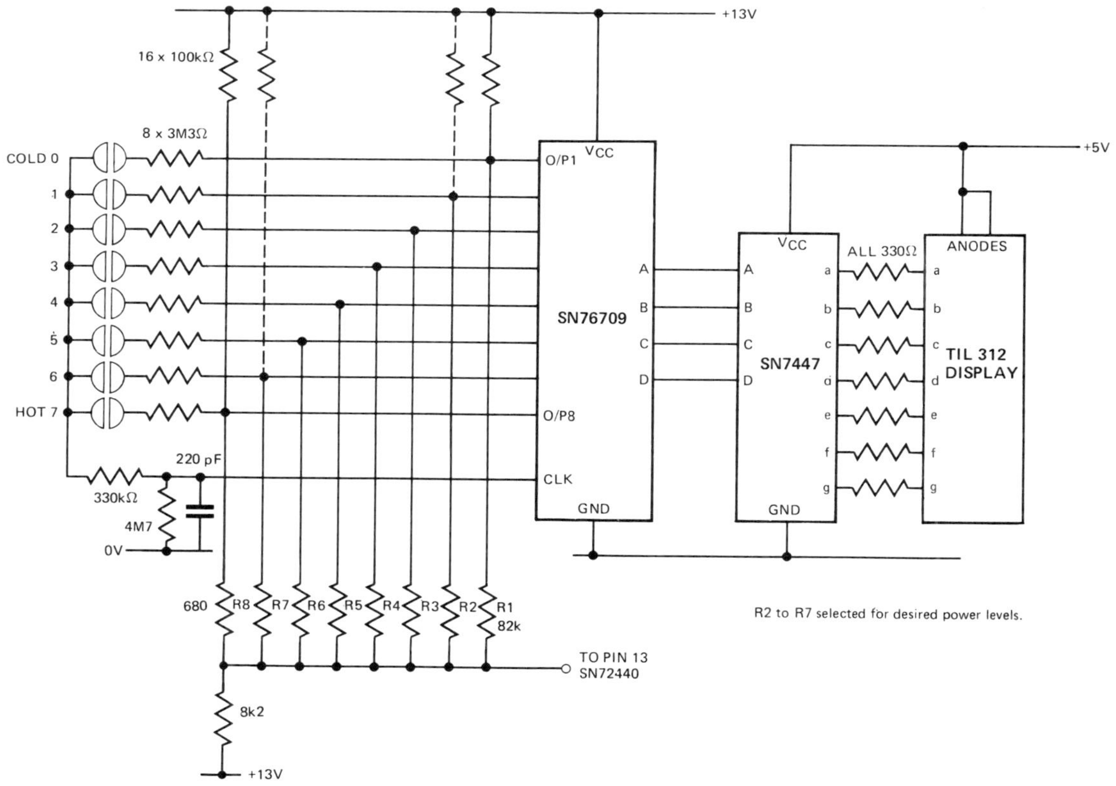

R2 to R7 selected for desired power levels.

FIGURE 16. Electronic Control of Heating Element.

power section of the control circuit (Figure 17 page 86 Vol IV) as the new selection circuit interfaces directly into the same point, but the power supply has to be modified in that a 5V supply has to be derived for the SN7447 and display if a numerical indication of power level is required. If a 'tab' l.e.d. display is chosen then the supply needs no modification.

REFERENCES

1. Applications Laboratory Staff of Texas Instruments Incorporated, *Electronic Power Control and Digital Techniques,* McGraw-Hill Book Company, New York, 1976, pp. 82-90.

2. Applications Laboratory Staff of Texas Instruments Incorporated, *Electronic Power Control and Digital Techniques,* McGraw-Hill Book Company, New York, 1976, pp. 84-86.

SECTION 4

MICROPROCESSORS/MICROCOMPUTERS

XI AN INTRODUCTION TO MICROPROCESSORS

by
Howard Cook

A microprocessor is a device containing functions equivalent to a small computer's Central Processor Unit (C.P.U.). It is thus capable of performing basic computer functions and can be incorporated into system designs where such functions are required. The fact that one semiconductor large scale integrated (l.s.i.) circuit can perform these computer functions means that computer techniques are now available at very low cost.

The microprocessor device has probably made a larger impact upon the electronics industry than any other single development since the first integrated circuit. Systems designed to use microprocessors are, in all but the simplest of cases, normally cheaper to design and produce, more reliable, physically smaller, consume less power and are inherently more flexible than a design using smaller logic devices.

Since the microprocessor is essentially a computer-on-a-chip, much of the terminology used in describing the device characteristics and operation originates from the computer sector of the industry. This can be a problem for engineers from non-computer environments when first evaluating microprocessors. Hence an attempt will be made in this chapter to explain the basic functions and operation in everyday terminology, introducing the microprocessor 'jargon' as it becomes relevant. A glossary at the end contains all such jargon with a brief explanation of the meaning.

The previous volume contained two chapters about microprocessors where their concepts, various systems and some applications were described[1]. However, it would be beneficial for the reader, particularly one not familiar with microprocessors, to read this and may be some of the later chapters in this book before graduating to those in the previous book.

COMPUTER ORGANISATION

A computer is made up of three basic blocks, which may vary in size and complexity but are common to most machines. The 'heart' of the computer is the C.P.U. This is the section which performs the actual 'work', since it is capable of arithmetic, data manipulation, etc. The C.P.U. performs many functions and is controlled by a set of inputs to which instructions are supplied in sequence. An Instruction is a control word containing enough information to cause the C.P.U. to perform one of its predetermined functions.

Associated with the C.P.U. there must be some data storage facility for two reasons. One is to store the data that is being worked on at any time and to store the results of the operations, etc. The second requirement is to store the Instructions which control the operation of the C.P.U.

The third block in the computer system is the Input/Output (I/O) function. To be of any use the computer must be capable of having data and instructions entered into memory and the C.P.U. and also it must be capable of 'outputting' data to the outside world. The arrangement of these three main functions in a computer system is shown in Figure 1.

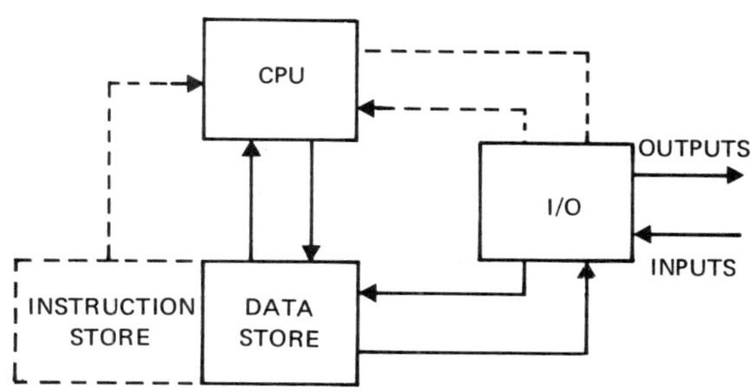

FIGURE 1. Basic Computer Configuration

A separate block is shown dotted, and labelled 'Instruction Store'. Although it is all part of the system memory it is convenient to consider it as a slightly different function from the data store. The other dotted lines, between the C.P.U. and the I/O function indicate that data can be input and output directly to and from the C.P.U. without going via the memory in many cases.

This basic computer configuration is also used in system designs using a microprocessor device. The microprocessor forms the C.P.U. function in the system, and data storage and I/O facilities are added to it to make the system fit the particular application. In general, the term 'microprocessor' is becoming accepted as meaning a single chip for integrated circuit (i.c.) implementation of the C.P.U. function. In actual fact there are some multi-chip versions, but the term microprocessor in this text will be used to define the single chip C.P.U. device. When a microprocessor is used to form the C.P.U. function in a system, the system is referred to as a microcomputer. So a microcomputer has a C.P.U., I/O and memory, and can operate as a computer system. Just to confuse the situation there are some devices available called 'single chip microcomputers'. These have all the elements of the system shown in Figure 1 included on a single device, and are a low cost method of implementing a system, with certain restrictions on performance and complexity.[2]

THE MICROPROCESSOR DEVICE

The microprocessor, like the computer C.P.U., has to be capable of arithmetic and logic functions, data manipulation and control functions, all according to the instruction being supplied to it at any time. Associated with the design of the microprocessor there is a set of instructions which the device will recognise and respond to. By supplying these instructions to the microprocessor in a particular sequence the system can be made to perform a particular task. The sequence of instructions for a given task is called the program and the job of determining the sequence of instructions initially is referred to as 'writing' the Program, or 'programming'. A generic term for programs and related information is Software, as opposed to the term covering the actual devices in the system, which is Hardware.

The microprocessor responds to instructions in the program, and in accordance with these it performs its basic functions on the data in the memory and the system inputs and outputs. The program of instructions has to be presented to the processor not only in the correct sequence, but also at the right times. The way this is achieved is to store the program in the system memory in locations which have been pre-defined in some manner. Normally the program is stored sequentially, so that successive instructions in the program are stored in successive memory locations according to some known address sequence. Assuming that the address sequence is the normal binary count, then Figure 2 shows instruction words of a program stored in a block of memory locations. A diagram of this kind which shows the utilisation of memory locations is often referred to as a Memory 'Map'.

Once the instructions are stored in the required sequence in a block of memory locations the processor can interrogate these locations each time it requires a new instruction. This is normally achieved by having a counter within the processor which can be preset, loaded, incremented, etc. The output from this counter is used to address the memory locations containing the instructions. This counter is called the 'Program Counter' in most processors. Referring to Figure 2 again, to begin the execution of this program the program counter would be set to 10010000, which addresses instruction 1. The processor then 'reads' instruction 1 from the memory and operates accordingly. At the end of the execution of this instruction the program counter is automatically incremented by 1, which then addresses instruction 2, and the process continues. For reasons of flexibility, the program counter is frequently a register rather than a hard-wired counter, and the processor uses its arithmetic capability to add to the contents of this register to increment the count. It is thus very easy for the program counter content to be modified by any positive or negative amount as well as being incremented. This allows areas of program to be

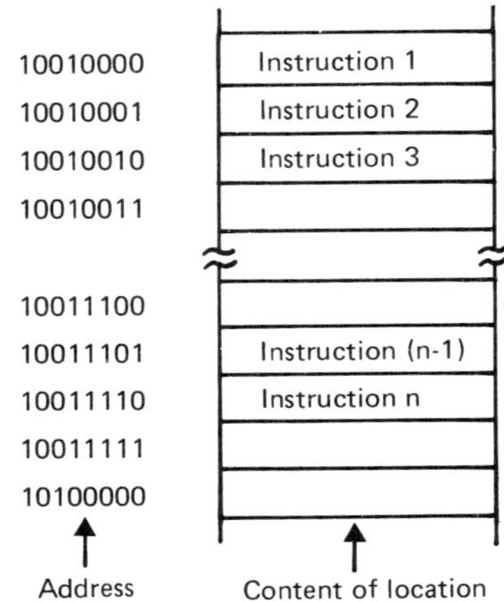

FIGURE 2. Memory Map of Instructions in Sequence

missed out or areas to be repeated, as required. This would be caused by 'Branch' or 'Jump' instructions, for example.[3]

Having obtained an instruction from memory the processor then performs the task defined by that instruction. In order to perform the arithmetic and logic functions, one of the major blocks within the processor is usually an Arithmetic Logic Unit (ALU). This is a circuit which has two sets of data inputs and one set of outputs and performs arithmetic and logic functions between the two input words and presents the result at the output. This circuit also responds to a set of control inputs which determine what function the ALU performs at any given time. This is shown in Figure 3 with a list of typical functions. By using these functions to operate on the data inputs, any logical or mathematical function can be implemented.

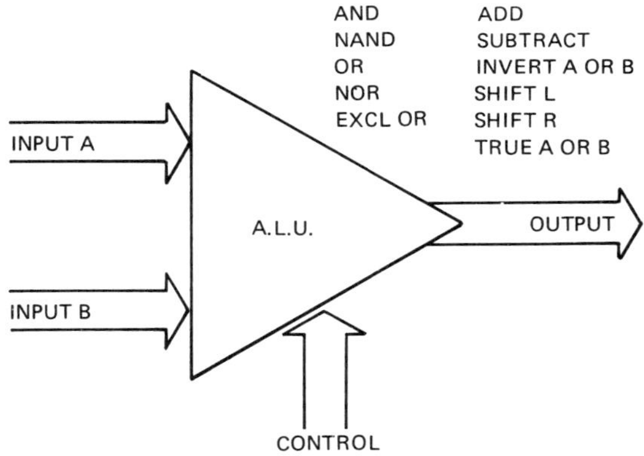

FIGURE 3. ALU Block Diagram and Functions

The control inputs to the ALU are derived from the instruction to the processor. In general the instructions supplied to the microprocessor imply several ALU functions and data manipulation functions. For example, if an instruction to the microprocessor said, 'add content of memory location A into content of memory location B', the sequence of events within the microprocessor would be similar to the list on Table 1. This sequence of events has to be derived from the single instruction to the processor, Add A to B. To do this an instruction decode and sequencer, or 'micro-sequence controller', forms another major function within the CPU.

TABLE 1. Add A to B. Sequence of Events within CPU.

- Output address A to memory.
- Read content of location A into CPU.
- Output address B to memory.
- Read content of location B into CPU.
- Add content of A into content of B.
- Write sum into location B in memory.
- Increment Program Counter.
- Output instruction address to memory.
- Read next instruction.

This can be made up of a counter and Read Only Memory (ROM) Arrays, as shown in Figure 4. The instruction is decoded by ROM I. This produces one set of outputs which represent a starting address for ROM II. Another set of outputs control how many times the counter, which supplies the remaining addresses to ROM II, will be incremented. Thus a sequence of control words appear at the outputs of ROM II. There are several ways of implementing this function, another of which is to use Programmable Logic Arrays (PLA),but the requirement and the function are identical.

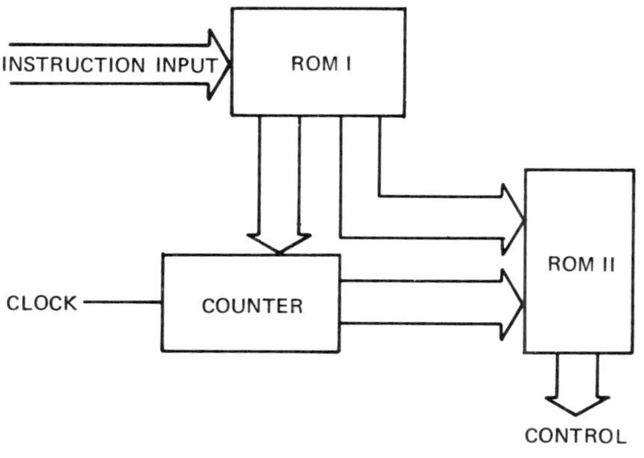

FIGURE 4. Instruction Decoder and Sequencer

There is one more major function within the CPU, and that is a working storage area. This is a small amount of memory either within the CPU or available to the CPU for immediate data storage. It is readily accessible by the CPU usually at a faster rate than addressing a memory location through a processor instruction. There are two important configurations for this storage area. The most common at present is to incorproate a number of words of storage on the CPU in a Register File. This is a number of registers which can be randomly addressed, and they are incorporated within the microprocessor device. The second method is to use the memory which is connected to the processor to perform this data storage function. When this method is used, a register within the processor has an address stored in it to indicate the area being used in memory for working 'registers'.[4]

One final feature of the microprocessor is usually a Status register. This is one storage register dedicated to indicating information concerning the last event to have taken place. For example, if a mathematical function resulted in an overflow, then a bit in the status register would be set accordingly. Similarly if the result of a comparison was equality, then the 'equal' status bit would be set, etc.

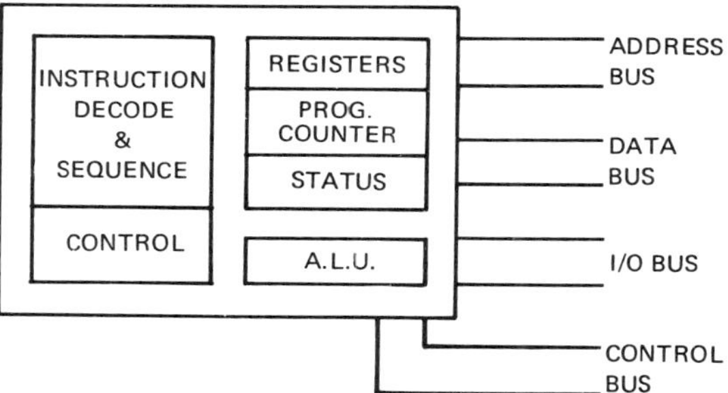

FIGURE 5. The CPU Block Diagram

Figure 5 shows the features of the microprocessor which have been discussed. The device contains the ALU, the instruction decoder and sequencer and some registers, including Program Counter, Status registers and possibly a working register file. The processor must also communicate with memory devices, input and output devices, etc. and it does this by means of a data bus, an address bus, a control bus, and an I/O bus. These are simply multi-wire 'highways', and on various microprocessors there are various combinations of these four. For example, many microprocessors do not have a separate I/O bus, but make use of the same data bus for I/O functions as for memory communication. There are trade-offs to be made with respect to the required peripheral circuits, operating speed, wiring, package pin count, etc. and different microprocessors designed for different application areas make use of different combinations.

BUILDING A SYSTEM

The microprocessor device requires a certain minimum amount of support devices to be connected to it to form a functional system. These are to perform the data memory, program memory and I/O functions. Whereas some microprocessors have specialised dedicated devices designed to work with them,[5] these tend to be expensive and, whilst they minimise the number of devices required in a system, they do not necessarily reduce the system cost. Other microprocessors have been designed to make full use of standard logic and memory devices in a system and these can offer a significant cost saving over the former approach.[6]

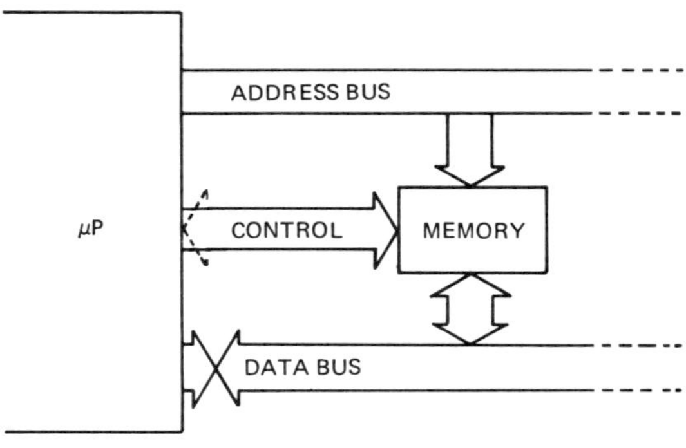

FIGURE 6. Memory Bus Structure

Memory devices connected to the microprocessor require three types of information transfer. They require addresses from the processor to determine which storage location is being accessed. They require control information to determine exactly when the device is to be active and also whether the memory access is a 'read' or a 'write' function (i.e. whether data is being transferred from the addressed memory location to the processor or vice versa). The third connection must be to actually transfer the memory data to and from the processor.

In the majority of microprocessor devices the memory bus structure is as shown in Figure 6. The address bus is unidirectional and outputs address information from the processor to the memory. The control bus outputs control information to the memory, and may also communicate timing information from the memory back to the processor. The data bus is bi-directional and is used to transfer data both to and from the memory. One of the control signals on the control bus indicates whether the data bus connections to the processor are in the input mode or the output mode at any given time.

There are two basic types of memory devices used in microcomputer systems. The data memory has data entered into it and read from it and hence must be capable of both Read and Write functions. The common type of device used for this form of storage is Random Access Memory (RAM).[7] This name does not explicitly define that the device has both Read and Write capability, but nevertheless has become accepted in the industry as being synonymous with this function. RAM (or Read/Write memory) is used as the data store, but it is not always the best medium for storing the program instructions. This is due to the fact that most semiconductor RAM devices are volatile, i.e. when the power supply is disconnected the data is lost. If this form of storage is used for the program instructions, the program must be re-loaded from paper tape or magnetic disc/tape, etc. each time the system is powered up. This is fine for computer systems where the program is probably changed regularly, but in many microprocessor based systems the system function will be dedicated to one particular application. In this situation it is usual to store the program instructions in a storage device which will not change its content when power is removed. Since the processor does not need to write data into the memory area which is storing the program, this area of memory can be made up of Read Only Memory (ROM) devices. These devices have a data pattern or code built into them at manufacture which cannot be altered (i.e. mask programmed).[8] The disadvantage of using mask programmed ROMs is that the program has to be tried, tested and proven before devices are manufactured to that code, and then there must be a requirement for many hundreds of identical devices to warrant their manufacture. The alternative is to use programmable ROMs (PROMs). With these the user enters his program code into the device via some specified electrical procedure.[9] Depending on the type of device used this procedure may be totally non-reversible (e.g. fusing metal links) or physically erasable (by irradiating with U.V. light). Whatever type is used, these are more suitable for prototype and small production run usage than mask programmed ROMs.

Since data memory and program memory is often implemented in two different types of device (RAM and ROM) the storage areas are thus often divided between different packages in the physical layout. Because of this and partly for convenience, program and data memory are normally represented by separate blocks in microcomputer system block diagrams. In terms of addressing, however, they are all memory, and the programmer has to know which addresses correspond to program memory and which correspond to data memory. The total addressing capability of the microprocessor is defined by the number of address bits it transfers via the address bus in any one addressing operation. For 'n' address bits the addressing capability is 2^n words of memory. Hence a device with a non-multiplexed address bus of 16 lines can address 2^{16} = 64k words of memory ($1k \simeq 2^{10} = 1024$).

To connect input and output devices to the microprocessor there are several methods which can be used. The most common method is 'memory mapped' I/O, whereby address combinations are decoded from the address bus to 'Enable' buffer devices (both input and output) connected to the data bus. The distinction between input and output

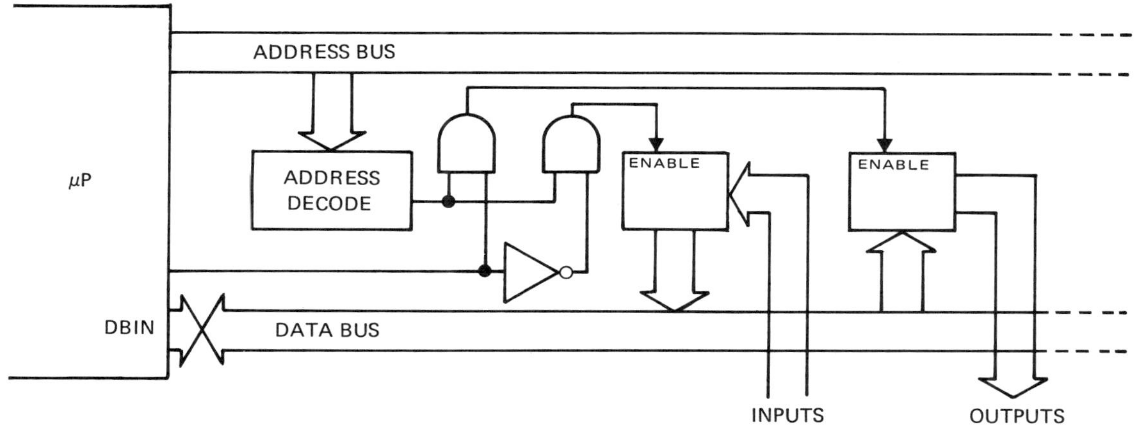

FIGURE 7. Memory Mapped I/O

device enable is performed by the processor's control output DBIN, which indicates whether the data bus is in the input or output mode. Figure 7 shows a parallel input port and a parallel output port implemented in this manner.

Any number of parallel input/output port pairs may be implemented this way up to the addressing capability of the processor. However, any address combination used for this is thus committed and hence encroaches on the true size of memory which can be used. For a small number of I/O ports this is insignificant, but with many I/O ports in a system this may become a problem. Some devices have the capability of differentiating between memory locations and I/O ports, even though they are addressed in the same manner. This may be by using a different instruction to output data to an output port at a particular address, than to output data to a memory location at that address. The physical result could be achieved by using a 'Memory Enable' control line which is only driven to the 'Enable' state by the processor in the latter case and not the former.

Memory Mapped I/O techniques provide fast parallel data transfer to and from the system, since the time to input or output one data word is the same as for a read or write operation to memory. One disadvantage of this system is that data transfers of less than a whole word are not effected economically, since the processor cannot address less than a full word I/O port. In control applications it is frequently required to input or output single bits of data. An example would be to test whether a switch has been closed, or to turn on a valve, etc. To cater for these requirements some microprocessors have additional methods of inputting and outputting data. An example of such a system is the Communications Register Unit (CRU) interface provided by the 990 family of devices and systems. 'Memory Mapping' techniques and the CRU interface are described fully in a latter chapter.

REAL TIME CONSIDERATIONS

The features and operation of microprocessors as described so far all relate to a device operating sequentially at a fixed rate, as defined by a clock input from an oscillator. The data sheet for the microprocessor device will define how long it takes to perform an instruction (Execution Time) in terms of clock cycles. The processor will work through the sequence of instructions as stored in program memory, taking its specified number of clock cycles per instruction and 'inputting' and 'outputting' data as required by the instructions. If the processor is required to respond to an external event, e.g. a switch being operated, then the program must be written to cause the processor to input the state of the switch occasionally and determine whether it was closed or open. This will occur at fixed intervals depending upon the execution time of the instructions which are being operated on in the meantime. Hence there may be an appreciable time between the external event taking place and the processor recognising it.

A way of improving this situation is to provide the processor with an 'Interrupt' input. This is a facility via which the processor can be disturbed from the function it is performing at any instant and be made to perform a different function. If the external switch, in the previous example, is connected to the interrupt input to the processor, when the switch is operated the processor immediately responds by changing function to another pre-defined program. The actual implementation of this is straightforward. At the time that the interrupt occurs the processor is already performing a task, with data for that task, etc. It is frequently required that the processor should return to this 'background' task after it has serviced the interrupt. To make this possible, sufficient information, regarding the current position in the program, the status and any data held in working memory within the processor, must be stored in a known area in memory. Then when the interrupt operation is completed, this information may be retrieved and the original operation continued at the exact point where it was left. This is represented diagrammatically in Figure 8.

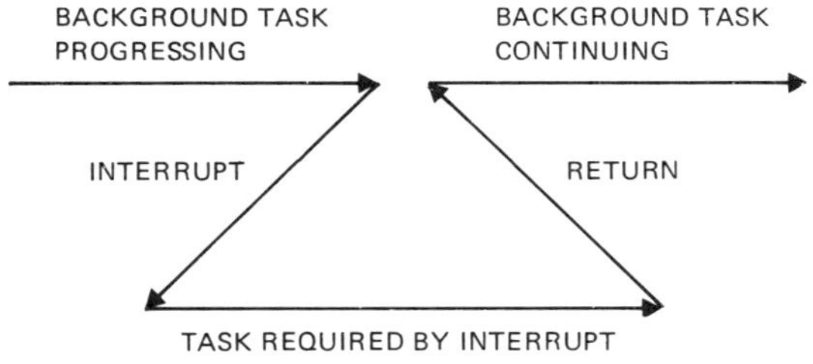

FIGURE 8. Interrupt.

In many applications it is an advantage to have a number of interrupt input facilities to the processor. If a number of switches are connected to a single interrupt input, and the processor always responds to this input, then the situation can arise where the interrupt task itself is interrupted by another switch being closed, etc. To provide some means of controlling whether the processor responds to some or all of the interrupt sources a system of prioritised interrupts is often employed. This uses either a number of interrupt inputs, each with a priority associated with it, or a single interrupt request input and a number of interrupt code inputs. In this case a code word is applied to the code inputs by the interrupt source to identify the source to the processor. Once again, different levels of interrupt, as identified by the interrupt code in this case, have different priority levels.

With a prioritised interrupt system an Interrupt 'Mask' can be set via the program. This simply defines the lowest priority interrupt that will be recognised by the processor at any time. Hence lower priority interrupts are masked out. This feature can also be used to ensure that when the processor is servicing a certain level interrupt, it can only be interrupted again by a higher priority interrupt.

A number of different ways are used to implement the change of task when the interrupt occurs. Probably the most common system is the use of vectored interrupt technique, whereby the processor is directed, by some means, to a new program in memory. This may rely on the interrupt source logic placing an address on the data bus, which the processor reads and transfers to its program counter. Alternatively the incidence of a particular level of interrupt may cause the processor to read the content of a certain memory location allocated to that interrupt level by the structure of the processor. The memory location is called a 'Trap', and its content is an address to be loaded into the program counter. Since the address stored in the trap location directs the processor to a new program area, it is called the 'Trap Vector'.

SOFTWARE

Having described the microprocessor device, how it is included in a system and some of its features, this next section covers the subject of software. The hardware which makes up a microcomputer system is useless until a program is supplied to it to make it operate. The program, by the time it is supplied to the microcomputer system, is in the form of instruction words of logic noughts and ones. As previously described these are loaded into memory (either ROM or RAM) and then executed in sequence by the system.

At this stage the sequence of words of '0's and '1's is called the 'Object Code'. The data sheet for the microprocessor will define the list of instructions to which the device will respond. This is the instruction set. The data sheet will also give the object code version of each instruction in one of the standard representations of the binary word (i.e. binary, octal, binary coded decimal, hexadecimal). Whilst it is assumed that the reader of this report is familiar with binary code, an explanation of the other systems is given in the Appendix

For convenience of use, each instruction is also represented by a Mnemonic. This is just a short 'name' which is usually made up of letters relevant to the function of that instruction. For example, the 'Branch and Load Workspace Pointer' instruction in the 990 instruction set has the mnemonic BLWP. These mnemonics allow the programmer to write down instructions on paper very much more easily than if the full written title of the instruction, or even the object code version, had to be used. The list of mnemonics representing a program is called the 'Source Code'. Having 'written' a program, i.e. decided in what order the available instructions need to be supplied to the processor and with what data, this information needs to be turned into the binary object code form. This then has to be loaded into the program memory of the microcomputer system to make it run.

SOFTWARE AIDS

The process of transcribing the source code, i.e. the list of mnemonics, into the binary object code by hand is tedious and prone to errors. For this reason, amongst others, there is an aid to the programmer in the form of another program. The microprocessor instruction set will almost certainly be supported by an 'Assembler' program, provided by the microprocessor vendor for use by programmers. The Assembler program converts source code into object code and, in addition, it allows the use of some easier methods of keeping trace of data locations, etc. in the program. It also performs some checks to determine whether the source code statements are valid (i.e. if the mnemonic exists for the particular instruction set) and provides some useful information about the program.[10] The mnemonics of the instructions, combined with other control words recognised by the assembler program, constitute a 'language' in which the microprocessor program can be written. This is known as the 'Assembly Language', and is probably the most common means of writing microprocessor programs. It forms a higher level language than programming in object code (i.e. actually writing '1's and '0's on paper) but is still a fairly basic and efficient method. Higher level languages exist, e.g. FORTRAN, BASIC, COBOL, etc., and these take care of more and more of the basic 'housekeeping' functions of the program. In a similar way to the processor decoding its input instructions into a sequence of 'micro-events', high level language program statements have to be decoded into a sequence of microprocessor instructions. This task is performed by another program called a 'Compiler', which performs a similar function for a high level language program as an assembler does for an assembly language program. The levels of complexity are shown diagrammatically in Figure 9.

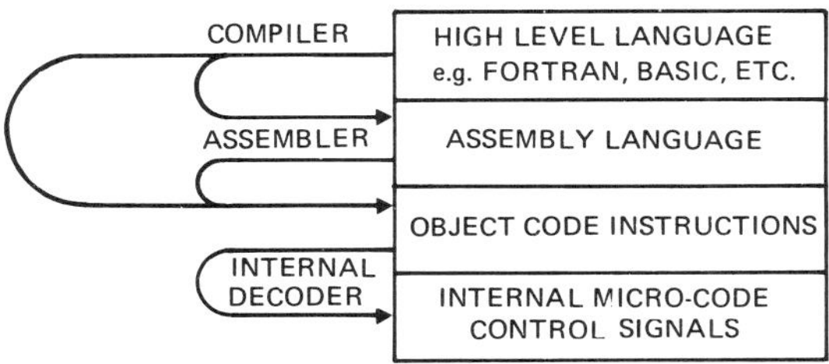

FIGURE 9. Levels of Program Code.

The assembler and compiler programs are aids to the programmer, and are not part of the end system. They do not even have to run on the same type of machine. Providing they have been written accordingly, they can be run on whatever computer the programmer has convenient access to, and still produce code for the microprocessor in question. If they operate in this method then they are referred to as a Cross Assembler and a Cross Compiler, and are known collectively as cross support. The third software aid to the programmer, which is used when the program is written and its functional accuracy needs to be checked, is a Simulator. This method of program verification is used normally when the actual system hardware is not available for testing, or even if it is available there is no way to monitor its (internal) operation. The simulator program is a method of indicating the data, at any or all locations in the device or system being simulated, as the program instructions are supplied to it. In this way the programmer can obtain a list of the way in which the device would respond to his program instructions at each step, and determine whether the program is operating correctly. The process of finding errors in the program and correcting them is often called 'de-bugging' the program.

This has not been a complete description of all the software aids available to the programmer, but the aids described do indicate the way in which the various level programming languages are handled. Another software aid which is commonly used is an Editor program. This assists the programmer in actually writing the source statements (high level or assembly level) and manipulating them. It stores the source statements in the memory of the computer being used as they are entered from a terminal (or other source). Once in memory they can be changed, deleted, new statements inserted, etc., by the use of various edit commands via a terminal. The facilities and commands available are a function of the editor program, and will be described in its documentation.

Having written the program, compiled or assembled it, if necessary simulated it, and finally de-bugged it, the resultant object code can be loaded into the program memory of the microprocessor system with a fair degree of certainty that it will work, assuming the hardware itself is correct.

THE SIGNIFICANCE OF MICROPROCESSORS

A system based on the use of a microprocessor offers a number of advantages to the design and production engineer, namely:

- Smaller Size
- Lower Cost
- Greater Reliability and Flexibility
- Component Standardisation
- Shorter Design Cycle Time.

How these advantages occur can best be explained with reference to Figure 10, showing the basic needs of any system. Here the outputs respond in a certain pre-determined manner according to the input states and changes, regardless of the technology used to implement the system between them. Examples of technology are obviously; electromechanical, dedicated (Hard-Wired) logic such as t.t.l., c.m.o.s., e.c.l. etc., and now software controlled logic (microprocessor + memory + program).

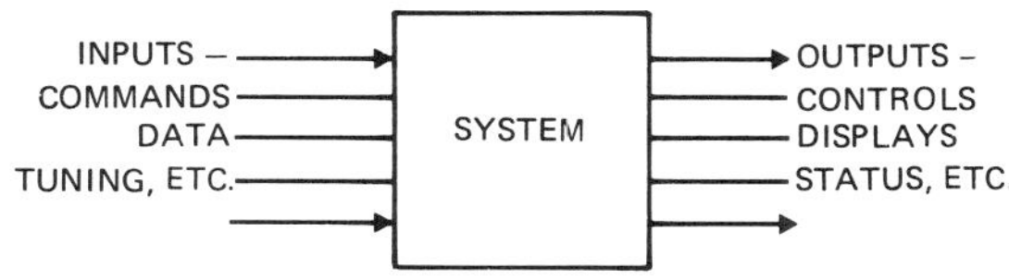

FIGURE 10. The Universal System Concept.

Size

In all but the smallest of system designs the microprocessor system will use less devices than its immediate predecessor, a system in t.t.l. logic, say. The overall reduction in the number of connections and integrated circuit pins will give a reliability improvement discussed later. The decrease in size when using the microprocessor results from the basic concept of its operation. Consider the following points:

The component count in a microprocessor system is largely dependent upon the length of the program, i.e. the number of instruction steps. A reasonable approximation is that one instruction corresponds to one logic function, since it instructs the microprocessor to perform one task. The memory section of the system stores data in the conventional one/zero manner. Because it is more convenient to enter data more than one bit at a time, the memory is organised to operate on a certain number of bits of data at any one time. The parallel combination of bits for which the memory is designed to handle most efficiently is referred to as the memory 'Word', and the memory is organised to store a number of these words. As each instruction is stored in one word of program memory in most cases, each word of memory corresponds to one logic function in the system. The memory word is usually between 8 and 16 bits in length, i.e. 8-16 bits of memory replace one logic gate of the t.t.l. system previously used.

If the average t.t.l. logic integrated circuit contains 8 to 16 logic gate functions, this corresponds to 128-256 bits of memory. Thus the figures for Table 2 can be deduced which shows that, for instance, a 4096 bit capacity memory (known as a 4k device) could replace from 16-32 logic devices. This effective increase in the number of logic functions per device can result in the overall system being considerably smaller than a hardwired logic system performing the same function. Associated with the reduction in package count will also be benefits in terms of cost and power dissipation.

TABLE 2. Comparison of Memory Size to Logic Functions

Standard Memory Device Capacity	Logic Devices lo	hi
1024 (1k)	4	8
2048 (2k)	8	16
4096 (4k)	16	32
8192 (8k)	32	64
16384 (16k)	64	128

Cost

A reduction in cost is brought about, as described above, from the lower device count resulting in a smaller system size and printed circuit board (p.c.b.) area. There will also be lower related overheads, e.g. from purchasing, inventory, etc. and Table 3 details system manufacturing expenses. Note that the related expenses amount to approximately twice the cost of the i.c. itself, indicating considerable cost reduction potential by using a microprocessor system.

TABLE 3. System Manufacturing Costs per Integrated Circuit

ITEM	APPROX. COST (£)	($)
I.C.	.25	.43
Incoming Inspection	.02	.04
Printed Circuit Board	.25	.43
Assembly	.02	.04
Test and Rework	.05	.09
Interconnection	.07	.12
Power supplies	.05	.09
Cabinet, Cooling, etc.	.05	.09
TOTAL	.76	1.33

Reliability

The largest passive source of failure in a system is from interconnections, which include soldered joints, i.c. bonds, plated-through holes, edge connectors, etc. The reduction in package count thus means a reduction in the number of connections which need to be made in a system. Thus there is an increase in the reliability of the system due to this factor in addition to the higher reliability due to fewer active components themselves.

Flexibility

In general, a system using one of the standard families of logic devices will be designed to perform a particular function and the result will be a dedicated piece of hardware. Such hardware, although adequate for doing the task for which it is designed, is nearly always no use at all for performing any other task. Even a fairly simple modification of the specification to which the hardware was designed may well result in a considerable amount of redesigning of the logic system. This will almost certainly also give rise to a new p.c.b. being required, with the associated cost, delay, etc. This modified design may, of course, have to run concurrently in production with the original system thus increasing load on production line, documentation and component stores etc. However, with a microprocessor system its inherent flexibility, due to being software controlled, largely alleviates this problem. It is often quite feasible to review an entire product range, both current and proposed, and to define a set of parameters common to the majority of products. Such parameters, in terms of the system shown in Figure 10, would be the number of inputs, number of outputs and required operating speed. To meet these common parameters it will often be possible to design a common circuit board containing a microprocessor and peripheral components suitable for use in all these systems. Thus the same microprocessor device type can be used to implement a wide range of functions, allowing standardisation on that product.

Standardisation

From an i.c. point of view, this standardisation allows the device to be manufactured in large volume which leads to low selling prices by the i.c. manufacturers. The system function is readily modified by just changing the program r.o.m. Thus no hardware or p.c.b. changes are necessary for complete range of production equipment. From a production point of view, therefore, there is a minimum manufacturing line overhead, minimum range of components in the store, maximum servicing efficiency and any additions to the product range are easily implemented. (Vacant sockets can be left in a system card where a particular application is not making full use of the system's capability.)

Design

The basic parameters for design are usually operating speed, number of inputs, number of outputs, memory capacity and length of program. In a conventional hardwired system, as mentioned, a re-design is required for every new product. However, in a microprocessor system the tried and proven hardware remains the same, only a new program being required. Thus the design cycle time is considerably shorter and any change can be achieved very quickly.

The use of a microprocessor does imply that in the design stage the systems engineer must have programming ability, either himself or available elsewhere, or else be prepared to adapt to this. The i.c. manufacturers, recognising the change in responsibility from logic designers to programmers, have invested considerably in customer support and offer various aids, e.g. extensive documentation, training sessions, development aids both hardware and software and program libraries. In some cases they will also undertake software development contracts for customers, or else be able to recommend an agent who is able to do so.

MICROPROCESSOR EVALUATION

The choice of a microprocessor for a given application or range of applications can appear to be a very complex task. In reality, however, it is straightforward. Of the microprocessors currently available there are distinct groups, segregated by certain major parameters. These are typically operating speed, system cost, input/output capability, support and second sourcing. However, some of these factors are related, e.g. operating speed with I/O capability, and I/O with system cost.

The first of these parameters, operating speed, may or may not be a crucial factor in a given application. Assuming it is of importance then it is necessary to understand the contributing factors to the time taken to perform a task. In general these are clock frequency, number of clock cycles per machine cycle, number of machine cycles per instruction, I/O organisation and number of instructions per function. The first four of these will be defined in the data sheet for a microprocessor, but the latter two need to be evaluated for the particular application. To compare the operating speed of two different microprocessors is not straightforward. To arrive at any meaningful result the best way is to generate 'Benchmark' program routines relevant to the final application. A Benchmark is simply a common function requirement. Software is written for each microprocessor to perform the benchmark function and then from the device data sheets the execution time, memory space, etc. can be derived. Only at this level can the different processors be compared for speed and efficiency of memory usage. An application involving a large amount of calculation in its execution will be best serviced by a microprocessor with high speed arithmetic capability. In system control applications, on the other hand, there may be little calculation involved, in which case a flexible I/O system will be an advantage.

In almost any application, one of the most important factors will be system cost. Assuming that a number of different microprocessors are capable of performing the required application, then the commercial aspects become the deciding factors. These are primarily cost and also second sourcing and available support. The cost factor is of obvious importance. The cheapest way of doing the job is obviously the most desirable, assuming all other things being equal.

To evaluate the system cost it is necessary to consider not only the cost of the microprocessor device itself, but also the cost of memory and peripheral devices that are also included in the system. To evaluate the memory cost requires an estimate of the amount of memory necessary for the given application, both for program storage and working memory. This, once again, is best achieved by a benchmarking process. The peripheral device cost depends to a large extent on how much the processor relies on specialised support devices, which tend to cost more than standard logic family devices. If the system can be efficiently implemented by using standard devices, then the system cost will benefit from this.

Most major systems manufacturers do not like to commit themselves to a particular product as major as a microprocessor unless they can purchase it from more than one vendor, and unless it is manufactured in more than one place. This requirement for second sourcing of a product is normally satisfied in the semiconductor industry by either two or more independent manufacturers designing and building the product to a common specification, or the manufacturer who originated the product to sell or give the production masks to another manufacturer under a cross license agreement. This then allows the second manufacturer to quickly put the device into production, thus aiding the initial designer/manufacturer by providing the required second source. Occasionally another situation arises where a single manufacturer produces the same function in the same or different technologies in two or more different manufacturing facilities, ending up with electrically and functionally equivalent devices manufactured independently of one other. This meets the requirement for second sourcing of the device. Such an example is the TMS/SBP9900 microprocessor. The TMS version is made in MOS in at least three different places around the world. The SBP device uses a totally different process i.e. i^2l. However all devices are electrically equivalent.

The final aspect to consider is support. What software support is available for the microprocessor, what hardware aids, development systems, etc. and what service can the manufacturer or vendor of the microprocessor offer you to solve your particular problems? The software support and development systems are important to most potential microprocessor users. The customer service aspect, however, tends to be most important to potential users with limited prior experience. Facilities such as the microprocessor customer centres provided by i.c. manufacturers and many of their distributors allow customer training, problem solving and system design support to be offered to customers, with all necessary hardware and software aids on hand.

All system designers considering a new project that will involve more than about £5 worth of standard logic devices should bear in mind the rapidly falling cost of microprocessors and all their advantages as previously described. In addition to microprocessors, the one-chip microcomputer devices, mentioned briefly at the beginning of this report, offer a cost effective replacement for electro-mechanical or purely mechanical control systems as well as electronic systems. The range of integrated circuit software controlled logic devices now available provides designers with a set of tools which will enable them to produce systems more compact, powerful and at lower cost than ever before.

REFERENCES

1. Applications Laboratory Staff of Texas Instruments Incorporated, *Electronic Power Control and Digital Techniques,* McGraw-Hill Book Company, New York, 1976, pp. 103-137.
2. Applications Laboratory Staff of Texas Instruments Incorporated, *Electronic Power Control and Digital Techniques,* McGraw-Hill Book Company, New York, 1976, pp. 116-123.
3. The Engineering Staff of Texas Instruments, Semiconductor Group, *TMS9900 Microprocessor Data Manual,* p. 24-25.
4. *990 Computer Family Systems Handbook,* Manual 945250-9701, Texas Instruments Inc., p.2-5.
5. The Engineering Staff of Texas Instruments Inc, MOS Houston, TMS5501, I/O Controller in TMS8080A Microprocessor Systems, Texas Instruments Inc. *Application Report CA185.*
6. The Engineering Staff of Texas Instruments Incorporated, MOS Houston, 'Minimum System Design TMS9900 16-bit Microprocessor', Texas Instruments *Application Report CA184.*
7. Applications Laboratory Staff of Texas Instruments Incorporated, *MOS and Special-Purpose Bipolar Integrated Circuits and R-F Power Transistor Circuit Design,* McGraw-Hill Book Company, New York, 1976, pp. 31-48.
8. Applications Laboratory Staff of Texas Instruments Incorporated, *MOS and Special-Purpose Bipolar Integrated Circuits and R-F Power Transistor Circuit Design,* McGraw-Hill Book Company, New York, 1976, pp. 91-106.
9. Applications Laboratory Staff of Texas Instruments Incorporated, *Electronic Power Control and Digital Techniques,* McGraw-Hill Book Company, New York, 1976, pp. 139-145.
10. 9900 Assembly Language Programmers Guide, ISBN 0-904047-1712, Texas Instruments Inc.

APPENDIX

Numbering Systems

Notation: Since Decimal, Octal and Hexadecimal systems use certain common characters and in the different systems identical character groups represent different numbers, some means is necessary to identify the system being used. In this appendix, the radix will be shown following the number. For example, Decimal 14 will be written 14_{10}, Octal 14 will be written 14_8 and Hexa Decimal 14 will be 14_{16}. If no radix is indicated then the number can be assumed to be in decimal representation.

Decimal: The decimal numbering system operates with a radix of 10, uses the ten characters 0-9 and is familiar to everybody. The least significant digit represents multiples of 10^0, the next significant digit represents multiples of 10^1, etc.

Octal: The octal numbering system uses a radix of 8 and employs the characters 0-7. The least significant digit represents multiples of 8^0, the next significant digit represents multiples of 8^1, etc. Octal is often used in the computer industry because it is easily converted to Binary and vice-versa. Since it is more compact than Binary for writing, etc., it is more convenient. To convert Binary to Octal, the Binary word is divided into groups of three digits, starting with the least significant bit, (l.s.b.) and adding leading zeros in the most significant positions to make up the last group as necessary. Since a group of three Binary digits must represent a number between 1 and 7, each group can be converted to a number in this range. Thus 001101 in Binary becomes 15^8.

Hexa-decimal: The Hexa-decimal system uses a radix of 16 and employs 16 characters 0-9 and A-F. The least significant character represents multiples of 16^0, the next significant character represents multiples of 16^1, etc. Conversion from Binary to Hexa-decimal involves the Binary word being considered in groups of four bits, starting from the l.s.b. Each group of four bits represents a number in the range $0\text{-}F_{16}$ and can be written as such. Hexa-decimal is convenient for dealing with Binary word lengths in multiples of four bits, as is usually the case with microprocessor systems.

Binary: The Binary system uses a radix of 2 and employs two characters, 0 and 1. The least significant character represents multiples of 2^0, the next significant character represents multiples of 2^1, etc. Binary numbering is used in electronic systems since its two characters 0 and 1 can be represented by the two electrical states 'On' and 'Off' or vice-versa.

Binary Coded Decimal (b.c.d.): B.c.d. replaces each individual character in a decimal number with a four bit binary word. Since the decimal characters are 0-9, there are six of the available sixteen combinations of the four bit word not used. B.c.d. is a convenient way of handling Decimal numbers in a digital system.

Table A1

Decimal	Octal	Hexa-Dec	Binary	B.C.D.
0	0	0	000000	0000 0000
1	1	1	000001	0000 0001
2	2	2	000010	0000 0010
3	3	3	000011	0000 0011
4	4	4	000100	0000 0100
5	5	5	000101	0000 0101
6	6	6	000110	0000 0110
7	7	7	000111	0000 0111
8	10	8	001000	0000 1000
9	11	9	001001	0000 1001
10	12	A	001010	0001 0000
11	13	B	001011	0001 0001
12	14	C	001100	0001 0010
13	15	D	001101	0001 0011
14	16	E	001110	0001 0100
15	17	F	001111	0001 0101
16	20	10	010000	0001 0110
17	21	11	010001	0001 0111
18	22	12	010010	0001 1000
19	23	13	010011	0001 1001
20	24	14	010100	0010 0000

In all cases the least significant digit is on the right hand side.

GLOSSARY OF TERMS

Term	Definition
Arithmetic Logic Unit	A circuit which produces arithmetic or logic functions of its inputs at its outputs, according to the state of its control inputs. An integral part of most microprocessors.
A.L.U.	Abbreviation for Arithmetic Logic Unit.
Assembler	A computer program which converts assembly language statements into object code and checks for non valid statements or incomplete definitions, etc.
Assembly Language	A means of representing program instructions in mnemonics and conveniently handling memory addressing in symbolic terms.
Benchmark	A common operation for the implementation of which program routines can be written, to determine the efficiency of different microprocessors in this operation.
Central Processor Unit	The part of a computer system which performs the calculation and data manipulation functions.
C.P.U.	Abbreviation for Central Processor Unit.
Compiler	A computer program which converts high level programming language statements to either assembly language statements or object code.
Cross Support	Computer programs which aid the writing and checking of programs for one type of machine, but which actually run on a different type of machine. Commonly – Assembler, Compiler and Simulator.
Debug	To debug a program is to locate and correct errors, either in writing or actual function.
Editor	A computer program which allows program statements to be entered, listed, modified and manipulated; to ease program writing.
Execution Time	The time taken to perform an instruction in terms of clock cycles.
Hardware	The electrical and mechanical components making up a system.
Instruction	The combination of logic high and low states which must be supplied to the microprocessor as a control word to cause it to perform a particular function. Represented in several ways, commonly assembler mnemonics.
Instruction Set	The list of instructions to which a particular microprocessor will respond.
Interrupt	A signal to the microprocessor which will cause it to change from its present task to another task. A means of operating in real time.
Interrupt Mask	An internal control word, set by software, which defines the levels of interrupt which the processor will accept or ignore at any given time.
I/O	Abbreviation for Input/Output, referring to data inputs and outputs to or from the computer system.
Memory	The part of the system which stores data (working data or instruction object code).
Memory Map	A diagram indicating the usage of available memory space in terms of memory addresses.
Memory Mapped I/O	A technique of implementing input/output facilities by addressing I/O ports as if they were memory locations.
Microcomputer	A computer system constructed by making extensive use of large scale integrated circuits.
Microcomputer (single chip)	A complete computer system (i.e. RAM, ROM, I/O, CPU, etc.) implemented in a single large scale integrated circuit.
Microprocessor	A computer CPU implemented by making extensive use of large scale integrated circuits. Frequently implemented in a single large scale integrated circuit.
Mnemonic	A name, usually made up of relevant letters of the function of an instruction.
Object Code	The control word of logic '1's and '0's as actually supplied to the processor as an instruction.
Prioritised Interrupts	Multiple interrupt inputs to a processor with a priority level associated with each input, thus enabling less important interrupts to be masked out. See 'Interrupt Mask'.

Program	A sequence of instructions generated by the programmer to cause the computer to perform a specific task.
Programmable Read Only Memory	A read only memory which is manufactured containing no data, which can have data entered into it by the user at a subsequent date, but is non volatile.
Program Counter	A counter or register within a processor, which contains the address of the memory location containing the next instruction in the program being executed.
PROM	Abbreviation for Programmable Read Only Memory.
Random Access Memory	A memory device or system which may have data written into any location or read from any location where the time taken to do so is independent of the particular location.
RAM	Abbreviation for Random Access Memory.
Read Only Memory	A memory device or system which has its data content established as part of its manufacture and cannot be changed.
ROM	Abbreviation for Read Only Memory.
Simulator	A computer program which evaluates the response of a system or device to instruction inputs, in terms of the data content of storage locations, status flags and I/O ports.
Software	A collective term for programs and related documentation, etc.
Source Code	The list of statements (in whatever programming language is being used) that makes up the program.
Trap	A pre-defined location in memory which the processor will read the contents of, as the result of a particular condition or operation.
Vector	A memory address, provided to the processor to direct it to a new area in program memory, as a result of an interrupt, for example.
Volatile	Used to describe memory devices, it means that the data content will be lost if the power supply to the device is removed.

XII A 16-BIT MICROPROCESSOR

by
Howard Cook and Jonathan Dell

The first generation of microprocessor was able to implement systems previously using discrete devices, standard i.c.s, custom designed i.c.s, or incorporating mini-computers. Low cost systems, i.e. those not employing a mini-computer, were however, no longer tied to dedicated end products. The use of a microprocessor gave economic flexibility for later product modifications, and introduced 'software' rather than 'hardware' as the controlling function. A second generation of microprocessor, for example the TMS8080, with separate data and address busses reduced the required system 'hardware', it no longer being necessary to de-multiplex data and address information from the same bus, increasing the system operating speed[1]. These devices have a more powerful and wider range of instructions, thus requiring less program memory to store the requirements for a given operation, and fewer memory accesses by the processor, speeding the operations. With a reduced number of instructions, the programmer generates less errors and the program takes a shorter time to fault find or 'debug'. A further advantage of this second generation of microprocessors is their more advanced computer type functions, including multiple vectored interrupt capability, provision for direct memory access (d.m.a.) system operations, and controlled interface or 'handshake' operation with memory devices and peripherals of mixed speed. With a wider bus, typically 16 bits for address and 8 bits for data, 2^{16} 8 bit words of memory can be addressed at the same time and the 8 bit (one byte) data word can be transferred simultaneously. However, this generation of microprocessor still has limited driving ability from the busses requiring buffers, the data instruction and status is on one bus, specialised support devices are required, and the software is incompatible with both first generation devices and minicomputers.

The arrival of a third generation device, e.g. the TMS9900, 16 bit microprocessor or central processing unit (c.p.u.) brings with it the advantage of being designed to be completely compatible, from both software and hardware point of view, with a whole range of computing products, from mini-computers, through printed circuit boards, to peripheral i.c.s. Using memory to memory architecture means they are fast in operation, and with a flexible input/output system efficient data handling is achievable. Their normal 'clocked' program can be efficiently interrupted to allow more important tasks to be performed. After describing briefly the '9900 microprocessor itself, this chapter deals in depth with the major third generation advantages mentioned above; its special input/output facilities, i.e. interfacing with the communication register unit, and interrupt operation. Other members of the '9900 family are briefly discussed at the end of the chapter.

THE TMS9900 MICROPROCESSOR

The block diagram of the TMS9900 16 bit microprocessor, given in Figure 1, shows the connections to the device. Although fabricated in n-channel silicon gate m.o.s. technology, all its inputs and outputs, except the clock inputs, are t.t.l. compatible to allow direct interface with standard t.t.l. and m.o.s. logic and memory devices.[2,3]

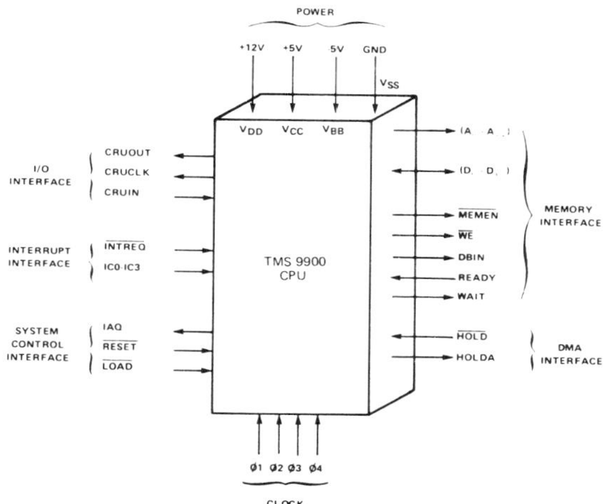

FIGURE 1. The TMS9900 Microprocessor

The data bus (D_0-D_{15}) is a 16 bit bi-directional data highway via which the c.p.u. communicates with memory devices and other 16 bit wide peripherals addressed as memory. Addressing is via the 15 bit address bus (A_0-A_{14}) which gives the capability of addressing 32k (32,768) words of memory, each being 16 bits wide. However, the processor is equally suited to applications where data is to be handled in 8 bit bytes since a 16th address bit is used within the processor to distinguish between the two bytes in a data word. Use of this facility is made straightforward by the inclusion of 'byte' instructions as well as 'word' instructions in the instruction set. Thus the c.p.u. can be made to perform on bytes or words according to the instruction used. When a byte instruction is used, the integrity of the unused byte making up the remainder of the word containing the required byte is preserved.

The TMS9900 uses memory to memory architecture to achieve a very fast context switching characteristic. The '9900 c.p.u. does not use an on-chip register file for working data storage, but organises blocks of words in memory for this purpose. There are three user-accessible registers in the c.p.u., and these are Program Counter, Status and Workspace Pointer. The first two are self explanatory, but the latter is used to 'point' to a block of memory locations. The Workspace Pointer register is loaded by the user with an even 16 bit address. This addresses a word location in memory which the c.p.u. will use as the first of a block of 16 register locations. The 16 word block in memory is termed a 'workspace', and workspaces can be changed simply by changing the content of the workspace pointer register. Any number of workspaces can be used in memory, and, if required, they can be made to overlap, thus conserving memory usage where all 16 registers are not going to be used. Figure 2 indicates the difference between the architecture of a register-type processor such as the TMS8080 and that of the TMS9900. Note the registers for the latter

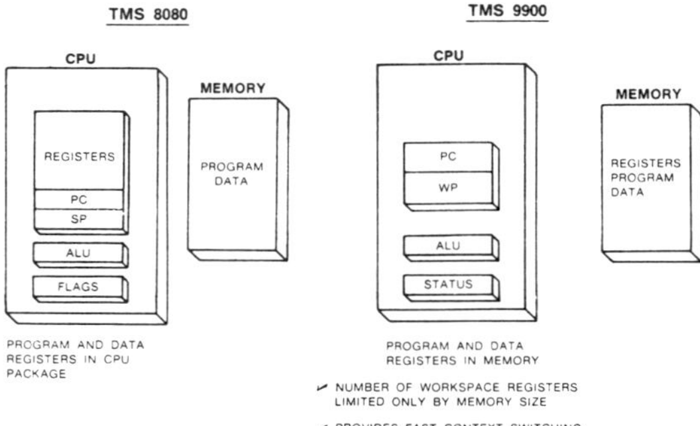

FIGURE 2. Architecture Comparison.

are implemented in memory, rather than within the c.p.u., as is the case with the '8080. The advantages of this organisation, in addition to not having to incorporate a considerable sized register file in the chip design, are mainly related to the time taken to change from one operation to another, or to perform a 'context switch'. (Also the space saved allows more advanced instructions, such as multiply and divide, to be implemented). A context switch takes place as a result of an interrupt originated from outside the system, or a subroutine call initiated by the software. When a context switch is to occur there is no requirement to store the content of a register file into memory, as is the case with a register machine, since the 'registers' are already in memory. All that is necessary is to store the Program Counter, Status, and Workspace Pointer registers as links to enable a complete return to the original environment. When a context switch is initiated, new values of workspace pointer and program counter are provided, either by trap vectors in memory associated with the interrupt level or program interrupt instruction (XOP), or as part of the calling instruction. Thus a new workspace in memory is being identified and the c.p.u. stores the old values of Program Counter, Status and Workspace Pointer in the last three 'registers' in the new workspace. To return to the original environment these values are simply transferred back into the appropriate registers in the c.p.u. For the '9900 to change context takes 8μs and to return takes 4-6μs, viz 27 + 25μs for the '8080.

INPUT/OUTPUT TECHNIQUES

General

In addition to the Input and Output facilities provided by most other microprocessor devices, the '9900 microprocessor has a three line serial interface facility called the Communications Register Unit, c.r.u. This allows the implementation of very low cost and flexible input/output systems using t.t.l. devices, and capable of efficiently handling any number of data bits from 1 to 16. The memory interface controls are provided to allow conventional interface to memory devices or to feed inputs and outputs along the data bus, i.e. memory mapped techniques.

The Communication Register Unit (C.R.U.)

The c.r.u. lines are a serial data input, CRUIN; a serial data output, CRUOUT, and an output clock, CRUCLK. These three lines are used in conjunction with address bits A_3 to A_{14} inclusive for data input/output functions, the address bits A_0 to A_2 being used in other operations involving the 'external' instructions.

The '9900 has a set of fine instructions which utilise the c.r.u. input/output function. Three of these allow manipulation of single bits while the other two can handle any word length, up to 16 bits. The c.r.u. part addresses are always derived from the contents of register 12 (R12) in the current workspace file. A full explanation of the c.r.u. is given elsewhere[4]. The use of the c.r.u. to implement low cost interfaces is best illustrated by some examples.

Keyboard Scan Example: A common requirement in control systems, apart from the control interface itself, is some form of keyboard data entry system. Figure 3 shows an 8 x 8 matrix keyboard interfaced to the '9900 c.p.u. using two t.t.l. devices. The horizontal lines are pulled up to 5V by a resistor on each line, and the logic state of each of these 8 lines can be connected to the CRUIN line to the processor via the SN74LS251 8 line to 1 line multiplexer i.c. This latter device is controlled by 3 address bits, in this case $A_{12} - A_{14}$. The vertical lines in the matrix are connected to the outputs of the SN74LS156 3 line to 8 line decoder. Three more address bits, $A_9 - A_{11}$, control which of these eight lines is driven to logic '0' at any time. Hence, when an address is established on the address bus, one vertical line is driven to logic zero, according to $A_9 - A_{11}$, and one horizontal line (normally at logic '1') is connected to CRUIN, according to $A_{12} - A_{14}$. However, if the key at the crosspoint of these two lines has been pressed (i.e. closed) then the horizontal line will be pulled down to logic '0'. This operation can be implemented by using the TB instruction, which will transfer the state of the key, at the addressed crosspoint in the matrix, to the 'equal' bit in the status register. For the circuit shown in Figure 3, the addresses of the 64 keys are in the range 0000 to> 007E.

The c.r.u. base address can be chosen to be any value within the range of the +127, −128 displacement limits for the TB instruction, relative to these addresses:

i.e. >007E − 127_{10} = >FFFF
and >0000 + 128_{10} = >0080

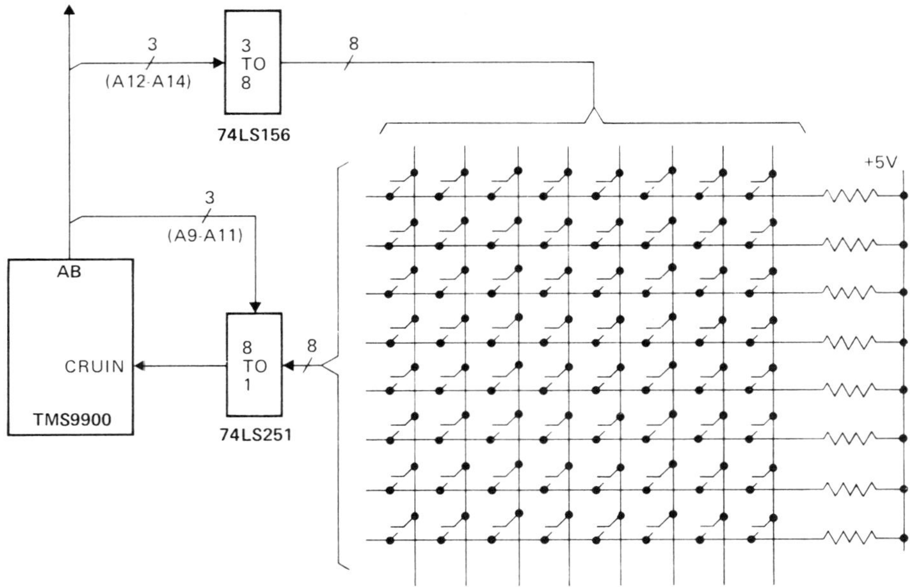

FIGURE 3. Keyboard Data Entry System.

If the c.r.u. base is chosen to be >FFFF then the instruction TB127 will test the key at >FFFF + 127_{10} which is >007E. Similarly, if the c.r.u. base address is chosen to be >0080, then the instruction TB −128 will test the key at >0080 −128_{10}, which is 0000.

A convenient value for the c.r.u. base address would be 007F. The use of a '1' in the l.s.b. can be an aid if the content of R12 is also being used as a loop counter. Consider the keyboard scan routine in Table 1. In this routine the TB instruction always operates with the c.r.u. base address and no displacement. The initial value of the c.r.u. base is not even, so that as it is repeatedly decremented by 2 until the value of 0001 is eventually reached. This is still greater than 0 (even though the 16th bit of R12 is not used in the actual addressing) and the corresponding value of $A_3 - A_{14}$ is all zeros. In this way every combination of these six address bits, from all ones to all zeros, is exercised by this routine. The next DECT instruction will cause R12 to be less than zero and the JGT will not take place. Instead the following unconditional JMP will cause routine to repeat.

The circuit in Figure 3 does not decode higher order addresses to enable this or other circuits connected to the c.r.u. system. The requirement for this will depend upon whether other circuits are to be operated by the c.r.u. in the particular application. If it is necessary to include higher order addresses in the selection of a particular facility then these must also be considered in the selection of the c.r.u. base address.

Table 1. Keyboard Scan Routine

SCAN	LI	R12,>007F	Set c.r.u. base address
LOOP	TB	0	Test bit defined by A_3 – A_{14} of base address
	JNE	KEY	Jump if key is pressed
	DECT	R12	Decrement c.r.u. base by 2
	JGT	LOOP	Jump to next test is R12> 0
	JMP	SCAN	Jump back to beginning if R12 ⩽ 0
KEY			Beginning of de-bounce routine, etc.

UART Interface Example: Figure 4 shows the diagram of the second interface example where a TMS6011 universal asynchronous receiver transmitter (u.a.r.t.)[5] device is interfaced to the microprocessor via the c.r.u. Recapping, the '6011 has a transmitter section which takes a parallel input data word and converts it to serial format for transmission on a serial line, and a receiver section which receives serial data on a line and converts it to parallel output. There are various control inputs to the device which determine the transmitter and receiver data formats. There are also error outputs to indicate whether the received data was of an acceptable format.

The transmitter section contains a buffer register, and as soon as the buffer register is empty new data may be loaded into it from the processor. The transmitter buffer

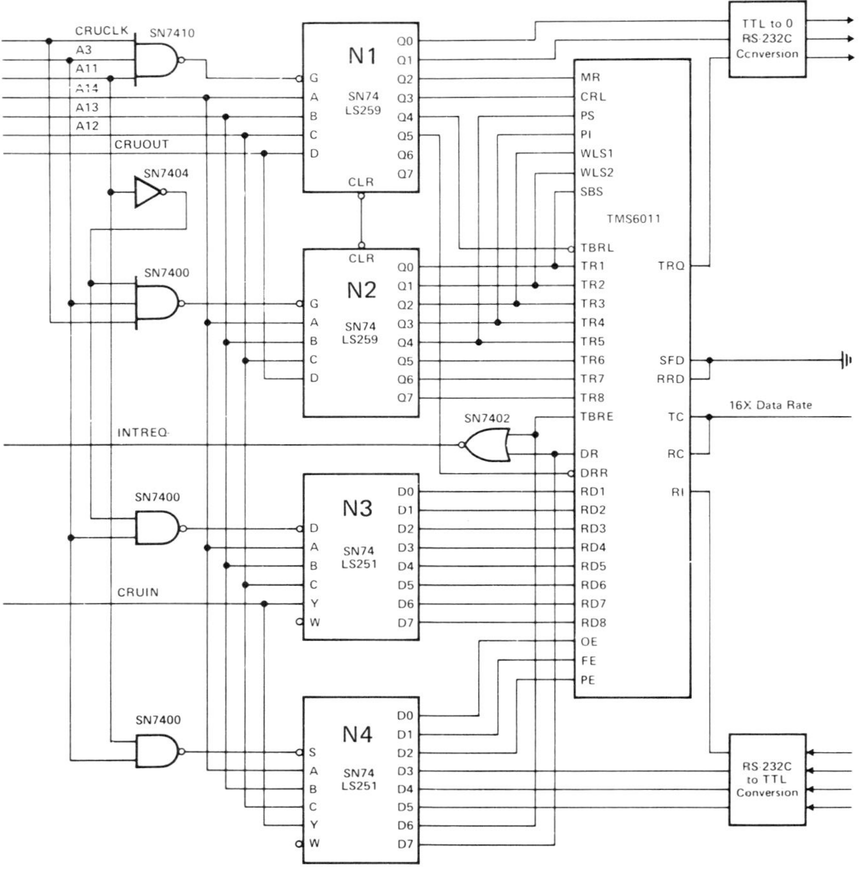

FIGURE 4. U.A.R.T. Interface System.

register empty flag, TBRE, indicates that this register is empty and is supplied to the processor's interrupt request line via the SN7402 OR gate i.c. The receiver section of the device has a Data Ready output to indicate that the data outputs of the device have valid data on them. This also is connected to the interrupt request input of the processor via the SN7402 i.c. When either one of these outputs from the '6011 occurs, the processor is interrupted, and its first task is to determine which if these outputs caused the interrupt. These two outputs are also connected to inputs of the SN74LS251 data multiplexer i.c. N4, whose output is connected to the CRUIN line to the processor. By addressing these two multiplexer inputs, the two flags from the '6011 can be examined in turn by the processor. The data outputs from the '6011 are also connected to inputs of the 'LS251 multiplexers and so these in turn can be addressed by the processor. The CRUOUT line from the processor is connected to the data inputs of the two 'LS259 addressable latch devices. The outputs from these devices supply the parallel inputs to the transmitter section of the '6011 device, as well as the control inputs to this device. By operating the Transmitter Buffer Register Load input to the '6011 the data present on the transmitter inputs will be loaded into the buffer register. By operating the Control Register Load input to the '6011 the control data on the inputs will be loaded into the control register of the device. The addressing of these various functions is shown in Table 2. The whole circuit is enabled by address bit 3 which must be a '1' to select this function.

The flow diagram shown in Figure 5 shows the sequence of events for controlling the '6011 device. When an interrupt occurs from this device the Transmitter Buffer Register Empty flag is examined to determine whether it is set, and hence whether it caused the interrupt. If it was set, then the transmitter routine is entered. If it was set, then the interrupt must have been caused by the Data Ready flag and so the receiver routine is entered. Note that in order to achieve the length of strobe pulse on the Control Register Load input to the '6011 it is necessary to set the input to a 'one' and then set it to a 'zero' with consecutive instructions. Similarly, for the TBRL and DRR inputs. In the transmitter routine the control data is first loaded into

Table 2 U.A.R.T. I/O Address Map

A_3	A_{11}	A_{12}	A_{13}	A_{14}	CRU OUTPUT	CRU INPUT
0	X	X	X	X	–	–
1	0	0	0	0	TR1/SBS	RD1
1	0	0	0	1	TR2/WLS2	RD2
1	0	0	1	0	TR3/WLS1	RD3
1	0	0	1	1	TR4/PI	RD4
1	0	1	0	0	TR5/PS	RD5
1	0	1	0	1	TR6	RD6
1	0	1	1	0	TR7	RD7
1	0	1	1	1	TR8	RD8
1	1	0	0	0		OE
1	1	0	0	1		FE
1	1	0	1	0	MR	PE
1	1	0	1	1	CRL	
1	1	1	0	0	TBRL	
1	1	1	0	1	DRR	
1	1	1	1	0		TBRE
1	1	1	1	1		DR

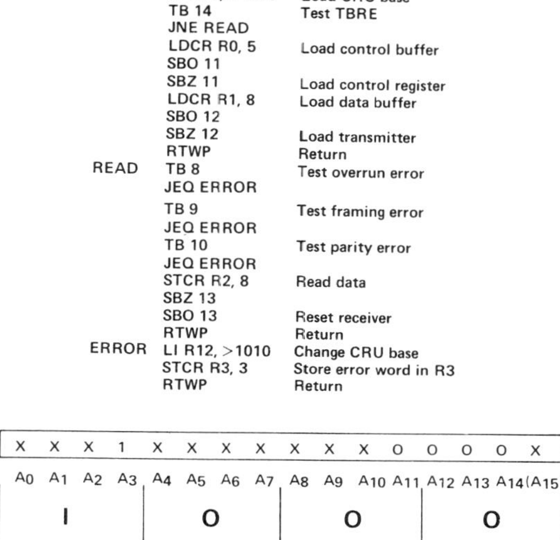

```
        LI R12, >1000    Load CRU base
        TB 14            Test TBRE
        JNE READ
        LDCR R0, 5       Load control buffer
        SBO 11
        SBZ 11           Load control register
        LDCR R1, 8       Load data buffer
        SBO 12
        SBZ 12           Load transmitter
        RTWP             Return
READ    TB 8             Test overrun error
        JEQ ERROR
        TB 9             Test framing error
        JEQ ERROR
        TB 10            Test parity error
        JEQ ERROR
        STCR R2, 8       Read data
        SBZ 13
        SBO 13           Reset receiver
        RTWP             Return
ERROR   LI R12, >1010    Change CRU base
        STCR R3, 3       Store error word in R3
        RTWP             Return
```


FIGURE 6. Interrupt Routine.

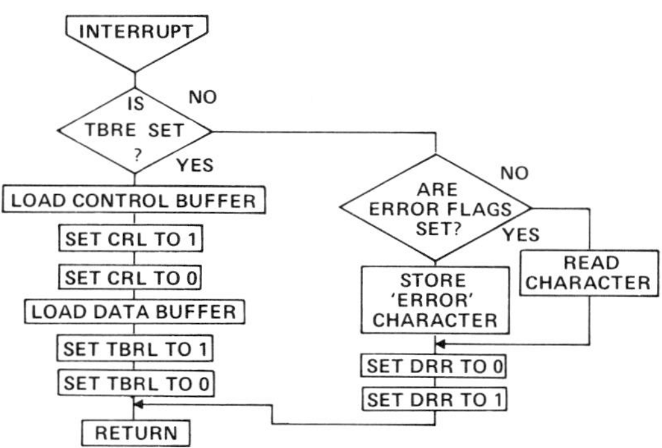

FIGURE 5. U.A.R.T. Flow Diagram.

the control register, to determine the format in which the data is to be transmitted. Then the data is loaded into the transmitter buffer register then the processor is returned to its original function. Had the Transmitter Buffer Register Empty flag not been set then 'read' part of the routine would have been entered. The error flags from the receiver section of the '6011 are examined to determine whether there was any error in reception. If there was no error then the character at the receiver output is read and the Data Ready Reset input to the device is set to a 'zero' and set to a 'one' to reset the data output. However, had there been an error, then an error character would be stored in place of the data character. Then, once again, Data Ready would be reset and the background routine returned to.

Figure 6 shows the routine for this function. From the address map shown in Table 2 the suitable c.r.u. base address can be derived and this would be hexa-decimal 1000. The first instruction is to load this value into the c.r.u. base address register. Then the Transmitter Buffer Register Empty flag is tested to determine whether it caused the interrupt. If this flag was not set, then the 'JNE READ' takes place and the 'read' routine is entered. However, if TBRE was set then the routine continues. The output instruction LDCR RO,5 causes five bits of control information to be output from register zero to the '6011. The two instructions SBO and SBZ for c.r.u. bit 11 strobe this control information into the '6011 using the Control Register Load input. Then 8 bits of data from register 1 are passed to the device and these are strobed into the transmitter buffer register by the SBO and SBZ instructions on c.r.u. bit 12, which is the Transmitter Buffer Register Load input. The RTWP instruction then returns the processor to its previous task. Had the 'JNE READ' taken place at the beginning of this routine, the jump to the label 'READ' would have entered the routine for handling data from the receiver section of the '6011. This begins by testing the error flags in sequence with Test Bit 8, Test Bit 9 and Test Bit 10 instructions. After each instruction, a 'jump on equal' to the label ERROR is used so that a single error on any of these flags will cause the error routine to be entered. If there is no error the next instruction is STCR R2,8 which causes the 8 data bits from the '6011 to be entered into register 2. The first instruction in the error routine is a change of the c.r.u. base address to hexa decimal 1010 which is the address at the first error flag. The instruction STCR R3,3 causes the 3 error bits to be loaded into register 3 as an error word. This is followed by a return instruction, to return the processor to its previous task.

Memory Mapped I/O Techniques

The logic required to interface a 16 bit memory mapped input/output port, is shown in Figure 7. The input is via two SN74S241 three state buffers which are enabled only when the three signals shown below are all active, i.e.

1. DBIN (Data Bus In) – when this output is active 'high' it indicates that the '9900 has disabled its output buffers to allow the memory (in this case an input port addressed as memory) to place data on the data bus during the period when $\overline{\text{MEMEN}}$ is 'low!'
2. $\overline{\text{MEMEN}}$ Memory Enable – when this output is active 'low' it indicates that the address bus contains a memory address.
3. Address decode logic – generates an active 'high' signal only when the desired appears on the address bus.

The output is taken via two SN74LS273 Octal D-Type Flip-Flops which are clocked by the following edge of Write Enable ($\overline{\text{WE}}$) if Address Decode and $\overline{\text{MEMEN}}$. When active 'low' the $\overline{\text{WE}}$ output indicates that data is available from the '9900 to be written into MEMORY.

Address Decode: Figure 8 shows a circuit for the address decode logic which will produce an active 'high' output for a unique address; in this case the address combination, 0111, 0011, 0110, 0110, in hexi-decimal 7366, is recognised. Both input and output circuits in this example are enabled by the same combination of address bits. It should be noted that, in a practical system, the high order addresses bits will be decoded elsewhere to select different parts of the memory, so it may be possible to considerably reduce the decode logic required to enable the I/O port by making use of these signals. It is also unlikely that the system will have so many I/O ports and so much memory that a unique address has to be allocated to the I/O port. For example, if a block of 256 address can be allocated to the I/O port, decoding the least significant eight address bits (7-14) can be omitted. Figure 9 shows an example of such a decoding scheme, here the I/O port will be enabled by any address in the range 6200_H to $63FE_H$.

Software: It has already been mentioned that data transfer between the I/O port and the microprocessor is accomplished by a move (MOV) instruction. Reference to the '9900 Microprocessor Data Manual shows that MOV is a dual operand instruction with multiple addressing modes for source and destination operands. In general the I/O port will be given a symbolic name, i.e. INOUT, but the other operand will depend on the location of the data to be transferred. Table 3 shows some possible instructions with their execution times.

Table 3. Instructions and Execution Times

Type	Output	Input	Clock Cycles	Time
1	MOV R2, @ INOUT	MOV @ INOUT, R2	22	7.3μs
2	MOV *R2 +, @ INOUT	MOV @ INOUT, *R2+	30	10μs
3	MOV R2, R1	MOV R1, R2	14	4.6μs

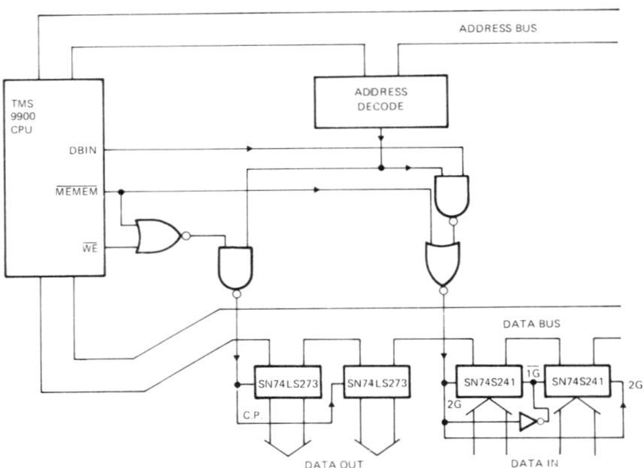

FIGURE 7. Memory Mapped Input/Output.

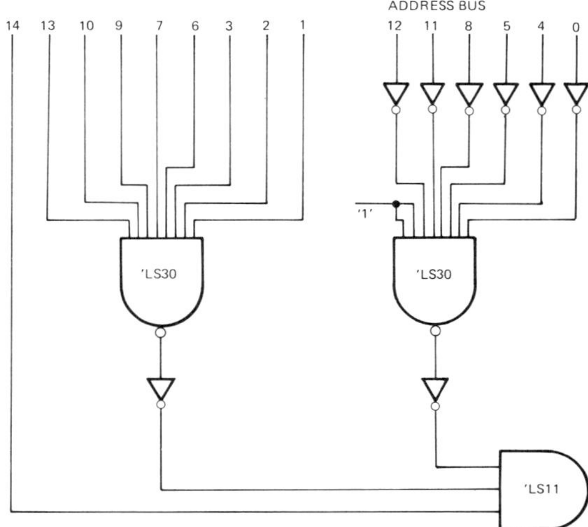

FIGURE 8. Address Decode Logic.

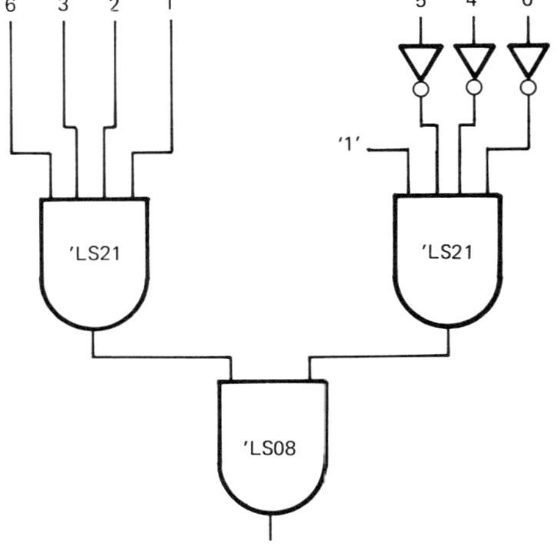

FIGURE 9. I/O Decoding.

Instructions of type 1 in Table 3 transfer the data between the port and a workspace register so the data must be placed in or fetched from the register as a separate exercise. Instructions of type 2. however, transfer the data between the port and a general location in memory addressed by the contents of the workspace register. In this case the contents of the register is also incremented after each execution of the instruction so transfer of the data between the port and a block of successive memory locations is facilitated. The fastest data transfer with the MOV instruction is achieved when only workspace addressing is employed, instruction type 3. So if the I/O port is configured as a workspace register a significant speed improvement is obtained. This arrangement will require a full decode of the address (similar to Figure 8) appropriate to the workspace register being used for I/O. The decoded address will also be required to disable the memory where the rest of the workspace registers are located.

A short program to transfer a block of words in memory between addresses START and ENDLOC to the output port is shown in Table 4. The number of clock cycle for the execution of each instruction is also shown in the Table 4, adding these together a new word is output every 54 clock cycles or 18μs. The symbolic addresses START, INOUT, and ENDLOC must be defined by equate statements, e.g. INOUT EQU > 7366 before the program can be assembled.

Table 4. Short Transfer Program

	LI	R2, START	LOAD REGISTER 2 WITH BLOCK START ADDRESS
LOOP	MOV	*R2+, @ INPUT	30 MOVE WORD AND INCREMENT REGISTER 2
	CI	R2, ENDLOC + 2	14 COMPARE VALUE IN R2 WITH BLOCK END ADDRESS +1
	JNE	LOOP	10 JUMP BACK UNTIL FINISHED
	CONTINUE		54 x .33 = 18μs

Interrupt Facility

In the block diagram of the '9900 microprocessor, shown in Figure 1, the interrupt interface is shown as an interrupt request line, $\overline{\text{INTREQ}}$, and four interrupt code inputs IC_0 to IC_3. These four inputs give provision for sixteen independent interrupts to the processor. The interrupt system is prioritised with level zero being the highest. An interrupt mask is set, in bits 12 to 15 of the status register and this determines what levels of interrupt will be accepted by the processor at any instant. However, level zero cannot be masked out. There are also two inputs to the processor which cause level zero interrupts in addition to the interrupt interface itself. These are the Reset input and Load input.

Figure 10 shows how external circuits can be interfaced to the interrupt inputs of the processor. The SN74148

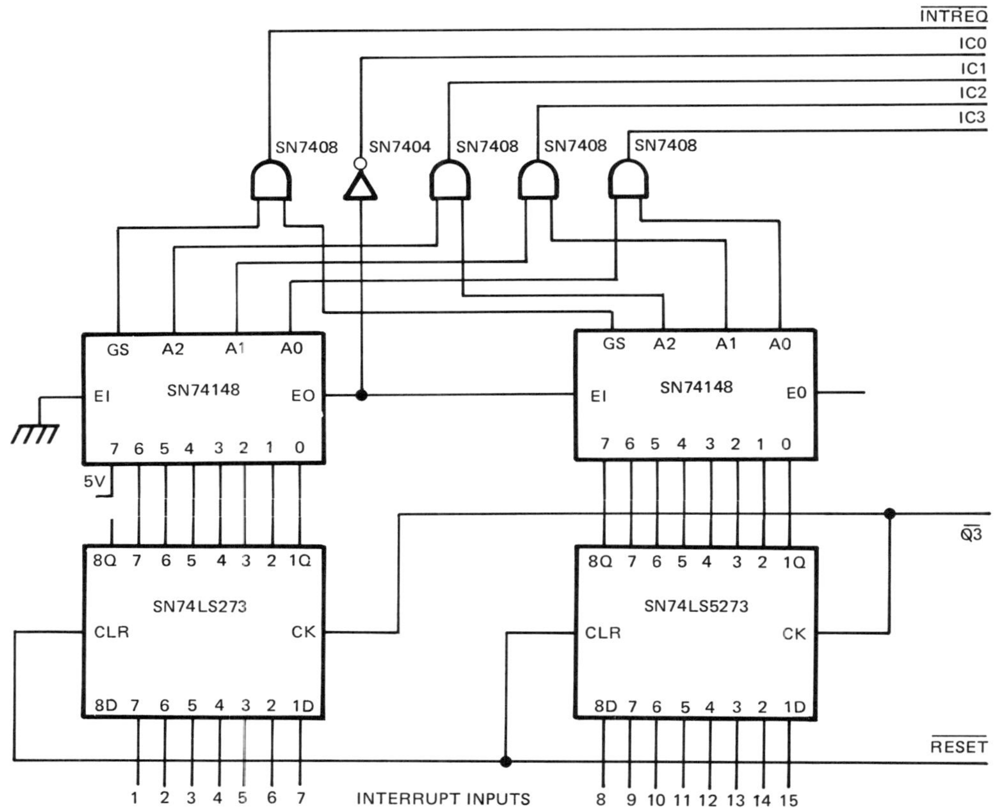

FIGURE 10. Interrupt Interface.

priority encoder devices generate an interrupt code to the processor corresponding to the highest priority interrupt input line valid at any time. However, the system is totally flexible and 1 to 4 interrupts can be implemented without resorting to these devices. The interrupt mask is controlled by the instruction 'Load Interrupt Mask Immediate', or LIMI. This instruction places the immediate operand into bits 12-15 of the status register. The processor uses the interrupt mask to identify the lowest level of interrupt that will be accepted. Figure 11 indicates this by showing the interrupt mask set at 8, and interrupt levels 0-8 being allowed and levels 9-15 not being allowed. When an interrupt does occur at a level that is accepted, the interrupt mask is automatically changed to mask out lower priority interrupts than the one which is being executed at that time. This is shown in the lower part of Figure 11 where a level 5 interrupt has been accepted, and the interrupts mask has been changed to 4. Thus here, only higher priority interrupts can interrupt the routine that is being executed. unless the LIMI instruction is used to lower the interrupt mask again. At the end of this level 5 interrupt, when the return to the background task is completed, the interrupt mask will be returned to its original value of, in this case 8.

When an interrupt is accepted the first instruction of the interrupt routine will always be executed even if the higher priority interrupt is trying to interrupt the current one. This does allow the interrupt mask to be changed by the first instruction of the interrupt routine if so required. The interrupt input must be latched to ensure that it will be available when the power samples it. This latch must be cleaned, however, before the interrupt sequences is completed, or the processor will do it again. This can be achieved by using the c.r.u. Figure 12 shows how the interrupt request latch is clock by 3, and can be rest by the output from an address decoder gated with the c.r.u. clock pulse. All that is required is an instruction in the interrupt service routine. This causes an output function to the address, which is recognised by the decoder in the circuit. The logic state of CRUOUT is immaterial, since only the address decoder output and the c.r.u. clock are required to generate a clear pulse to the interrupt latches.

The '9900 microprocessor uses a system of vectored interrupts, and there are two vectors stored in memory corresponding to each level of interrupt. These vectors are a Workspace Pointer and a Program Counter. The address in memory in which each of these is stored is defined by the architecture of the microprocessor. The memory map showing these locations is shown in Figure 13. When an interrupt occurs, for example at level 1, the processor will fetch the contents of memory addresses 0004 and 0006 and place them in the Workspace Pointer register and Program

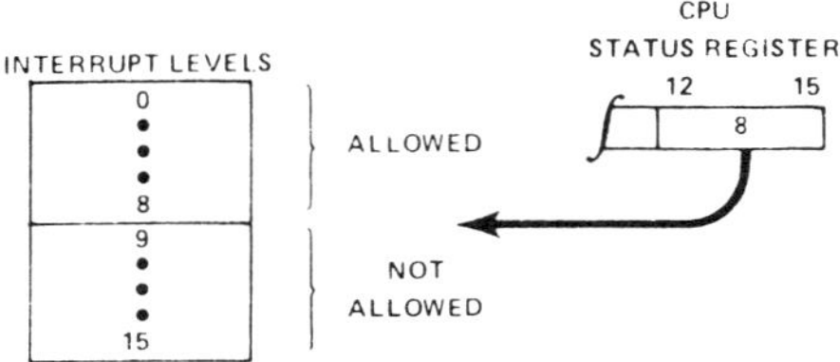

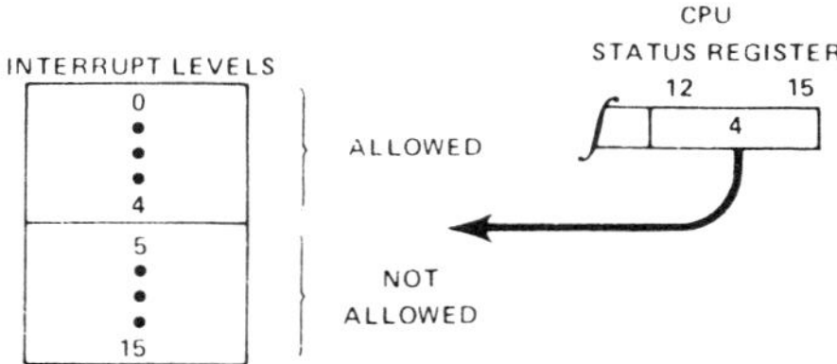

FIGURE 11. Interupt Operation.

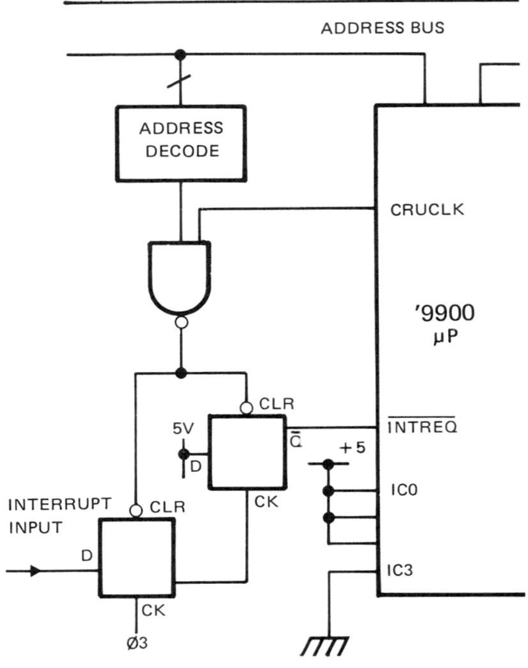

FIGURE 12. Interrupt Reset via C.R.U.

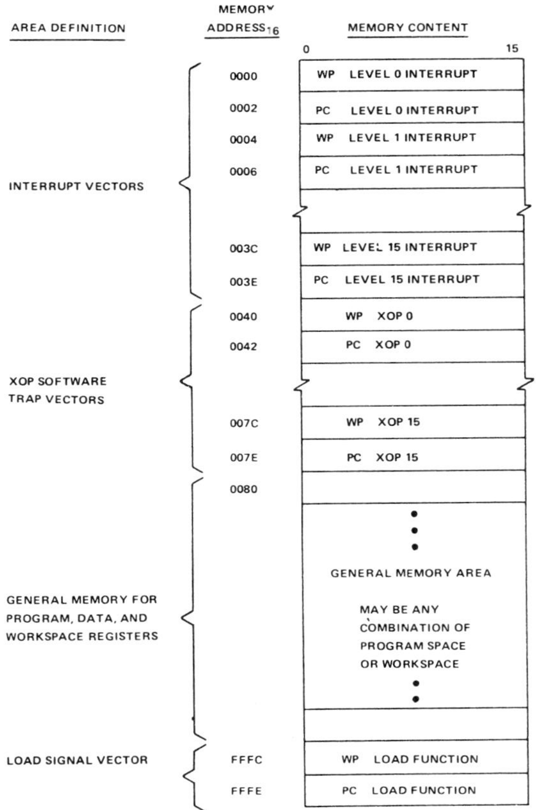

FIGURE 13. Location Memory Map,

Counter register respectively in the c.p.u. The previous values of these registers, and the Status Register, are stored in registers 13, 14 and 15 of the new workspace defined by the interrupt Workspace Pointer vector. As in the case of context switches resulting from a sub-routine called by a 'Branch and Load Workspace Pointer' instruction, BLWP, the context switch caused by an interrupt input can be imple-text switches resulting from a sub-routine called by a 'Branch and Load Workspace Pointer' instruction, BLWP, the context switch caused by an interrupt input can be implemented in a very short period of time by this microprocessor. This is due to the fact that the contents of a large number of internal registers does not have to be stored in memory, as is the case with register type processors, i.e. '8080.

To minimise the number of devices required by the system to implement the interrupt priority logic, another member of the device family is available i.e. the TMS9901 programmable systems interface described later.

OTHER FAMILY PRODUCTS

SPB9900 C.P.U.

This device is similar to the TMS9900 but has been designed to operate over the full military temperature range (–55 to +125°C) by fabricating it in i^2l. From its block diagram shown in Figure 14 it can be seen that it thus has all the key features of the '9900, i.e. full '9900 instruction set, 15 levels of vectored interrupt, d.m.a. capability, 16 bit data and 15 bit address busses, separate i/o interface (c.r.u.); and is compatible to it.[7] However, being made in i^2l, it has the extra advantages of a single power supply which can be easily provided[8], a single t.t.l. clock, static logic and bipolar reliability. It is also likely that its speed capability will better that of its n.m.o.s. counterpart.

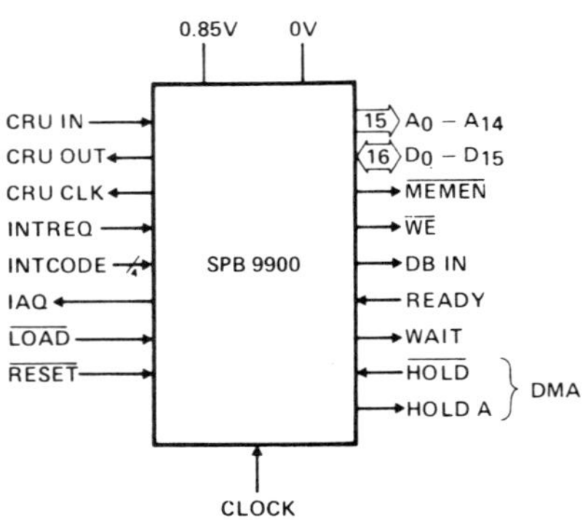

FIGURE 14. The SBP9900 Microprocessor.

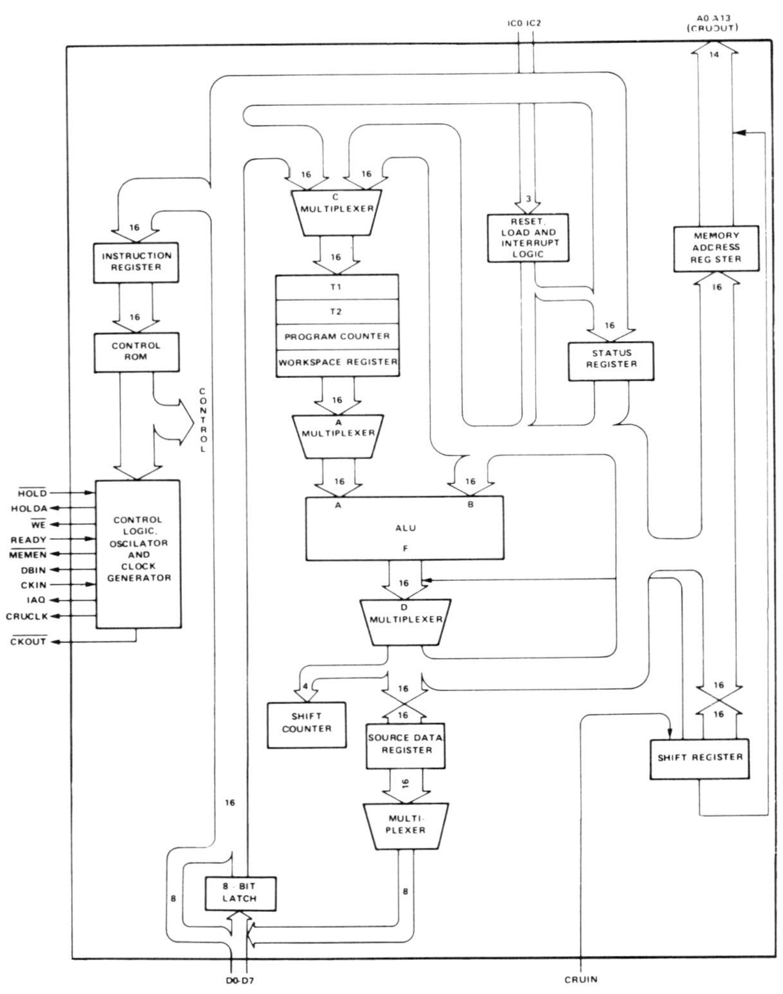

FIGURE 15. Block Diagram of the TMS9980 Microprocessor.

TMS9980 Microprocessor

Designed to minimise the cost for smaller systems, the TMS9980 is again a single chip 16-bit c.p.u. made in n-channel silicon gate m.o.s.[9] However, it has an 8-bit data bus, on-chip clock and is in a 40 pin package, with inputs and outputs as shown in Figure 15. Its instruction set is exactly the same as that for the '9900 and it has the same features, e.g. memory to memory architecture, etc.

TMS9940 Single Chip Microcomputer

Being a microcomputer the '9940 has r.o.m., r.a.m., c.p.u., i/o, and clock generators, as well as a timer, all on the same chip[10]. This is shown in its block diagram given in Figure 16. It uses a sub-set of '9900 instructions, including multiply and divide. Two versions are available, one with mask programmable r.o.m. and the other with electrically re-programmable r.o.m. (e.p.r.o.m.). Made in n.m.o.s., it operates from a 5V power supply with a 'power down' facility.

TMS9901 Programmable Systems Interface

This is a multifunctioned component designed to provide economical interrupts and i/o ports in a '9900/9980 microprocessor system[11]. It interfaces to the microprocessor directly and provides 22 interrupt and i/o ports. Six of these are dedicated interrupt inputs, 7 are dedicated i/o ports and the other nine are programmable and can be defined as either interrupt of i/o. The device is fabricated in n-channel m.o.s. and requires a single 5V power supply. It takes care of all the synchronization and prioritization functions that can be required by the processor for the interrupt inputs. It then provides to the processor and interrupt request line and the 4 interrupt code inputs. A programmable real time clock is included in it. A diagram showing the '9901 basic configuration is shown in Figure 17.

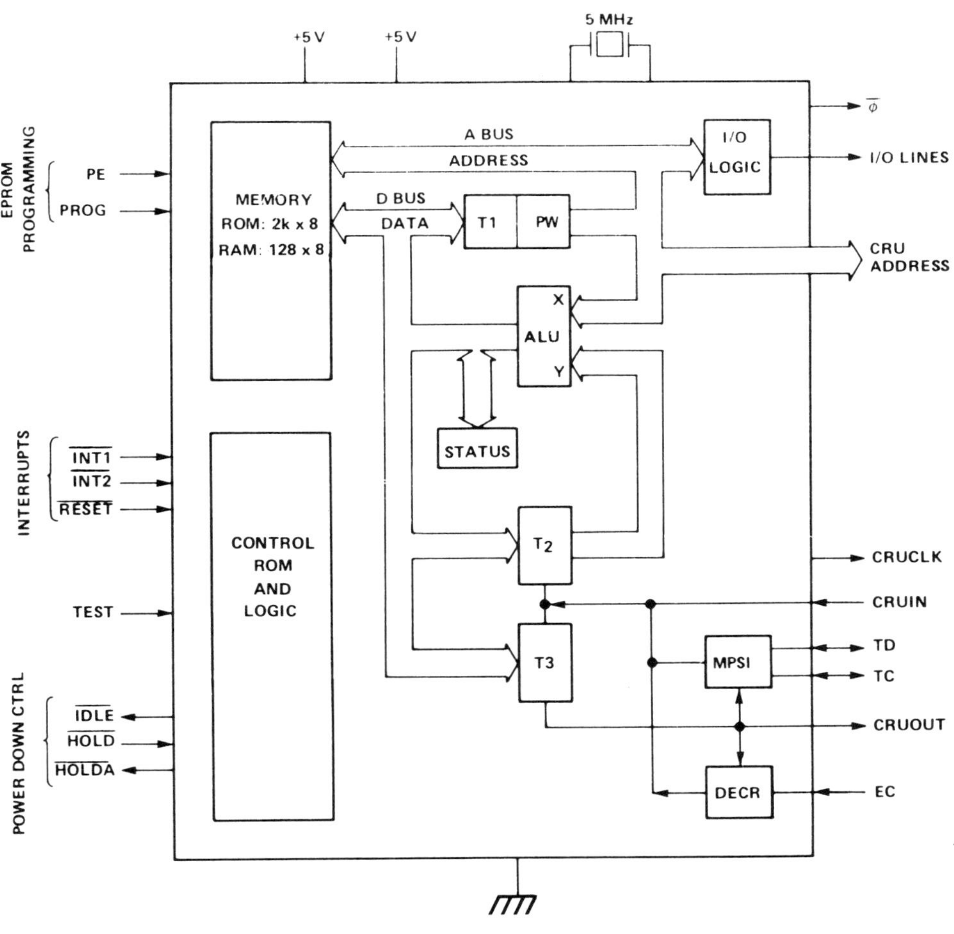

FIGURE 16. The TMS9940 Microcomputer Block Diagram.

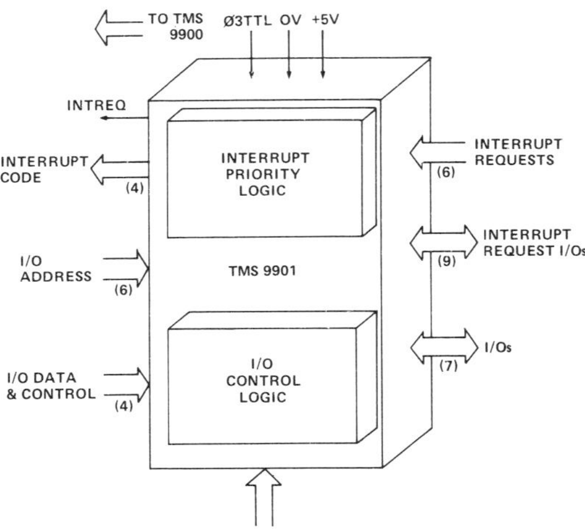

FIGURE 17. The TMS9901 Programmable Interrupt & I/O Controller.

TMS9902/3 Communications Controllers

The asynchronous version, the '9902[12], provides the interface between the microprocessor and a serial asynchronous channel, performing the timing and data serialization and de-serialization necessary to control that channel. A typical system using the '9902 is shown in Figure 18. The device allows choice of character length (5 to 8 bit), stop bits (1, 1½ or 2), and parity (even, odd or no parity).

The synchronous version, the '9903[13], provides the interface between the microprocessor and a serial synchronous channel. Again the device allows choice of character length (5 to 9 bits) and parity, as well as choice of internal or external character synchronisation and data clock rate input. It will operate with serial standard protocols and will perform various polynomials of cyclical redundancy checks (c.r.c.) generation and detection.

The SN54S/74S481 4 Bit Slice Processor Element[14, 15]

These devices, built in Schottky t.t.l. for speed, are designed to be compatible with the '9900 and memory to memory architecture. They have dual input/output ports and an address port, and are pre-programmed to perform multiply, divide and cyclical redundancy generation making these algorithms very fast. For example, four devices in cascade can perform 16 bit by 16 bit double precision divide in 3μs.

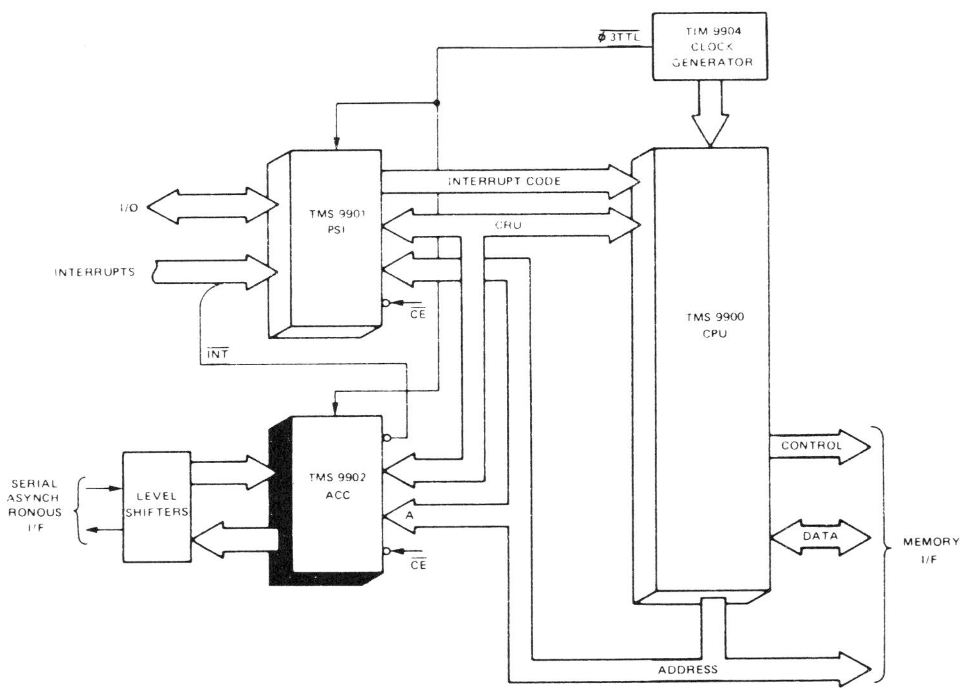

FIGURE 18. Typical System Using TMS9902 A.C.C. With the TMS9900 Microprocessor.

REFERENCES

1. Applications Laboratory Staff of Texas Instruments Incorporated, *Electronic Power Control and Digital Techniques,* McGraw-Hill Book Company, New York, 1976, pp. 104-106.
2. The Engineering Staff of Texas Instruments Inc., MOS Houston, 'TMS9900 System Development Manual', *Texas Instruments Application Report B199 or MOSA2.*
3. The Engineering Staff of Texas Instruments Inc., MOS Houston, 'Minimum System Design with the TMS9900 16-bit Microprocessor', *Texas Instruments Application Report CA184.*
4. Howard Cook and Jonathan Dell, 'Utilising the TMS9900 Communications Register Unit', *Texas Instruments Application Report B192.*
5. Applications Laboratory Staff of Texas Instruments Incorporated, *Electronic Power Control and Digital Techniques,* McGraw-Hill Book Company, New York, 1976, pp. 153-165.
6. The Engineering Staff of Texas Instruments Semiconductor Group, *TMS9900 Microprocessor Data Manual,* Texas Instruments Ltd, March 1977.
7 The Engineering Staff of Texas Instruments Semiconductor Group, *SBP9900* I^2L *16-bit Microprocessor Data Manual,* Texas Instruments, October 1976.
8. Applications Laboratory Staff of Texas Instruments Incorporated, *Electronic Power Control and Digital Techniques,* McGraw-Hill Book Company, New York, 1976, p. 113.
9. The Engineering Staff of Texas Instruments Semiconductor Group, *TMS9980 Microprocessor Data Manual,* Texas Instruments Ltd., March 1977.
10. John D. Bryant and Rick Longley, 'TMS9940 Single Chip Microcomputer', *Texas Instruments Inc.*
11. The Engineering Staff of Texas Instruments Semiconductor Group, *TMS9901 Programmable Systems Interface Data Manual,* Texas Instruments, October 1976.
12 The Engineering Staff of Texas Instruments Semiconductor Group, *TMS9902 Asynchronous Communication Controller,* Texas Instruments, January 1976.
13. Yogi Pandya/Steve Davis, 'TMS9903 Universal Synchronous Receiver Transmitter', *Texas Instruments,* March 1976.
14. The Engineering Staff of Texas Instruments Semiconductor Group, *SN54S481, SN74S481 4-Bit Slice Schottky Processor Elements Data Manual,* Texas Instruments, November 1976.
15. Chris Gare, 'An Introduction to the SN54/74S481 Bit Slice', *Texas Instruments Application Report B184.*

XIII ANALOGUE TO DIGITAL CONVERSION USING A MICROPROCESSOR

by
David Parratt

The conversion of analogue inputs into digital form is a common requirement for many systems especially those employing microprocessors. The designer has several methods available to him by which this data received from an analogue source may be converted to digital.[1] Essentially the choice is between using one of the currently available monolithic analogue to digital converters (a.d.c.), or using the microprocessor itself as part of the a.d.c. circuit.

In the first method the a.d.c. is selected by the microprocessor as an input port by means of a signal decoded from the address bus. The addition of output latches and three-state buffers is often required as the a.d.c.s are generally not designed to interface easily with the data bus of a microprocessor. It may also be necessary to incorporate logic which will prevent erroneous data being transferred should the microprocessor attempt to read the a.d.c. output before a conversion is completed. The use of such monolithic devices can give rise to fast conversions where the conversion rate is limited primarily by the conversion time of the external a.d.c. However, the design may incur an unacceptable overhead in the form of additional hardware.

It is usually possible to reduce the required number of devices by adopting the second alternative, i.e. to incorporate the microprocessor itself in the a.d.c. circuit. The advantages gained by this approach vary considerably between the many different microprocessors on the market, but the TMS9900 is for instance, particularly well suited to this design technique. The '9900's 16 bit register and data bus organisation allow the most frequently required analogue to digital conversion accuracies (10 or 12 bits) to be achieved. In addition its serial input/output facility via the communications register unit (c.r.u.) is ideal for the technique of successive approximation conversion. This method of analogue to digital conversion is briefly reviewed prior to describing the use of the TMS9900 in this application.

SUCCESSIVE APPROXIMATION CONVERSION

Figure 1 shows that the converter has two inputs; a known voltage, V_{ref}, which is set to a convenient reference level, and an unknown voltage, V_X. The output in this example consists of ten lines which will indicate the bit values within the binary representation of the value V_X. Since there are 10 lines, the output can indicate to an accuracy of $1/2^{10}$ or 1/1024 of V_{ref}. The first step in the successive approximation is to determine the value ('1' or '0') of the most significant bit (m.s.b.). If the value of V_X is equal to or greater than half of the reference voltage then the m.s.b. is set to '1'. Conversely the m.s.b. is set to a zero if the value of V_X is less than half of V_{ref}. The converter then directs its attention to the half of the voltage range of V_{ref} as now designated by the value of the m.s.b. It then determines which half of the newly

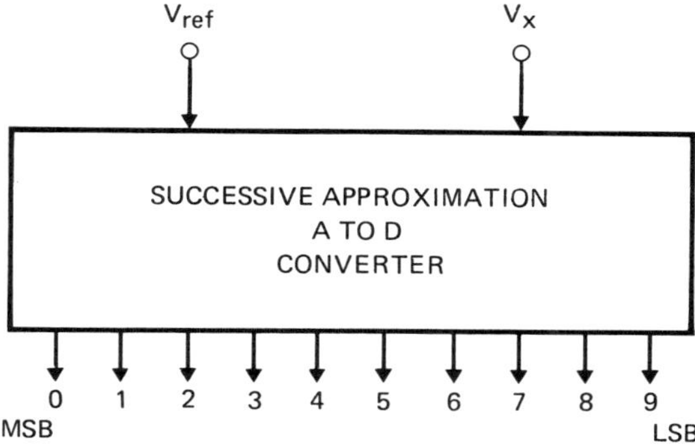

FIGURE 1. Converter.

designated V_{ref} range (i.e. zero to $V_{ref}/2$ or $V_{ref}/2$ to V_{ref}) contains the remaining value of V_X and sets the value of the second bit to a '1' or '0' accordingly. The converter continues to divide in half the appropriate range of the reference voltage as designated by the immediately previous operation until all ten bits are determined. Each successive output bit then represents an analogue input value of one half the value of that represented by the previous bit. For convenience in the following example let V_{ref} = 10.240V. Figure 2 shows a 'map' diagram of the output bits and the voltage ranges they represent. When the m.s.b. = 1 it represents a value of 5.120V and similarly when the l.s.b. = 1 it represents a value of 0.01V.

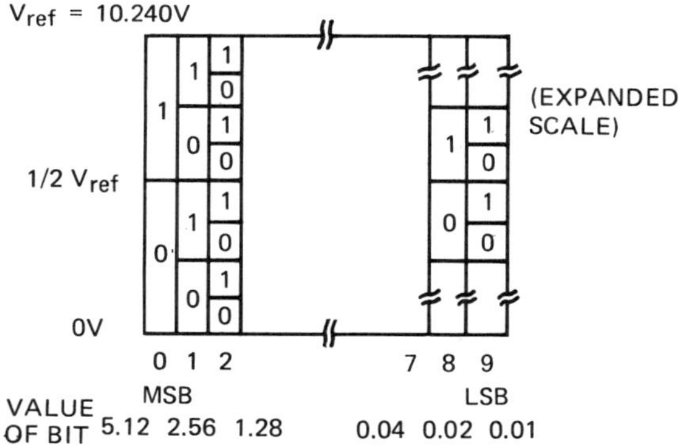

FIGURE 2. 'Map' Diagram of the Output Bits.

Thus if $V_X = 6.820V$, then the sequence of events will be as shown in Table 1.

Table 1. Sequence of Events.

	Comparison			Action		
	6.82	>	5.12	set bit	0 = 1	(m.s.b.)
(6.82 – 5.12 = 1.70)	1.70	<	2.56	set bit	1 = 0	
	1.70	>	1.28	set bit	2 = 1	
(1.70 – 1.28 = 0.42)	0.42	<	0.64	set bit	3 = 0	
	0.42	>	0.32	set bit	4 = 1	
(0.42 – 0.32 = 0.10)	0.10	<	0.16	set bit	5 = 0	
	0.10	>	0.08	set bit	6 = 1	
(0.10 – 0.08 = 0.02)	0.02	<	0.04	set bit	7 = 0	
	0.02	=	0.02	set bit	8 = 1	
(0.02 – 0.02 = 0.00)	0.00	<	0.01	set bit	9 = 0	(l.s.b.)

l.s.b. is in the '1' position and all other switches are in the '0' position. If the network is broken at point A and look to the left a resistance of R, formed by 2R in parallel with 'R + R', and an open circuit voltage of $\frac{1}{2}V_{ref}$ will be seen.

This equivalent circuit, as shown in Figure 4, can be substituted at point A and the circuit can be broken at point B. Once again to the left there is a resistance of R formed by 2R in parallel with 'R plus the R from circuit A' and an open circuit voltage of '$\frac{1}{2}V_{ref}/2$' or $\frac{1}{4}V_{ref}$. This analysis can be carried on until point N is reached and at each break point the equivalent open circuit voltage is divided by 2. Thus the voltage added to V_{out} by the nth switch is $V_{ref}/2^n$.

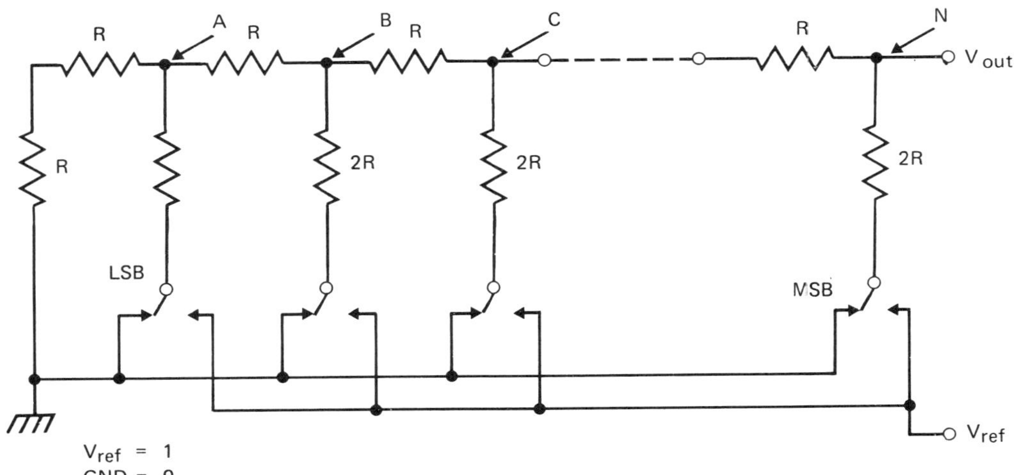

FIGURE 3. R/2R Ladder Network D.A.C.

The binary word thus obtained, i.e. 1010101010 = 682 can be seen to be a true binary representation of the nalogue input 6.820 volts providing that whatever scaling is required is pre-defined.

PRACTICAL CONVERTERS

One of the practical ways to build a successive approximation converter is to use an R/2R ladder network and some switches connected to form a digital to analogue converter as shown in Figure 3. Each switch represents a bit beginning with the m.s.b. at the right. Each switch can 'make' to either V_{ref} (bit = 1) or ground (bit = 0).

When the m.s.b. = 1 and all the other bits = 0, $V_{out} = \frac{1}{2} V_{ref}$. Similarly, the next successive switch to the left (bit 1) adds a value to V_{out} equal to one half the value added by the m.s.b. switch. That is, when bit 1 = 1 a value of $\frac{1}{4}V_{ref}$ is added to V_{out}. Each successive switch to the left when set to a 1 contributes a value to V_{out} equal to one half the value contributed by the previous switch to the right.

To see how this occurs, the circuit can be analysed with a series of Thevenin equivalent circuits. Suppose the

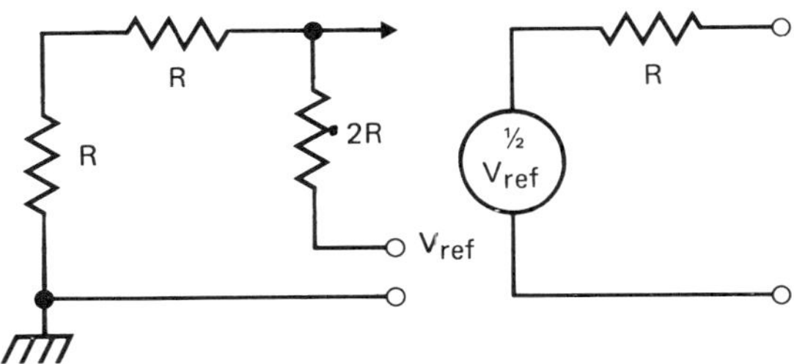

FIGURE 4. Equivalent Circuits.

Continuing the practical approach to building the converter, the switches can be replaced with semiconductor analogue switch devices which in turn can be controlled by standard logic gates. Thus the switches may be activated by some chosen standard logic levels (Figure 5). A buffer amplifier is used to isolate the ladder network and provide a high impedance load for it.

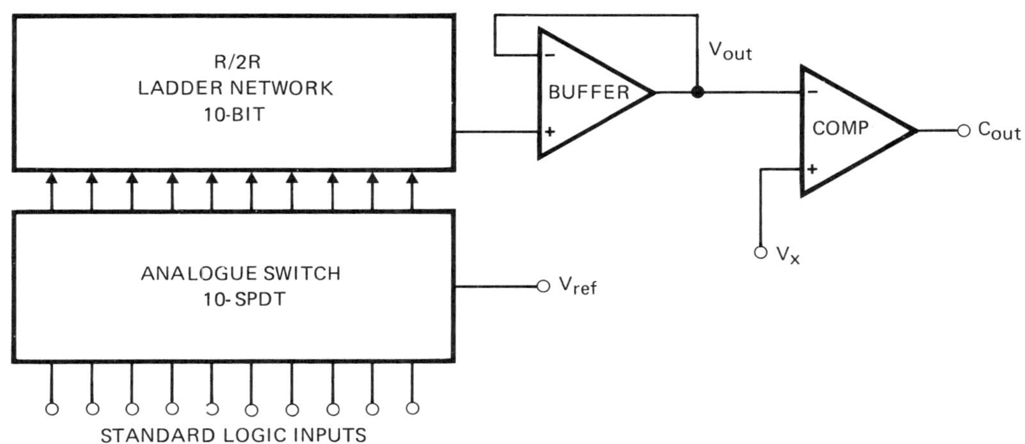

FIGURE 5. Using Analogue Switch Devices.

A comparator has one input connected to V_{out} from the buffer, and the other input is connected to V_X. The comparator output will be in the '1' state for $V_X > V_{out}$ and in the '0' state for $V_X < V_{out}$. The voltage V_X can now be converted into digital form as follows. With all the logic inputs at '0' V_{out} = 0V and C_{out} = 1, the switch for the m.s.b. is closed and the comparator output checked. If C_{out} = 1, then V_X is greater than $\frac{1}{2}V_{ref}$ and the m.s.b. = 1. The m.s.b. switch is left closed and the switch corresponding to bit 1 is also closed. The comparator output is then checked again. If C_{out} = 0, then

$$(\tfrac{1}{2}V_{ref} + \tfrac{1}{4}V_{ref}) > V_X > \tfrac{1}{2}V_{ref}.$$

Switch 1 is then opened and switch 2 closed and the comparator output checked. For each switch closure resulting in C_{out} = 1 the switch is left closed. If C_{out} = 0 the switch is re-opened and the process proceeds to the next less significant bit until all 10 bits are correctly set. The resulting bit pattern at the logic inputs contains the digital form of V_X.

Although d.a.c.s of this type can be constructed from standard components it is recommended that a propriety converter giving the required accuracy is used.

INTERFACE TO MICROPROCESSOR

The circuits which completes the analogue to digital conversion now needs to be interfaced to the microprocessor in order to achieve system control. The design of this interface is particularly easy to implement economically with the TMS9900 by utilising the c.r.u. By using this technique the need for the analogue switch in the previous circuit is eliminated as the CRUOUT line is used to provide all the bit signals to the digital to analogue converter in the system. The comparator output is read via the CRUIN line such that its state can be monitored. To implement the input/output function one SN74LS251 i.c. (an 8 to 1 multiplexer) for an 8 bit parallel input port and two SN74LS259 i.c.s (8 bit addressable latches) for a 16 bit parallel output port can be used. The complete circuit diagram of the a.d.c. system is shown in Figure 6.

The steps involved in performing a general successive approximation conversion are summarised in the flow chart of Figure 7 and the specific technique employed with the TMS9900 microprocessor is shown in Figure 8, where the carry flag is used to indicate the completion of a conversion sequence. Table 2 gives the full TMS9900 assembly listing for a 10 bit conversion routine. Workspace register 1 is used to count the number of bits in the conversion in addition to pointing to the appropriate bit being operated upon at any given time. Register 2 is used to store the successive approximations building up to the final result and Register 12 contains the c.r.u. base address.

The first instruction (CLR R2) clears the contents of register 2 by replacing the operand with a full 16-bit word of zeros. The second instruction (LI R1, >0400) loads register 1 with a 16-bit binary word consisting of 15 '0's and a single '1' at data bit 5. This is used to determine the number of bits to be converted. The instruction (LI R12, DAC) is used to load the c.r.u. base address representing the least significant bit of the digital to analogue converter. (This address is equated to the symbolic name DAC). (SRL R1, 1) shifts the contents of register 1 to the right by one place and fills the vacated bit with a zero. The status bits affected are logical greater than, arithmetic greater than, equal and carry. As the l.s.b. is shifted into the carry bit by this instruction, the '1' in the bit 5 position will be shifted into the carry bit only after all ten bits of the conversion have been determined. The (JOC FIN) instruction is used to detect this state and jump out of the loop to the label FIN which marks the end of the conversion and the beginning of the next function. If, after the SRL instruction, the carry bit is clear, the next instruction to be executed is SOC R1, R2 (set ones corresponding). The effect of this instruction is to set to '1' any bit in register 2 which corresponds to a '1' in register 1, i.e.ORing R1 and R2 in effect. Since only one

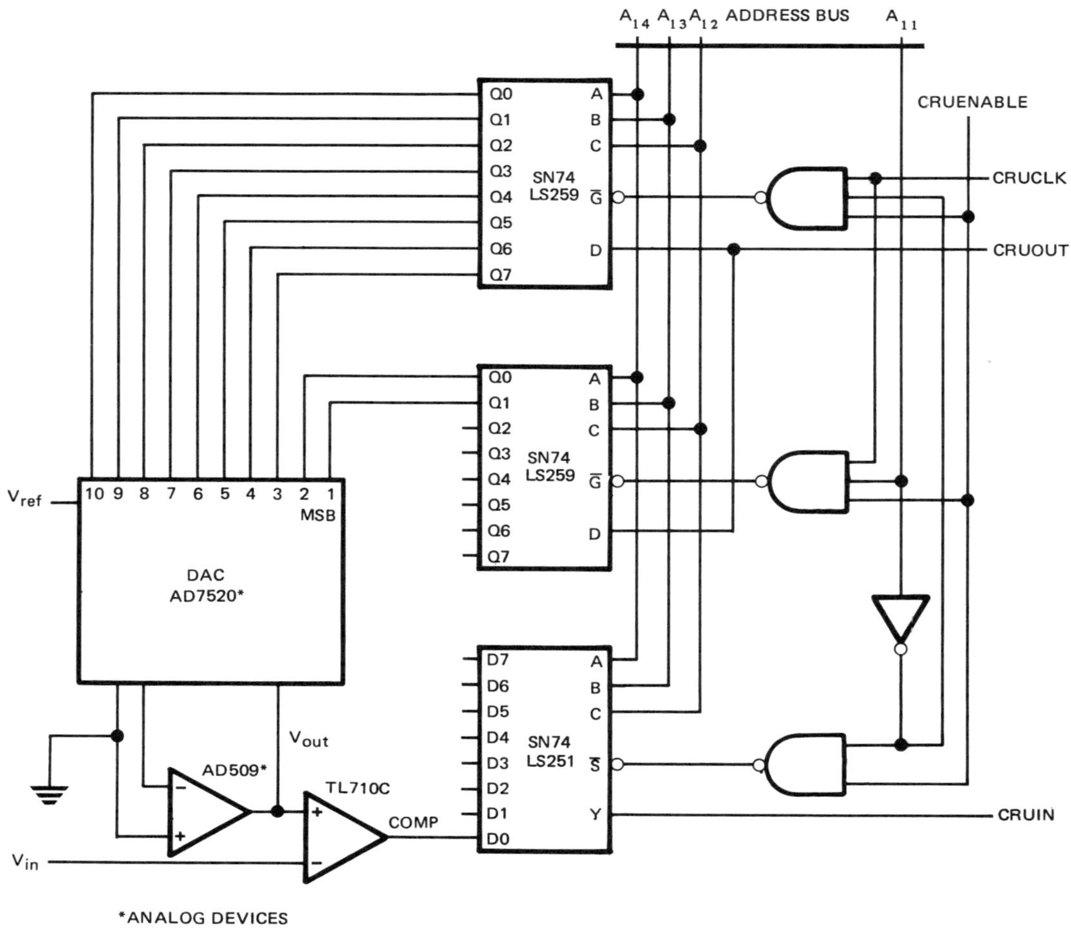

FIGURE 6. Analogue to Digital Converter.

Table 2. Full Assembly Listing

LABEL	INSTRUCTION		COMMENT	NUMBER OF CYCLES CLOCK	MEMORY
ADC	CLR	R2	CLEAR RESULT REGISTER	10	3
	LI	R1, > 0400	LOAD BIT COUNTER	12	3
	LI	R12, DAC(LSB)	LOAD CRU BASE		
LOOP	SRL	R1, 1	SHIFT LSB INTO CARRY	22	4
	JOC	FIN	JUMP WHEN CARRY = 1	{ 8 10	1 1
	SOC	R1, R2	SET '1' IN RESULT REGISTER	14	4
	LDCR	R2,10	OUTPUT 10 BITS OF R2	40	3
	TB	0	EXAMINE COMPARATOR O/P	12	2
	JEQ	LOOP	JUMP IF '1'	{ 8 10	1 1
	SZC	R1, R2	RESET '1' TO '0' IN RESULT	14	4
	JMP	LOOP	NEXT BIT	10	1
FIN	------------------------- -------------------------		END OF CONVERSATION		

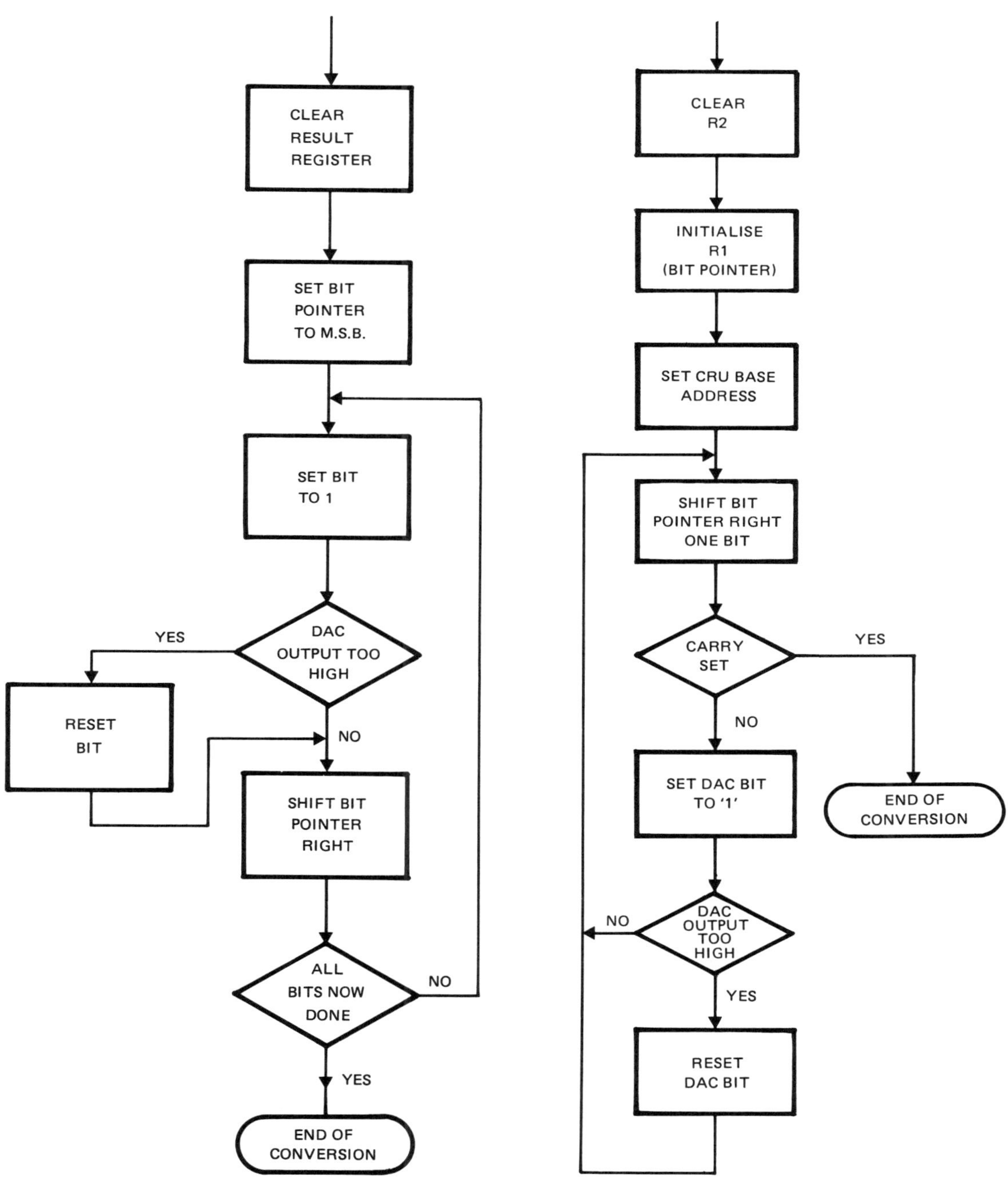

FIGURE 7. Flow Chart of Successive Approximation Conversion

FIGURE 8. Microprocessor Conversion Flow Chart

bit in R1 is at '1', this instruction sets the corresponding bit in R2 to 1. (LDCR R2, 10) then transfers the 10 least significant bits of R2 via the c.r.u. to the output lines connected to the d.a.c. inputs. The d.a.c. output is compared to the analogue input via the comparator. The output of this device is tested with the (TB 0) instruction which reads the bit of data at the addressed port (CRU Base address) via the CRUIN line and sets the 'equal' status bit to the logic value of the comparator output.

The output of the d.a.c. and the comparator must have settled by the time the microprocessor reads the CRU input. With the software as shown in Table 2 the CRU input is tested immediately after the digital word is transferred and study of the operation of the CRU instructions shows that the CRU Bit will be tested 8.65μs after the last bit of the digital word is transferred to the d.a.c. Notice also that with the circuit shown m.s.b. of the digital word is transferred last which means that the d.a.c. always gives its worst case settling time. To account for the settling time of the d.a.c. and the comparator a delay loop may have to be inserted between the LDCR and TB instructions.

```
        LDCR                    Clock Cycles

        LI    R6, DELAY              12
DLY     DEC   R6                     10
        JNE   DLY                    10
        TB
```

This will introduce a delay of 4 + n(6.66)μs where n is the delay count if the processor is running at 3MHz.

Alternatively, for a short extra delay, a series of NOP instructions could be inserted which will each introduce a delay of 2μs.

```
LDCR
NOP
NOP
NOP
TB
```

In this case settling time must be less than about 14μs. If the comparator output, and therefore the equal bit, are set to a logic '0' the d.a.c. output is too high and the last bit to be set is reset at a logic '1'. The program then returns to label 'LOOP' at the (SRL R1, 1) instruction where the bit pointer is shifted to select the next lowest order bit. This process is continued until a full 10 bit conversion is completed. The time taken for a 10 bit conversion by this method is approximately 420μs when the microprocessor is operated at a 3MHz clock rate.[2] The exact conversion time will depend upon the actual value being converted.

Essentially the only limitation to this conversion time is the speed of operation of the comparator since valid data must be present before the CRUIN line is read.

This method of analogue to digital conversion demonstrates the ease by which individual bits may be manipulated and controlled by utilising the communication register unit in the TMS9900 microprocessor. In addition the interface circuits required are standard catalogue parts which are both easy to implement and are low cost.

REFERENCES

1. Applications Laboratory Staff of Texas Instruments Incorporated, *MOS and Special-Purpose Bipolar Integrated Circuits and R-F Power Transistor Circuit Design,* McGraw-Hill Book Company, New York, 1976, p. 102.
2. *TMS 9900 Microprocessor Data Manual,* Texas Instruments Limited, p. 28, March, 1977.

XIV SOFTWARE GENERATION USING TIMESHARING SERVICES

by
Jonathan A. Dell

Microprocessor programs can be developed advantageously by using programs which have been installed on various host computers of commercial Timesharing networks, viz. timesharing cross support programs. Once these programs are available, e.g. there are three for the '9900 microprocessor[1], they can be used by anyone with a suitable terminal, acoustic modem and a telephone, and offer the cheapest way of getting 'hands-on' experience with a microprocessor software. When a particular network has been chosen, it is necessary to contact them and make an agreement. The timesharing company will provide a User number, a Password, and a telephone number which accesses a connection to the computer network. The charges for use of the timesharing services are accumulated against the User number. The Password is usually arranged to be unreadable on the printed output from the terminal to protect the account from unauthorised access.

```
HHHH
U::=BBQ44999,
PASSWORD
$$$$$$$$$$$$$
READY
RUN VSDI
VSDI CONNECTED TO CUU=0E6
LOGON BQ44999
ENTER PASSWORD FOR BQ44999-
$$$$$$$$$
:BQ44999 LOGON IN PROGRESS AT 11:30:33 ON JUNE 22,1976
NO BROADCAST MESSAGES
READY

LOGOFF
BQ44999 LOGGED OFF CRISP- 11:34:42 ON JUNE 22, 1976+

VSDI DISCONNECTED
BYE
                    ______________________________
O
CSS ONLINE - HSYS

>LINK HSYS
>LOGIN ABCDE999
PASSWORD:
$$$$$$$$
A/C INFO:
>
HSYS READY AT 04.58.23 ON 24JUNE76
CSS.300 06/15/76

04.58.25 >
05.02.15 >LOGOUT
15.03 VPU'S, .08 CONNECT HRS, 309 I/O
LOGGED OFF AT 05.02.28 ON 24JUNE76
                    ______________________________
PLEASE TYPE YOUR TERMINAL IDENTIFIER E
-1042-06--
PLEASE LOG IN:
USER NAME: ABCDEF:42
PASSWORD:
PROJECT CODE:
LOGMSG - 19:19:48 EST THURSDAY 03/04/76
•PLEASE Q LOGMSG FOR WEEKEND SCHEDULE.
LOGON AT 10:40:27 EST FRIDAY 03/05/76
C>
C>LOG
CONNECT= 00:03:09 TRU=      1.99
LOGOFF AT 08:56:50 EST FRIDAY 03/05/76
```

FIGURE 1. Logging on Procedures

LOGGING ON

Logging on is the name given to the sequence by which a user sets up a connection to the timesharing computer. Unless a special modem is installed it will be necessary to dial the telephone number and, when a response is obtained, place the receiver into the acoustic modem. A character is then entered at the keyboard which signals to the network the character rate of the terminal in use. Entering the User number and Password are the next operations, usually prompted by outputs at the terminal, and a mask is printed on the line where the password is entered. As the timesharing networks may contain several computers, it is necessary to establish the link to the appropriate one and the Logging On sequence will have to include instructions to set up this link. A detailed listing of the Logging on sequence, which differs in detail for the various networks, is shown in Figure 1. When a connection has been achieved the terminal will print a message, or prompt, to show that the computer is available for work.

The information which is required as source or control for the development programs is entered into a File. A file can contain data, mnemonics, a message or a complete program. The user must give each of his files a unique name if he wishes the contents to remain uncorrupted. Before defining a new file, it is advisable to inspect a list of the filenames stored previously by calling for a list to be printed with a command such as LISTFILES. The creation and modification of these files is accomplished by engaging the Edit mode of the timesharing computer.

EDITOR

The edit mode is invoked by entering EDIT with a filename and filetype on the keyboard, e.g. EDIT EXAMPLE DATA. Filenames and filetypes can each contain up to eight alphanumeric characters such as TEST DATA or TMS9900 PROGRAM. The filetype will probably be common for a number of user files. If a previously unused filename is entered the computer goes to Input mode allowing the user to write his statements into the file.

To modify an existing file a number of subcommands are available in the edit mode such as LOCATE, CHANGE, DELETE and INSERT. For the three timesharing networks that are used for the '9900 microprocessor, these commands are detailed in Table 1, but full explanations can be found in the Manuals provided by the individual companies.

```
06.43.08 >E EXAMPLE DAD@TA
EDIT:
>P 99
        TITL      ' TMS9900 TIMESHARING DEMONSTRATION '
        TITL      '  SIGNED MULTIPILICATION USING XOP '
*
*
        OPTION    XREF,SYMT,OBJ
        IDT 'SIGNX'
        DEF    START,XOP2,NEG,END
START   LWPI >0100            DEFINE WORKSPACE
        LI   R1,XOP2          LOAD R1 WITH ADDRESS OF
XOP2    EQU  >0922            LABEL XOP2,I.E. 0922HEX
        MOV  R1,@>004A        SET PC TRAP VECTOR
MASK    EQU >300              LABLE OF MASK WORD
        LI   R2,>8000         LOAD R2 WITH MASK WORD
        MOV  R2,@MASK         LOAD MASK INTO MEMORY
        LI   R1,>0700         LOAD R1 WITH WP ADDRESS
        MOV  R1,@>0048        MOVE WP TO WP TRAP
        TITL     'LOCATE DATA                                    '
        PAGE
        LI   R3,>0010         LOAD MULTIPLIER
        LI   R5,>8002         LOAD MULTIPLICAND
        LI   R1,>0106         LOAD MULTIPLICAND ADDRESS IN R1
        XOP  *R1,2            CALL XOP2
        TITL  'XOP2                                              '
             PAGE
        AORG XOP2
        MOV  @4(11),R1        MOVE MULTIPLICAND INTO NEW R1
        XOR  *R11,R1          EXCLUSIVE 'OR'
        JLT  NEG              JUMP IF MSB OF RESULT IS 1
        CLR  @2(11)           SET SIGN FLAG TO 0
        RTWP                  RETURN
NEG     LI   R1,>FFFF         SET SIGN FLAG TO 1
        MOV  R1,@2(11)
        RTWP
        TITL 'EXECUTE                                            '
             PAGE
        RORG
        SZC  @MASK,R3         REMOVE SIGN
        SZC  @MASK,R5         REMOVE SIGN
        MPY  R3,R5            MULTIPY
        CI   R4,0             DETERMINE SIGN
        JEQ  END              JUMP IF ANSWER POSITIVE
        SOC  @MASK,R5         SET SIGN BIT TO 1
        TITL '                                         '
END
*       CONTINUE PROGRAM
      END
EOF:
```

FIGURE 2. Example Data Listing

In the TMS9900 instruction mnemonics, the @-sign is used to signify Indexed and Symbolic addressing modes. However, the @-sign is often set up as a Character Delete symbol in that part of the executive program which determines the terminal parameters when logging on. This may be changed by defining a new symbol such as ← for character delete, a procedure which is fully described in the system manuals.

For input to microprocessor development programs, a file containing the users program, mnemonic statements, assembler directives, titles and comments, is required. An example program which contains all these items is shown in Figure 2.

DEVELOPMENT PROGRAMS

The development programs for the microprocessor are contained in various packages, for example, as in the TI Microcomputer Package (TIMCP). These programs are invoked by causing the package to execute on the host computer by a command such as RUN TIMCP or ATTACH

Table 1. Editor Command Index

	G.E/HONEYWELL	CSS INTERNATIONAL	TYMSHARE
EDIT	E NAME TYPE	E NAME TYPE	E NAME TYPE
INPUT	I	I	I
INPUT/	I LINENO	I	I
INSERT	IN CHARSTRING		
SAVE	S NAME. TYPE	S NAME TYPE	S NAME TYPE
DELETE	D N	DE /N / STRING	DEL N
UP	UP N	U /N / STRING	UP N
DOWN	DOWN N	DO/N STRING /	DOWN N
TOP	TOP	T	TOP
BOTTOM	B	B	B
FIND	F = STRING = COL	F STRING	F STRING
LOCATE	F STRING	L/STRING/	LOCATE/STRING/
LIST/ PRINT/ TYPE	L	P	TYPE
CHANGE	C/OLD/NEW/	C/OLD/NEW	C/OLD/NEW
END/ QUIT	END	Q	QUIT

TIMCP depending on the network in use.

To control the development programs the computer requires answers to a series of questions, the first of these is the device type on which development is to take place, e.g. the TMS9900. This is followed by the option required, Assembly (ASM) or Simulation (SIM) for example.

ASSEMBLER

The assembler program operates on a file of source statements, i.e. assembly language mnemonics, data, and addressing information, and generates a file of object code and an assembly listing. The assembly listing can be printed at the terminal or stored in a file for future reference. Whenever a file is referenced by the assembler program the name and type of that file is requested and must be entered at the keyboard.

The program EXAMPLE DATA, Figure 2, has been used as the source for the assmebler. Figure 3 shows the terminal output during the set up sequence for an assembly run, and the resulting output is shown in Figures 4 to 6, which also illustrate the effect of the Assembler Directives. The CSS International network was used to produce this assembly, but the other networks produce similar results. All the directives which affect the operation of the assembler can be used, and some with reference to the EXAMPLE PROGRAM (Figure 2), will be described. The directives are listed in Table 2 and explained in detail in the Assembly Language programmers guide[2].

A program description follows the Title directive TITL at the top of the file and causes this to head the first page of assembler output. If no further Titles were included in the program this would also be placed in the heading of each subsequent page.

```
06.46.20 >ATTACH TIMCP
TIMCP    ATTACHED AS 192,(T)
TEXAS INSTRUMENTS MICROPROCESSOR SIMULATION SYSTEM
COPYRIGHT (C) 1975 TEXAS INSTRUMENTS INCORPORATED
ENTER DEVICE (TMS1000,TMS8080,TMS9900)>TMS9900
WOULD YOU PREFER THE SAMPLE(PREDEFINED) PROGRAMMED
MODE OF OPERATION: (YES OR NO)>NO
ENTER OPTION(ASM,SIM,UTL,END)>ASM
ENTER ASM OBJECT FILE NAME>TMS9900 OBJECT
ENTER ASM SOURCE FILE NAME>EXAMPLE DATA
ASM LISTING ( FILE 06 ) AT ? (TERMINAL,FILE)
>TERMINAL
FT08F001 CON  RECFM FA  LRECL 00133 BLKSIZE 00133 U
FT29F001 DSK  RECFM FB  LRECL 00133 BLKSIZE 01330 ASMTEMP  DATA     Y
FT03F001 DSK  RECFM FB  LRECL 00080 BLKSIZE 00080 TMS9900  OBJECT   P
TYPE YES TO EXECUTE>YES
EXECUTION:
```

FIGURE 3. Engaging the Assembler

```
 MS9900 ASSEMBLER (VERSION A.1 10/15/75)        12/9/76          06:48:09
COPYRIGHT (C) 1975 TEXAS INSTRUMENTS INCORPORATED
TEXAS INSTRUMENTS OWNS AND IS RESPONSIBLE FOR ASM9900

SIGNX     TMS9900 TIMESHARING DEMONSTRATION                         PAGE    1


RECD     LOC OBJ      SOURCE STATEMENT

0001                             TITL       ' TMS9900 TIMESHARING DEMONSTRATION '
0002                             TITL       '  SIGNED MULTIPILICATION USING XOP '
0003                  *
0004                  *
0005                             OPTION     XREF,SYMT,OBJ
0006                             IDT 'SIGNX'
0007                             DEF     START,XOP2,NEG,END
0008   0000 02E0  START          LWPI >0100               DEFINE WORKSPACE
       0002 0100
0009   0004 0201                 LI    R1,XOP2            LOAD R1 WITH ADDRESS OF
       0006 0922
0010        0922  XOP2           EQU   >0922              LABEL XOP2,I.E. 0922HEX
0011   0008 C801                 MOV   R1,@>004A          SET PC TRAP VECTOR
       000A 004A
0012        0300  MASK           EQU >300                 LABLE OF MASK WORD
0013   000C 0202                 LI    R2,>8000           LOAD R2 WITH MASK WORD
       000E 8000
0014   0010 C802                 MOV   R2,@MASK           LOAD MASK INTO MEMORY
       0012 0300
0015   0014 0201                 LI    R1,>0700           LOAD R1 WITH WP ADDRESS
       0016 0700
0016   0018 C801                 MOV   R1,@>0048          MOVE WP TO WP TRAP
       001A 0048
0017                             TITL     'LOCATE DATA
0018                             PAGE




SIGNX     LOCATE DATA                                               PAGE    2


RECD     LOC OBJ      SOURCE STATEMENT

0019   001C 0203                 LI    R3,>0010           LOAD MULTIPLIER
       001E 0010
0020   0020 0205                 LI    R5,>8002           LOAD MULTIPLICAND
       0022 8002
0021   0024 0201                 LI    R1,>0106           LOAD MULTIPLICAND ADDRESS IN R1
       0026 0106
0022   0028 2C91                 XOP   *R1,2              CALL XOP2
0023                             TITL  'XOP2
0024                                   PAGE
```

FIGURE 4. Assembly Listing

The OPTION statement causes cross reference and symbol tables, together with the object code, to be included with the assembly listing. The Object code is automatically recorded in a separate file defined in response to the ASM OBJECT FILE NAME request at the start of the sequence calling the assembler (see Figure 3), so it may not be required again in the assembler listing.

IDT, the program identification directive, must precede any statements resulting in object code and defines a program name which will be included at the beginning of the object code.

The DEF statement causes the following labels to be defined in the object code also so that they are available for reference by other programs which only see the object

```
SIGNX     XOP2                                                      PAGE    3

RECD     LOC OBJ      SOURCE STATEMENT

0025     0922                     AORG XOP2
0026     0922 C06B                MOV  @4(11),R1       MOVE MULTIPLICAND INTO NEW R1
         0924 0004
0027     0926 285B                XOR  *R11,R1         EXCLUSIVE 'OR'
0028     0928 1103                JLT  NEG             JUMP IF MSB OF RESULT IS 1
0029     092A 04EB                CLR  @2(11)          SET SIGN FLAG TO 0
         092C 0002
0030     092E 0380                RTWP                 RETURN
0031     0930 0201   NEG          LI   R1,>FFFF        SET SIGN FLAG TO 1
         0932 FFFF
0032     0934 CAC1                MOV  R1,@2(11)
         0936 0002
0033     0938 0380                RTWP
0034                              TITL 'EXECUTE
0035                                   PAGE
```

```
SIGNX     EXECUTE                                                   PAGE    4

RECD     LOC OBJ      SOURCE STATEMENT

0036     002A                     RORG
0037     002A 40E0                SZC  @MASK,R3        REMOVE SIGN
         002C 0300
0038     002E 4160                SZC  @MASK,R5        REMOVE SIGN
         0030 0300
0039     0032 3943                MPY  R3,R5           MULTIPY
0040     0034 0284                CI   R4,0            DETERMINE SIGN
         0036 0000
0041     0038 1302                JEQ  END             JUMP IF ANSWER POSITIVE
0042     003A E160                SOC  @MASK,R5        SET SIGN BIT TO 1
         003C 0300
0043                              TITL
0044     003E        END
0045                 *            CONTINUE PROGRAM
0046                           END

*0000* NO.OF ERRORS IN THIS ASSEMBLY= 0000

NO. OF RELOCATABLE LOCATIONS USED = 003E
```

FIGURE 5. Assembly Listing

code listing.

The TITL and PAGE directives together cause the contents of the TITL to be printed as the heading of the following page in the assembler output.

Absolute object code is defined for the section of the Example Program called XOP2 by the statement AORG XOP2, the absolute location of the first statement being defined by the value of label XOP2.

No particular origin is specified for the first sections of program so the assembler automatically assumes that they are Relocatable. After an AORG directive, the following code is absolute until a Relocatable RORG directive is again encountered.

The Object code output with the assembly listing is shown in Figure 6. Tag characters are used to show the meaning of each word; a list of all possible tag characters is shown in Table 3 and a full description of each can be found in the Assembly Language Programmers Guide[2].

If a T1733ASR Terminal is available, the Object code can be taken out on cassette at this stage and transferred to

```
**OBJECT CODE(HEX)**

0 003E SIGNX    A 0000  B 02E0  B 0100  B 0201  B 0922  B C801  B 004A  B 0202
 B 8000  B C802  7 F243  F   SIGN   1
A 0012  B 0300  B 0201  B 0700  B C801  B 0048  B 0203  B 0010  B 0205  B 8002
 B 0201  B 0106  7 F359  F   SIGN   2
A 0028  B 2C91  9 0922  B C06B  B 0004  B 285B  B 1103  B 04EB  B 0002  B 0380
 B 0201  B FFFF  7 F29D  F   SIGN   3
9 0934  B CAC1  B 0002  B 0380  A 002A  B 40E0  B 0300  B 4160  B 0300  B 3943
 B 0284  B 0000  7 F308  F   SIGN   4
A 0038  B 1302  B E160  B 0300  5 0000 START  6 0922 XOP2   6 0930 NEG    5 003
E END     7 F203  F          SIGN   5
:       12/9/76          06:48:09
                             SIGN   6

# OF OBJECT RECORDS OUTPUT=    6


SIGNX                                                              PAGE    5


**CROSS REFERENCE TABLE**

   SYMBOL        VALUE    DEFN     REFERENCES

   END           003E'    DEF        44     7    41
   MASK          0300      12        14    37    38    42
   NEG           0930     DEF        31     7    28
   R0            0000               NOT REFERENCED
   R1            0001                 9    11    15    16    21    22    26    27
                                     31    32
   R10           000A               NOT REFERENCED
   R11           000B                27
   R12           000C               NOT REFERENCED
   R13           000D               NOT REFERENCED
   R14           000E               NOT REFERENCED
   R15           000F               NOT REFERENCED
   R2            0002                13    14
   R3            0003                19    37    39
   R4            0004                40
   R5            0005                20    38    39    42
   R6            0006               NOT REFERENCED
   R7            0007               NOT REFERENCED
   R8            0008               NOT REFERENCED
   R9            0009               NOT REFERENCED
   SIGNX         IDT        6       NOT REFERENCED
   START         0000'    DEF         3     7
   XOP2          0922     DEF        10    25     7     9
----END OF ASSEMBLY
```

FIGURE 6. Object Code & Cross Reference Listing

a dedicated prototyping system such as the 990/4 computer.

The cross reference and symbol table completes the assembler output, Figure 6.

SIMULATOR

The simulator section of the cross support programs allows the user to test and 'debug' the object coded programs which he has created with the aid of the assembler program. When a simulation is requested the names of the files referenced as source, control and output must be specified in response to the questions printed at the terminal. The terminal output during a 'set up for simulation' is shown in Figure 7. Before a simulation can take place the object code must be loaded into the sections of program memory where it will reside in the final system. This is accomplished with the help of the Linking Loader. The Linking Loader takes modules of object code, generated from a current assembly or stored from previous assemblies, and places them into the simulated memory at locations

Table 2. Assembler Directives

Directive	Syntax	Force Word Boundary	Note
Output Options	OPTION <keyword>[,<keyword>] . . .	NA	5
Page Title	[<label>] TITL <string>	NA	
Program Identifier	[<label>] IDT <string>	NA	
External Definition	[<label>] DEF <symbol>[,<symbol>] . . .	NA	
External Reference	[<label>] REF <symbol>[,<symbol>] . . .	NA	
Absolute Origin	[<label>] AORG <wd expr>	No	
Relocatable Origin	[<label>] RORG [<expr>]	No	1, 3
Dummy Origin	[<label>] DORG <wd expr>	No	
Block Starting with Symbol	[<label>] BSS <wd expr>	No	
Block Ending with Symbol	[<label>] BES <wd expr>	No	
Initialize Word	[<label>] DATA <expr>[,<expr>] . . .	Yes	
Initialize Text	[<label>] TEXT [-] <string>	No	2
Define Extended Operation	[<label>] DXOP <symbol>,<term>	NA	
Define Assembly-Time Constant	<label> EQU <expr>	NA	3
Word Boundary	[<label>] EVEN	Yes	
No Source List	[<label>] UNL	NA	
List Source	[<label>] LIST	NA	
Page Eject	[<label>] PAGE	NA	
Initialize Byte	[<label>] BYTE <wd expr> [,<wd expr>] . . .	No	
Program End	[<label>] END [<symbol>]	NA	4

NOTES

1. The expression must be relocatable.
2. The minus sign causes the assembler to negate the rightmost character.
3. Symbols in expressions must have been previously defined.
4. Symbol must have been previously defined.
5. Keywords are XREF, OBJ, SYMT, NOLIST, and TEXT.

Table 3. Object Output Tag Characters

Tag Character	Hexadecimal Field (Four Characters)	Second Field	Meaning
0	Length of all relocatable code	8-character Program Identifier	Program Start
1	Entry address	None	Absolute Entry Address
2	Entry address	None	Relocatable Entry Address
3	Location of last appearance of symbol	6-character symbol	External Reference last used in relocatable code
4	Location of last appearance of symbol	6-character symbol	External Reference last used in absolute code
5	Location	6-character symbol	Relocatable External Definition
6	Location	6-character symbol	Absolute External Definition
7	Checksum for current record	None	Checksum
9	Load address	None	Absolute load address
A	Load address	None	Relocatable load address
B	Data	None	Absolute data
C	Data	None	Relocatable data
F	None	None	End-of-record
G	Location	6-character symbol	Relocatable symbol definition
H	Location	6-character symbol	Absolute symbol definition

```
ENTER OPTION(ASM,SIM,UTL,END)>SIM
ENTER LOADER COMMAND FILE NAME>LOAD DATA
ENTER LOADER INCLUDE FILE DATA (DDNAME NAME TYPE MODE OR C/R)
>FT03F001 TMS9900 OBJECT P
>
SIM CONTROL ( FILE 05 ) AT ? (TERMINAL,FILE)
>TERMINAL
ENTER ABSOLUTE OBJECT FILE NAME>TMS9900 AOBJ
SIM LISTING ( FILE 06 ) AT ? (TERMINAL,FILE)
>TERMINAL
FT04F001 DSK  RECFM FC  LRECL 00080 BLKSIZE 00080 LOAD     DATA    P
FT03F001 DSK  RECFM FC  LRECL 00080 BLKSIZE 00080 TMS9900  OBJECT  P
FT17F001 DSK  RECFM FB  LRECL 00080 BLKSIZE 00080 TMS9900  AOBJ    P
TYPE YES TO EXECUTE>YES
EXECUTION:
```

FIGURE 7. Engaging the Simulator

specified by the user in the Loader Command File. It also resolves any external references, or links, between the program modules.

```
06.57.30 >E LOAD DATA
EDIT:
>P 9
ORIGIN >1000
INCLUDE FT03F001
SAVE ABS OBJECT
ENTRY START
EOF:
>Q
```

FIGURE 8. Load Data Listing

The file LOAD DATA, shown in Figure 8, was used to control the loading of the Example Program, and contains the four types of Loader command which are available. These are fully detailed in the Cross Support System Users Guide[3]. An ORIGIN statement defines the starting location for the relocatable code; an INCLUDE statement references the source of object code; a SAVE causes a file containing the Absolute object code to be created; and ENTRY defines the start of program execution at the label START.

When the load has been completed a Loader Map is printed at the terminal. This lists the names of the sections of program, the starting location, the length of that section and also defines the location of any labels used in each section. A very simple loader map produced when the EXAMPLE PROGRAM was loaded for simulation is shown in Figure 9. A stating location of Hex 1000 was specified for the relocatable part of the program, the locations of the XOP were absolutely specified in the object code so they are not modified by the loader.

When the load has been completed control passes to the Simulator program and the control statements, previously entered into a file, or entered now at the keyboard, are executed in turn. A full list of the control statements which can be employed are shown in Table 4, and each is explained fully in a Cross Support System Users Guide[3]. For the simulation of the EXAMPLE PROGRAM only two control statements were used TRACE and RUN. TRACE causes, for a specified location or range of locations, a printed output of the LOCATION, INSTRUCTION REGISTER, INSTRUCTION MNEMONIC, SOURCE ADDRESS, DESTINATION ADDRESS, PROGRAM COUNTER, STATUS REGISTER and the AFFECTED WORKSPACE REGISTER. Also, when a new Workspace is called in the program, the current contents of all the registers in that workspace are printed. RUN causes program execution to start from a specified location, or the current Program counter value. A limit of the number of instructions to be executed will prevent any closed loop from using excessive computer time before it is discovered. For each instruction executed within the trace request a trace output, as described above, will be printed.

The output of a SIMULATION run on the Example Program is shown in Figure 10. A breakpoint is detected at the end of the program because the last location contains no instruction. Control then passes to the next control statement. An entry of /* defines the last control statement and the end of the simulation run.

```
*******************LOADER MAP*******************

NAME     LOCATION  LENGTH     ENTRY NAME  LOCATION
                              XOP2        0922
                              NEG         0930
                              --------------------

SIGNX    1000      003E       --------------------
                              START       1000
                              END         103E

ENTRY = >1000

 -RELOCATED DECK PUNCHED-

*****************LOAD COMPLETED*****************
```

FIGURE 9. The Loader Map

Table 4. Simulator Command Index

SUMMARY OF CONTROL LANGUAGE STATEMENTS

The formats of the control statements are shown, with a brief description, as follows:

Format	Description
[label] {R / RUN} [*] {F / FOR} n [{FR / FROM} i1] [{T / TO} i2] [,label]	Specifies where to start and stop simulation. Control passes to statement at label operand when a breakpoint occurs.
[label] {T / TRACE} [list]	Specifies locations to be traced.
[label] {NOT / NOTRACE} [list]	Disables trace for specified locations.
[label] {RE / REFER} [list]	Specifies locations for reference breakpoint.
[label] {NOR / NOREFER} [list]	Disables reference breakpoint at specified locations.
[label] {A / ALTER} [list]	Specifies locations for alteration breakpoint.
[label] {NOA / NOALTER} [list]	Disables alteration breakpoint at specified locations.
[label] {P / PROTECT} [list]	Specifies areas for memory protection.
[label] IF (logical expression) label	Conditional transfer of control program.
[label] {J / JUMP} label	Unconditional transfer of control program.
[label] {TI / TIME} [n]	Prints the value of 9900 time and optionally sets a new value.
[label] {D / DISPLAY} [D] {C / CPU} [register list]	Prints contents of registers.
[label] {D / DISPLAY} [D / C] {M / MEMORY} list	Prints contents of memory.
[label] {D / DISPLAY} {S / SYMBOL} [$ / symbol / number]	Prints values from symbol table.
[label] {D / DISPLAY} {CR / CRU} {I / INPUT / O / OUTPUT} list	Prints CRU values.
[label] {S / SET} {C / CPU} register-value list	Places values into registers.
[label] {S / SET} {M / MEMORY} location-value list	Places values into memory.
[label] {S / SET} {I / INT} level, n_1 [,n_2,n_3]	Sets up one or more interrupts.
[label] {E / END}	Disables breakpoints and traces, and initializes simulation. Passes control to next control statement.
[label] {EB / EBCDIC}	Specifies EBCDIC code for characters of input.
[label] {AS / ASCII}	Specifies ASCII code for characters of input.
[label] {I / INPUT} {n / n_1 TO n_2} [F / FIRST / L / LAST / A / ALL] [data]	Defines input lines and fields, and supplies data for program being simulated.
[label] {O / OUTPUT} {n / n_1 TO n_2}	Defines output lines and fields, or prints output of program being simulated.
[label] {CONN / CONNECT} list	Connects input CRU lines to output CRU lines.
[label] {C / CONVERT} expression-list	Evaluates and prints values of expressions in decimal and hexadecimal form.
[label] {B / BATCH}	Specifies batch mode.
[label] {L / LOAD}	Loads WP and PC from locations $FFFC_{16}$ and $FFFE_{16}$.
[label] {CL / CLOCK} t	Specify clock period.
[label] {M / MEMORY} {RA / RAM / RO / ROM} {R / READ} = n_1 [{W / WRITE} = n_2] list	Define available memory. Default is 32K RAM.
[label] {SA / SAVE}	Create absolute object module.
• [label] {W / WIDTH} n	Specifies number of columns available for printing.

```
 MS9900 SIMULATOR (VERSION A.2 04/26/76) 12/9/76 07:13:59
COPYRIGHT (C) 1975 TEXAS INSTRUMENTS INCORPORATED
TEXAS INSTRUMENTS OWNS AND IS RESPONSIBLE FOR TMS9900 SIMULATOR
*  1:
>TRACE >900 TO >1038
*  2:
>RUN FOR 100
LOC   IR        S-AD D-AD  PC   ST
1000 02E0 LWPI 1002       1004 0000 WP 0100 R0 0000 R1 0000 R2 0000
   R3 0000 R4 0000 R5 0000 R6 0000 R7 0000 R8 0000 R9 0000 RA 0000
   RB 0000 RC 0000 RD 0000 RE 0000 RF 0000
1004 0201 LI   1006 0102 1008 C000 R1 0922
1008 C801 MOV  0102 004A 100C C000 R1 0922
100C 0202 LI   100E 0104 1010 8000 R2 8000
1010 C802 MOV  0104 0300 1014 8000 R2 8000
1014 0201 LI   1016 0102 1018 C000 R1 0700
1018 C801 MOV  0102 0048 101C C000 R1 0700
101C 0203 LI   101E 0106 1020 C000 R3 0010
1020 0205 LI   1022 010A 1024 8000 R5 8002
1024 0201 LI   1026 0102 1028 C000 R1 0106
1028 2C91 XOP  0048      0922 C200 WP 0700 R0 0000 R1 0000 R2 0000
   R3 0000 R4 0000 R5 0000 R6 0000 R7 0000 R8 0000 R9 0000 RA 0000
   RB 0106 RC 0000 RD 0100 RE 102A RF C000
0922 C06B MOV  010A 0702 0926 8200 R1 8002 RB 0106
0926 285B XOR  0106 0702 0928 8200 R1 8012 RB 0106
0928 1103 JLT            0930 8200
0930 0201 LI   0932 0702 0934 8200 R1 FFFF
0934 CAC1 MOV  0702 0108 0938 8200 R1 FFFF RB 0106
0938 0380 RTWP 071A      102A C000 WP 0100 R0 0000 R1 0106 R2 8000
   R3 0010 R4 FFFF R5 8002 R6 0000 R7 0000 R8 0000 R9 0000 RA 0000
   RB 0000 RC 0000 RD 0000 RE 0000 RF 0000
102A 40E0 SZC  0300 0106 102E C000 R3 0010
102E 4160 SZC  0300 010A 1032 C000 R5 0002
1032 3943 MPY  0106 010A 1034 C000 R3 0010 R5 0000 R6 0020
1034 0284 CI   1036 0108 1038 8000 R4 FFFF
1038 1302 JEQ            103A 8000
* BREAK POINT - PC=103E - ILLEGAL OPERATION CODE
EXECUTION TRANSFER TO NEXT CONTROL STATEMENT
*  3:
>/*

END OF FILE ON SIMULATOR CONTROL DATA SET
ENTER OPTION(ASM,SIM,UTL,END)>END
DEV 192 DETACHED
```

FIGURE 10. Simulator Listing

A third option is sometimes available, e.g. as in the TI Microprocessor Package, known as Utility (UTL). This program produces an output, in the form of punched paper tape or 80 column cards, to enable the manufacture of r.o.m.s. or p.r.o.m.s. to be programmed. Various data formats are available and full descriptions of these can be found for instance, in the TMS8080 Simulator Manual[4].

REFERENCES

1. Examples of the three networks on which the Texas Instruments programs are installed are: Honeywell/G.E. of Honeywell Timesharing; CSS International of CSS International, U.K., Limited; and Tymshare of Tymcom Limited.

2. *9900 Assembly Language Programmers Guide,* ISBN 0-904047-17 2, Texas Instruments Feb. '76.

3. *Cross Support System User's Guide,* ISBN 0-904047-18-0, Texas Instruments Feb. '76.

4. The Engineering Staff of Texas Instruments Incorporated, Semiconductor Group, *Simulator Manual – TMS8080 Microprocessor,* Texas Instruments Inc. CM125.

XV SERIAL CODE GENERATION USING A MICROPROCESSOR/MICROCOMPUTER

by
Chris Gare

With the spread of the microprocessor into many low-cost consumer products there is now great demand for cheap methods of entering data. Conventionally a keyboard has been used for this function which can utilise various types of mechanical or solid-state systems of encoding. It is now feasible to scan a keyboard, decode which key was activated, and generate a serial code with the aid of a single microprocessor device. This has distinct advantages over all other techniques as its simplicity and reduced number of parts lead to a marked decrease in production costs.

CODES & KEYBOARDS

Today's communication, computer and consumer industries employ the use of many serial codes, which have been precisely defined[1] to allow compatibility between independently designed and sited equipment. For instance, computer-to-computer communication in distributed processing systems are probably the most complex, and terminal to central processor unit (c.p.u.) links the least complex examples. In other areas alternate forms of code are encountered; the telephone and radio networks for Telex, telegram and news agencies; microprocessor controlled games machines; viewer information services for European television; message switching networks and instrumentation. All of these growth areas require the use of cheap methods of entering and extracting alpha-numeric information. As far as data entry is concerned the most popular operator interface is, by far, a keyboard. This varies in size from just a few keys in the case of simple instrumentation, up to a full alpha-numeric keyboard for computer and message data generation.

Numerous types of keyboard encoders are to be found but they can be broadly split up into two sections, mechanical and electronic. The standard mechanical system, used in teletypes and teleprinters, utilises a network of rods and cams driven by a motor to operate a microswitch connected to the electrical interface. This system suffers, as most mechanical systems do, from unreliability and an acoustically noisy operation. The electronic keyboard overcomes all the problems inherent in mechanical versions but necessitates the use of quite a number of complex integrated circuits to perform the required encoding, e.g. multiplexers and counters[2], or special MOS i.c.s with associated circuits[3], or a character generation read only memory (r.o.m.) and a universal asynchronous receiver transmitter (u.a.r.t.) system as shown in Figure 1. By replacing the above mentioned integrated circuits with a single microprocessor the complexity of the keyboard's circuitry is drastically reduced, producing an item that can be made cheap enough for even the most price conscious area of electronics; the consumer industry.

There are as many types of code in existance as there are methods of keyboard encoding; thus any attempt to describe them all would be self-defeating. But there are at least three codes that predominate above all others in terms of usage and familiarity: Murray, used by the telegraph networks; USASCII, used by the majority of computer installations, and Morse, although gradually being superceded in the commercial communication field, by cable and telephony. All of these codes, and the majority of others, can be very effectively generated by a microprocessor using similar techniques but with modified character look-up tables and serialising routines. The format of the three above mentioned codes will now be outlined to indicate what the processor needs to generate.

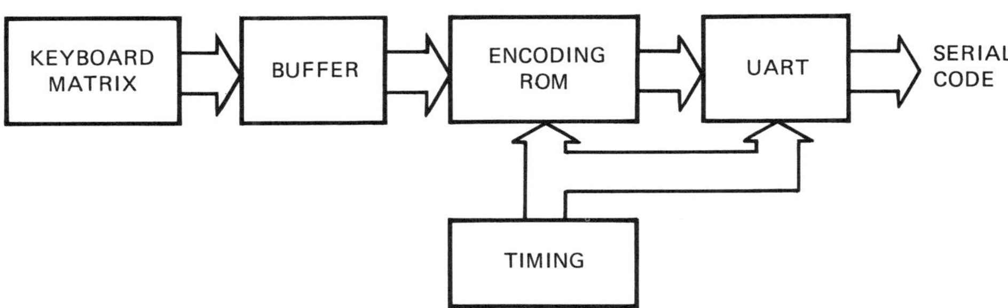

FIGURE 1. Conventional Keyboard Encoder

Murray or Baudot Code

Murray code, although not utilised in any application other than Telex and telgram networks, is one of the most widely used codes purely due to the volume of such traffic. Most business premises are equipped with a teleprinter unit driven by a special telephone cable. These devices are mechanical in operation and have remained unchanged in basic design for many years. The code itself is of a straightforward nature (Figure 2) and is composed of a five-bit data word with the least significant digit being transmitted first.

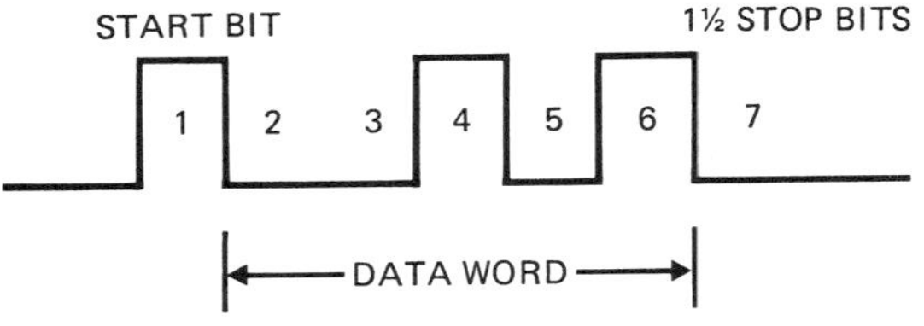

FIGURE 2. Murray Code

This is preceded by a start bit which is needed to inform the receiver that a data word is approaching. After the data words are added one and a half stop bits to ensure that the printer relays stops in a space, not a mark condition. The code generator then controls a bistable Carpenter relay which switches a ± 80V power supply onto the transmission line, + 80V for a mark and –80V for a space. As there are only 5 data bits in the code, allowing a maximum of 32 unique characters, a shift function is required. When upper-case numerals and syntax characters are required a shift key is hit to inform the receive station that the next character is upper-case. At the end of an upper-case sequence the shift key is again hit to restore the alpha-character set. It is the receiver which decides whether the character is upper or lower-case, not the transmitter.

USASCII Code

USASCII code, together with EBDIC and Hollerith, is widely used by the computer and consumer fields as a standard code for data transmission. Not only is the code precisely defined, but also the physical interfaces to ensure electrical as well as codal standardisation. Examples of this are the RS232 where a space is –12V and a mark + 12V and the teletype current interface where + 20mA is a mark and a lack of current a space. Both require a specialised interface device or logic between the code generator and the transmission medium. The code itself consists of an eight-bit data word allowing a maximum of 128 unique characters which can be split up into eight fields. Broadly speaking field 0 and 1 contains control characters; field 2 contains syntactic characters; field 3 numerals, fields 4 and 5 contain upper and lower-case alpha characters and field 5 through 7 contain syntactic characters. The code is transmitted least significant bit first preceded by a start bit and terminated by one stop bit of opposite polarity to the start bit. This ten-bit code can be transmitted at any predefined rate but the generally accepted speeds lie in the range of 100 Baud (10 characters/second) to 2400 baud. The lower rates being allocated to printers and teletypes while the faster ones are reserved for direct computer-to-computer links or visual display units which are capable of accepting such high data rates.

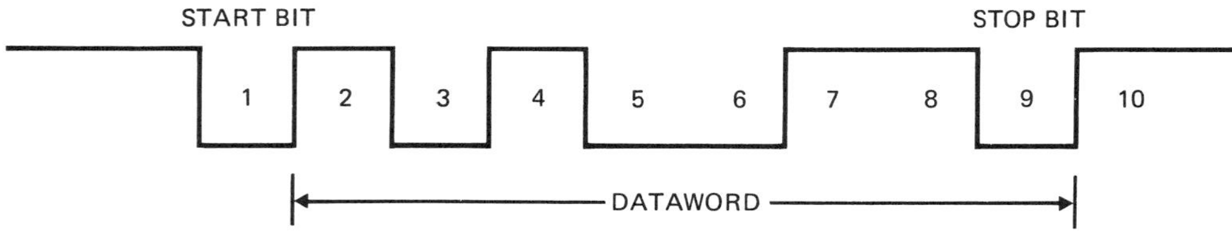

FIGURE 3. USASCII Code

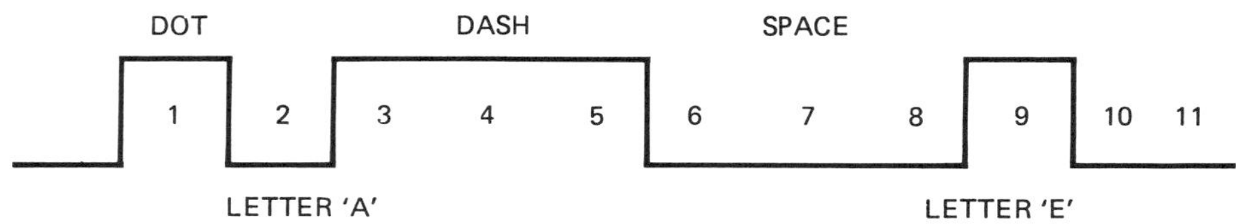

FIGURE 4. Morse Code

Morse

Although it could be considered to be a rather odd example of a serial code it is possible, using the similar techniques to that used to generate USASCII, to construct Morse code using a microprocessor. In fact, it is more technically difficult to generate morse code than any other serial code. Although Morse is not used as much today as it used to be, with the advent of sophisticated telephony techniques, it can still be widely encountered on ship-to-shore and inter-country communications where reliable contact between stations is mandatory. In computer terms a dot consists of one logic '1' bit followed by a logic '0' bit while the dash consists of three logic '1' bits followed by one logic '0' bit. The inter-character spacing is three logic '0's while the interword spacing is six logic '0' bits. The processor, after a key press, constructs the required character out of dots and dashes and outputs them to a first-in first-out (f.i.f.o.) buffer which effectively removes keyboard typing hesitations between characters. A fuller description will follow later in the chapter.

THE MICROCOMPUTER

Using a microprocessor allows the implementation of serial code generation to be performed in a simple fashion. In particular the choice of the TMS1000 device gives a very elegant solution to the problem.

Hardware

A description of the TMS1000 is given in full in the previous volume[4]. The main factors which led to its choice for the keyboard encoder are, however, as follows. The device is a one-chip microcomputer needing no external integrated circuits in the system design, other than an interface package to match its p.m.o.s. output to an RS232 or a current loop standard. Eight of the microcomputer data out pins and its 4-bit data-in bus can be used to scan a keyboard, one output being reserved for the serial data port. From a passive component point of view, only two external resistors and two capacitors are required to govern the frequency of the system clock and to form an initial reset pulse.

Software

The standard instruction set for the TMS1000 series is also given in the previously mentioned TMS1000 description[4]. The manner to which the software is applied for the encoders is given later in the respective encoder descriptions.

THE ASCII ENCODER

Hardware

A full logic diagram of the keyboard to serial ASCII or Murray code can be seen in Figure 5. The alpha-numeric keyboard is wired as an array of keys 10 columns by 4 rows. At each column-row intersection is a press-to-make

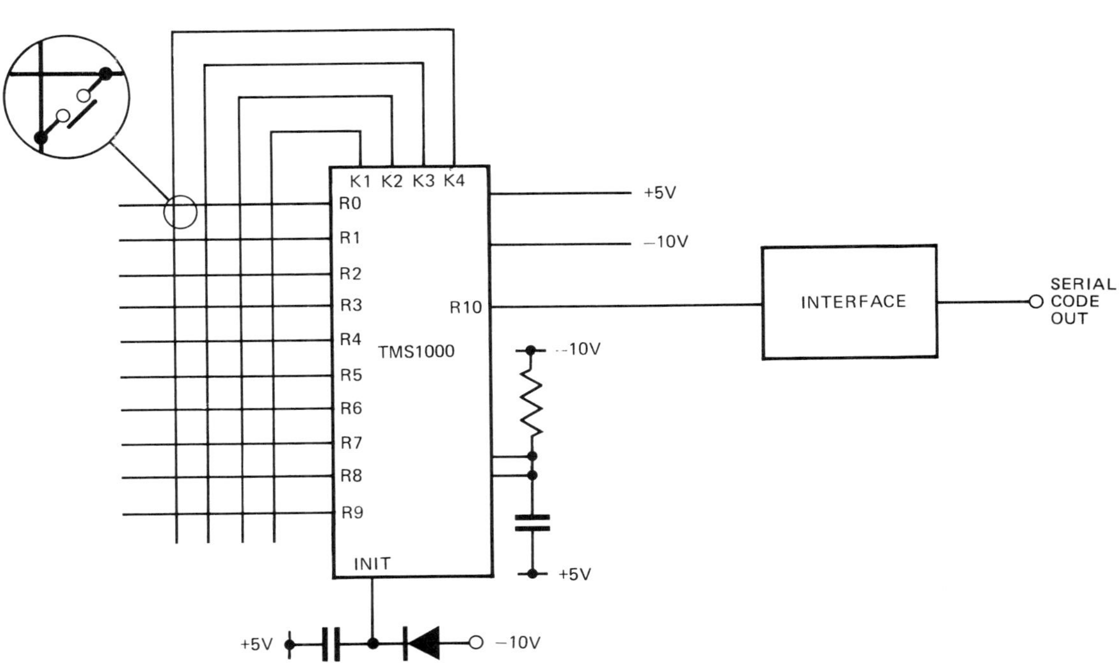

FIGURE 5. ASCII Code Generator

key contact so that when a key is pressed a specific R-column is connected to one K-row. The keyboard rows are then placed on the K-bus of the processor. To find out if a key has been pressed a logic '1' is placed sequentially on each R-output and the K-bus is tested to see whether it contains a logic '1'. If it does, the processor services the key press after 'debouncing' it; if it does not, the R-output is reset and the (N+1) output is set and the test sequence repeated. When an activated key has been found by the scan routine a 'debounce' sequence is initiated to check the validity of the key-press. One of the R-outputs is reserved for the serial data output port and it is this which is connected to the transmission line. The diode/capacitor network is used to generate a hardware reset pulse on the application of the power supply. This forces the program counter to address 00000 and the page address to 1111, i.e. the last page. This implies that the programmer must place his initialisation routine at this location or at least place a branch instruction to vector to it. The resistor/capacitor network control the internal clock oscillator and, as mentioned earlier, enable the clock frequency to be set anywhere in the range 100kHz to 400kHz. If precise timing of the serial code is required the processor can be driven by an external crystal clock entered by one of the timing component pins. As most of the keys require a dual function (upper and lower case) one of them is reserved to act as a shift key. When this key is pressed a character is not transmitted but a software 'flag' is set in an allocated status register to inform the character generation routine that the next key press is an upper-case, not a lower-case, character. This 'flag' can be unset by the first key press after the shift key or on a re-press of the shift key. This is purely a software controlled operation and its action depends on the functional specification of the unit as required by the user.

The interface block connected between the microprocessor and the transmission-line is required to convert the MOS output of the computer to one of the standard interfaces. This could be RS232, 20mA current loop for ASCII, ± 80V for teleprinter operation, or even an audio frequency modulation if the use of a MODEM is envisaged.

The above paragraphs describe the hardware aspects of the encoder and it can be seen to be very simple, the complex part of the project is the software which provides the actual operational control of the system. It is into this area that most of the effort needs to be put to implement such a design solution. As the encoder is entirely controlled by software it is possible to modify the functional capabilities right through the development phase as unforeseen problems or operational requirements are encountered. This is the main advantage in using a microprocessor rather than hard-wired logic.

Software

The block diagram of the software tasks is shown in Figure 6. It is straight forward in that it is purely sequential in terms of flow. The majority of segment interfacing is achieved through direct branch instructions, the only subroutines being the delays required for switch debounce and

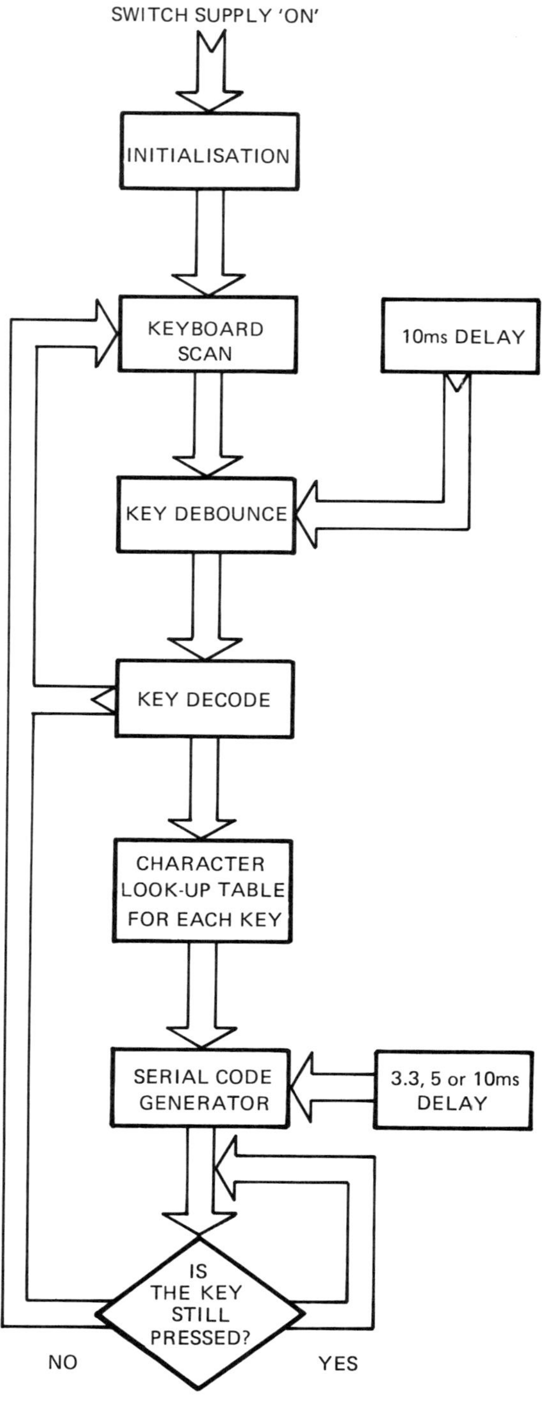

FIGURE 6. Software Tasks

the timing control of the output serialising routine. The program is developed in the conventional manner by first defining the operational/functional aspects of the encoder, generating a block flow diagram of the routines necessary for correct implementation and then actually transforming the blocks into mnemonic coding ready for cross-assembling on a suitable machine. A brief outline of each program segment will now be given ending up with an actual routine in mnemonic form as an example of the complexity level.

Initialisation: When power is first applied to the microprocessor the program counter is automatically loaded with address '0' of the r.o.m. At this address the programmer places his initialisation routines. In this instance all the r.a.m. locations are cleared to zero which also unsets all the software flags. In most applications flags must be set in these routines to ensure safe start-up of the controlled machine. Once the microprocessor registers have been put into a zero state, control is passed to the next routine.

Automatic Keyboard Scan: The microprocessor now has to find out whether the operator has pressed a key; it does this by carrying out a keyboard scan routine. This is achieved by using 10 of the R-outputs and the 4 K-inputs. The processor sequentially places a logic '1' on each output and checks to see whether there is a logic '1' on the K-bus which would be the case if a key has been pressed in the activated column. When one has been detected the column address and the K-input bus are stored and control passed to a switch-debounce routine to ensure the key press was valid.

Switch Debounce: The key press is debounced in software by calling a 10ms delay as soon as a key has been activated. If, after this delay, the key is still pressed then a decision is made that it was valid and the program passes onto the decode routines. More complex routines are possible which might be needed if the processor is used in an electrically noisy environment.

Key Decode: After debounce the processor proceeds to a series of decode routines to discover which particular key was activated and then pass control to a program segment associated with that particular key. The R-column and the K-input for the activated key have already been saved so these are compared to constants. When a match is found a program branch occurs.

Character Look-up Tables: The character look-up tables are routines for every key on the keyboard, each of which is referenced in the key decode routines outlined above. The first procedure in the table is to check whether the shift-key flag has been set by a previous press of the shift key. If it has, then the routine loads the code of the upper-case character into two register locations. If it was not, then the lower-case code is loaded. A control counter held in another storage register tells the routine where to load the character. Afterwards the counter is incremented.

Delays: A software delay is obtained by loading two registers with a known count and decrementing them. When both registers reach zero this is detected and the program returns to the calling address.

This routine is not only used to debounce a key-press but also controls the transmission rate of the serially generated character so if required, the preset count can be loaded from the keyboard thus allowing key control of the data transmission rate.

Serial Code Generator: Once the character code has been loaded into the registers it is the function of the serial code generator to output the stored code in serial form to one of the R-outputs. This is achieved by a process of testing each bit in the code sequentially and loading them to the selected output every 10ms to generate the required transmission rate of 100 Baud. Before this is done, however, the output is put to a logic '0' for 10ms to create the start bit and after the code has been scanned to a logic '1' to form the stop bit. For Murray code the time delay would be 22ms.

Is the Key still Pressed? The above program segments require a maximum time of 110ms to sequence through so it is quite possible that the operator is still pressing the key at the end of transmission. This routine checks to see if that is the case and if so loops on itself until the key is released. The processor then recommences the keyboard scan looking for another key activation.

THE MORSE ENCODER

Hardware

Generating morse code (Figure 7) is slightly more difficult than other code generators because, unlike all others, the inter-character spacing is precisely defined so it is necessary to buffer the outgoing serial data to remove the operator typing hesitations between key hits. This is easily achieved by passing the generated code through a f.i.f.o. buffer. The processor loads the Morse code into the buffer at the full speed of the microcomputer immediately a key is hit. The output of the buffer is read, synchronously at a much slower rate, so that it 'flows' at constant speed and spacing. The data level within the f.i.f.o. is monitored by the processor by changing the K1 input over from the keyboard to the f.i.f.o. level indicator. This is done by using an R-output to control the multiplexer, if the buffer begins to fill up the operator is flagged to slow down his typing rate. If the processor is generating a long, repetitive automatic message greater than the storage capability of the f.i.f.o., the processor checks to see if the f.i.f.o. is full and if it is sits in a wait loop until the f.i.f.o. empties sufficiently to be able to load more characters.

Software

The actual system of generating the code, as far as the software is concerned, is similar to that used to generate ASCII. Actual examples are given below of two of the program segments. Table 1 is the keyboard scan routine that looks for, detects and debounces a key press. This is shown in flow diagram form in Figure 8. Table 2 is the shift key routine in the character look-up table that sets a shift flag in a status register as described earlier.

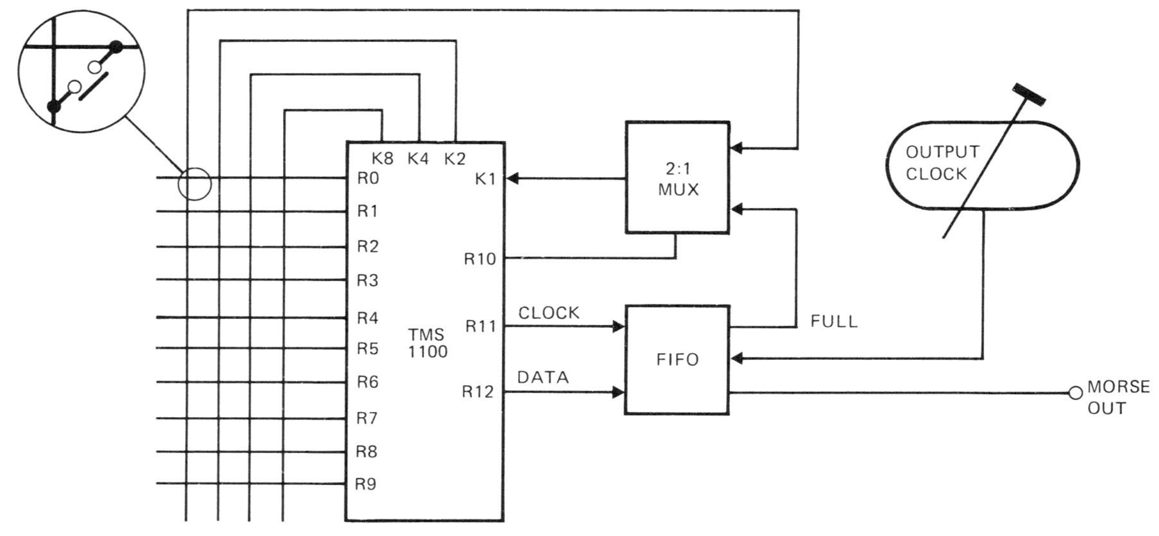

FIGURE 7. Morse Code Generator

Table 1. The Scan Routine

LABEL	OP. CODE	OPERAND	COMMENTS
SCAN	TCY	9	Set Y register to point to R9 output.
SNC	SETR		Set R(X) to 1 (initially R9).
	TYA		Transfer (Y) to accumulator.
	TCY	COLA	Point to memory register COLA.
	TAM		Store R(X) in COLA.
	TAY		Restore R(X) to Y register.
	KNEZ		Test K-bus for any logic '1's.
	BR GO1		If yes, branch to GO1.
GO	TCY	COLA	
	TMY		Put R(X) to Y register.
	RSTR		Reset R(X) output.
	DYN		Decrement Y register, ie R(X-1).
	YNEC		Overflow? ie end of scan?
	BR	SNC	No. Go to next R output R(X-1)
	BR	SCAN	Yes. Restart scan at R9.
GO1	CALL	DELAY	Call debounce delay.
	KNEZ		Is the key still active?
	BR ACKEY		YES – Valid key hit.
	BR GO		Restart scan – key hit not valid.
ACKEY			
	Decode routines		

Table 2. Shift Key Routine

SHIFT	TCY	STATUS	Point to status register.
	SBIT	SHIF	Set shift flag.
RESL	KNEZ		Is the shift key still pressed?
	CALL	DELAY	If yes call delay.
	KNEZ		Is the shift key still pressed?
	BR	RESL	Yes. Stay in this loop.

POSTSCRIPT

The use of the TMS1000 range of microcomputers in high volume keyboard encoders produces a very elegant solution. This should suit the requirements of volume manufacturers, whose main aim is a reduction in parts count and hence reduced production costs. As the device contains r.o.m.s it must be mask programmed by the manufacturer after software development. This involves a masking charge which is of a 'one-off' nature so it can be reclaimed over the production run of the equipment. Development is not a problem because of the existance of the TMS1099 which allows external r.a.m./p.r.o.m. to be used for software 'debugging'. (The use of the TMS1099 itself in a finished product can only be justified if a small production run is envisaged.)

REFERENCES

1. Applications Laboratory Staff of Texas Instruments Incorporated, *MOS and Special-Purpose Bipolar Integrated Circuits and R-F Power Transistor Circuit Design,* McGraw-Hill Book Company, New York, 1976, pp. 12-15.

2. Applications Laboratory Staff of Texas Instruments Incorporated, *Electronic Power Control and Digital*

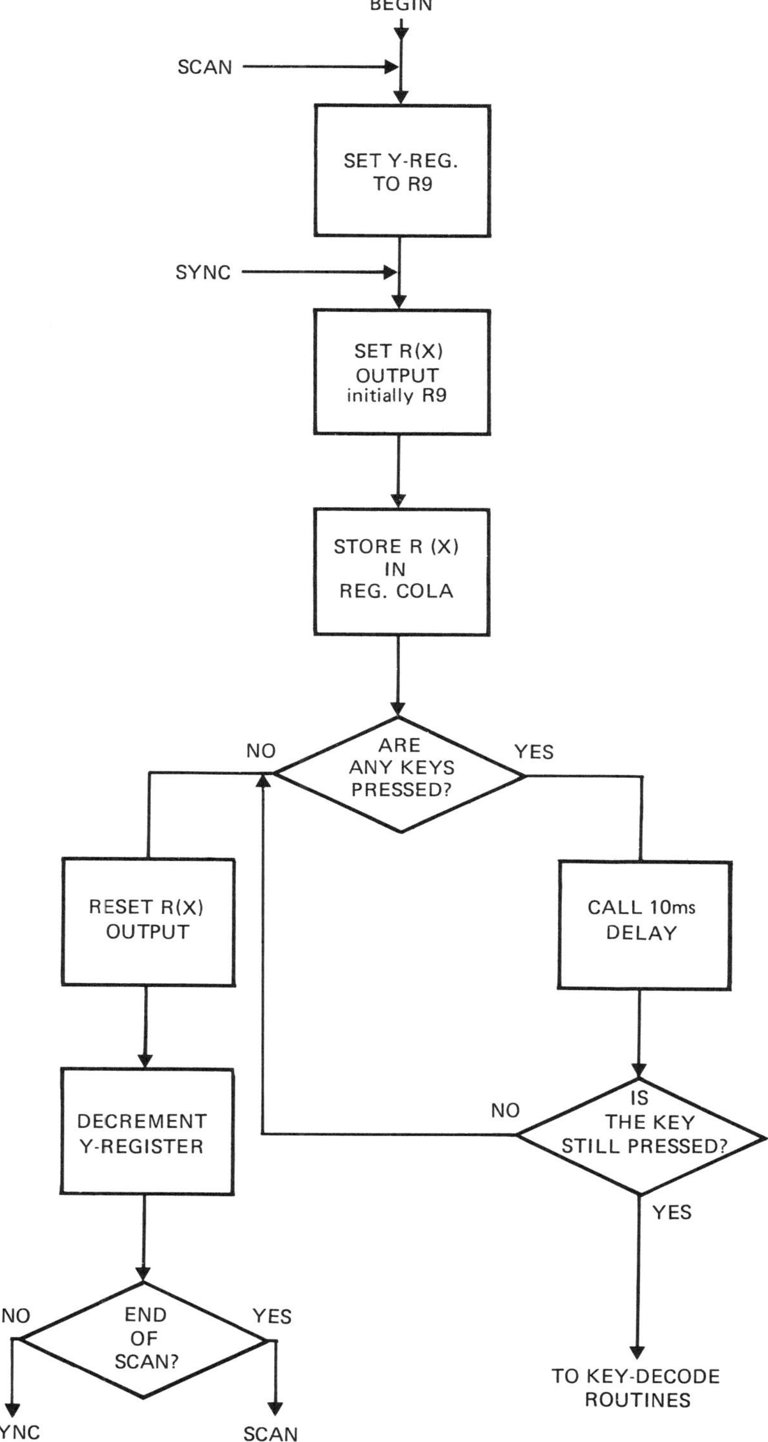

FIGURE 8. Keyboard Scan

Techniques, McGraw-Hill Book Company, New York, 1976, pp. 185-186.

3. Applications Laboratory Staff of Texas Instruments Incorporated, *MOS and Special-Purpose Bipolar Integrated Circuits and R-F Power Transistor Circuit Design,* McGraw-Hill Book Company, New York, 1976, pp. 24-26.
4. Applications Laboratory Staff of Texas Instruments Incorporated, *Electronic Power Control and Digital Techniques,* McGraw-Hill Book Company, New York, 1976, pp. 116-123.

XVI USING A MICROCOMPUTER IN CONSUMER APPLICATIONS

by
David A. Bonham

With the continually falling price of microprocessors/microcomputers and their increasing usefulness with ever increasing functions provided, it is inevitable that they will be used in everyday high volume equipment previously dominated by electro-mechanical controls, e.g. cookers, weighing scales, copying machines, petrol pumps, the keyboard encoders described in the previous chapter, toys and even cars, etc. In addition a new range of products using them will become viable, for example, automatic telephone diallers, personal communications and security systems. The major part of this chapter describes how a microcomputer is employed as a programmable controller for a domestic oven. Most of the explanation applies, however, equally well to any machine that performs a control function according to data from sensors and/or a keyboard, and perhaps also displays some parameters.

AUTOMATIC COOKER

General

The automatic cooker controller to be described runs an oven via a keyboard. For simplicity the functional concept of the controller is the same as existing electromechanical oven controllers, most of which can be preset in an automatic mode. This controller works with electric ovens, or gas ovens using a magnetic gas valve. It has a clock display that normally shows the time (real time). This clock can be set from the keyboard. The oven has a manual mode when a temperature can be selected and the oven will simply cook at that temperature. The other mode is automatic. Times are selected for the food to be ready (stop time) and for the required cooking time (cook time). The oven will then be switched 'on' and switched 'off' at the correct times. The times and temperature can be set in any order. As times are entered they appear on the display. If the keyboard is left for more than several seconds the time of day will automatically return to the display.

For a manufacturer to accept the use of microprocessor or microcomputer solution he must be convinced that it will be low cost. It must either be cheaper than his present solution or it must offer some enhanced features to allow him to increase his customers' acceptance. By using the TMS1000 microcomputer the manufacturer has the opportunity of meeting one or both of these criteria, as it contains all of the elements necessary for a working computer/microprocessor control system. In the one device are a microprocessor, a program read only memory (r.o.m.), a data random access memory (r.a.m.), a clock generator and it has an excellent input/output (I/O) arrangement[1]. It has eleven individual latched outputs and eight outputs encoded by the programmable logic array, p.l.a., which is also in the device. It is micro programmable – i.e. some of the instructions can be redefined thus giving the microcomputer a different repertoire of instructions. The power supply is simple, being a single 15V rail at 6mA. It is made using the p-m.o.s. technologies in a 4 mask process where the fourth mask defines the customer's program and his choice of output p.l.a.

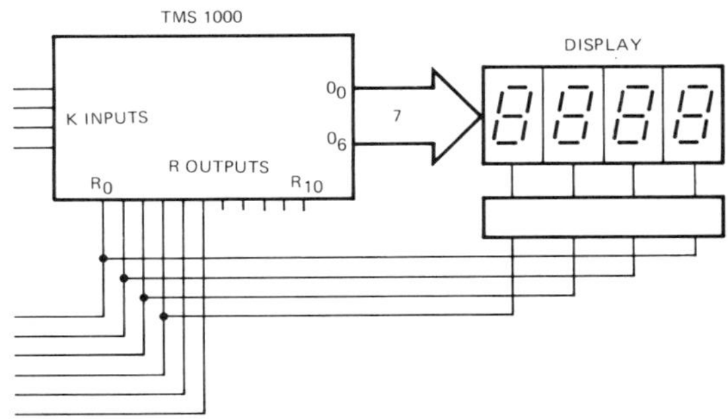

FIGURE 1. Display Driving

Circuit Design

Display: Figure 1 shows how conveniently display driving can be implemented. The display digits, which are common cathode, seven segments light emitting diodes (l.e.d.s) say, have like segments commoned at their anodes. The O outputs, encoded by the p.l.a., drive the segments. The number to be displayed is held in the r.a.m., preferably in consecutive locations in a file. The common cathodes of each digit are driven by an R output, which corresponds to the Y location of the relevant digit. The first location is accessed and the first digit is transferred to the output p.l.a., and this transforms it into seven segment code. The R latch is set and the digit appears. The R output is eventually reset and the next location accessed and output via the p.l.a. The corresponding R is set and the next digit appears. This is repeated along the display, strobing each digit in turn as the value is output. It is, of course, performed at a speed which causes the eye to believe that the whole number is present all the time. Because of the strobing, the actual segment currents are high and a digit driver is necessary. According to the brightness required and the total number of digits, there may also need to be segment drivers.

Keyboard: Figure 2 shows basic arrangement for a keyboard input using depression keys. It is similar to the display circuit in that the R outputs strobe the matrix columns in turn. The K inputs, if floating, are pulled down

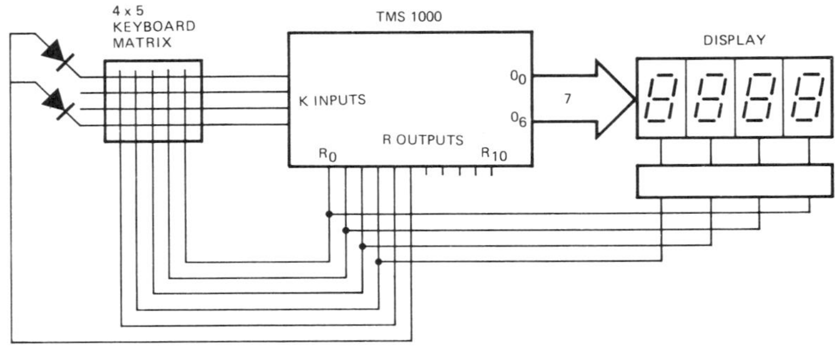

FIGURE 2. Keyboard Scan

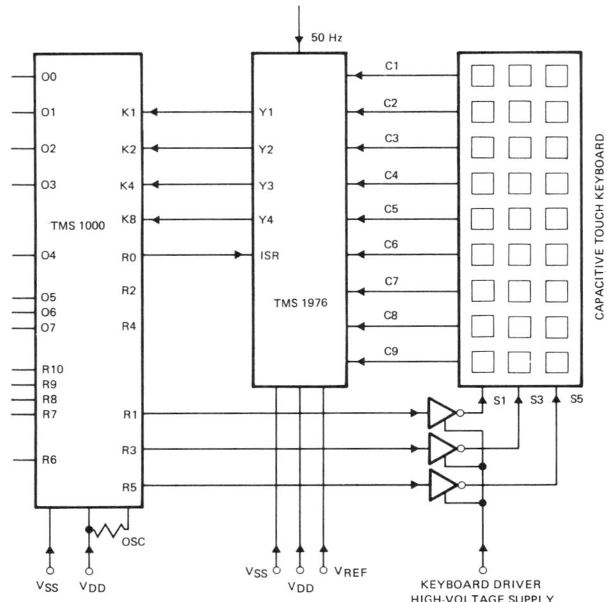

FIGURE 3. Capacitive Touch Keyboard

by an internal resistor. If an R output is taken 'high' and a K input then goes 'high', the processor knows that a key is being pressed. Knowing the R value and the K value determines which key on the matrix this is. An important feature is that the same R outputs can be used for both keyboard and display driving.

Figure 3 shows how a capacitive touch keyboard can be used with the TMS1000 microcomputer. Capacitive touch keys are a necessity on many appliances, particularly those used in the kitchen, because of the environment. Dirt and grease are problems on a cooker which make depression keys unreliable. The TMS1976 i.c. is a device which interfaces between the TMS1000 and high impedance key plates. It prioritises and encodes them. It also has a separate input available for synchronisation or timing such as 50Hz.

Analogue to Digital Conversion: An oven, unlike the simple ring or plate on a hob, is used with feedback control. The temperature of the oven is sensed and compared with the required setting and the heat switched 'on' or 'off' accordingly. In present systems a thermostat is used. One disadvantage is its hysteresis. One electronic solution is to use a sensitor but then the analogue resistance or a voltage must be converted to a digital form so that it can be compared with the required setting. Figure 4 shows how this is performed. A ladder network of resistors is controlled by outputs from the microcomputer and their resultant is compared in an operational amplifier or comparitor with the sensor output. Using this circuit it is possible to iteratively determine the analogue voltage if required. A comparison is, however, simpler. The required control setting is output to the resistors from the microcomputer and the output of the amplifier shows whether the temperature is too high or too low. This technique has an advantage over a thermostat. The thermostat can only be set to one temperature by the person cooking. So one can only tell from it, whether the temperature is too high or low. Using a sensitor the controller can regulate to a different temperature as time progresses. Alternatively, with the microcomputer one can measure the temperature and so know the difference from the required setting. This allows proportional control of the heating. The accuracy of temperature control required during cooking does not demand proportional control, but note that it could be included without adding or changing the components at all. This is typical of the additional features at no extra cost that a microcomputer can bring. Again because the converter is used at an instant when the keyboard is not being read and it can be arranged that the displays are blank, the same R outputs, which strobe the display and keyboard, can also control the resistor switches of the a.d.c.

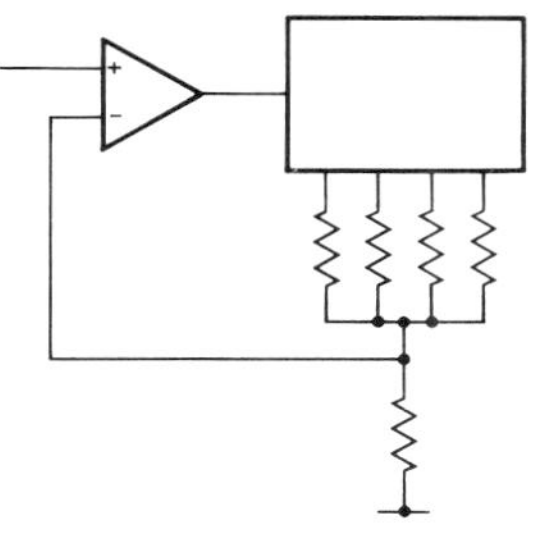

FIGURE 4. A to D Conversion using the TMS 1000

Circuit Diagram: The overall circuit is shown in Figure 5. The 'real time' clock, derived from the mains, can come from a secondary winding of the transformer of the power supply and the zero crossing timing for the triac control can be produced by a simple two transistor circuit[2]. Alternatively, the zero crossing function can be generated at the microcomputer's input, although it then may need to be set up at test.

As said before the manufacturer wants the lowest cost solution that meets his market requirement. The main variables that will affect the unit cost of production are the circuitry (hardware), and development cost. Development cost per unit decreases as production volume increases. So for a high volume design, the design engineer must first of all be constrained to reduce the hardware cost. The circuitry must be arranged so that it needs the minimum number of components. For example, the microcomputer can do input decoding rather than using external gates.

Programming

The microcomputer is controlled by a sequence of instructions, its program or software, which determine how it will carry out the application. Naturally the same microcomputer can perform a new application if given a new program. Also the same microcomputer with the same surrounding circuits can perform the same application differently if given a variation of the original program. Thus having decided upon a circuit layout, the program must be developed. This is best done by dividing the program into software sections to operate the various sections

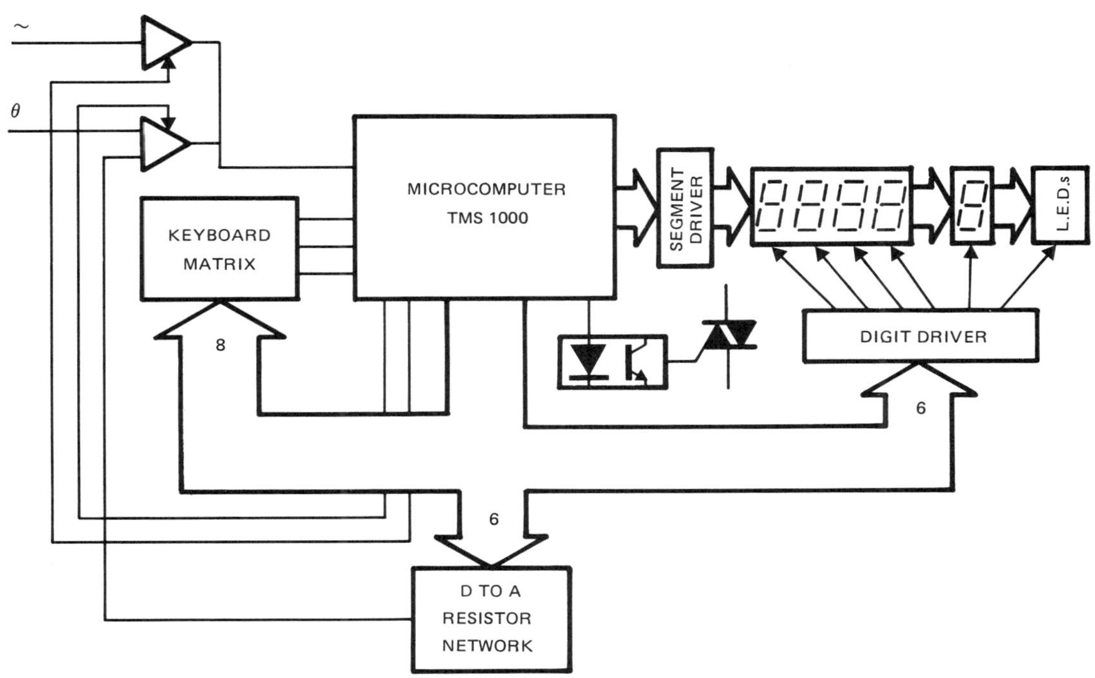

FIGURE 5. Cooker Hardware

of hardware. Examples are shown in Figure 6. At this stage the r.a.m. locations are allocated to various parameters. Figure 7 shows how this might be. This allocation and the order of R connections is chosen to give the most convenient configuration. For example, if temperature is in location Y = 0 then R0 is used to strobe the temperature display and also the output R0 is used to strobe key 0 (zero) on the keyboard matrix.

Software Routines: Having designed the basic hardware then there are many different ways it could operate as an oven controller. The clock could be 12 hour and 24 hour. Temperature control could be proportional or 'on'/'off' or even combine integral and differential terms. The differences might be simpler: does the time of day automatically reappear on the display after Cooking Time has been set, and how long is the pause before this happens?

A specification should be decided with this amount of detail. A flow chart should be drawn to determine how best to service the various requirements of this specification. It is necessary for instance to strobe the display and keyboard. Also needed, although at a much lower rate, is a check on the temperature, and, if in automatic cooking mode, to compare certain times. Figure 8 gives one solution. One outcome of the flow chart is that the requirement for 'flags' and loop counters will be shown. (A flag being an indicator to show that a condition has occurred at some time previous. Whether the flag is 'set' or not is shown by the presence of a number or a bit in a known position in the memory. A loop counter allows a sequence of instructions to be used repeatedly for a number of times before going on to the rest of the program.) In Figure 8 the keyboard and display are strobed twice per mains transition (with 2 mains transitions per 20ms) and a flag is used to remember whether the first or second strobing is due. There are other cases such as heating – the decision to heat or not is made in the middle of the flowchart, whereas action is taken at the beginning.

The blocks of the flow chart must perform the following:

a) Start Routine – In this application, as in many others, it is important that the condition of the system after applying power is a known one and also that the oven is OFF. R.a.m. contents are cleared. Certain flags are set or reset to put cooker in safe 'off' condition. Some registers are initialised, e.g. Display 01.00 am. Typical of 'additional features for no more hardware' would be a flashing display upon switching the mains supply 'on'. This would indicate that the power has been OFF and the clock needs setting.

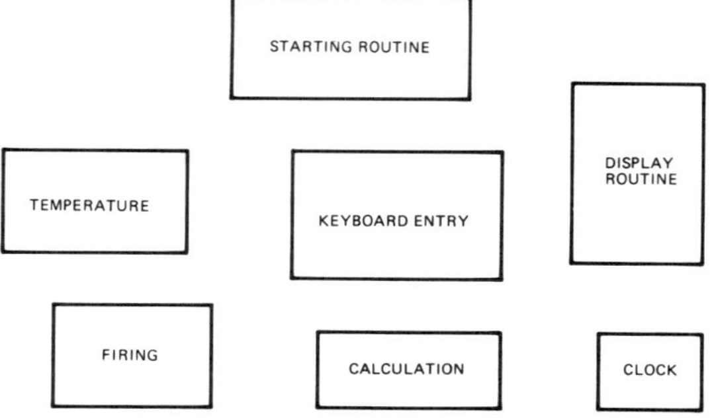

FIGURE 6. Software Modules

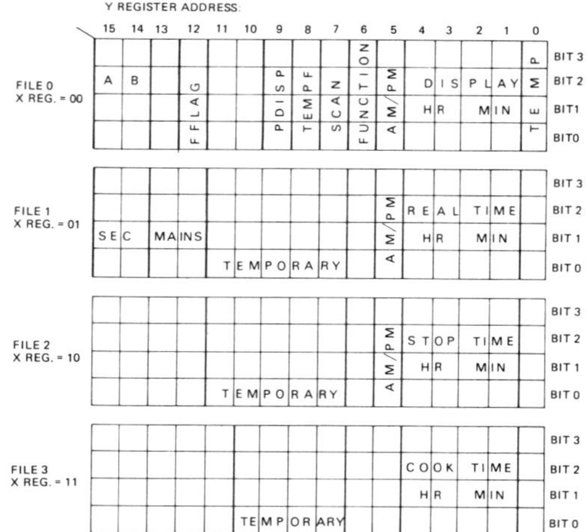

FIGURE 7. R.A.M. Allocation

b) Keyboard Entry – Entry of information can be as with a calculator, or entry by incrementing the display until the required value is reached. This latter reduces key requirement although the significance is lost if using capacitive touch keys because additional keys can be made at negligible extra cost. Key 'debounce' is performed in software. Any key input can be examined several times to make sure it is steady and the contacts are not bouncing. Decoding of the keys in the matrix causes branching to the relevant routine called up by the key.

c) Display Routine – Display of temperature as Regulo – Mark number and a time in hours and minutes with a.m. and p.m. if needed. A variation could be to show the required temperature in degrees.

d) Triac Firing Control – To enable the triac to be fired nearer to zero crossing of the mains, and thereby reduce the interference from the load, the routine is written twice, one or the other being used according to whether the heat flag is set or not. Each routine examines the state of the mains and waits for it to change before proceeding.

e) Real Time Clock – Time is kept by counting the mains half cycles. The clock is a software analogue of the counter one would build in t.t.l. say. The units are counted in the first stage and overflows are then counted in the second stage (tens), etc. The time taken to execute the complete flowchart

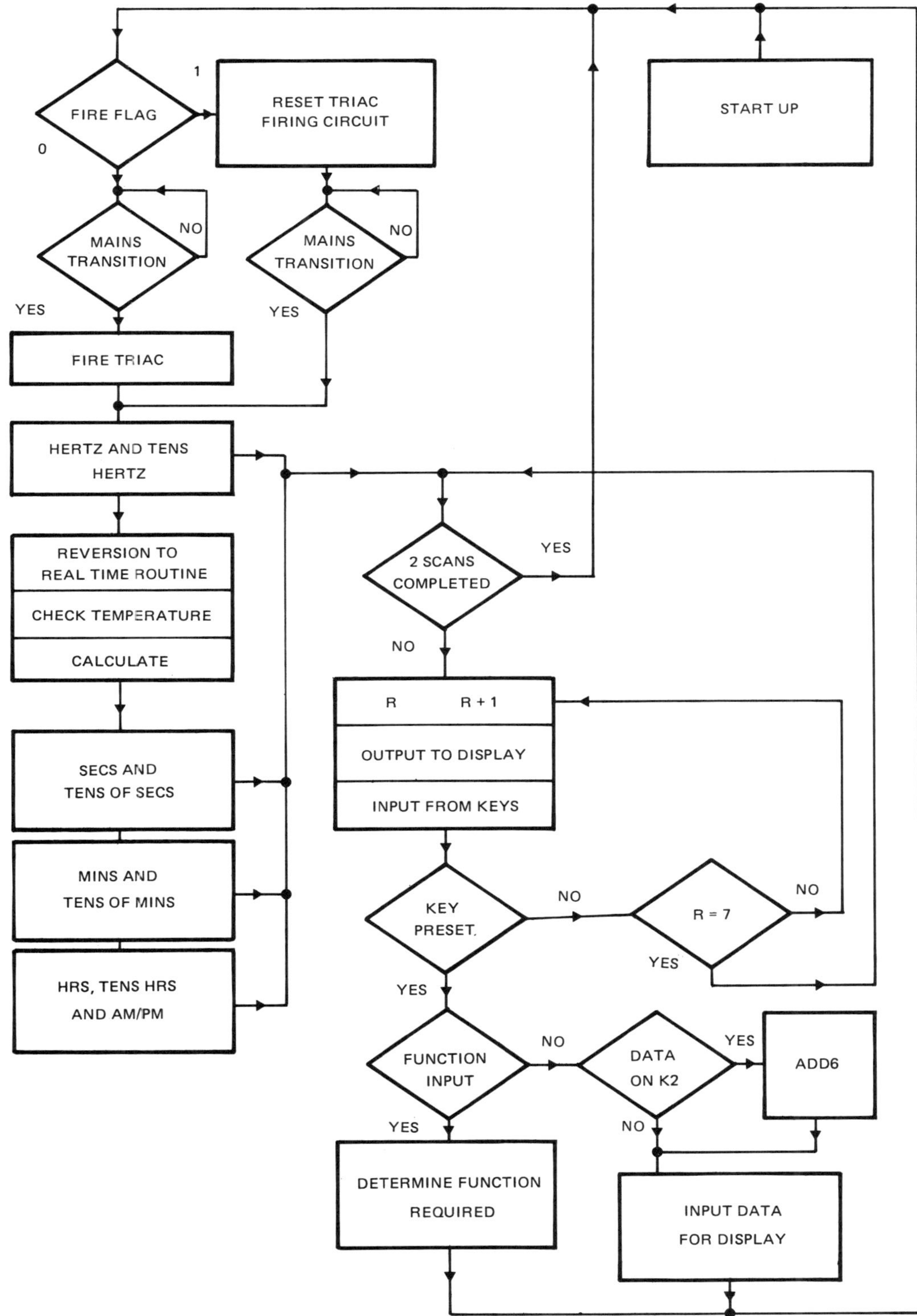

FIGURE 8. Simplified Flowchart of Cooker Controller

loop and return to the mains zero crossing detect routine is just less than 10ms. This gives good noise immunity because the clock cannot react to noise on the mains in the middle of a cycle. Again this is analogous to using a monostable at the input of a t.t.l. clock/counter to lock out the input pulses until just before the next is due.

f) Temperature Control– The inputs from the user are of a Regulo or Mark number type. This is equivalent to a temperature which is in turn equivalent to a resistance or voltage from the sensor circuit. Neither conversion may be linear. The simple solution is to have a look up table which selects a value for the Mark number input. This value is then used directly to set the required resistors in the temperature sensing resistor ladder.

g) Calculation – In the automatic mode the inputs from the user are Stop Time and Cooking Time. (Here is another example of how the format might be changed without changing the hardware – apart from a different engraving on a key! The inputs could be any two from start time, stop time and cooking time). To determine when to switch 'on', the microcomputer has to subtract the Real Time and Cook Time from the Stop Time, and to switch 'off', has to subtract Real Time from Stop Time. Some corrections have to be made to allow for a.m. and p.m., complicated by the fact that 12xx p.m. is one hour before 01xx p.m., and also that 12.00 a.m. is followed by 12.01 p.m.

Examples of the Clock Routine and Input Routine are given in the Appendix.

Program Development and Prototyping

There are several ways of developing a product. One way is to use computer timesharing described in Chapter XIV. This can be used to develop the product to an advanced state, or to simply assemble the program so that development can be carried out on the hardware.

Timesharing: Having written a module of the software, it is typed into a file on a timesharing network. As stated a listing of the program with the correct op-codes can be produced. Programs can also be simulated as if they were being run on a TMS1000 microcomputer. Thus for this (and other) applications input conditions can be set up and changed and the computer will simulate what would occur if actual hardware was being used. An output on the terminal can be obtained which shows the state of every register and input and output for each instruction step, or one can simplify the output by suppressing parts of the print out and/or restricting the occurrence of print outs (i.e. Print outs will only be when an input is read).

Another feature of timesharing which could be useful here is the facility to produce a paper tape of the program (and of the op-code p.l.a. whether standard or microprogrammed. Also the output p.l.a. which the customer will wish to define for his application). These can be used to program p.r.o.m.s or r.o.m.s, or program the HE1. The latter is a machine which is a t.t.l./m.o.s. emulation of the microcomputer with a loadable r.a.m. program memory, op-code p.l.a. and output p.l.a. It has displays to show the contents of all registers in the microcomputer. It can be set to execute a program and stopped on a break point or it can be connected to a hardware system and perform in-circuit emulation. Thus it is of great use in developing a program before committing to the mask of a TMS1000 microcomputer.

As well as the TMS1000 there is another microprocessor called the TMS1099 which is identical to the '1000 except that the r.o.m. is no longer on the chip. This means that a single TMS1099 can be run with any number of different programs by changing an external r.o.m./p.r.o.m. A printed circuit board has been designed for the TMS1099, which takes p.r.o.m. for program, p.r.o.m. to simulate the output p.l.a., and buffering, to run from the on-chip clock or an external clock. P.r.o.m.s allow the designer to make changes to his program as it nears completion. It is however possible to develop the whole program using the TMS1099, on a LL221 printed circuit board, together with the hardware decided upon and shown in Figure 4, using a piece of equipment called ROMSYM. (ROMSYM is a programmable r.o.m. of one/two thousand bytes. It is made of r.a.m. which can be loaded by paper tape [as produced by timesharing] or by individual bit switches. It is mains powered but has a power down mode and battery back-up allowing retention of data for a week. It allows complete freedom to quickly and cheaply alter a section or words of the program and at the same time test the relationship with the surrounding hardware.) Although the '1099 has a data sheet minimum clock frequency of 100kHz, a typical device at room temperature will operate at almost one instruction per second. This can allow one to check the route of the program visually.

Prototyping: A development which obviates the need to use timesharing is a TMS1000 cross support package on a 990-4 minicomputer[3]. The 990-4 and a data terminal form a prototyping system which can be used to develop programs for the TMS1000 microcomputer as well as the TMS9900/9980 and 9940 microprocessors/microcomputers. There is also a low cost prototyping system called EP1 that gives the same sort of features as the HE1. These are all developments paths which allow the manufacturer's engineers to develop expertise in microcomputers. After the first project they will see other opportunities to use a microcomputer to good effect and will now be able to implement them even quicker.

Cooker Program Development: Much of the cooker program was developed on the HE1 (because it was available) but the '1099 plus ROMSYM could have been used exclusively. A short routine could have been written which was branched to, which transferred any desired register content to the display. Most of the program was written in detail first to get an overall shape. This shows up the need for flags and explicit addressing (where address incrementing would otherwise have been used) when modules of program were broken up by the insertion of other modules. An example is the clock which basically goes from Hertz to Hours and a.m./p.m. It is split into two parts by the a. to d. conversion and a calculation of times.

The testing of the program was done by modules. For example the clock mentioned above was isolated as a whole, with unconditional jumps substituted around the a.d.c. and calculations. When the lower significance counters had been checked their moduli were reduced by changing one instruction (ALEC 9 to ALEC 1). Changing a single instruction like this is very quick using the bit switches of either HE1 or ROMSYM – there is obviously no need to reassemble and produce another tape! To prove the clock counter no external connections to the HE1 are required. If the zero crossing is removed then the counter can free run. The final instruction in the counter is made to be a branch which returns the program to the beginning. Obviously the clock will not perform at the correct timing but we are only concerned at this stage with the sequence.

Before much more can be proved it is preferable to 'debug' the input routine and the display routine. Although these contain a lot of statements they have been written before for the microcomputer, and this 'library' module only needs a few small alterations to adapt it to any particular application. With the keyboard and display operative, small sections such as the shift left routine can be examined (new digits are entered on the right of the display and the existing number is shifted left), followed by the copying from display to store and the calling up from store to display. With the ability to set in data via the keyboard it is now possible to check the operation of the calculation algorithms. It is easiest to check these if the real time is not changing. Therefore, the clock counter can be by-passed by changing an instruction temporarily to a branch.

The policy is to check-out only the smallest section possible at any time running it with the portions of program that are known to run correctly. The display is a most useful output to show what is happening and is therefore one of the first modules to be debugged.

Debugging of Hardware: If the ROMSYM and TMS1099 have been used then the hardware will have been debugged concurrently with the software. There may still be some modifications such as the display brightness but these will be small. When the HE1 is used then a similar situation can exist. The keyboard is obviously the best tool for entering data into the HE1. It (the HE1) has its own 16 digit display showing the output of the p.l.a. strobed by the R outputs. This is what is required to check the display routine software. Nevertheless the real display hardware can also be driven from the device outputs of the HE1 to test this portion of the final hardware. It can be powered by its actual power supply. The same is true of the a.d.c. It only remains for the keyboard, display and converter to be connected to a TMS1099 together with the ROMSYM or some p.r.o.m.s and the prototype can be tested.

Extra Facilities

Such a program as discussed here used about two thirds of the available r.o.m. and r.a.m. Many extra features could be added such as a Minitimer, alarms and 'keep warm' options. If there are a large number of other functions required such as a 'weight of joint' input, or quality of cook, i.e. rare, medium, well done, then it might be that the basic one thousand instructions are exceeded and a larger microcomputer is needed. There are two devices in the TMS1000 family with twice the r.a.m. and r.o.m. Another pair of devices have high voltage inputs and outputs. These six devices have basically the same architecture but those with twice the r.o.m. and r.a.m. have some different instructions to allow addressing of the extra memory. The basic features and differences of these six devices are shown in Table 1. There is another member of the family without r.o.m. (TMS1098) to allow prototyping of these twice size devices and a version of the HE1 (HE2). The ROMSYM is designed to be easily expanded to 2k bytes.

Table 1. 4-Bit Microcomputer Features

	TMS 1000	TMS 1200	TMS 1070	TMS 1270	TMS 1100	TMS 1300
Package Pin Count	28 Pins	40 Pins	28 Pins	40 Pins	28 Pins	40 Pins
Instruction Read Only Memory	1024 X 8 Bits (8,192 Bits)		1024 X 8 Bits (8,192 Bits)		*2048 X 8 Bits (16,384 Bits)*	
Data Random Access Memory	64 X 4 Bits (256 Bits)		64 X 4 Bits (256 Bits)		*128 X 4 Bits (512 Bits)*	
"R" Individually Addressed Output Latches	11	13	11	13	11	*16*
"O" Parallel Latched Data Outputs	8 Bits		8 Bits	*10 Bits	8 Bits	
Maximum-Rated Voltage (O, R, and K)	20 V		*35 V*		20 V	
Working Registers	2-4 Bits Each		2-4 Bits Each		2-4 Bits Each	
Instruction Set	See Table 2, Page 9		See Table 2, Page 9		See Table 3, Page 15	
Programmable Instruction Decoder	Yes		Yes		Yes	
On-Chip Oscillator	Yes		Yes		Yes	
Power Supply/Typical Dissipation	15 V/90 mW		15 V/90 mW		15 V/105 mW	
Time-Share Assembler Support	Yes		Yes		Yes	
Time-Share Simulator Support	Yes		Yes		Yes	
Hardware Evaluator and Debugging Unit	HE-2		HE-2		HE-2	
System Evaluator Device with External Instruction Memory	SE-1 (TMS1099 JL)		SE-1 (TMS 1099 JL)		SE-2 (TMS 1098 JL)	

*The HE-2 does not have a decoder for the extra O outputs.

AUTOMOTIVE APPLICATIONS

General

In addition to being able to handle a large matrix of inputs, have easy feed from latched outputs and/or scan a numeric display, control a sequence, perform timing and calculate, the microcomputer used in car engine control must be fast. Also the inputs to be measured are likely to be in analogue form so these must be converted to digital values.

A device which is suited to such applications is the TMS9940 microcomputer. This, as previously mentioned in Chapter XII is part of the '9900 family of processors, has therefore all the family features, and uses the same language with a 16-bit instruction word. R.o.m., r.a.m. and a 14 bit timer are all on the chip. Another advantage is that it has 32 programmable and latched I/O ports. 8 of these ports could be used to address a multiplexed analogue to digital converter. The addressing, in a single instruction, would select the analogue input to be converted and output the resulting digital value serially to the processor. This technique, which the '9900 family has, allows the transfer of parallel information to a parallel register but via a serial line thus simplifying design.

Practical Example

In a motor car control of the spark timing or fuel requirement is calculated from a number of parameters such as throttle opening, load, engine speed, manifold depression, air temperature and engine temperature. A microcomputer would combine these parameters together mathematically to give two major factors. These factors would then be used to 'look up' the relevant output signal (such as the spark advance time). As there are two factors the 'look up table' would need to be three dimensional (known as a 'look up surface'). To save the storage space that a suitable surface would need, a low resolution surface would be used which requires significantly less points to be stored. Then an intermediate point can be produced by inter-polation between surrounding points. Thus an 8 by 8 surface together with interpolation of 16 intermediate fractions of each co-ordinate is approximately equivalent to a surface with 16,384 points. This obviously saves a large r.o.m. but uses a lengthy interpolation program which in turn means that the speed of the '9940 microcomputer would be required to complete its task in the time available. At the same time that the processor is performing the calculation and look up for the next output it must be controlling the present output. That is two tasks have to be performed simultaneously. This probably is possible theoretically with clever programming but it is easier and produces less constraints if there is a separate timer to time the spark advance say. Figure 9 shows how elegant such an automotive system would be using the '9940 and a multiplexing analogue to digital converter i.c. This arrangement can monitor 10 anologue inputs as well as controlling a further, 16 say, digital I/O ports.

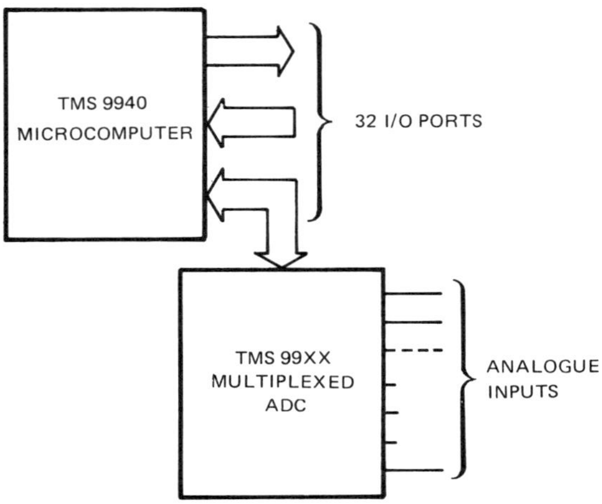

FIGURE 9. Automotive System.

REFERENCES

1. Applications Laboratory Staff of Texas Instruments Incorporated, *Electronic Power Control and Digital Techniques,* McGraw-Hill Book Company, New York, 1976, pp. 116-123.
2. Applications Laboratory Staff of Texas Instruments Incorporated, *Electronic Power Control and Digital Techniques,* McGraw-Hill Book Company, New York, 1976, pp. 91, 95-96.
3. *990 Computer Family Systems Handbook,* Manual 945250-9701, Texas Instruments Inc.

APPENDIX

Clock/Counter Module

The first part of this module is listed in Table 2.

Table 2. Clock Counter Listing

	Label	Instruction	Comment
1.	HZ	LDX 1	load X with 1 address
2.		TCY 12	transfer constant (12) to Y location
3.		IMAC	increment value in memory at accumulator
4.		ALEC 9	is this value in acc. less or equal to 9?
5.		BR LTAM	if yes, branch to the label LTAM
6.		TCMIY 0	if no, transfer C (0) to memory and also increment Y
7.	THZ	IMAC	
8.		ALEC 9	
9.		BR LTAM	
10.		TCMIY 0	
11.	SEC	IMAC	divide by 10, seconds counter
12.		ALEC 9	
13.		BR LTAM	
14.		TCMIY 0	
15.	TSEC	IMAC	divide by 6, tens of seconds counter
16.		ALEC 5	
17.		BR LTAM	
18.		TCMIY 0	

A flowchart of the routine is shown in Figure 10. Previous to statement 1 the triac had been controlled. Therefore the program flow comes to statement 1 every half cycle. Statements 1 and 2 set the r.a.m. addressing (by the X and Y registers) to address the location containing the units Hertz count. The value is incremented by statement 3, the result of the incrementation being loaded into the accumulator. Here its value is tested to see if the counter is going to overflow 9. Statement 4 is the test and in common with other conditional statements the branch is taken (if the next statement is a BRANCH), if the statement is true. The branch (statement 5) is to another statement found by its label LTAM. LTAM is a statement elsewhere in the program which is the instruction r.a.m. – transfer accumulator to memory. Therefore, to summarise: if the value in the memory has been incremented and it is still 9 or less it is returned in incremented form to the memory, and the program flow now following on from LTAM continues. If the branch was not taken because now a 10 is in the accumulator, that memory location is loaded with 'zero' and a 'one' carried over, i.e. the tens of Hertz counter is incremented.

Using ALEC 9 gives a modulo 10 counter, using ALEC 5 gives a module 6 counter. Thus the Hz and THz divide by 10 x 10 = 100, which gives seconds from half cycles of a 50 cycles input, and SEC and TSEC divide by 10 x 6 which gives a minutes output.

Input Routine

To understand this next example, it is important to know how the keys have been placed on the matrix. It has been chosen that the function keys, manual, automatic, temperature, etc., are all connected to the K1 input. Keys for the values 0 to 7 are on K4 and their value is matched by the value of R that strobes them: e.g. R3 strobes Key 3, R4 key 4, etc. Keys 8 and 9 are connected to K2 and strobed by R2 and R3 respectively. All this is shown in Figure 11. With the displays and keyboard being driven by the same group of R outputs, it is convenient to set an R and then perform both display output and keyboard input before progressing to the next R. In the previous section of program the display value has been output and a certain R output has just been set. The next section of the program, shown in Table 3, then reads the keyboard matrix, by strobing it.

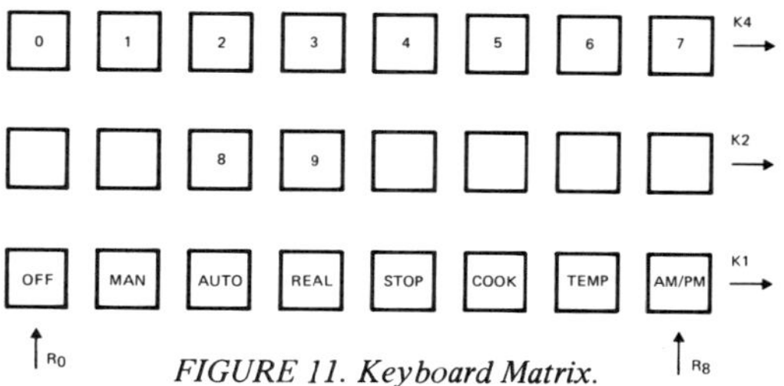

FIGURE 11. Keyboard Matrix.

The progress of the strobing is remembered by storing the R (and Y) value in a designated location (SCAN).

The state of the K inputs is transferred to the accumulator by Statement 3. If there was no signal on K8 from the mains time input then the value in the accumulator will be 7 or less. If it is not adding 8 to the accumulator affectively gives us the value without K8 (Statements 5 and 6). Statement 7 checks that some key has been pressed. If not then the strobing is continued with the next R. Statements 9, 10, 11 and 12, give a delay of 5 or 6ms. Then the inputs are read again and masked and tested by statements 13 to 18. According to the structure of the program and its

Table 3. Input Routine Listing.

	Label	Instruction	Comment
1.		TCY SCAN	Address location 'SCAN' and
2.		TAM	transfer current R (and Y) value in to it from accumulator.
3.		TKA	
4.		ALEC 7	
5.		BR K1	
6.		A8AAC	
7.	K1	ALEC 0	
8.		BR NOK	
9.	DELAY	DAN	
10.		BR DELAY	Keybounce
11.		DYN	delay
12.		BR DELAY	
13.		TKA	
14.		ALEC 7	
15.		BR K2	Mask K8
16.		A8AAC	
17.	K2	ALEC 0	
18.		BR NOK	No key pressed
19.		ALEC 1	
20.		BR I FUN	
21.		TCY SCAN	
22.		XMA	
23.		TBITI 2	
24.		BR K4	
25.		A6AAC	Correct for 8 and 9
26.	K4	BR INPUT	

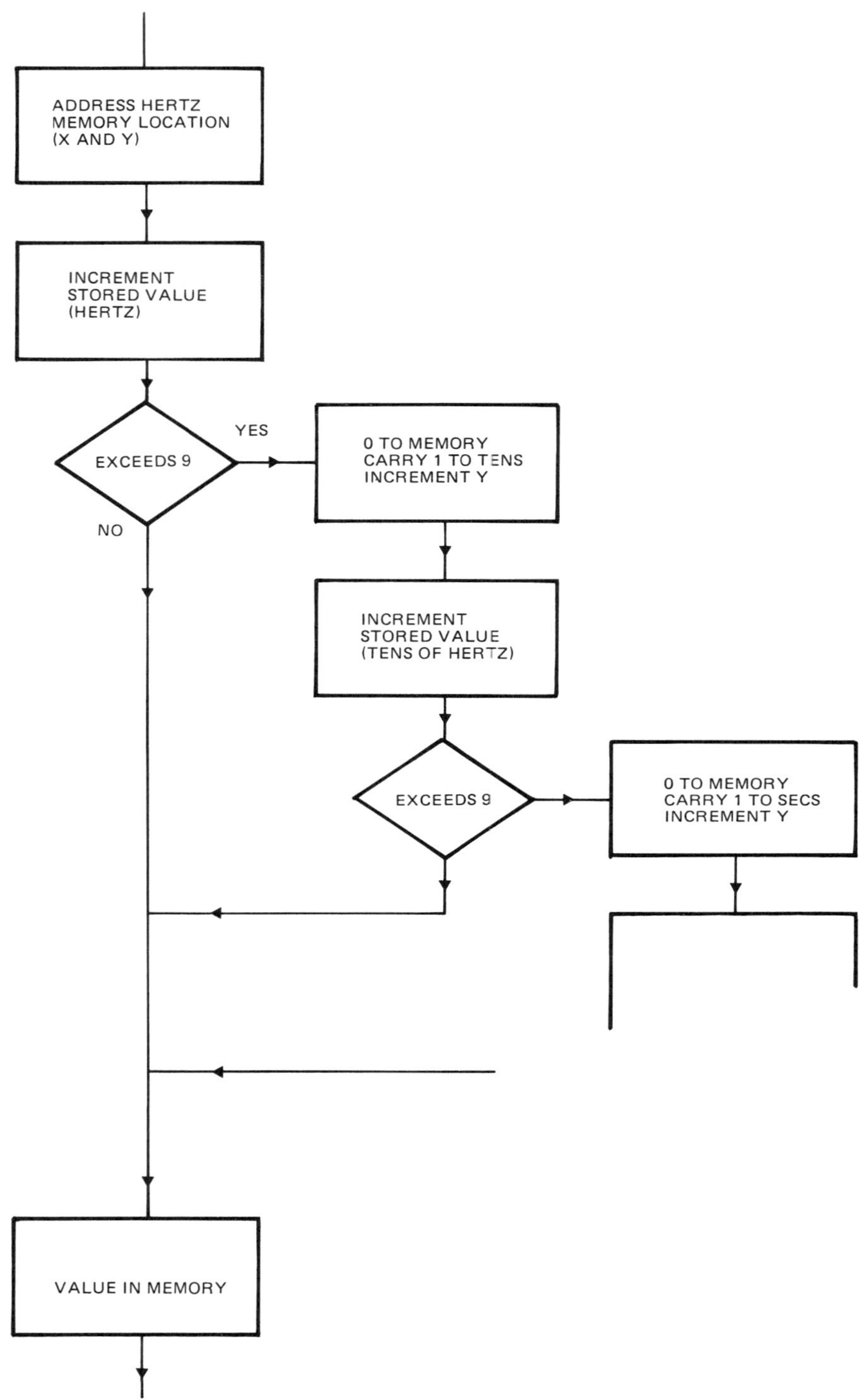

FIGURE 10. Part of a Clock Flowchart.

flowchart then one probably could use a subroutine call to statements 3 to 8 to replace statements 13 to 18.

Statement 19 tests to see if the input is at K1. Referring to the keyboard matrix in Figure 11 shows that if ACC = 1 (K1) then an input function has been selected. Statement 20 branches the program to a selection routine which determines the actual function by referring to the present R value.

If the program proceeds to statement 21 instead, then the input must be on K2 or K4. By returning to the memory location previously loaded in statement 2 we can find the present R value. Exchanging memory and accumulator puts R into acc. and the input value into memory. When in memory the individual bits of data can be examined and this is used to determine whether K2 or K4 is present. If K4 then the R value is the actual value of the key. If K2 is present (by elimination) then by adding 6 to the R value the key value is obtained and the data is then entered into a register by a suitable routine.

Index